# More iOS6 Development

## Further Explorations of the iOS SDK

Alex Horovitz
Kevin Kim
Jeff LaMarche
David Mark

Apress·

## More iOS6 Development

ISBN-13 (pbk): 978-1-4302-3807-2

ISBN-13 (electronic): 978-1-4302-3808-9

President and Publisher: Paul Manning
Lead Editor: Steve Anglin
Technical Reviewer: Nick Waynik
Editorial Board: Steve Anglin, Mark Beckner, Ewan Buckingham, Gary Cornell, Louise Corrigan, Morgan Ertel, Jonathan Gennick, Jonathan Hassell, Robert Hutchinson, Michelle Lowman, James Markham, Matthew Moodie, Jeff Olson, Jeffrey Pepper, Douglas Pundick, Ben Renow-Clarke, Dominic Shakeshaft, Gwenan Spearing, Matt Wade, Tom Welsh
Coordinating Editor: Brigid Duffy
Copy Editor: Mary Behr
Compositor: SPi Global
Indexer: SPi Global
Artist: SPi Global
Cover Designer: Anna Ishchenko

Distributed to the book trade worldwide by Springer Science+Business Media New York, 233 Spring Street, 6th Floor, New York, NY 10013. Phone 1-800-SPRINGER, fax (201) 348-4505, e-mail orders-ny@springer-sbm.com, or visit www.springeronline.com. Apress Media, LLC is a California LLC and the sole member (owner) is Springer Science + Business Media Finance Inc (SSBM Finance Inc). SSBM Finance Inc is a Delaware corporation.

For information on translations, please e-mail rights@apress.com, or visit www.apress.com.

Apress and friends of ED books may be purchased in bulk for academic, corporate, or promotional use. eBook versions and licenses are also available for most titles. For more information, reference our Special Bulk Sales–eBook Licensing web page at www.apress.com/bulk-sales.

Any source code or other supplementary materials referenced by the author in this text is available to readers at www.apress.com. For detailed information about how to locate your book's source code, go to www.apress.com/source-code.

*To Annie, for all her love and support.*

# Contents at a Glance

# Contents

# About the Authors

**Dave Mark** is a longtime Mac developer and author who has written a number of books on Mac and iOS development, including *Beginning iPhone 4 Development* (Apress, 2011), *More iPhone 3 Development* (Apress, 2010), *Learn C on the Mac* (Apress, 2008), *Ultimate Mac Programming* (Wiley, 1995), and The *Macintosh Programming Primer* series (Addison-Wesley, 1992). Dave was one of the founders of MartianCraft, an iOS and Android development house. Dave loves the water and spends as much time as possible on it, in it, or near it. He lives with his wife and three children in Virginia.

**Jeff LaMarche** is a Mac and iOS developer with more than 20 years of programming experience. Jeff has written a number of iOS and Mac development books, including *Beginning iPhone 4 Development* (Apress, 2011), *More iPhone 3 Development* (Apress, 2010), and *Learn Cocoa on the Mac* (Apress, 2010). Jeff is a principal at MartianCraft, an iOS and Android development house. He has written about Cocoa and Objective-C for MacTech Magazine, as well as articles for Apple's developer web site. Jeff also writes about iOS development for his widely read blog at www.iphonedevelopment.blogspot.com.

**Kevin Kim** is a co-founder and developer at AppOrchard LLC, a Tipping Point Partners company focused on sustainable iOS development. A graduate of Carnegie Mellon University, he was first exposed to the NeXTStep computer (the ancestor of today's iPhone) as a programmer at the Pittsburgh Supercomputing Center and has been hooked ever since. His career has spanned finance, government, biotech, and technology, including Apple where he managed the Apple Enterprise Services team for the New York metro area. Kevin was also a co-author of *Pro iOS 5 Tools* (Apress, 2011). He currently resides in the Alphabet City section of New York City with his wife and a clowder of rescued cats.

# About the Technical Reviewer

**Nick Waynik** has been working in the IT field for over 13 years and has done everything from network administration to web development. He started writing iOS apps when the SDK was first released. Since then he has gone on to start his own business focusing on iOS development. He loves spending his free time with his wife, Allison, and son, Preston; sometimes he even plays golf. He blogs at nickwaynik.com and can be found on Twitter as @n_dubbs.

# Acknowledgments

Writing a book like this one is more than the effort of us, the authors. Even though our names are on the cover, it is the result of the hard work of many people.

First, I would like to thank Dave Mark and Jeff LaMarche for writing the first version of the book, and for giving me a solid foundation from which to build and expand upon.

I would like to thank the staff at Apress for making sure this book was completed as close to schedule as possible. Brigid Duffy provided the guidance and oversight to make sure I completed this book. Tom Welsh made sure I stayed on topic and kept things clear. Mary Behr made the manuscript look beautiful. I'd also like to thank Brandon Levesque for making sure people knew this book was coming.

Thanks to the technical reviewers Nick Waynick and Mark Dalrymple for making sure the code I wrote actually works. Any mistakes that still exist are mine.

Thanks to my friends and colleagues at AppOrchard for their patience through the last several months of curmudgeonly behavior and for helping me make this project successful.

A great deal of thanks to my wife, Annie, for making sure I worked on this book when I would have rather been watching baseball or playing guitar. Thanks to my cats, PK, Manny, and Leela, for wanting to be fed when I needed a break. An extra thanks goes to Manny for being the subject of many of the examples in this book.

Finally, thanks to you, the reader, for buying this book. We like to think of programming as a scientific discipline, but, at times it feels more like a black art. If this book helps you on your journey of understanding iOS programming, then it is all worthwhile.

# Chapter 1

# Here We Go Round Again

So, you're still creating iPhone applications, huh? Great! iOS and the App Store have enjoyed tremendous success, fundamentally changing the way mobile applications are delivered and completely changing what people expect from their mobile devices. Since the first release of the iOS Software Development Kit (SDK) way back in March 2008, Apple has been busily adding new functionality and improving what was already there. It's no less exciting a platform than it was back when it was first introduced. In fact, in many ways, it's more exciting, because Apple keeps expanding the amount of functionality available to third-party developers like us.

Since the last release of this book, *More iPhone 3 Development* (Apress 2010), Apple has released a number of frameworks, tools, and services. These include, but aren't limited to

- **Core frameworks**: Core Motion, Core Telephony, Core Media, Core View, Core MIDI, Core Image, and Core Bluetooth

- **Utility frameworks**: Event Kit, Quick Look Framework, Assets Library, Image I/O, Printing, AirPlay, Accounts and Social Frameworks, Pass Kit

- **Services and their frameworks**: iAds, Game Center, iCloud, Newsstand

- **Developer-centric enhancements**: Blocks, Grand Central Dispatch (GCD), Weak Linking Support, Automatic Reference Counting (ARC), Storyboards, Collection Views, UI State Preservation, Auto Layout, UIAutomation

and many more…

Obviously, there are too many changes to cover completely in a single book. But we'll try our best to make you comfortable with the ones that you'll most likely need to know.

## What This Book Is

This book is a guide to help you continue down the path to creating better iOS applications. In *Beginning iOS 6 Development* (Apress, 2012), the goal was to get you past the initial learning curve and to help you get your arms around the fundamentals of building your first iOS applications. In this book, we're assuming you already know the basics. So, in addition to showing you how to use several of the new iOS APIs, we're also going to weave in some more advanced techniques that you'll need as your iOS development efforts grow in size and complexity.

In *Beginning iOS 6 Development*, every chapter was self-contained, each presenting its own unique project or set of projects. We'll be using a similar approach in the second half of this book, but in Chapters 2 through 8, we'll focus on a single, evolving Core Data application. Each chapter will cover a specific area of Core Data functionality as we expand the application. We'll also be strongly emphasizing techniques that will keep your application from becoming unwieldy and hard to manage as it gets larger.

# What You Need To Know

This book assumes that you already have some programming knowledge and that you have a basic understanding of the iOS SDK, either because you've worked through *Beginning iOS 6 Development* or because you've gained a similar foundation from other sources. We assume that you've experimented a little with the SDK, perhaps written a small program or two on your own, and have a general feel for Xcode. You might want to quickly review Chapter 2 of *Beginning iOS Development*.

---

### COMPLETELY NEW TO IOS?

If you are completely new to iOS development, there are other books you probably should read before this one. If you don't already understand the basics of programming and the syntax of the C language, you should check out *Learn C on the Mac for OS X and iOS* by David Mark and James Bucanek (Apress, 2012), which is a comprehensive introduction to the C language for Macintosh programmers (www.apress.com/9781430245339).

If you already understand C but don't have any experience programming with objects, check out *Learn Objective-C on the Mac* (Apress, 2012), an excellent and approachable introduction to Objective-C by Mac programming experts Scott Knaster, Wagar Malik, and Mark Dalrymple (www.apress.com/9781430218159).

Next, navigate over to the Apple iPhone Development Center and download a copy of *The Objective-C 2.0 Programming Language*, a very detailed and extensive description of the language and a great reference guide at *http://developer.apple.com/library/ios/#documentation/Cocoa/Conceptual/ObjectiveC/ Introduction/introObjectiveC.html*.

Once you have a firm handle on Objective-C, you need to master the fundamentals of the iOS SDK. For that, you should check out the prequel to this book, *Beginning iOS 6 Development: Exploring the iOS SDK* by David Mark, Jack Nutting, Jeff LaMarche, and Fredrik Olsson (Apress 2011, www.apress.com/9781430245124).

---

# What You Need Before You Can Begin

Before you can write software for iOS devices, you need a few things. For starters, you need an Intel-based Macintosh running Lion (Mac OS X 10.7 or later). Any Macintosh computer—laptop or desktop—that has been released since 2008 should work just fine, but make sure your machine is Intel-based and is capable of running Lion.

This may seem obvious, but you'll also need an iPhone (3GS or later), iPod touch (3rd generator or later), or an iPad (iPad 2 or later). While much of your code can be tested using the iPhone/iPad simulator, not all programs will run in the simulator. And you'll want to thoroughly test any application you create on an actual device before you ever consider releasing it to the public.

Finally, you'll need to sign up to become a Registered iOS Developer. If you're already a Registered iOS Developer, go ahead and download the latest and greatest iPhone development tools, and skip ahead to the next section.

If you're new to Apple's Registered iOS Developer programs, navigate to `http://developer.apple.com/ios/`, which will bring you to a page similar to that shown in Figure 1-1. Just below the iOS Dev Center banner, on the right side of the page, you'll find links labeled Log in and Register. Click the Register link. On the page that appears, click the Continue button. Follow the sequence of instructions to use your existing Apple ID or create a new one.

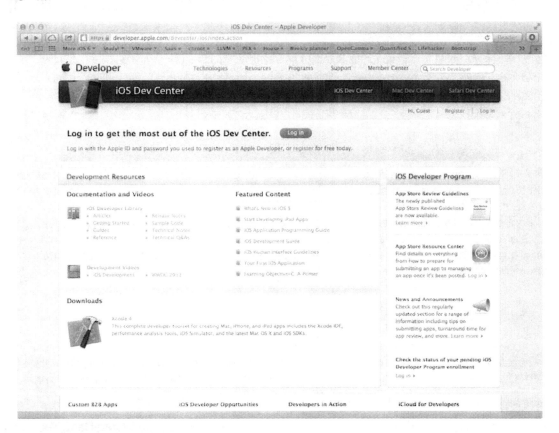

*Figure 1-1. Apple's iOS Dev Center web site*

At some point, as you register, you'll be given a choice of several paths, all of which will lead you to the SDK download page. The three choices are free, commercial, and enterprise. All three options give you access to the iOS SDK and Xcode, Apple's integrated development environment (IDE). Xcode includes tools for creating and debugging source code, compiling applications, and performance-tuning the applications you've written. Please note that although you get at Xcode through the developer site, your Xcode distribution will be made available to you via the App Store.

The free option is, as its name implies, free. It lets you develop iOS apps that run on a software-only simulator but does not allow you to download those apps to your iPhone, iPod touch, or iPad, nor sell your apps on Apple's App Store. In addition, some programs in this book will run only on your device, not in the simulator, which means you will not be able to run them if you choose the free solution. That said, the free solution is a fine place to start if you don't mind learning without doing for those programs that won't run in the simulator.

The other two options are to sign up for an iOS Developer Program, either the Standard (commercial) Program or the Enterprise Program. The Standard Program costs $99. It provides a host of development tools and resources, technical support, distribution of your application via Apple's App Store, and, most important, the ability to test and debug your code on an iPhone rather than just in the simulator. The Enterprise Program, which costs $299, is designed for companies developing proprietary, in-house applications for the iPhone, iPod touch, and iPad. For more details on these two programs, check out `http://developer.apple.com/programs/`.

> **Note**    If you are going to sign up for the Standard or Enterprise Program, you should go do it right now. It can take a while to get approved, and you'll need that approval to be able to run applications on your iPhone. Don't worry, though—the projects in the early chapters of this book will run just fine on the iPhone simulator.

Because iOS devices are connected mobile devices that utilize a third party's wireless infrastructure, Apple has placed far more restrictions on iOS developers than it ever has on Macintosh developers, who are able to write and distribute programs with absolutely no oversight or approval from Apple. Apple is not doing this to be mean, but rather to minimize the chances of people distributing malicious or poorly written programs that could degrade performance on the shared network. It may seem like a lot of hoops to jump through, but Apple has gone through quite an effort to make the process as painless as possible.

# What's In this Book

As we said earlier, Chapters 2 through 7 of this book focus on Core Data, Apple's primary persistence framework. The rest of the chapters cover specific areas of functionality that are either new with iOS SDK or were simply too advanced to include in *Beginning iOS 6 Development*.

Here is a very brief overview of the chapters that follow:

*Chapter 2, The Anatomy of Core Data*: In this chapter, we'll introduce you to Core Data. You'll learn why Core Data is a vital part of your iPhone development arsenal. We'll dissect a simple Core Data application and show you how all the individual parts of a Core Data-backed application fit together.

*Chapter 3, A Super Start*: *Adding, Displaying, and Deleting Data*: Once you have a firm grasp on Core Data's terminology and architecture, you'll learn how to do some basic tasks, including inserting, searching for, and retrieving data.

*Chapter 4, The Devil in the Detail View*: In this chapter, you'll learn how to let your users edit and change the data stored by Core Data. We'll explore techniques for building generic, reusable views so you can leverage the same code to present different types of data.

*Chapter 5, Preparing for Change: Migrations and Versioning*: Here, we'll look at Apple tools that you can use to change your application's data model, while still allowing your users to continue using their data from previous versions of your application.

*Chapter 6, Custom Managed Objects*: To really unlock the power of Core Data, you can subclass the class used to represent specific instances of data. In this chapter, you'll learn how to use custom managed objects and see some benefits of doing so.

*Chapter 7, Relationships, Fetched Properties, and Expressions*: In this final chapter on Core Data, you'll learn about some mechanisms that allow you to expand your applications in powerful ways. You'll refactor the application you built in the previous chapters so that you don't need to add new classes as you expand your data model.

*Chapter 8, iCloud Storage*: The iCloud Storage APIs are among the coolest features of iOS. The iCloud APIs will let your apps store documents and key-value data in iCloud. iCloud will wirelessly push documents to a user's device automatically and update the documents when changed on any device—automatically. You'll enhance your Core Data application to store information on iCloud.

*Chapter 9, Peer-to-Peer Over Bluetooth Using GameKit*: The GameKit framework makes it easy to create programs that communicate over Bluetooth, such as multiplayer games for the iPhone and iPod touch. You'll explore GameKit by building a simple two-player game.

*Chapter 10, CoreLocation and MapKit*: This chapter explores another great new piece of functionality added to the iOS SDK: an enhanced CoreLocation. This framework now includes support for both forward and reverse geocoding location data. You will be able to convert back and forth between a set of map coordinates and information about the street, city, country (and so on) at that coordinate. Plus, you'll explore how all this interoperates with enhanced MapKit.

*Chapter 11, Messaging: Mail, Social, and iMessage*: Your ability to get your message out has gone beyond e-mail. In this chapter, we'll take you through the core options of Mail, the Social Framework, and iMessage and you'll see how to leverage each appropriately.

*Chapter 12, Media Library Access and Playback*: It's now possible to programmatically get access to your users' complete library of audio tracks stored on their iPhone or iPod touch. In this chapter, you'll look at the various techniques used to find, retrieve, and play music and other audio tracks.

*Chapter 13, Locking it Down: iOS Security*: In this chapter, you'll be taking a look at the Security framework (Security.framework), which provides a standard set of security-related services for iOS applications. In addition to the basic interfaces of this framework, you will utilize some additions for managing credentials that are not specified by standards but that are required by many applications.

*Chapter 14, Keeping Your Interface Responsive*: Long-running programming tasks can easily bog down the iOS user interface. In this chapter, you'll take a look at implementing advanced Storyboarding techniques so that your application remains responsive.

*Chapter 15, Unit Testing, Debugging, and Instruments*: No program is ever perfect. Bugs and defects are a natural part of the programming process. In this chapter, you'll learn various techniques for preventing, finding, and fixing bugs in iOS SDK programs.

*Chapter 16, The Road Goes Ever On…:* Sadly, every journey must come to an end. We'll wrap up this book with fond farewells and some resources we hope you'll find useful.

As we said in *Beginning iOS 6 Development*, iOS is an incredible computing platform, an ever-expanding frontier for your development pleasure. In this book, we're going to take you further down the iPhone development road, digging deeper into the SDK, touching on new and, in some cases, more advanced topics.

Read the book and be sure to build the projects yourself—don't just copy them from the archive and run them once or twice. You'll learn most by doing. Make sure you understand what you did, and why, before moving on to the next project. Don't be afraid to make changes to the code. Experiment, tweak the code, observe the results. Rinse and repeat.

Got your iOS SDK installed? Turn the page, put on some iTunes, and let's go. Your continuing journey awaits.

# Chapter 2

# Core Data: What, Why, and How

Core Data is a framework and set of tools that allow you to save (or persist) your application's data to an iOS device's file system automatically. Core Data is an implementation of something called object-relational mapping (ORM). This is just a fancy way of saying that Core Data allows you to interact with your Objective-C objects without having to worry about how the data from those objects is stored and retrieved from persistent data stores such as relational database (such as SQLite) or into a flat file.

Core Data can seem like magic when you first start using it. Core Data objects are, for the most part, handled just like plain old objects, and they seem to know how to retrieve and save themselves automagically. You won't create SQL strings or make file management calls, ever. Core Data insulates you from some complex and difficult programming tasks, which is great for you. By using Core Data, you can develop applications with complex data models much, much faster than you could using straight SQLite, object archiving, or flat files.

Technologies that hide complexity the way Core Data does can encourage "voodoo programming," that most dangerous of programming practices where you include code in your application that you don't necessarily understand. Sometimes that mystery code arrives in the form of a project template. Or, perhaps you download a utilities library that does a task for you that you just don't have the time or expertise to do for yourself. That voodoo code does what you need it to do, and you don't have the time or inclination to step through it and figure it out, so it just sits there, working its magic… until it breaks. As a general rule, if you find yourself with code in your own application that you don't fully understand, it's a sign you should go do a little research, or at least find a more experienced peer to help you get a handle on your mystery code.

The point is that Core Data is one of those complex technologies that can easily turn into a source of mystery code that will make its way into many of your projects. Although you don't need to know exactly how Core Data accomplishes everything it does, you should invest some time and effort into understanding the overall Core Data architecture.

This chapter starts with a brief history of Core Data and then it dives into a Core Data application. By building a Core Data application with Xcode, you'll find it much easier to understand the more complex Core Data projects you'll find in the following chapters.

# A Brief History of Core Data

Core Data has been around for quite some time, but it became available on iOS with the release of iPhone SDK 3.0. Core Data was originally introduced with Mac OS X 10.4 (Tiger), but some of the DNA in Core Data actually goes back about 15 years to a NeXT framework called Enterprise Objects Framework (EOF), which was part of the toolset that shipped with NeXT's WebObjects web application server.

EOF was designed to work with remote data sources, and it was a pretty revolutionary tool when it first came out. Although there are now many good ORM tools for almost every language, when WebObjects was in its infancy, most web applications were written to use handcrafted SQL or file system calls to persist their data. Back then, writing web applications was incredibly time- and labor-intensive. WebObjects, in part because of EOF, cut the development time needed to create complex web applications by an order of magnitude.

In addition to being part of WebObjects, EOF was also used by NeXTSTEP, which was the predecessor to Cocoa. When Apple bought NeXT, the Apple developers used many of the concepts from EOF to develop Core Data. Core Data does for desktop applications what EOF had previously done for web applications: it dramatically increases developer productivity by removing the need to write file system code or interact with an embedded database.

Let's start building your Core Data application.

# Creating a Core Data Application

Fire up Xcode and create a new Xcode project. There are many ways to do this. When you start Xcode, you may get the Xcode startup window (Figure 2-1). You can just click the area titled "Create a New Xcode Project." Or you can select **File ➤ New ➤ Project**. Or you can use the keyboard shortcut ⇧⌘N. Whatever floats your boat. Going forward, we're going to mention the options available in the Xcode window or the menu options, but we won't use the keyboard shortcut. If you know and prefer the keyboard shortcuts, feel free to use them. Let's get back to building your app.

*Figure 2-1.  Xcode startup window*

Xcode will open a project workspace and display the Project Template sheet (Figure 2-2). On the left are the possible template headings: iOS and OS X. Each heading has a bunch of template groups. Select the Application template group under the iOS heading, and then select Master-Detail Application template on the right. On the bottom right, there's a short description of the template. Click the Next button to move the next sheet.

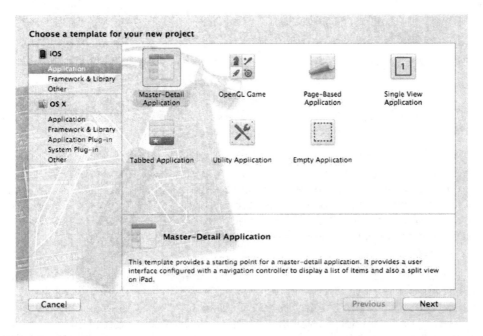

*Figure 2-2.  Project Template sheet*

The next sheet is the Project Configuration sheet (Figure 2-3). You'll be asked to provide a product name; use the name **CoreDataApp**. The Organization Name and Company Identifier fields will be set automatically by Xcode; by default these will read MyCompanyName and com.mycompanyname. You can change these to whatever you like, but for the Company Identifier, Apple recommends using the reverse domain name style (such as com.apporchard).

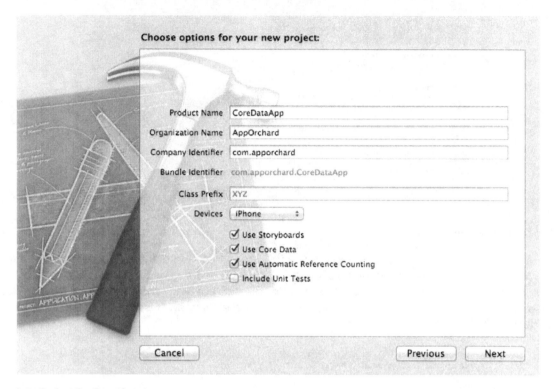

*Figure 2-3. Project Configuration sheet*

Note that the Bundle Identifier field is not editable; rather it's populated by the values from the Company Identifier and Product Name fields. The Class Prefix field is an option to add a prefix (i.e., NS) before all your project's classes. You can leave this blank.

The Devices drop-down field lists the possible target devices for this project: iPad, iPhone, or Universal. The first two are self-explanatory. "Universal" is for applications that will run on both the iPad and iPhone. It's a blessing and a curse to have to a single project that can support both iPads and iPhones. But for the purposes of this book, you'll stick with iPhone. Since you'll be using storyboards, make sure the "Use Storyboards" checkbox is checked. You obviously want to use Core Data, so check its checkbox. Finally, make sure the "Use Automatic Reference Counting" checkbox is checked.

Click Next, and choose a location to save your project (Figure 2-4). The checkbox on the bottom will set up your project to use Git (www.git-scm.com), a free, open-source version control system. It's useful to use so you can leave it checked. We won't discuss it, but if you don't know about version control or git, we suggest you get familiar with them. Click Create. Xcode should create your project, and it should look like Figure 2-5.

*Figure 2-4.  Choose a location to put your project*

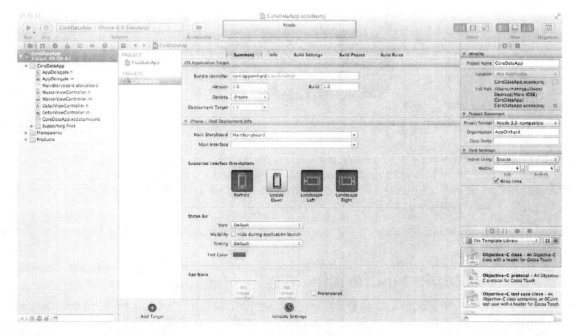

*Figure 2-5.  Voila, your project is ready!*

Build and run the application. Either press the Run button on the Toolbar, or **Product ➤ Run**. The simulator should appear. Press the Add (+) button in the upper right. A new row will insert into the table that shows the exact date and time the Add button was pressed (Figure 2-6). You can also use the Edit button to delete rows. Exciting, huh?

*Figure 2-6. CoreDataApp in action*

Under the hood of this simple application, a lot is happening. Think about it: without adding a single class, or any code to persist data to a file or interact with a database, pressing the Add button created an object, populated it with data, and saved it to a SQLite database created for you automatically. There's plenty of free functionality here.

Now that you've seen an application in action, let's take a look at what's going on behind the scenes.

# Core Data Concepts and Terminology

Like most complex technologies, Core Data has its own terminology that can be a bit confusing to newcomers. Let's break down the mystery and get your arms around Core Data's nomenclature.

Figure 2-7 shows a simplified, high-level diagram of the Core Data architecture. Don't expect it all to make sense now, but as you look at different pieces, you might want to refer back to this diagram to cement your understanding of how they fit together.

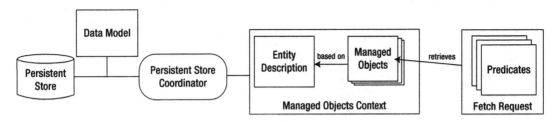

*Figure 2-7. The Core Data architecture*

There are five key concepts to focus on here. As you proceed through this chapter, make sure you understand each of the following:

- ▓ Data Model
- ▓ Persistent Store
- ▓ Persistent Store Coordinator
- ▓ Managed Object and Managed Object Context
- ▓ Fetch Request

Once again, don't let the names throw you. Follow along and you'll see how all these pieces fit together.

# The Data Model

What is a data model? In an abstract sense, it's an attempt to define the organization of data and the relationship between the organized data components. In Core Data, the data model defines the data structure of objects, the organization of those objects, the relationships between those objects, and the behavior of those objects. Xcode allows you, via the model editor and inspector, to specify your data model for use in your application.

If you expand the CoreDataApp group in the Navigator content pane, you'll see a file called CoreDataApp.xcdatamodel. This file is the default data model for your project. Xcode created this file for you because you checked the "Use Core Data" checkbox in the Project Configuration sheet. Single-click CoreDataApp.xcdatamodel to bring up Xcode's model editor. Make sure the Utility pane is visible (it should be the third button on the View bar), and select the Inspector. Your Xcode window should look like Figure 2-8.

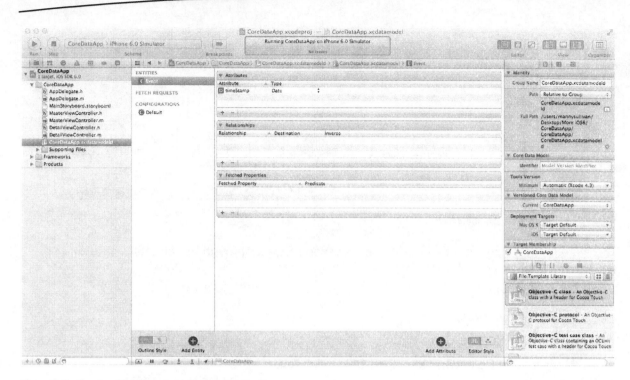

*Figure 2-8.  Xcode with the model editor and inspector*

When you selected the data model file, `CoreDataApp.xcdatamodel`, the Editor pane changed to present the Core Data model editor (Figure 2-9). Along the top, the jump bar remains unchanged. Along the left, the gutter has been replaced by a wider pane, the Top-Level Components pane. The Top-Level Components pane outlines the entities, fetch requests, and configurations defined in the data model (we'll cover these in detail in a little bit). You can add a new entity by using the Add Entity button at the bottom of the Top-Level Components pane. Alternately, you can use the **Editor ➤ Add Entity** menu option. If you click and hold the Add Entity button, you will be presented with a pop-up menu of choices: Add Entity, Add Fetch Request, and Add Configuration. Whatever option you choose, the single-click behavior of the button will change to that component and the label of the button will change to reflect this behavior. The menu equivalents for adding fetch requests and configurations can be found in the Editor menu below the **Add Entity** menu item.

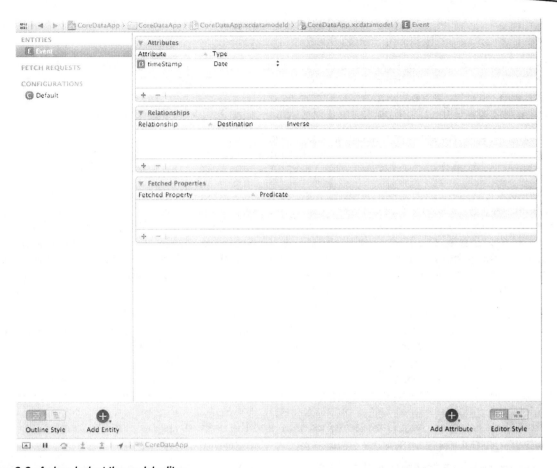

*Figure 2-9. A close look at the model editor*

The Top-Level Components pane has two styles: list and hierarchical. You can toggle between these two styles by using the Outline Style selector group found at the bottom of the Top-Level Components pane. Switching styles with the CoreDataApp data model won't change anything in the Top-Level Components pane, as there's only one entity and one configuration, so there's no hierarchy to be shown. If you had a component that depended on another component, you'd see the hierarchical relationship between the two with the hierarchical outline style.

The bulk of the Editor pane is taken up by the Detail editor. The Detail editor has two editor styles: table and graph. By default (and pictured in Figure 2-9), the Detail editor is in table style. You can toggle between these styles by using the Editor Style selector group on the bottom right of the Editor pane. Try it. You can see the difference in the two styles.

When you select an entity in the Top-Level Components pane, the Detail editor will display, in table style, three tables: Attributes, Relationships, and Fetched Properties. Again, we'll cover these in detail in a little bit. You can add a new attribute by using the Add Attribute button below the Detail editor. Similar to the Add Entity button, a click-and-hold will reveal a pop-up menu of choices: Add Attribute, Add Relationship, and Add Fetched Property. Again, the single-click behavior of this button will change depending on your choice, with its label reflecting that behavior. Under the Editor menu there are three menu items: Add Attribute, Add Relationship, and Add Fetched Property. These are only active when an entity is selected in the Top-Level Components pane.

If you switch the Detail editor to graph style, you'll see a large grid with a single rounded square in the center. This rounded square represents the entity in the Top-Level Components pane. The template you used for this project creates a single entity, Event. Selecting Event in the Top Level Components pane is the same as selecting the rounded rectangle in the graph view.

Try it. Click outside the entity in the Detail editor grid to deselect it, and then click the Event line in the Top-Level Components pane. The entity in the graph view will also be selected. The Top Level Components pane and the graph view show two different views of the same entity list.

When unselected, the title bar and lines of the Event entity square should be pink. If you select the Event entity in the Top-Level Components pane, the Event entity in the Detail editor should change color to a blue, indicating it's selected. Now click anywhere on the Detail editor grid, outside the Event rounded square. The Event entity should be deselected in the Top Level Components pane and should change color in the Detail editor. If you click on the Event entity in the Detail editor, it will be selected again. When selected, the Event entity should have a resize handle (or dot) on the left and right sides, allowing you to resize its width.

You are currently given the Event entity. It has a single attribute, named timeStamp, and no relationships. The Event entity was created as part of this template. As you design your own data models, you'll most likely delete the Event entity and create your own entities from scratch. A moment ago, you ran your Core Data sample application in the simulator. When you pressed the + icon, a new instance of Event was created. Entities, which we'll look at more closely in a few pages, replace the Objective-C data model class you would otherwise use to hold your data. We'll get back to the model editor in just a minute to see how it works. For now, just remember that the persistent store is where Core Data stores its data, and the data model defines the form of that data. Also remember that every persistent store has one, and only one, data model.

The inspector provides greater detail for the item(s) selected in the model editor. Since each item could have a different view in the inspector, we'll discuss the details as we discuss the components and their properties. That being said, let's discuss the three top-level components: entities, fetch requests, and configurations.

## Entities

An entity can be thought as the Core Data analogue to an Objective-C class declaration. In fact, when using an entity in your application, you essentially treat it like an Objective-C class with some Core Data-specific implementation. You use the model editor to define the properties that define your entity. Each entity is given a name (in this case, Event), which must begin with a capital letter. When you ran CoreDataApp earlier, every time you pressed the Add (+) button, a new instance of Event was instantiated and stored in the application's persistent store.

Make sure the Utility pane is exposed, and select the Event entity. Now look at the inspector in the Utility pane (make sure the enspector is showing by selecting the Inspector button in the Inspector selector bar). Note that the Inspector pane now allows you to edit or change aspects of the entity (Figure 2-10). We'll get to the details of the inspector later.

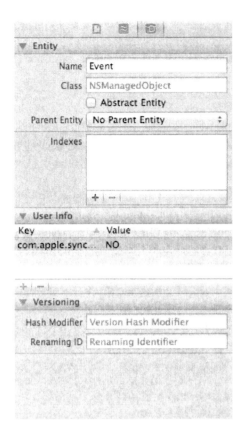

*Figure 2-10. The inspector for the Event entity*

## Properties

While the Editor pane lists all the data model's entities, the Inspector pane allows you to "inspect" the properties that belong to the selected entity. An entity can be made up of any number of properties. There are three different types of properties: attributes, relationships, and fetched properties. When you select an entity's property in the model editor, the property's details are displayed in the Inspector pane.

## Attributes

The property that you'll use the most when creating entities is the attribute, which serves the same function in a Core Data entity as an instance variable does in an Objective-C class: they both hold data. If you look at your model editor (or at Figure 2-10), you'll see that the Event entity has one attribute named timeStamp. The timeStamp attribute holds the date and time when a given Event instance was created. In your sample application, when you click the + button, a new row is added to the table displaying a single Event's timeStamp.

Just like an instance variable, each attribute has a type. There are two ways to set an attribute's type. When the model editor is using the table style, you can change an attributes type in the Attributes table in the Detail editor (Figure 2-11). In your current application, the timeStamp

You will create many fetch requests programmatically in the next few chapters, and you'll be looking at a simple one a little later in this chapter in the "Creating a Fetched Results Controller" section.

## Configurations

A configuration is a set of entities. Different configurations may contain the same entity. Configurations are use to define which entities are stored in which persistent store. Most of the time, you won't need anything other than the default configuration. We won't cover using multiple configurations in this book. If you want to learn more, check the Apple Developer site or *Pro Core Data for iOS, 2nd Edition* (www.apress.com/9781430236566).

## The Data Model Class: NSManagedObjectModel

Although you won't typically access your application's data model directly, you should be aware of the fact that there is an Objective-C class that represents the data model in memory. This class is called NSManagedObjectModel, and the template automatically creates an instance of NSManagedObjectModel based on the data model file in your project. Let's take a look at the code that creates it now.

In the Navigation pane, open the CoreDataApp group and AppDelegate.m. In the Editor jump bar, click the last menu (it should read No Selection) to bring up a list of the methods in this class (see Figure 2-13). Select -managedObjectModel in the Core Data Stack section, which will take you to the method that creates the object model based on the CoreDataApp.xcdatamodel file.

*Figure 2-13. The editor pane set to show counterparts will allow you to see the declaration and implementation*

The method should look like this:

```
// Returns the managed object model for the application.
// If the model doesn't already exist, it is created from the application's model.
- (NSManagedObjectModel *)managedObjectModel
{
    if (_managedObjectModel != nil) {
        return _managedObjectModel;
    }
    NSURL *modelURL = [[NSBundle mainBundle] URLForResource:@"CoreDataApp"
                                              withExtension:@"momd"];
    _managedObjectModel = [[NSManagedObjectModel alloc] initWithContentsOfURL:modelURL];
    return _managedObjectModel;
}
```

The first checks the instance variable _managedObjectModel to see if it's nil. This accessor method uses a form of lazy loading. The underlying instance variable doesn't actually get instantiated until the first time the accessor method is called. For this reason, you should never, ever access _managedObjectModel directly (except within the accessor method itself, of course). Always make sure to use the accessor methods. Otherwise, you could end up trying to make calls on an object that hasn't been created yet.

> **Tip**  The data model class is called NSManagedObjectModel because, as you'll see a little later in the chapter, instances of data in Core Data are called managed objects.

If _managedObjectModel is nil, you can go get your data model. By default XCode should have written the following two lines of code to accomplish this for you:

```
NSURL *modelURL = [[NSBundle mainBundle] URLForResource:@"CoreDataApp"
                                          withExtension:@"momd"];
_managedObjectModel = [[NSManagedObjectModel alloc] initWithContentsOfURL:modelURL];
```

Remember how we said that a persistent store was associated with a single data model? Well, that's true, but it doesn't tell the whole story. You can combine multiple .xcdatamodel files into a single instance of NSManagedObjectModel, creating a single data model that combines all the entities from multiple files. If you are planning on having more than one model, you can change those two lines of code to one.

This one line of code will take any .xcdatamodel files that might be in your Xcode project and combines them together into a single instance of NSManagedObjectModel:

```
_managedObjectModel = [NSManagedObjectModel mergedModelFromBundles:nil];
```

So, for example, if you create a second data model file and add it to your project, that new file will be combined with CoreDataApp.xcdatamodel into a single managed object model that containes the contents of both files. This allows you to split up your application's data model into multiple smaller and more manageable files.

The vast majority of iOS applications that use Core Data have a single persistent store and a single data model, so the default template code will work beautifully most of the time. That said, Core Data does support the use of multiple persistent stores. You could, for example, design your application to store some of its data in a SQLite persistent store and some of it in a binary flat file. If you find that you need to use multiple data models, remember to change the template code here to load the managed object models individually using `mergedModelFromBundles:`.

## The Persistent Store and Persistent Store Coordinator

The persistent store, which is sometimes referred to as a backing store, is where Core Data stores its data. By default, on iOS devices Core Data uses a SQLite database contained in your application's `Documents` folder as its persistent store. But this can be changed without impacting any of the other code you write by tweaking a single line of code. We'll show you the actual line of code to change in a few moments.

> **Caution**    Do not change the type of persistent store once you have posted your application to the App Store. If you must change it for any reason, you will need to write code to migrate data from the old persistent store to the new one, or else your users will lose all of their data—something that will almost always make them quite unhappy.

Every persistent store is associated with a single data model, which defines the types of data that the persistent store can store.

The persistent store isn't actually represented by an Objective-C class. Instead, a class called `NSPersistentStoreCoordinator` controls access to the persistent store. In essence, it takes all the calls coming from different classes that trigger reads or writes to the persistent store and serializes them so that multiple calls against the same file are not being made at the same time, which could result in problems due to file or database locking.

As is the case with the managed object model, the template provides you with a method in the application delegate that creates and returns an instance of a persistent store coordinator. Other than creating the store and associating it with a data model and a location on disk (which is done for you in the template), you will rarely need to interact with the persistent store coordinator directly. You'll use high-level Core Data calls, and Core Data will interact with the persistent store coordinator to retrieve or save the data.

Let's take a look at the method that returns the persistent store coordinator. In `CoreDataAppDelegate.m`, select `-persistentStoreCoordinator` from the function pop-up menu. Here's the method:

```
// Returns the persistent store coordinator for the application.
// If the coordinator doesn't already exist, it is created and the application's store added to it.
- (NSPersistentStoreCoordinator *)persistentStoreCoordinator
{
    if (_persistentStoreCoordinator != nil) {
        return _persistentStoreCoordinator;
    }
```

```objc
NSURL *storeURL = [[self applicationDocumentsDirectory]
                    URLByAppendingPathComponent:@"CoreDataApp.sqlite"];

NSError *error = nil;
_persistentStoreCoordinator = [[NSPersistentStoreCoordinator alloc]
                                    initWithManagedObjectModel:[self managedObjectModel]];
if (![_persistentStoreCoordinator addPersistentStoreWithType:NSSQLiteStoreType
                                    configuration:nil
                                            URL:storeURL
                                        options:nil
                                            error:&error]) {
    /*
    Replace this implementation with code to handle the error appropriately.

    abort() causes the application to generate a crash log and terminate. You should not use
    this function in a shipping application, although it may be useful during development.

    Typical reasons for an error here include:
    * The persistent store is not accessible;
    * The schema for the persistent store is incompatible with current managed object model.
    Check the error message to determine what the actual problem was.

    If the persistent store is not accessible, there is typically something wrong with the file
    path. Often, a file URL is pointing into the application's resources directory instead of a
    writeable directory.

    If you encounter schema incompatibility errors during development, you can reduce their
        frequency by:
    * Simply deleting the existing store:
            [[NSFileManager defaultManager] removeItemAtURL:storeURL error:nil]
    * Performing automatic lightweight migration by passing the following dictionary as the
        options parameter:
    @{NSMigratePersistentStoresAutomaticallyOption:@YES,
            NSInferMappingModelAutomaticallyOption:@YES}

    Lightweight migration will only work for a limited set of schema changes; consult "Core Data
    Model Versioning and Data Migration Programming Guide" for details.
    */
    NSLog(@"Unresolved error %@, %@", error, [error userInfo]);
    abort();
}

return _persistentStoreCoordinator;

}
```

As with the managed object model, this persistentStoreCoordinator accessor method uses lazy loading and doesn't instantiate the persistent store coordinator until the first time it is accessed. Then it creates a path to a file called CoreDataApp.sqlite in the Documents directory in your application's sandbox. The template will always create a filename based on your project's name. If you want to use a different name, you can change it here, though it generally doesn't matter what you call the file since the user will never see it.

> **Caution**   If you do decide to change the filename, make sure you don't change it after you've posted your application to the App Store, or else future updates will cause your users to lose all of their data.

Take a look at this line of code:

```
if (![_persistentStoreCoordinator addPersistentStoreWithType:NSSQLiteStoreType
                                 configuration:nil
                                 URL:storeURL
                                 options:nil
                                 error:&error]) {
```

The first parameter to this method, NSSQLiteStoreType, determines the type of the persistent store. NSSQLiteStoreType is a constant that tells Core Data to use a SQLite database for its persistent store. If you want your application to use a single, binary flat file instead of a SQLite database, you could specify the constant NSBinaryStoreType instead of NSSQLiteStoreType. The vast majority of the time, the default setting is the best choice, so unless you have a compelling reason to change it, leave it alone.

> **Note**   A third type of persistent store supported by Core Data on iOS devices is called in-memory store. The primary use of this option is to create a caching mechanism, storing the data in memory instead of in a database or binary file. To use an in-memory store, specify a store type of NSInMemoryStoreType.

## Reviewing the Data Model

Before you move on to other parts of Core Data, let's quickly review how the pieces you've looked at so far fit together. You might want to refer back to Figure 2-7.

The persistent store (or backing store) is a file on an iOS device's file system that can be either a SQLite database or a binary flat file. A data model file, contained in one or more files with an extension of .xcdatamodel, describes the structure of your application's data. This file can be edited in Xcode. The data model tells the persistent store coordinator the format of all data stored in that persistent store. The persistent store coordinator is used by other Core Data classes that need to save, retrieve, or search for data. Easy enough, right? Let's move on.

# Managed Objects

Entities define the structure of your data, but they do not actually hold any data themselves. The instances of data are called managed objects. Every instance of an entity that you work with in Core Data will be an instance of the class NSManagedObject or a subclass of NSManagedObject.

# Key-Value Coding

The NSDictionary class allows you to store objects in a data structure and retrieve an object using a unique key. Like the NSDictionary class, NSManagedObject supports the key-value methods valueForKey: and setValue:forKey: for setting and retrieving attribute values. It also has additional methods for working with relationships. You can, for example, retrieve an instance of NSMutableSet representing a specific relationship. Adding managed objects to this mutable set or removing them will add or remove objects from the relationship it represents.

If the NSDictionary class is new to you, take a few minutes to fire up Xcode and read about NSDictionary in the documentation viewer. The important concept to get your head around is key-value coding, or KVC. Core Data uses KVC to store and retrieve data from its managed objects.

In your template application, consider an instance of NSManagedObject that represents a single event. You could retrieve the value stored in its timeStamp attribute by calling valueForKey:, like so:

```
NSDate *timeStamp = [managedObject valueForKey:@"timeStamp"];
```

Since timeStamp is an attribute of type date, you know the object returned by valueForKey: will be an instance of NSDate. Similarly, you could set the value using setValue:forKey:. The following code would set the timeStamp attribute of managedObject to the current date and time:

```
[managedObject setValue:[NSDate date] forKey:@"timeStamp"];
```

KVC also includes the concept of a keypath. Keypaths allow you iterate through object hierarchies using a single string. So, for example, if you had a relationship on your Employee entity called whereIWork, which pointed to an entity named Employer, and the Employer entity had an attribute called name, then you could get to the value stored in name from an instance of Employee using a keypath like so:

```
NSString *employerName = [managedObject valueForKeyPath:@"whereIWork.name"];
```

Notice that you use valueForKeyPath: instead of valueForKey:, and you provide a dot-separated value for the keypath. KVC parses that string using the dots, so in this case, it would parse it into two separate values: whereIWork and name. It uses the first one (whereIWork) on itself and retrieves the object that corresponds to that key. It then takes the next value in the keypath (name) and retrieves the object stored under that key from the object returned by the previous call. Since Employer is a to-one relationship, the first part of the keypath would return a managed object instance that represented the Employee's employer. The second part of the keypath would then be used to retrieve the name from the managed object that represents the Employer.

> **Note** If you've used bindings in Cocoa, you're probably already familiar with KVC and keypaths. If not, don't worry—they will become second nature to you before long. Keypaths are really quite intuitive.

## Managed Object Context

Core Data maintains an object that acts as a gateway between your entities and the rest of Core Data. That gateway is called a managed object context (often just referred to as a context). The context maintains state for all the managed objects that you've loaded or created. The context keeps track of changes that have been made since the last time a managed object was saved or loaded. When you want to load or search for objects, for example, you do it against a context. When you want to commit your changes to the persistent store, you save the context. If you want to undo changes to a managed object, you just ask the managed object context to undo. (Yes, it even handles all the work needed to implement undo and redo for your data model).

When building iOS applications, you will have only a single context the vast majority of the time. However, iOS makes having more than one context easy. You can create nested managed object contexts, in which the parent object store of a context is another managed object context rather than the persistent store coordinator.

In this case, fetch and save operations are mediated by the parent context instead of by a coordinator. You can imagine a number of usage scenarios, including things like performing background operations on a second thread or queue and managing discardable edits from an inspector window or view. A word of caution: nested contexts make it more important than ever that you adopt the "pass the baton" approach of accessing a context (by passing a context from one view controller to the next) rather than retrieving it directly from the application delegate.

Because every application needs at least one managed object context to function, the template has very kindly provided you with one. Click AppDelegate.m again, and select -managedObjectContext from the Function menu in the Editor Jump Bar. You will see a method that looks like this:

```
// Returns the managed object context for the application.
// If the context doesn't already exist, it is created and bound to the persistent store coordinator
for the application.
- (NSManagedObjectContext *)managedObjectContext
{
    if (_managedObjectContext != nil) {
        return _managedObjectContext;
    }

    NSPersistentStoreCoordinator *coordinator = [self persistentStoreCoordinator];
    if (coordinator != nil) {
        _managedObjectContext = [[NSManagedObjectContext alloc] init];
        [_managedObjectContext setPersistentStoreCoordinator:coordinator];
    }
    return _managedObjectContext;
}
```

This method is actually pretty straightforward. Using lazy loading, _managedObjectContext is checked for nil. If it is not nil, its value is returned. If managedObjectContext is nil, you check to see if your NSPersistentStoreCoordinator exists. If so, you create a new _managedObjectContext, then use setPersistentStoreCoordinator: to tie the current coordinator to your managedObjectContext. When you're finished, you return _managedObjectContext.

> **Note**    Managed object contexts do not work directly against a persistent store; they go through a persistent store coordinator. As a result, every managed object context needs to be provided with a pointer to a persistent store coordinator in order to function. Multiple managed object contexts can work against the same persistent store coordinator, however.

## Saves On Terminate

While you're in the application delegate, scroll up to another method called applicationWillTerminate:, which saves changes to the context if any have been made. The changes are saved to the persistent store. As its name implies, this method is called just before the application exits.

```
- (void)applicationWillTerminate:(UIApplication *)application
{
    // Saves changes in the application's managed object context before the application
    // terminates.
    [self saveContext];
}
```

This is a nice bit of functionality, but there may be times when you don't want the data to be saved. For example, what if the user quits after creating a new entity, but before entering any data for that entity? In that case, do you really want to save that empty managed object into the persistent store? Possibly not. You'll look at dealing with situations like that in the next few chapters.

## Load Data From the Persistent Store

Run the Core Data application you built earlier and press the plus button a few times (see Figure 2-6). Quit the simulator, and then run the application again. Note that the timestamps from your previous runs were saved into the persistent store and loaded back in for this run.

Click MasterViewController.m so you can see how this happens. As you can probably guess from the filename, MasterViewController is the view controller class that acts as your application's, well, master view controller. This is the view controller for the view you can see in Figure 2-6.

Once you've clicked the filename, you can use the Editor jump bar's Function menu to find the viewDidLoad: method, although it will probably be on your screen already since it's the first method in the class. The default implementation of the method looks like this:

```
- (void)viewDidLoad
{
    [super viewDidLoad];
    // Do any additional setup after loading the view, typically from a nib.
    self.navigationItem.leftBarButtonItem = self.editButtonItem;

    UIBarButtonItem *addButton =
        [[UIBarButtonItem alloc] initWithBarButtonSystemItem:UIBarButtonSystemItemAdd
                                                     target:self
                                                     action:@selector(insertNewObject:)];
    self.navigationItem.rightBarButtonItem = addButton;
}
```

The first thing the method does is call super. Next, it sets up the Edit and Add buttons. Note that MasterViewController inherits from UITableViewController, which in turn inherits from UIViewController. UIViewController provides a property named editButtonItem, which returns an Edit button. Using dot notation, you retrieve editButtonItem and pass it to the leftBarButtonItem property of the navigationItem property. Now the Edit button is the left button in the navigation bar.

Now let's focus on the Add button. Since UIViewController does not provide an Add button, use alloc to create one from scratch and the add it as the right button in the navigation bar. The code is fairly straightforward:

```
UIBarButtonItem *addButton =
    [[UIBarButtonItem alloc] initWithBarButtonSystemItem:UIBarButtonSystemItemAdd
                                                 target:self
                                                 action:@selector(insertNewObject:)];
self.navigationItem.rightBarButtonItem = addButton;
```

So, with the basic user interface set up, it's time to look at how the fetched results controller works.

## The Fetched Results Controller

Conceptually speaking, the fetched results controller isn't quite like the other generic controllers you've seen in the iOS SDK. If you've used Cocoa bindings and the generic controller classes available on the Mac, such as NSArrayController, then you're already familiar with the basic idea. If you're not familiar with those generic controller classes, a little explanation is probably in order.

Most of the generic controller classes in the iOS SDK (such as UINavigationController, UITableViewController, and UIViewController) are designed to act as the controller for a specific type of view. View controllers, however, are not the only types of controller classes that Cocoa Touch provides, although they are the most common. NSFetchedResultsController is an example of a controller class that is not a view controller.

NSFetchedResultsController is designed to handle one very specific job, which is to manage the objects returned from a Core Data fetch request. NSFetchedResultsController makes displaying data from Core Data easier than it would otherwise be because it handles a bunch of tasks for you. It will, for example, purge any unneeded objects from memory when it receives a low-memory warning and reload them when it needs them again. If you specify a delegate for the fetched results controller, your delegate will be notified when certain changes are made to its underlying data.

## Creating a Fetched Results Controller

You start by creating a fetch request and then use that fetch request to create a fetched results controller. In your template, this is done in `MasterViewController.m`, in the `fetchedResultsController` method. `fetchedResultsController` starts with a lazy load to see if there is already an active instantiated `_fetchedResultsController`. If that is not there (resolves to nil), it sets out to create a new fetch request. A fetch request is basically a specification that lays out the details of the data to be fetched. You need to tell the fetch request which entity to fetch. In addition, you want to add a sort descriptor to the fetch request. The sort descriptor determines the order in which the data is organized.

Once the fetch request is defined appropriately, the fetched results controller is created. The fetched results controller is an instance of the class `NSFetchedResultsController`. Remember that the fetched results controller's job is to use the fetch request to keep its associated data as fresh as possible.

Once the fetched results controller is created, you do your initial fetch. You do this in `MasterViewController.m` at the end of `fetchedResultsController` by sending your fetched results controller the `PerformFetch` message.

Now that you have your data, you're ready to be a data source and a delegate to your table view. When your table view wants the number of sections for its table, it will call `numberOfSectionsInTableView:`. In your version, you get the section information by passing the appropriate message to `fetchResultsController`. Here's the version from `MasterViewController.m`:

```
- (NSInteger)numberOfSectionsInTableView:(UITableView *)tableView
{
    return [[self.fetchedResultsController sections] count];
}
```

The same strategy applies in `tableView:numberOfRowsInSection:`

```
- (NSInteger)tableView:(UITableView *)tableView numberOfRowsInSection:(NSInteger)section
{
    id<NSFetchedResultsSectionInfo> sectionInfo =
        [self.fetchedResultsController sections] objectAtIndex:section];
    return [sectionInfo numberOfObjects];
}
```

You get the idea. You used to need to do all this work yourself. Now you can ask your fetched results controller to do all the data management for you. It's an amazing time-saver!

Let's take a closer look at the creation of the fetched results controller. In `MasterViewController.m`, use the function menu to go to the method `-fetchedResultsController`. It should look like this:

```
- (NSFetchedResultsController *)fetchedResultsController
{
    if (_fetchedResultsController != nil) {
        return _fetchedResultsController;
    }
```

```
    NSFetchRequest *fetchRequest = [[NSFetchRequest alloc] init];
    // Edit the entity name as appropriate.
    NSEntityDescription *entity = [NSEntityDescription entityForName:@"Event"
                        inManagedObjectContext:self.managedObjectContext];
    [fetchRequest setEntity:entity];

    // Set the batch size to a suitable number.
    [fetchRequest setFetchBatchSize:20];

    // Edit the sort key as appropriate.
    NSSortDescriptor *sortDescriptor = [[NSSortDescriptor alloc] initWithKey:@"timeStamp"
                                                                ascending:NO];

    NSArray *sortDescriptors = @[sortDescriptor];

    [fetchRequest setSortDescriptors:sortDescriptors];

    // Edit the section name key path and cache name if appropriate.
    // nil for section name key path means "no sections".
    NSFetchedResultsController *aFetchedResultsController = [[NSFetchedResultsController alloc]
                            initWithFetchRequest:fetchRequest
                            managedObjectContext:self.managedObjectContext
                            sectionNameKeyPath:nil cacheName:@"Master"];
    aFetchedResultsController.delegate = self;
    self.fetchedResultsController = aFetchedResultsController;

        NSError *error = nil;
        if (![self.fetchedResultsController performFetch:&error]) {
            // Replace this implementation with code to handle the error appropriately.
            // abort() causes the application to generate a crash log and terminate. You should
            // not use this function in a shipping application, although it may be useful during
            // development.
            NSLog(@"Unresolved error %@, %@", error, [error userInfo]);
            abort();
        }

    return _fetchedResultsController;
}
```

As discussed earlier, this method uses lazy loading. The first thing it does is check _fetchedResultsController for nil. If _fetchedResultsController already exists, it is returned; otherwise, the process of creating a new fetchedResultsController is started.

As the first step, you need to create an NSFetchRequest and NSEntityDescription, and then attach the NSEntityDescription to the NSFetchRequest.

```
NSFetchRequest *fetchRequest = [[NSFetchRequest alloc] init];
// Edit the entity name as appropriate.
NSEntityDescription *entity = [NSEntityDescription entityForName:@"Event"
                                    inManagedObjectContext:self.managedObjectContext];
[fetchRequest setEntity:entity];
```

Remember, you're building a fetched results controller, and the fetch request is part of that. Next, set the batch size to 20. This tells Core Data that this fetch request should retrieve its results 20 at a time. This is sort of like a file system's block size.

```
// Set the batch size to a suitable number.
[fetchRequest setFetchBatchSize:20];
```

Next, build an NSSortDescriptor and specify that it use timeStamp as a key, sorting the timestamps in descending order (earlier dates last).

```
// Edit the sort key as appropriate.
NSSortDescriptor *sortDescriptor = [[NSSortDescriptor alloc] initWithKey:@"timeStamp" ascending:NO];
```

Now you create an array of sort descriptors. Since you'll be using only one, you pass in sortDescriptor and follow it with nil to let initWithObjects know you just have a single element in the array. (Note that the template could have used initWithObject instead).

```
NSArray *sortDescriptors = @[sortDescriptor];
[fetchRequest setSortDescriptors:sortDescriptors];
```

Try this experiment: change ascending:NO to ascending:YES and run the application again. What do you think will happen? Don't forget to change it back when you are finished.

> **Tip**   If you need to restrict a fetch request to a subset of the managed objects stored in the persistent store, use a predicate. There's an entire chapter dedicated to predicates in *Learn Objective-C on the Mac, 2nd Edition* by Mark Dalrymple, Scott Knaster, and Waqar Malik (Apress, 2012). The default template does not use predicates, but you'll be working with them in the next several chapters.

Now you create an NSFetchedResultsController using your fetch request and context. You'll learn about the third and fourth parameters, sectionNameKeyPath and cacheName, in Chapter 3.

```
// Edit the section name key path and cache name if appropriate.
// nil for section name key path means "no sections".
NSFetchedResultsController *aFetchedResultsController =
    [[NSFetchedResultsController alloc] initWithFetchRequest:fetchRequest
                                managedObjectContext:self.managedObjectContext
                                  sectionNameKeyPath:nil
                                           cacheName:@"Master"];
```

Next, you set self as the delegate and set fetchedResultsController to the fetched results controller you just created.

```
aFetchedResultsController.delegate = self;
self.fetchedResultsController = aFetchedResultsController;
```

Finally, you perform the fetch and, if there are no errors, you assign the results to your private instance variable _fetchedResultsController and return the results.

```
NSError *error = nil;
if (![self.fetchedResultsController performFetch:&error]) {
    // Replace this implementation with code to handle the error appropriately.
    // abort() causes the application to generate a crash log and terminate. You should not use this
    // function in a shipping application, although it may be useful during development.
    NSLog(@"Unresolved error %@, %@", error, [error userInfo]);
    abort();
}

return _fetchedResultsController;
```

Don't worry too much about the details here. Try to get your head around the big picture. As you make your way through the next few chapters, the details will come into focus.

## The Fetched Results Controller Delegate Methods

The fetched results controller must have a delegate, and that delegate must provide four methods, which you will describe in the pages that follow. These four methods are defined in the protocol NSFetchedResultsControllerDelegate. The fetched results controller monitors its managed object context and calls its delegates as changes are made to its context.

## Will Change Content Delegate Method

When the fetched results controller observes a change that affects it—such as an object it manages being deleted or changed, or when a new object is inserted that meets the criteria of the fetched results controller's fetch request—the fetched results controller will notify its delegate before it makes any changes, using the method controllerWillChangeContent:.

The vast majority of the time a fetched results controller will be used along with a table view, and all you need to do in that delegate method is to inform the table view that updates about to be made might impact what it is displaying. This is the method that ensures it gets done:

```
- (void)controllerWillChangeContent:(NSFetchedResultsController *)controller
{
    [self.tableView beginUpdates];
}
```

## Did Change Contents Delegate Method

After the fetched results controller makes its changes, it will then notify its delegate using the method controllerDidChangeContent:. At that time, if you're using a table view (and you almost certainly will be), you need to tell the table view that the updates you told it were coming in controllerWillChangeContent: are now complete. This is handled for you like so:

```
- (void)controllerDidChangeContent:(NSFetchedResultsController *)controller
{
    [self.tableView endUpdates];
}
```

## Did Change Object Delegate Method

When the fetched results controller notices a change to a specific object, it will notify its delegate using the method `controller:didChangeObject:atIndexPath:forChangeType:newIndexPath:`. This method is where you need to handle updating, inserting, deleting, or moving rows in your table view to reflect whatever change was made to the objects managed by the fetched results controller. Here is the template implementation of the delegate method that will take care of updating the table view for you:

```
- (void)controller:(NSFetchedResultsController *)controller didChangeObject:(id)anObject
      atIndexPath:(NSIndexPath *)indexPath forChangeType:(NSFetchedResultsChangeType)type
    newIndexPath:(NSIndexPath *)newIndexPath
{
    UITableView *tableView = self.tableView;

    switch(type) {
        case NSFetchedResultsChangeInsert:
            [tableView insertRowsAtIndexPaths:@[newIndexPath]
                       withRowAnimation:UITableViewRowAnimationFade];
            break;

        case NSFetchedResultsChangeDelete:
            [tableView deleteRowsAtIndexPaths:@[indexPath]
                       withRowAnimation:UITableViewRowAnimationFade];
            break;

        case NSFetchedResultsChangeUpdate:
            [self configureCell:[tableView cellForRowAtIndexPath:indexPath] atIndexPath:indexPath];
            break;

        case NSFetchedResultsChangeMove:
            [tableView deleteRowsAtIndexPaths:@[indexPath]
                       withRowAnimation:UITableViewRowAnimationFade];
            [tableView insertRowsAtIndexPaths:@[newIndexPath]
                       withRowAnimation:UITableViewRowAnimationFade];
            break;
    }
}
```

Most of this code is fairly straightforward. If a row has been inserted, you receive a type of `NSFetchedResultsChangeInsert` and you insert a new row into the table. If a row was deleted, you receive a type of `NSFetchedResultsChangeDelete` and you delete the corresponding row in the table. When you get a type of `NSFetchedResultsChangeUpdate`, it means that an object was changed and the code calls `configureCell` to ensure that you are looking at the right data. If a type of `NSFetchedResultsChangeMove` was received, you know that a row was moved, so you delete it from the old location and insert it at the location specified by `newIndexPath`.

## Did Change Section Delegate Method

Lastly, if a change to an object affects the number of sections in the table, the fetched results controller will call the delegate method `controller:didChangeSection:atIndex:forChangeType:`.

If you specify a `sectionNameKeyPath` when you create your fetched results controller, you need to implement this delegate method to take care of adding and deleting sections from the table as needed. If you don't, you will get runtime errors when the number of sections in the table doesn't match the number of sections in the fetched results controller. Here is the template's standard implementation of that delegate method that should work for most situations:

```
- (void)controller:(NSFetchedResultsController *)controller
        didChangeSection:(id<NSFetchedResultsSectionInfo>)sectionInfo
        atIndex:(NSUInteger)sectionIndex
        forChangeType:(NSFetchedResultsChangeType)type
{
    switch(type) {
        case NSFetchedResultsChangeInsert:
            [self.tableView insertSections:[NSIndexSet indexSetWithIndex:sectionIndex]
                    withRowAnimation:UITableViewRowAnimationFade];
            break;

        case NSFetchedResultsChangeDelete:
            [self.tableView deleteSections:[NSIndexSet indexSetWithIndex:sectionIndex]
                    withRowAnimation:UITableViewRowAnimationFade];
            break;
    }
}
```

Using these four delegate methods, when you add a new managed object, the fetched results controller will detect that, and your table will be updated automatically. If you delete or change an object, the controller will detect that, too. Any change that affects the fetched results controller will automatically trigger an appropriate update to the table view, including properly animating the process. This means that you don't need to litter your code with calls to `reloadData` every time you make a change that might impact your dataset. Very nice!

### Retrieving a Managed Object From the Fetched Results Controller

Your table view delegate methods have become much shorter and more straightforward, since your fetched results controller does much of the work that you previously did in those methods. For example, to retrieve the object that corresponds to a particular cell, which you often need to do in `tableView:cellForRowAtIndexPath:` and `tableView:didSelectRowAtIndexPath:`, you can just call `objectAtIndexPath:` on the fetched results controller and pass in the `indexPath` parameter, and it will return the correct object.

```
NSManagedObject *object = [[self fetchedResultsController] objectAtIndexPath:indexPath];
```

## Creating and Inserting a New Managed Object

From the function menu in the editor pane, select `insertNewObject`, which is the method that is called when the + button is pressed in the sample application. It's a nice, simple example of how to create a new managed object, insert it into a managed object context, and then save it to the persistent store.

```
- (void)insertNewObject:(id)sender
{
    NSManagedObjectContext *context = [self.fetchedResultsController managedObjectContext];
    NSEntityDescription *entity = [[self.fetchedResultsController fetchRequest] entity];
    NSManagedObject *newManagedObject =
        [NSEntityDescription insertNewObjectForEntityForName:[entity name]
                                      inManagedObjectContext:context];

    // If appropriate, configure the new managed object.
    // Normally you should use accessor methods, but using KVC here avoids the need to add a custom
class to the template.
    [newManagedObject setValue:[NSDate date] forKey:@"timeStamp"];

    // Save the context.
    NSError *error = nil;
    if (![context save:&error]) {
        // Replace this implementation with code to handle the error appropriately.
        // abort() causes the application to generate a crash log and terminate.
        // You should not use this function in a shipping application,
        // although it may be useful during development.
        NSLog(@"Unresolved error %@, %@", error, [error userInfo]);
        abort();
    }
}
```

Notice that the first thing the code does is to retrieve a managed object context from the fetched results controller. In this simple example where there's only one context, you could also have retrieved the same context from the application delegate. There are a few reasons why the default code uses the context from the fetched results controller. First of all, you already have a method that returns the fetched results controller, so you can get to the context in just one line of code.

```
NSManagedObjectContext *context = [self.fetchedResultsController managedObjectContext];
```

More importantly, though, a fetched results controller always knows which context its managed objects are contained by, so even if you decide to create an application with multiple contexts, you'll be sure that you're using the correct context if you pull it from the fetched results controller.

Just as you did when you created a fetch request, when inserting a new object, you need to create an entity description to tell Core Data which kind of entity you want to create an instance of. The fetched results controller also knows what entity the objects it manages are, so you can just ask it for that information.

```
NSEntityDescription *entity = [[self.fetchedResultsController fetchRequest] entity];
```

Then it's simply a matter of using a class method on NSEntityDescription to create the new object and insert it into a context.

```
NSManagedObject *newManagedObject =
    [NSEntityDescription insertNewObjectForEntityForName:[entity name]
                                  inManagedObjectContext:context];
```

It does seem a little odd that you use a class method on NSEntityDescription, rather than an instance method on the context you want to insert the new object into, but that's the way it's done.

Though this managed object has now been inserted into the context, it still exists in the persistent store. In order to insert it from the persistent store, you must save the context, which is what happens next in this method:

```
// Save the context.
NSError *error = nil;
if (![context save:&error]) {
    // Replace this implementation with code to handle the error appropriately.
    // abort() causes the application to generate a crash log and terminate.
    // You should not use this function in a shipping application,
    // although it may be useful during development.
    NSLog(@"Unresolved error %@, %@", error, [error userInfo]);
    abort();
}
```

As the comment says, you need to handle the error more appropriately than calling abort. We'll cover this more in the ensuing chapters. Also, notice that you don't call reloadData on your table view. The fetched results controller will realize that you've inserted a new object that meets its criteria and will call the delegate method, which will automatically reload the table.

## Deleteing Managed Objects

Deleting managed objects is pretty easy when using a fetched results controller. Use the function menu to navigate to the method called tableView:commitEditingStyle:forRowAtIndexPath:. That method should look like this:

```
- (void)tableView:(UITableView *)tableView
        commitEditingStyle:(UITableViewCellEditingStyle)editingStyle
        forRowAtIndexPath:(NSIndexPath *)indexPath
{
    if (editingStyle == UITableViewCellEditingStyleDelete) {
        NSManagedObjectContext *context = [self.fetchedResultsController managedObjectContext];
        [context deleteObject:[self.fetchedResultsController objectAtIndexPath:indexPath]];

        NSError *error = nil;
        if (![context save:&error]) {
            // Replace this implementation with code to handle the error appropriately.
            // abort() causes the application to generate a crash log and terminate.
            // You should not use this function in a shipping application,
            // although it may be useful during development.
            NSLog(@"Unresolved error %@, %@", error, [error userInfo]);
            abort();
        }
    }
}
```

The method first makes sure that you're in a delete transaction (remember that this same method is used for deletes and inserts).

```
if (editingStyle == UITableViewCellEditingStyleDelete) {
```

Next, you retrieve the context.

```
NSManagedObjectContext *context = [self.fetchedResultsController managedObjectContext];
```

Then the context is asked to delete that object.

```
[context deleteObject:[self.fetchedResultsController objectAtIndexPath:indexPath]];
```

Next, the managed object context's save: method is called to cause that change to be committed to the persistent store.

```
NSError *error = nil;
if (![context save:&error]) {
    // Replace this implementation with code to handle the error appropriately.
    // abort() causes the application to generate a crash log and terminate. You should not use this
    // function in a shipping application, although it may be useful during development.
    NSLog(@"Unresolved error %@, %@", error, [error userInfo]);
    abort();
}
```

No need to admonish you again about the call to abort, as we discussed this previously.

And that's all there is to deleting managed objects.

# Putting Everything in Context

At this point, you should have a pretty good handle on the basics of using Core Data. You've learned about the architecture of a Core Data application and the process of using entities and properties. You've seen how the persistent store, managed object model, and managed object context are created by your application delegate. You learned how to use the data model editor to build entities that can be used in your program to create managed objects. You also learned how to retrieve, insert, and delete data from the persistent store.

Enough with the theory! Let's move on and build us some Core Data applications, shall we?

# Chapter 3

# A Super Start: Adding, Displaying, and Deleting Data

Well, if that last chapter didn't scare you off, then you're ready to dive in and move beyond the basic template you explored in Chapter 2.

In this chapter, you're going to create an application designed to track some superhero data. Your application will start with the Master-Detail Application template, though you'll be making lots of changes right from the beginning. You'll use the model editor to design your superhero entity. Then you'll create a new controller class derived from `UIViewController` that will allow you to add, display, and delete superheroes. In Chapter 4, you'll extend your application further and add code to allow the user to edit her superhero data.

Take a look at Figure 3-1 to get a sense of what your app will look like when it runs. It looks a lot like the template app. The major differences lie in the entity at the heart of the application and in the addition of a tab bar at the bottom of the screen. Let's get to work.

*Figure 3-1. The SuperDB application as it will look once you've finished this chapter*

# Setting up the Xcode Project

Time to get your hands dirty. Launch Xcode if it's not open, and bring up your old friend, the new project assistant (Figure 3-2).

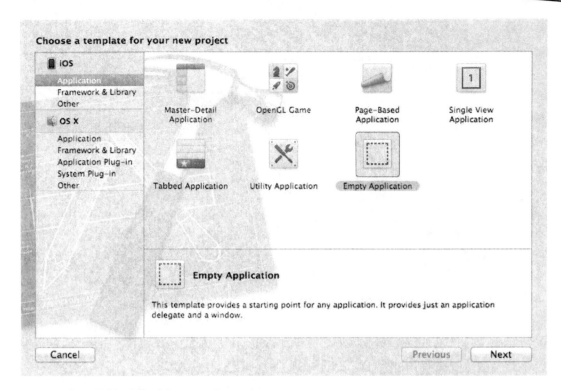

*Figure 3-2.  Your dear old friend, Xcode's new project assistant*

In the last chapter, you started with the Master-Detail Application template. When you're creating your own navigation applications, it's a good template to use as it gives you a lot of the code you're likely to need in your application. However, to make it easier to explain where to add or modify code and also to reinforce your understanding of how applications are constructed, you're going to build the SuperDB application from scratch, just as you did throughout most of *Beginning iOS 6 Development* by David Mark, Jack Nutting, and Jeff LaMarche (Apress).

Select Empty Application, and click Next. When prompted for a product name (Figure 3-3), type in **SuperDB**. Select iPhone for the device family, and make sure that the "Use Core Data" and "Use Automatic Reference Counting" checkboxes are checked. After clicking Next again, use the default location to save the project and click Create.

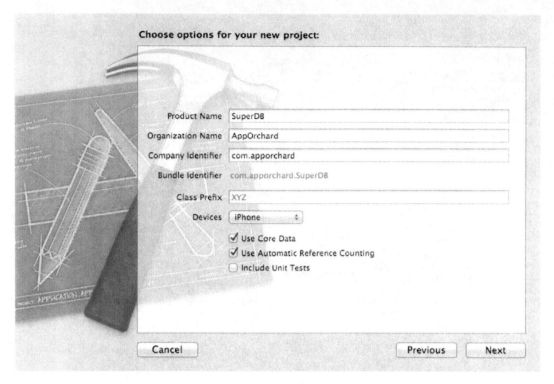

*Figure 3-3.  Entering project details*

You need to make some changes to use storyboards. Storyboards were a new feature added to Xcode with iOS 5. They make managing user interfaces and the transitions between those interface much easier. Xcode provides a visual editor, the storyboard editor, to aid in the layout and design of user interfaces. Where Interface Builder let you work with one view at a time, storyboards let you work the entire set of views and their behavior. By default, the Empty Application template did not give you a storyboard. This is easy enough to fix.

First, create a new storyboard file. Select the SuperDB group in the Navigator pane, and create a new file (type ⌘N or use the menu File ➤ New ➤ File). When the New File Assistant appears (Figure 3-4), select User Interface from under the iOS heading in the left pane, then select Storyboard from the right pane, and click the Next button. Choose iPhone as the device on the next assistant screen, and click Next again. Name the file **SuperDB.storyboard**, and save it in the project folder (Figure 3-6). The new file, SuperDB.storyboard, should appear in the Navigator pane.

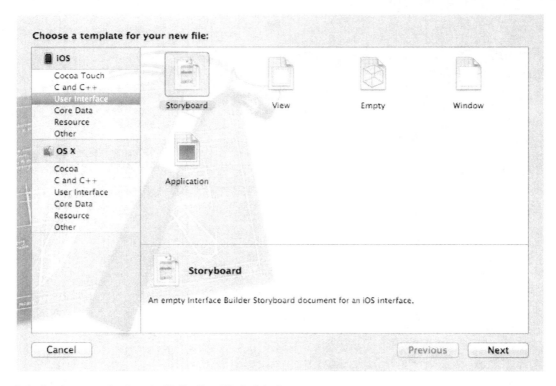

*Figure 3-4.  Create a new storyboard with the New File Assistant*

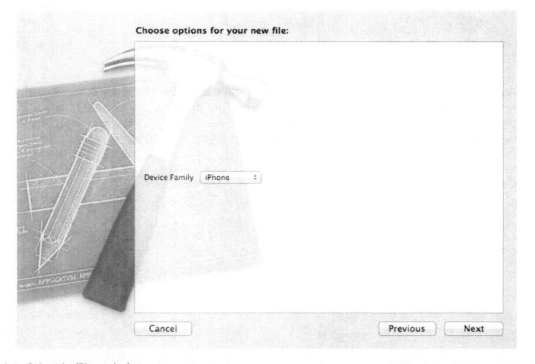

*Figure 3-5.  Select the iPhone device*

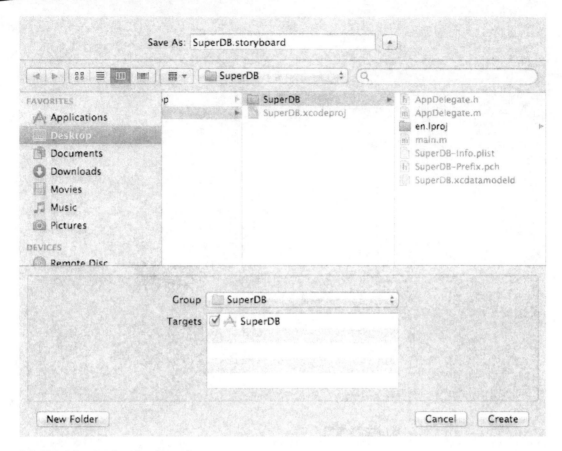

*Figure 3-6. Name the storyboard and save it*

Finally, you need to tell Xcode that you want to use the new SuperDB.storyboard file. Select the SuperDB project at the top of the Navigator pane. When the project editor appears, select the SuperDB Target and go to the project summary editor (Figure 3-7). In the section titled iPhone/iPod Deployment Info, enter the name **SuperDB** into the Main Storyboard field.

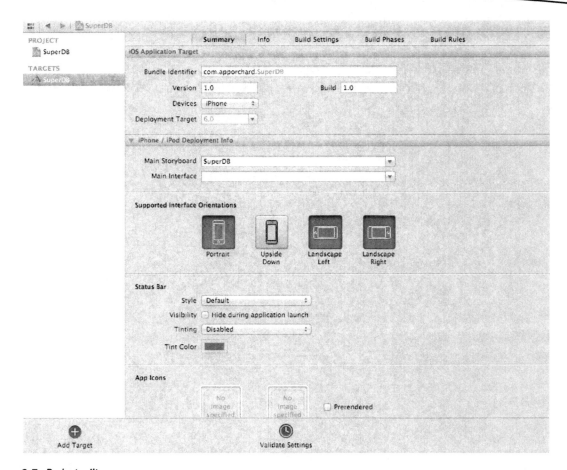

*Figure 3-7. Project editor*

Since you have configured SuperDB to use a storyboard, you need to clean up the application delegate. Select AppDelegate.m in the Navigator pane. The code editor should appear. Find the method

```
- (BOOL)application:(UIApplication *)application
        didFinishLaunchingWithOptions:(NSDictionary *)launchOptions
```

and edit it to read

```
-(BOOL)application:(UIApplication *)application
        didFinishLaunchingWithOptions:(NSDictionary *)launchOptions
{
        return YES;
}
```

Now you need to actually create your storyboard. Find and select SuperDB.storyboard in the Navigation pane. The editor pane should transform into the storyboard editor (Figure 3-8). Let's quickly review the storyboard editor. The content of the editor is a grid, similar to the model editor graph style. On the bottom left of the storyboard editor is a disclosure button. The arrow in the button should be pointing to the right. Click it.

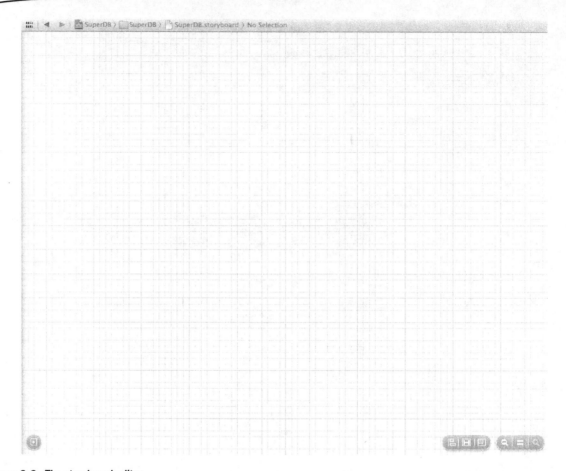

*Figure 3-8. The storyboard editor*

The storyboard document outline (Figure 3-9) should appear on the left of the storyboard editor. Right now this view is empty with no scenes (we'll define *scenes* in a little bit). Normally, the storyboard document outline provides a hierarchical view of the scenes, their view controllers, views and UI components.

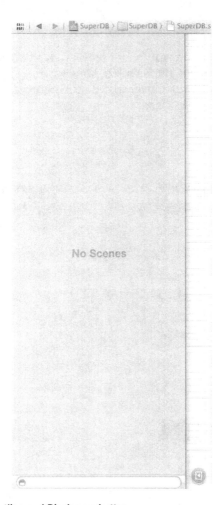

*Figure 3-9. The storyboard document outline and Disclosure button*

There is a pair of button groups on the bottom right of the editor (Figure 3-10). The button group on the left is for configuring auto layout of your views; we'll describe them in Chapter 4. The button group on the right has three buttons: Zoom Out, Zoom-to-Fit, and Zoom In. They change the zoom level of the storyboard editor.

*Figure 3-10. Storyboard editor button groups*

## Adding a Scene

Reset the Xcode workspace so that the storyboard editor looks like Figure 3-8. Open the Utility pane, and find the navigation controller in the Object library (which should be at the bottom of the Utility pane). Drag the navigation controller over to the storyboard editor. Your storyboard editor should look something like Figure 3-11.

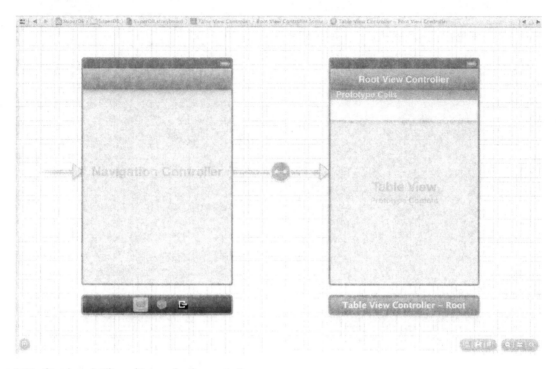

*Figure 3-11.  Storyboard editor with a navigation controller*

## Scenes and Segues

Interestingly, Xcode decided that along with the navigation controller, you wanted a table view controller and set it up. Click the Zoom-To-Fit (=) button on the lower right to fit everything in the storyboard editor. What you see now are two scenes, labeled Navigation Controller and Table View Controller - Root. Between the two scenes is a segue. It's the arrow pointing from the Navigation Controller to the Table View Controller - Root. It has an icon in the middle of it that tells you this is a manual segue.

A scene is basically a view controller. The leftmost scene is labeled Navigation Controller, rightmost is the Table View Controller - Root. The navigation controller is used to manage the other view controllers. In Chapter 2, the navigation controller managed the master and detail view controllers. The navigation controller also provided the navigation bar that allowed you to edit and add events in the master view controller and provided the Back button in the detail view controller.

A segue defines the transition from a scene to the next scene. In the application from Chapter 2, when you selected an event in the master view controller, you triggered the segue to transition to the detail view controller.

But what about the arrow to the left of the navigation controller? That simply tells you the navigation controller is the root view controller for this storyboard.

## Storyboard Document Outline

Now that you have something in your storyboard editor, let's take a look at the storyboard document outline. Open it up. Now you can see the hierarchical view of the scenes described earlier (Figure 3-12), with their view controllers, views, and UI components.

*Figure 3-12. The story document outline, populated*

Let's take a look at your work so far. Build and run the SuperDB app. You should see something like Figure 3-13.

*Figure 3-13.* *The SuperDB app so far*

# Application Architecture

There's no single right architecture for every application. One obvious approach would be to make the application a tabbed application, and then add a separate navigation controller for each tab. In a situation where each tab corresponds to a completely different view showing different types of data, this approach would make perfect sense. In Chapter 7 of *Beginning iOS 6 Development*, you used that exact approach because every single tab corresponded to a different view controller with different outlets and different actions.

In this case, however, you're going to implement two tabs (with more to be added in later chapters), but each tab will show exactly the same data, just ordered differently. When one tab is selected, the table will be ordered by the superhero's name. If the other tab is selected, the same data will be shown but ordered by the superhero's secret identity.

Regardless of which tab is selected, tapping a row on the table will do the same thing: drill down to a new view where you can edit the information about the superhero you selected (which you will add in the next chapter). Regardless of which tab is selected, tapping the Add button will add a new instance of the same entity. When you drill down to another view to view or edit a hero, the tabs are no longer relevant.

For your application, the tab bar is just modifying the way the data in a single table is presented. There's no need for it to actually swap in and out other view controllers. Why have multiple navigation controller instances all managing identical sets of data and responding the same way to touches? Why not just use one table controller and have it change the way it presents the data based on which tab is selected? This is the approach you're going to take in this application. As a result, your application won't be a true tabbed application.

Your root view controller will be a navigation controller, and you'll use a tab bar purely to receive input from the user. The end result that is shown to the user will be identical to what they'd see if you created separate navigation controllers and table view controllers for each tab. Behind the scenes you'll be using less memory and won't have to worry about keeping the different navigation controllers in sync with each other.

Your application's root view controller will be an instance of UINavigationController. You'll create your own custom view controller class, HeroListController, to act as the root view controller for this UINavigationController. HeroListController will display the list of superheroes along with the tabs that control how the heroes are displayed and ordered.

Here's how the app will work. When the application starts, an instance of HeroListController is loaded from the Storyboard file. Then an instance of UINavigationController is created with the HeroListController instance as its root view controller. Finally, the UINavigationController is set as the application's root view controller. The view associated with the HeroListController contains your tab bar and your superhero table view.

In Chapter 4, you'll add a table view controller into the mix to implement a detail superhero view. When the user taps on a superhero in the superhero list, this detail controller will be pushed onto the navigation stack and its view will temporarily replace the HeroListController's view in the UINavigationController's content view. No need to worry about the detail view now; we just wanted you to see what's coming.

# Designing the View Controller Interface

Your application's root view controller is now a stock UINavigationController. You didn't need to write any code for it; you just dropped a navigation controller object into your storyboard. Xcode also gave you a UITableViewController as the root of the navigation controller's stack. Even though you will be using a table to display the list of heroes, you're not going to subclass UITableViewController. Because you also need to add a tab bar to your interface, you're going to create a subclass of UIViewController and create your interface in the storyboard editor. The table that will display the list of heroes will be a subview of your view controller's content pane.

If not already selected, select the SuperDB.storyboard in the Navigation pane. Also make sure the Utility pane is exposed. The storyboard should have two scenes: the Navigation Controller and the Table View Controller - Root. Zoom out so that both scenes are visible. Select the Table View Controller - Root. Only the Table View Controller - Root scene and label should be highlighted blue. Delete the table view controller by hitting the Delete key or Edit ➤ Delete. You should now only have the navigation controller.

From the bottom of the Utility pane, select a view controller from the Object library and drag it to the storyboard editor. A view controller should appear; place it to the right of the navigation controller (Figure 3-14).

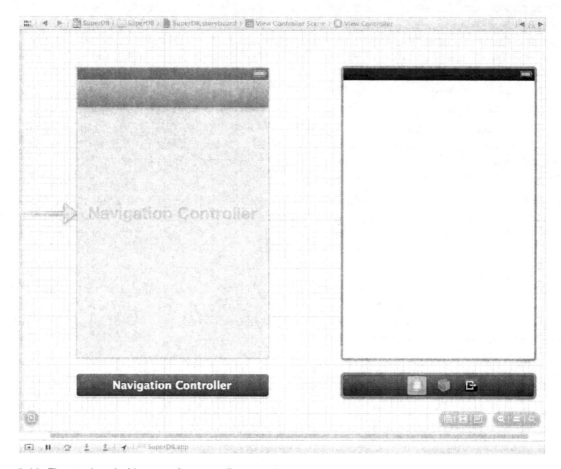

*Figure 3-14.* *The storyboard with a new view controller scene*

Before you lay out the new view controller, let's connect it to the navigation controller. Select the navigation controller. Click the Zoom In button until the navigation controller changes to display three icons (Figure 3-15). Hover the pointer over the left-most icon. A pop-up window should appear with the words navigation controller. Control-drag from the navigation controller icon to the view of the view controller. When you release the pointer, you should see a pop-up menu of possible segue assignments (Figure 3-16). Select root view controller in the Relationship Segue section. You should see a segue appear between the navigation controller and the view controller. Also, the view controller should now have a navigation bar along the top.

*Figure 3-15.* *Navigation controller label icons*

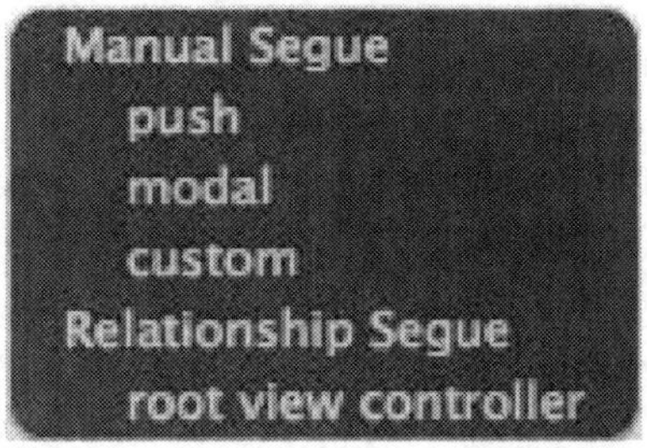

*Figure 3-16.* *Possible segue assignments*

Now you can design the view controller's interface. Let's add the tab bar first. Look in the library for a Tab Bar. Make sure you're grabbing a tab bar and not a tab bar controller. You only want the user interface item. Drag a tab bar from the library to the scene called View Controller, and place it snugly in the bottom of the window, as shown in Figure 3-17.

*Figure 3-17.* *The tab bar placed snugly against the bottom of the scene*

**Note**   You may need to zoom in to drop the tab bar into the view. You need to zoom in enough so the label changes from view controller to a series of icons. The bottom of Figure 3-17 shows this.

The default tab bar has two tabs, which is exactly the number you want. Let's change the icon and label for each. With the tab bar still selected, click the star above Favorites. Then click the Attributes Inspector button in the Utility pane selector bar (it should be the fourth button). Alternately, you can select View ➤ Utilities ➤ Show Attribute Inspector. The menu short cut is ⌥⌘4.

If you've correctly selected the tab bar item, the Attribute Inspector pane should say Tab Bar Item and the Identifier pop-up should say Favorites. In the Attribute Inspector, give this tab a title of **By Name** and an image of name_icon.png (Figure 3-18). Now click the three dots above the word More on the tab bar to select the right tab. Using the inspector, give this tab a title of **By Secret Identity** and an image of secret_icon.png.

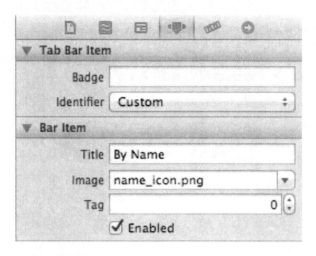

*Figure 3-18. Setting the attributes of the left tab*

**Note**    The files name_icon.png and secret_icon.png can be found in the download archive for this book.

Back in the Object library, look for a table view. Again, make sure you're getting the user interface element, not a table view controller. Drag this to the space above the tab bar. It should resize automatically to fit the space available. After you drop it, it should look like Figure 3-19.

*Figure 3-19.* *The table view in the scene*

Finally, grab a table view cell, and drag it on top of the table view. Xcode should automatically align it to the top the table view (Figure 3-20).

*Figure 3-20.* *The table view cell on the table view*

Select the table view cell, and expose the Attribute Inspector in the Utility pane. You need to change some of the attributes to get the behavior you want. First, set the style to Subtitle. This gives a table view cell with a large title text and a smaller subtitle text below the title. Next, give it an identifier value of HeroListCell. This value will be used later when creating table view cells. Finally, change the selection from Blue to None. This means when you tap on a table view cell, it won't highlight. Your Attribute Inspector should look like Figure 3-21.

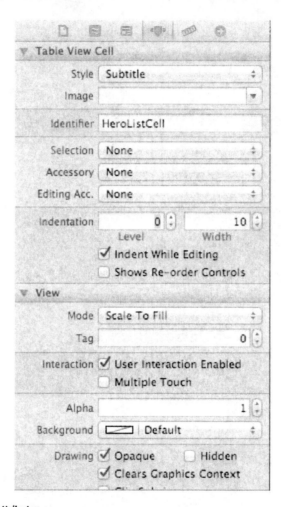

*Figure 3-21. The table view cell attributes*

Your interface is complete. Now you need to define your view controller interface in order to make the outlet, delegate, and datasource connections.

## Creating HeroListController

Single-click the SuperDB group in the Navigator pane. Now create a new file (⌘N or File ➤ New ➤ File). When the New File Assistant appears (Figure 3-22), select Cocoa Touch from under the iOS heading in the left pane, then select Objective-C class from the right pane, and click the Next button.

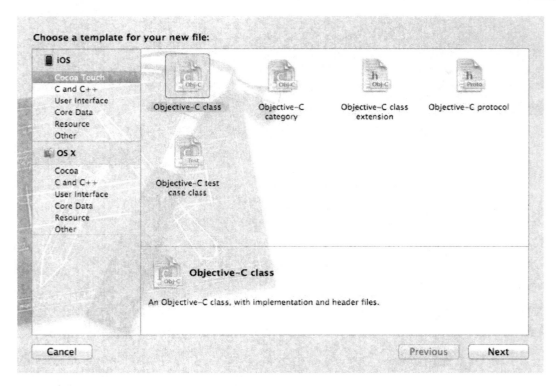

*Figure 3-22.* *Selecting the Objective-C class template in the new file assistant*

On the second file assistant pane (Figure 3-23), give the class a name of HeroListController and make it a subclass of UITableViewController. Make sure both the "Targeted for iPad" and "With XIB for user interface" items are unchecked. With that done, click the Next button. The file dialog should be selected to the SuperDB project folder, so just click Create. Two files should have been added to the project view: HeroListController.h and HeroListController.m.

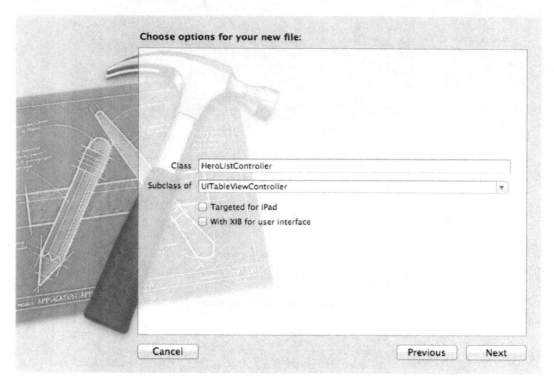

*Figure 3-23.  Selecting the UITableViewController in the file assistant*

Wait a minute. When you made the interface in MainStoryboard.storyboard, you used a plain
UIViewController, not a UITableViewController. And we said earlier that you didn't want to
use a UITableViewController. So why did we have you make HeroListController a subclass of
UITableViewController?

If you look back at Figure 3-1, you can see that your application displays a list of heroes in
a table view. That table view will need a data source and delegate. The HeroListController
will be that data source and delegate. By asking the New File Assistant to make a subclass of
UITableViewController, Xcode will use a file template that will predefine a bunch of table view data
source and delegate methods. Select HeroListController.m in the Navigator pane and take a look
at the file in the Editor pane. You should see the methods Xcode gave you for free.

However, you do need to make the HeroListController a subclass of UIViewController. Single-click
HeroListController.h in the Navigator pane. Find the @interface declaration, and change it from

```
@interface HeroListController : UITableViewController
```

to

```
@interface HeroListController : UIViewController <UITableViewDataSource, UITableViewDelegate>
```

Next, select HeroListController.m. Find the method

```
- (id)initWithStyle:(UITableViewStyle)style
{
```

```
        self = [super initWithStyle:style];
        if (self) {
        // Custom initialization
        }
        return self;
}
```

and delete it.

Now you need to connect to the table view data source and delegate to the HeroListController. While you're at it, create the outlets needed for the tab bar and table view. You could add them manually, but we assume you know how to do that. Let's try using an alternate method.

Select SuperDB.storyboard in the Navigator pane and expose the storyboard editor. Make sure your zoom level is such that that view controller label shows the three icons. Hover the pointer over the left-most icon, an orange circle with a white square. Xcode should pop up a label that reads View Controller. Single-click to select it. Over in the Utility pane, select the Identity Inspector (Figure 3-24). Change the Class field (under the Custom Class header) to HeroListController.

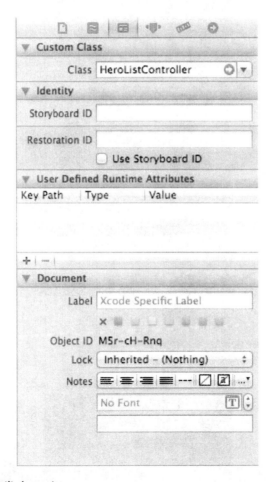

*Figure 3-24. View Controller's Identity Inspector*

What have you done here? You've told Xcode that your view controller is not a plain old `UIViewController`, but now a `HeroListController`. If you hover the pointer over the view controller icon, the pop-up will read Hero View Controller now.

## Making the Connections and Outlets

First, make the `HeroListController` the table view data source and delegate. Control-drag from the Table View area to the `HeroListController` (Figure 3-25). When you release, an Outlets pop-up window should appear (Figure 3-26). Select dataSource. Repeat the control-drag, this time selecting delegate.

*Figure 3-25. Control-drag from the table view to the HeroListController*

*Figure 3-26. Table view Outlets pop-up window*

Now you're going to add the outlets for the tab bar and table view. On the toolbar, change the editor from the Standard editor to the Assistant editor. The Editor pane should split into two views (Figure 3-27). The left view will have the storyboard editor; the right view will have a Code editor showing the interface file of HeroListController.

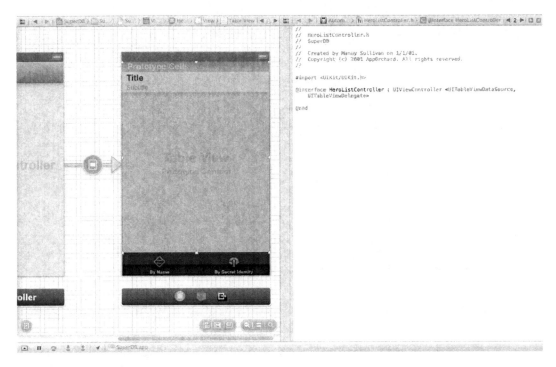

*Figure 3-27.* *The Assistant editor*

Again, control-drag from the Table View area, but this time go to the Code editor, just between the @interface and @end declarations (Figure 3-28). Once you release, a Connection pop-up window should appear (Figure 3-29). Enter heroTableView in the Name field and leave the rest of the fields at their default settings. Click the Connect button.

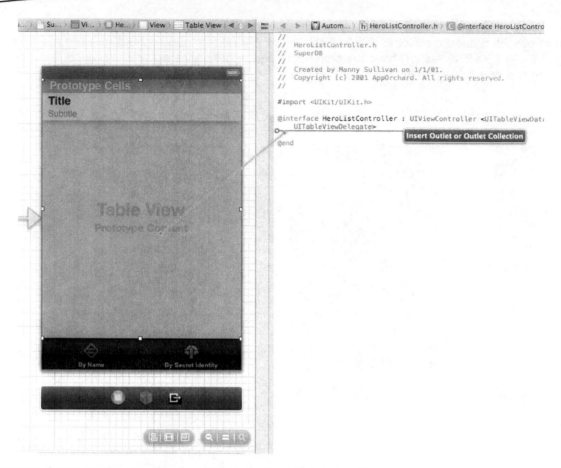

**Figure 3-28.** *Control-drag from the table view to the HeroListController interface file*

**Figure 3-29.** *The Connection pop-up window*

The following line should be added after the @interface declaration:

```
@property (weak, nonatomic) IBOutlet UITableView *heroTableView;
```

Repeat the process, this time control dragging from the tab bar to the just underneath the new @property declaration. Use **heroTabBar** for the name. You should get the following new @property declaration for the tab bar:

```
@property (weak, nonatomic) IBOutlet UITabBar *heroTabBar;
```

## Navigation Bar Buttons

If you build and run the SuperDB app, you should get something like Figure 3-30.

*Figure 3-30. SuperDB so far. Looking good!*

Let's add the Edit and Add (+) buttons. Make sure the Standard Editor toggle is selected in the toolbar, then select `HeroListController.m` in the Navigator pane. In the Editor pane, find the method

```
- (void)viewDidLoad
```

At the bottom of the method, you should see the following lines:

```
// Uncomment the following line to display an Edit button in the navigation bar for this view controller.
// self.navigationItem.rightBarButtonItem = self.editButtonItem;
```

Uncomment the second line and change the rightBarButtonItem to leftBarButtonItem, like so:

```
// Uncomment the following line to display an Edit button in the navigation bar for this view controller.
self.navigationItem.leftBarButtonItem = self.editButtonItem;
```

To add the Add (+) button, you need to go back to the storyboard editor. Select `SuperDB.storyboard` in the Navigator pane. Drag a bar button item from the Object library to the right side of the navigation bar in the Hero view controller. In the Utility pane, select the Attribute Inspector. You should see the Attribute Inspector for a bar button item (Figure 3-31). If not, make sure the bar button item you just added is selected. Change the Identifier field to Add. The bar button item's label should change from Item to +.

**Figure 3-31.** *Bar button item's Attribute Inspector*

Toggle back to the Assistant editor. Control-drag from the bar button item to just below the last `@property` in the `HeroListController` interface file. When the connection pop-up window appears, add a connection named **addButton**. Control-drag from the bar button item again to just above the `@end`. This time, when the connection pop-up appears, change the connection value to Action and set the name to **addHero** (Figure 3-32). Click connect. You should see a new method declaration:

```
- (IBAction)addHero:(id)sender;
```

*Figure 3-32. Adding the addHero: Action*

If you go to the `HeroListController` implementation file, you'll see the (empty) method implementation:

```
- (IBAction)addHero:(id)sender {
}
```

Build and run the app. Everything looks in place (Figure 3-33). Click the Edit button. It should turn into a Done button. Click the Done button, and it should go back to Edit. Press the Add (+) button. Nothing happens. That's because you haven't written the -addHero: method to do anything. You'll get to that soon.

*Figure 3-33. Everything is in the right place*

However, right now the tab bar does not have either tab button selected. When you start the app, both buttons are off. You can select one, then toggle between the two. But shouldn't one of the buttons be selected at launch? You'll implement that next.

# Tab Bar and User Defaults

You want the application to start with one of the tab bar buttons selected. You can do that pretty easily, by adding something like this

```
// Select the Tab Bar Button
UITabBarItem *item=[self.heroTabBar.items objectAtIndex:0];
[self.heroTabBar setSelectedItem:item];
```

to the viewDidLoad: method of the HeroListController. Go ahead and try it. The application starts and the By Name tab is selected. Now, select the By Secret Identity tab and stop the app in Xcode. Restart the app. The By Name tab is selected. Wouldn't it be nice if the application remembered your last selection? You can use user defaults to do that remembering for you.

In the HeroListController interface, add the following lines before the @interface declaration:

```
#define kSelectedTabDefaultsKey @"Selected Tab"

enum {
    kByName,
    kBySecretIdentity,
};
```

The kSelectedTabDefaultsKey is the key you'll use to store and retrieve the selected tab bar button index from the user defaults. The enumeration is just a convenience for the values 0 and 1.

Switch over to the HeroListController implementation file, and add the following to the end of the viewDidLoad: method:

```
// Select the Tab Bar button
NSUserDefaults *defaults = [NSUserDefaults standardUserDefaults];
NSInteger selectedTab = [defaults integerForKey:kSelectedTabDefaultsKey];
UITabBarItem *item = [self.heroTabBar.items objectAtIndex:selectedTab];
[self.heroTabBar setSelectedItem:item];
```

(If you entered the earlier tab bar selection code, make sure you make the changes correctly.)

Build and run the app. Toggle the tab bar. Quit the app, and make sure the By Secret Identity button is selected. Quit the app, and start it again. It should remember the selection, right? Not yet. You haven't written code to write the user default when the tab bar selection changes. You're only reading it at launch. Let's write the default when it changes.

Select the SuperDB.storyboard, and control-drag from the tab bar to the Hero view controller. When the Outlets pop-up appears, select delegate (it should be your only choice). Next, select HeroListController.h, and change the @interface declaration from

```
@interface HeroListController : UIViewController<UITableViewDataSource, UITableViewDelegate>
```

to

```
@interface HeroListController : UIViewController<UITableViewDataSource, UITableViewDelegate,
UITabBarDelegate>
```

Now UITabBarDelegate has a required method -tabBar:didSelectItem:. Select
HeroListController.m, and navigate the Editor to just above the -addHero: method. Add these lines:

```
#pragma mark - UITabBarDelegate Methods

- (void)tabBar:(UITabBar *)tabBar didSelectItem:(UITabBarItem *)item
{
    NSUserDefaults *defaults = [NSUserDefaults standardUserDefaults];
    NSUInteger tabIndex = [tabBar.items indexOfObject:item];
    [defaults setInteger:tabIndex forKey:kSelectedTabDefaultsKey];
}
```

Now when you quit and launch the application, it remembers your last tab bar selection.

# Designing the Data Model

Now you need define the application's data model. As we discussed in Chapter 2, the Xcode
model editor is where you design your application's data model. In the Navigator pane, click on
SuperDB.xcdatamodel. This should bring up the model editor (Figure 3-34).

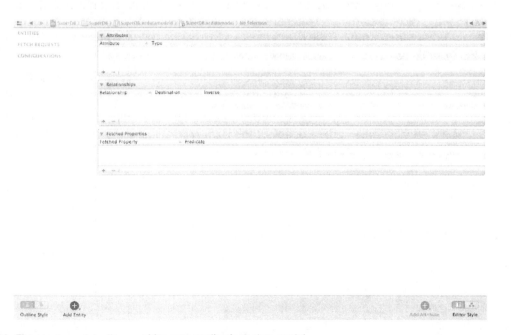

***Figure 3-34.*** *The empty model editor awaiting your application's data model*

Unlike the data model from Chapter 2, you should be starting with a completely empty data model. So let's dive right in and start building. The first thing you need to add to your data model is an entity. Remember, entities are like class definitions. Although they don't store any data themselves, without at least one entity in your data model, your application won't be able to store any data.

## Adding an Entity

Since the purpose of your application is to track information about superheroes, it seems logical that you're going to need an entity to represent a hero. You're going to start off simple in this chapter and track only a few pieces of data about each hero: name, secret identity, date of birth, and sex. You'll add more data elements in future chapters, but this will give you a basic foundation upon which to build.

Add a new entity to the data model. A new entity, named Entity, should appear in the Top-Level Components pane. This entity should be selected, and the text Entity should be highlighted. Type **Hero** to name this entity.

## Editing the New Entity

Let's verify that your new Hero entity has been added to the default configuration. Select the Default Configuration in the Top-Level Configuration pane. The Data Editor Detail pane to the right should have changed with a single table named Entities. There should be one entry in this table, the entity you just named Hero.

Next to Hero is a checkbox called Abstract. This checkbox allows you to create an entity that cannot be used to create managed objects at runtime. The reason why you might create an abstract entity is if you have several properties that are common to multiple entities. In that case, you might create an abstract entity to hold the common fields and then make every entity that uses those common fields a child of that abstract entity. Thus if you needed to change those common fields, you'd only need to do it in one place.

Next, the Class field should blank. This means the Hero entity is a subclass of NSManagedObject. In Chapter 6, you'll see how to create custom subclasses of NSManagedObject to add functionality.

You can see more detail by selecting this row, and then exposing the Utility pane. Let's expose the Utility pane. Once the Utility pane appears, select the Data Model Inspector (the third button on the Inspector Selector bar). The Utility pane should be similar to Figure 3-35.

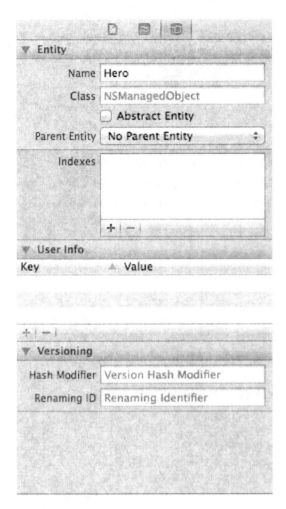

*Figure 3-35.* *The Utilities pane for the new Entity*

The first three fields (Name, Class, and Abstract Entity) mirror what you saw in the Data Detail pane. Below the Abstract Entity checkbox is a pop-up menu labeled Parent Entity. Within a data model, you have the ability to specify a parent entity, which is very similar to subclassing in Objective-C. When you specify another entity as your parent, the new entity receives all the properties of parent entity along with any additional ones that you specify. Leave the parenting pop-up set to No Parent Entity.

> **Note**    You may be wondering about the additional areas in the Data Model Inspector, titled User Info, Versioning and Entity Sync. These settings give you access to more advanced configuration parameters that are only rarely used. You won't be changing any of the configurations.
>
> If you're interested in finding out more about these advanced options, you can read more about them in *Pro Core Data for iOS, 2nd Edition* (www.apress.com/9781430236566). Apple has the following guides online as well: the Core Data Programming Guide at http://developer.apple.com/library/ios/#documentation/Cocoa/Conceptual/CoreData/cdProgrammingGuide.html and the Core Data Model Versioning and Data Migration Guide at http://developer.apple.com/library/ios/#documentation/Cocoa/Conceptual/CoreDataVersioning/Articles/Introduction.html.

# Adding Attributes to the Hero Entity

Now that you have an entity, you must give it attributes in order for managed objects based on this entity to be able to store any data. For this chapter, you need four attributes: name, secret identity, birth date, and sex.

## Adding the Name Attribute

Select the Hero entity in the data component pane, and add an attribute. Once added, an entry named `Attribute` should appear in the `Attributes Property` table in the detail pane. Just as when you created a new entity, the newly added attribute has been automatically selected for you. Type **name**, which will cause the name of the new attribute to be updated. The Attributes Property pane should look like Figure 3-36.

*Figure 3-36.  Attributes detail*

> **Tip**    It's not an accident that you chose to start your entity Hero with a capital H, but your attribute name with a lowercase n. This is the accepted naming convention for entities and properties. Entities begin with a capital letter; properties begin with a lowercase letter. In both cases, if the name of the entity or property consists of more than one word, the first letter of each new word is capitalized.

The Type column of the table specifies the data type of the attribute. By default, the data type is set to Undefined.

Now, let's expose the Utilities pane again (if it's not already open). Make sure the name attribute is selected in the detail pane, and choose the Data Model Inspector (Figure 3-37). The first field should be titled Name, and it should have the value of name.

*Figure 3-37. The Data Model Inspector for the new name attribute*

Below the Name field are three checkboxes: Transient, Optional, and Indexed. If Optional is checked, then this entity can be saved even if this attribute has no value assigned to it. If you uncheck it, then any attempt to save a managed object based on this entity when the name attribute is nil will result in a validation error that will prevent the save. In this particular case, name is the main attribute that you will use to identify a given hero, so you probably want to require this attribute. Single-click the Optional checkbox to uncheck it, making this field required.

The Transient checkbox allows you to create attributes that are not saved in the persistent store. They can also be used to create custom attributes that store non-standard data. For now, don't worry too much about Transient. Just leave it unchecked; you'll revisit this checkbox in Chapter 6.

The final checkbox, Indexed, tells the underlying data store to add an index on this attribute. Not all persistent stores support indices, but the default store (SQLite) does. The database uses an index to improve search speeds when searching or ordering based on that field. You will be ordering your superheroes by name, so check the Indexed checkbox to tell SQLite to create an index on the column that will be used to store this attribute's data.

> **Caution**    Properly used, indices can greatly improve performance in a SQLite persistent store. Adding indices where they are not needed, however, can actually degrade performance. If you don't have a reason for selecting Indexed, leave it unchecked.

## Attribute Types

Every attribute has a type, which identifies the kind of data that the attribute is capable of storing. If you single-click the Attribute Type drop-down (which should currently be set to Undefined), you can see the various datatypes that Core Data supports out of the box (Figure 3-38). These are all the types of data that you can store without having to implement a custom attribute, like you're going to do in Chapter 6. Each of the data types correspond to an Objective-C class that is used to set or retrieve values, and you must make sure to use the correct object when setting values on managed objects.

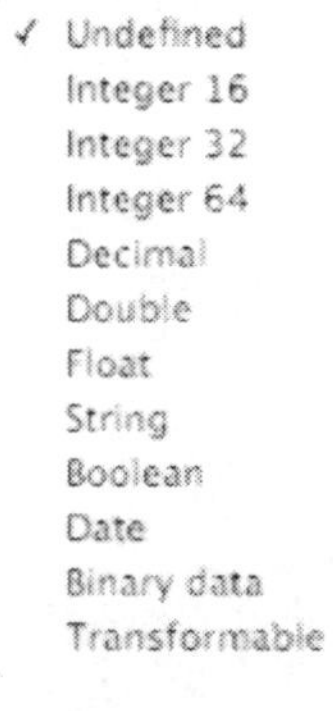

```
✓  Undefined
   Integer 16
   Integer 32
   Integer 64
   Decimal
   Double
   Float
   String
   Boolean
   Date
   Binary data
   Transformable
```

*Figure 3-38. The data types supported by Core Data*

### The Integer Data Types

Integer 16, Integer 32, and Integer 64 all hold signed integers (whole numbers). The only difference between these three number types is the minimum and maximum size of the values they are capable of storing. In general, you should pick the smallest-size integer that you are certain will work for your purposes. For example, if you know your attribute will never hold a number larger than a thousand, make sure to select Integer 16 rather than Integer 32 or Integer 64. The minimum and maximum values that these three data types are capable of storing are shown in Table 3-1.

*Table 3-1. Integer Type Minimums and Maximums*

| Data Type | Minimum | Maximum |
| --- | --- | --- |
| Integer 16 | −32,768 | 32, 767 |
| Integer 32 | −2,147,483,648 | 2,147,483,647 |
| Integer 64 | −9,223,372,036,854,775,808 | 9,223,372,036,854,77`5,807 |

At runtime, you set integer attributes of a managed object using instances of NSNumber created using a factory method such as numberWithInt: or numberWithLong:.

## The Decimal, Double, and Float Data Types

The decimal, double, and float data types all hold decimal numbers. Double and float hold floating-point representations of decimal numbers similar to the C datatypes of double and float, respectively. Floating-point representations of decimal numbers are always an approximation due to the fact that they use a fixed number of bytes to represent data. The larger the number to the left of the decimal point, the less bytes there are available to hold the fractional part of the number. The double data type uses 64 bits to store a single number while the float data type uses 32 bits of data to store a single number. For many purposes, these two datatypes will work just fine. However, when you have data, such as currency, where small rounding errors would be a problem, Core Data provides the decimal data type, which is not subject to rounding errors. The decimal type can hold numbers with up to 38 significant digits stored internally using fixed-point numbers so that the stored value is not subject to the rounding errors that can happen with floating-point numbers.

At runtime, you set double and float attributes using instances of NSNumber created using the NSNumber factory method numberWithFloat: or numberWithDouble:. Decimal attributes, on the other hand, must be set using an instance of the class NSDecimalNumber.

## The String Data Type

The string data type is one of the most common attribute types you will use. String attributes are capable of holding text in nearly any language or script since they are stored internally using Unicode. String attributes are set at runtime using instances of NSString.

## The Boolean Data Type

Boolean values (YES or NO) can be stored using the Boolean data type. Boolean attributes are set at runtime using instances of NSNumber created using numberWithBOOL:.

## The Date Data Type

Dates and timestamps can be stored in Core Data using the date data type. At runtime, date attributes are set using instances of NSDate.

## The Binary Data Type

The binary data type is used to store any kind of binary data. Binary attributes are set at runtime using NSData instances. Anything that can be put into an NSData instance can be stored in a binary attribute. However, you generally can't search or sort on binary data types.

## The Transformable Data Type

The transformable data type is a special data type that works along with something called a value transformer to let you create attributes based on any Objective-C class, even those for which there is no corresponding Core Data data type. You would use transformable data types to store a UIImage instance, for example, or to store a UIColor instance. You'll see how transformable attributes work in Chapter 6.

# Setting the name Attribute Type

A name, obviously, is text, so the obvious type for this attribute is string. Select string from the Attribute Type drop-down. After selecting it, a few new fields will appear in the Detail pane (Figure 3-39). Just like Interface Builder's inspector, the Detail pane in the model editor is context-sensitive. Some attribute types, such as the string type, have additional configuration options.

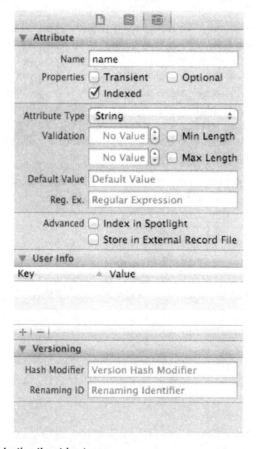

*Figure 3-39. The Detail pane after selecting the string type*

The Min Length: and Max Length: fields allow you to set a minimum and maximum number of characters for this field. If you enter a number into either field, any attempt to save a managed object that has less characters than the Min Length: or more characters than Max Length: stored in this attribute will result in a validation error at save time.

Note that this enforcement happens in the data model, not in the user interface. Unless you specifically enforce limitations through your user interface, these validations won't happen until you actually save the data model. In most instances, if you enforce a minimum or maximum length, you should also take some steps to enforce that in your user interface. Otherwise, the user won't be informed of the error until they go to save, which could be quite a while after they've entered data into this field. You'll see an example of enforcing this in Chapter 6.

The next field is labeled Default Value. You can use this to, well, set a default value for this property. If you type a value into this field, any managed object based on this entity will automatically have its corresponding property set to whatever value you type in here. So, in this case, if you were to type Untitled Hero into this field, any time you created a new Hero managed object, the name property would automatically get set to Untitled Hero. Heck, that sounds like a good idea, so type **Untitled Hero** into this field.

The last field is labeled Reg. Ex., which stands for regular expression. This field allows you to do further validation on the entered text using regular expressions, which are special text strings that you can use to express patterns. You could, for example, use an attribute to store an IP address in text and then ensure that only valid numerical IP addresses are entered by entering the regular expression \b\d{1,3}\.\d{1,3}\.\d{1,3}\. \d{1,3}\b. You're not going to use regular expressions for this attribute, so leave the Reg. Ex. field blank.

> **Note**    Regular expressions are a very complex topic on which many full books have been written. Teaching regular expressions is way beyond the scope of this book, but if you're interested in using regular expressions to do data model-level validation, a good starting point is the Wikipedia page on regular expressions at http://en.wikipedia.org/wiki/Regular_expression, which covers the basic syntax and contains links to many regular expression-related resources.

Finally, for good measure, save.

## Adding the Rest of the Attributes

Your Hero entity needs three more attributes, so let's add them now. Click the Add Attribute button again. Give this one a name of **secretIdentity** and a type of string. Since, according to Mr. Incredible, every superhero has a secret identity, you'd better uncheck the Optional check box. You will be sorting and searching on secret identity, so check the Indexed box. For Default Value, type in Unknown. Because you've made the field mandatory by unchecking the Optional check box, it's a good idea to provide a default value. Leave the rest of the fields as is.

> **Caution**    Be sure to enter default values for the name and secretIdentity attributes. If you don't, the program will behave badly. If your program crashes, check to make sure you've saved your source code files and your nib files.

Click the plus button a third time to add yet another attribute, giving it a name of **birthdate** and a type of date. Leave the rest of the fields at their default values for this attribute. You may not know the birthdate for all of your superheroes, so you want to leave this attribute as optional. As far as you know now, you won't be doing a lot of searching or ordering on birthdate, so there's no need to make this attribute indexed. You could do some additional validation here by setting a minimum, maximum, or default date, but there really isn't much need. There's no default value that would make sense, and setting a minimum or maximum date would preclude the possibility of an immortal superhero or a time-traveling one, which you certainly don't want to do!

This leaves you with one more attribute for this first iteration of your application: sex. There are a number of ways that you could choose to store this particular piece of information. For simplicity's sake (and because it will help us show you a few helpful techniques in Chapter 6), you're just going to store a character string of either Male or Female. Add another attribute and select a type of string. Let's leave this as an optional setting; there might just be an androgynous masked avenger or two out there. You could use the regular expression field to limit inputs to either Male or Female but, instead, you're going to enforce that in the user interface by presenting a selection list rather than enforcing it here in the data model.

Guess what? You've now completed the data model for the first iteration of the SuperDB application. Save it and let's move on.

# Declaring the Fetched Results Controller

In order to populate the table view, you need to fetch all the Hero entities stored in your persistent store. The best way to accomplish this is to use a fetched results controller inside the HeroListController. In order to use a fetched results controller, you need to define its delegate to be notified when the fetched results change. To make things easy, you'll make the HeroListController the fetched results controller delegate.

Select HeroListController and change the @interface declaration to this:

```
@interface HeroListController : UIViewController<UITableViewDataSource, UITableViewDelegate,
UITabBarDelegate, NSFetchedResultsControllerDelegate>
```

Now that you've declared the NSFetchedResultsControllerDelegate, you need the controller. You could declare the property in HeroListController.h, but you don't actually need this property to be public. You're only going use it within the HeroListController. So you'll make this a private property.

Select HeroListController.m, and scroll the editor to the top of the file, if necessary. Right above the @implementation declaration, you should add these lines:

```
#import "HeroListController.h"
@interface HeroListController ()
@end
```

The @interface declaration is actually a category declaration. Note the empty parenthesis at the end of the line. This is just a convention for declaring a category inside the implementation file. So you'll change it to read

```
#import "HeroListController.h"
#import "AppDelegate.h"

@interface HeroListController ()
@property (nonatomic, strong, readonly) NSFetchedResultsController *fetchedResultsController;
@end
```

You added the #import because you'll need it later on. Add the appropriate @synthesize declaration after the @implementation, like so:

```
@synthesize fetchedResultsController = _fetchedResultsController;
```

> **Note**   You may hear developers claim that using the underscore prefix is reserved by Apple and that you shouldn't use it. This is a misconception. Apple does, indeed, reserve the underscore prefix for the names of methods. It does not make any similar reservation when it comes to the names of instance variables. You can read Apple's naming convention for instance variables, which makes no restriction on the use of the underscore, at http://developer.apple.com/library/ios/#documentation/Cocoa/Conceptual/CodingGuidelines/Articles/NamingIvarsAndTypes.html.

Notice that the fetchedResultsController property is declared with the readonly keyword. You will be lazily loading the fetched results controller in the accessor method. You do not want other classes to be able to set fetchedResultsController, so you declare it readonly to prevent that from happening.

# Implementing the Fetched Results Controller

Somewhere in the @implemention of HeroListController you need your managedObjectContext and fetchedResultsController methods. Let's add it just above the addHero: method.

```
#pragma mark - FetchedResultsController Property

- (NSFetchedResultsController *)fetchedResultsController
{
}
```

Like they use to say, where's the beef? Well, we wanted to step through this line by line and explain the code. The full listing is available at the end of the chapter if you want to look ahead.

First, we said the fetched results controller was going to be lazily loaded, so here's the code to handle that:

```
if (_fetchedResultsController != nil) {
    return _fetchedResultsController;
}
```

If you get past this point, it means that the _fetchResultsController instance variable (or ivar) is nil, so you'll have to create one. First, you need to instantiate a fetch request.

```
NSFetchRequest *fetchRequest = [[NSFetchRequest alloc] init];
```

Now you get the entity description for your Hero entity and set the fetch request entity. While you're at it, set the fetch batch size, which breaks the fetch up into batches for performance reasons.

```
AppDelegate *appDelegate = (AppDelegate *)[[UIApplication sharedApplication] delegate];
NSManagedObjectContext *managedObjectContext = [appDelegate managedObjectContext];
NSEntityDescription *entity = [NSEntityDescription entityForName:@"Hero"
                                        inManagedObjectContext:managedObjectContext];
[fetchRequest setEntity:entity];
[fetchRequest setFetchBatchSize:20];
```

The order of the fetch results is going to depend on which tab you've selected, so you'll get that value. As a sanity check, read the user defaults if no tab is selected.

```
NSUInteger tabIndex = [self.heroTabBar.items indexOfObject:self.heroTabBar.selectedItem];
if (tabIndex == NSNotFound) {
    NSUserDefaults *defaults = [NSUserDefaults standardUserDefaults];
    tabIndex = [defaults integerForKey:kSelectedTabDefaultsKey];
}
```

Now you set the fetch request's sort descriptors. A sort descriptor is a simple object that tells the fetch request what property (attribute) should be used to compare instances of entities, and whether it should be ascending or descending. A fetch request expects an array of sort descriptors, the order of sort descriptors determines the order of priority when comparing.

```
NSString *sectionKey = nil;
switch (tabIndex) {
    // Notice that the kByName and kBySecretIdentity Code are nearly identical.
    // A refactoring opportunity?
    case kByName: {
        NSSortDescriptor *sortDescriptor1 = [[NSSortDescriptor alloc] initWithKey:@"name"
                                                                ascending:YES];
        NSSortDescriptor *sortDescriptor2 = [[NSSortDescriptor alloc] initWithKey:@"secretIdentity"
                                                                ascending:YES];
        NSArray *sortDescriptors =
            [[NSArray alloc] initWithObjects:sortDescriptor1, sortDescriptor2, nil];
        [fetchRequest setSortDescriptors:sortDescriptors];
        sectionKey = @"name";
        break;
    }
    case kBySecretIdentity:{
        NSSortDescriptor *sortDescriptor1 = [[NSSortDescriptor alloc] initWithKey:@"secretIdentity"
                                                                ascending:YES];
        NSSortDescriptor *sortDescriptor2 = [[NSSortDescriptor alloc] initWithKey:@"name"
                                                                ascending:YES];
        NSArray *sortDescriptors =
            [[NSArray alloc] initWithObjects:sortDescriptor1, sortDescriptor2, nil];
```

```
        [fetchRequest setSortDescriptors:sortDescriptors];
        sectionKey = @"secretIdentity";
        break;
    }
}
```

If the By Name tab is selected, you ask the fetch request to sort by the name attribute, then
the secretIdentity. For the By Secret Identity tab, you reverse the sort descriptors. You set a
sectionKey string, which you'll use next.

Now you finally instantiate the fetched results controller. Here's where you use the sectionKey,
and assign it a cache name of Hero. You assign the fetched results controller delegate to the
HeroListController.

```
_fetchedResultsController =
    [[NSFetchedResultsController alloc] initWithFetchRequest:fetchRequest
                                        managedObjectContext:managedObjectContext
                                          sectionNameKeyPath:sectionKey
                                                   cacheName:@"Hero"];

_fetchedResultsController.delegate = self;

return _fetchedResultsController;
```

Finally, you return the fetched results controller.

# Fetched Results Controller Delegate Methods

Since you assigned the fetched results controller delegate to the HeroListController, you need
to implement those methods. Add the following below the fetchedResultsController method you
just created:

```
#pragma mark - NSFetchedResultsControllerDelegate Methods

- (void)controllerWillChangeContent:(NSFetchedResultsController *)controller
{
    [self.heroTableView beginUpdates];
}

- (void)controllerDidChangeContent:(NSFetchedResultsController *)controller
{
    [self.heroTableView endUpdates];
}

- (void)controller:(NSFetchedResultsController *)controller
  didChangeSection:(id<NSFetchedResultsSectionInfo>)sectionInfo
           atIndex:(NSUInteger)sectionIndex
     forChangeType:(NSFetchedResultsChangeType)type
```

```
{
    switch(type) {
        case NSFetchedResultsChangeInsert:
            [self.heroTableView insertSections:[NSIndexSet indexSetWithIndex:sectionIndex]
                                    withRowAnimation:UITableViewRowAnimationFade];
            break;

        case NSFetchedResultsChangeDelete:
            [self.heroTableView deleteSections:[NSIndexSet indexSetWithIndex:sectionIndex]
                                    withRowAnimation:UITableViewRowAnimationFade];
            break;

    }
}

- (void)controller:(NSFetchedResultsController *)controller
    didChangeObject:(id)anObject
        atIndexPath:(NSIndexPath *)indexPath
     forChangeType:(NSFetchedResultsChangeType)type
      newIndexPath:(NSIndexPath *)newIndexPath
{
    switch(type) {
        case NSFetchedResultsChangeInsert:
            [self.heroTableView insertRowsAtIndexPaths:@[newIndexPath]
                                    withRowAnimation:UITableViewRowAnimationFade];
            break;

        case NSFetchedResultsChangeDelete:
            [self.heroTableView deleteRowsAtIndexPaths:@[indexPath]
                                    withRowAnimation:UITableViewRowAnimationFade];
            break;

        case NSFetchedResultsChangeUpdate:
        case NSFetchedResultsChangeMove:
            break;

    }
}
```

For an explanation of these methods, refer to the "Fetched Results Controller Delegate" section of Chapter 2.

# Making All Work

You're almost done. You still need to

- Implement the Edit and Add (+) buttons.

- Code the table view data source and delegate methods correctly.

- Make the tab bar selector sort the table view.

- Run the fetch request at launch.
- Handle errors.

It seems like a lot, but it's not. Let's start with the error handling first.

# Error Handling

You'll make things simple by using a simple alert view to display errors. In order to use an alert view, you need to implement an alert view delegate. Like the fetched results controller, you'll make the HeroListController the alert view delegate. Edit the HeroListController @interface declaration to read

```
@interface HeroListController : UIViewController<UITableViewDataSource, UITableViewDelegate,
UITabBarDelegate, NSFetchedResultsControllerDelegate, UIAlertViewDelegate>
```

In HeroListController.m, you'll add a simple alert view delegate method.

```
#pragma mark - UIAlertViewDelegate Methods

- (void)alertView:(UIAlertView *)alertView didDismissWithButtonIndex:(NSInteger)buttonIndex
{
    exit(-1);
}
```

All this method does is cause your application quit.

# Implementing Edit and Add

When you click the Add (+) button, the application does more than just add a row to the table view. It adds a new Hero entity to the managed object context. In the HeroListController.m file, modify the addHero method to read

```
- (IBAction)addHero:(id)sender
{
    NSManagedObjectContext *managedObjectContext =
        [self.fetchedResultsController managedObjectContext];

    NSEntityDescription *entity = [[self.fetchedResultsController fetchRequest] entity];
    [NSEntityDescription insertNewObjectForEntityForName:[entity name]
                                  inManagedObjectContext:managedObjectContext];

    NSError *error = nil;
    if (![managedObjectContext save:&error]) {
        UIAlertView *alert =
            [[UIAlertView alloc]
                initWithTitle:NSLocalizedString(@"Error saving entity",
                                                @"Error saving entity")
```

```
                 message:[NSString stringWithFormat:NSLocalizedString(@"Error was: %@, quitting.",
                                                    @"Error was: %@, quitting."),
                                    [error localizedDescription]]
                delegate:self
          cancelButtonTitle:NSLocalizedString(@"Aw, Nuts", @"Aw, Nuts")
          otherButtonTitles:nil];
        [alert show];
    }
}
```

When the Edit button is clicked, the `setEditing:animated:` method is automatically called. So you just need to add that method to your `HeroListController.m` without having declare it in the interface file.

```
- (void)setEditing:(BOOL)editing animated:(BOOL)animated
{
    [super setEditing:editing animated:animated];
    self.addButton.enabled = !editing;
    [self.heroTableView setEditing:editing animated:animated];
}
```

All you do here is call the super method, disable the Add (+) button (you don't want to be adding heroes while editing!), and call `setEditing:animated` on the table view.

## Coding the Table View Data Source and Delegate

Using the `CoreDataApp` from Chapter 2 as an example, you need to change the following table view data source methods:

```
- (NSInteger)numberOfSectionsInTableView:(UITableView *)tableView
{
        return [[self.fetchedResultsController sections] count];
}


- (NSInteger)tableView:(UITableView *)tableView numberOfRowsInSection:(NSInteger)section
{
        id<NSFetchedResultsSectionInfo> sectionInfo =
          [[self.fetchedResultsController sections] objectAtIndex:section];
        return [sectionInfo numberOfObjects];
}
```

Next, you handle the table view cell creation, like so:

```
- (UITableViewCell *)tableView:(UITableView *)tableView
        cellForRowAtIndexPath:(NSIndexPath *)indexPath
{
    static NSString *CellIdentifier=@"HeroListCell";
    UITableViewCell *cell = [tableView dequeueReusableCellWithIdentifier:CellIdentifier];
```

```
    // Configure the cell...
    NSManagedObject *aHero = [self.fetchedResultsController objectAtIndexPath:indexPath];
    NSInteger tab = [self.heroTabBar.items indexOfObject:self.heroTabBar.selectedItem];
    switch (tab) {
        case kByName:
            cell.textLabel.text = [aHero valueForKey:@"name"];
            cell.detailTextLabel.text = [aHero valueForKey:@"secretIdentity"];
            break;
        case kBySecretIdentity:
            cell.textLabel.text = [aHero valueForKey:@"secretIdentity"];
            cell.detailTextLabel.text = [aHero valueForKey:@"name"];
            break;
    }

    return cell;
}
```

Finally, you uncomment tableView:commitEditingStyle:forRowAtIndexPath: to handle deleting rows.

```
// Override to support editing the table view.
- (void)tableView:(UITableView *)tableView
        commitEditingStyle:(UITableViewCellEditingStyle)editingStyle
        forRowAtIndexPath:(NSIndexPath *)indexPath
{
    NSManagedObjectContext *managedObjectContext =[self.fetchedResultsController
managedObjectContext];

    if (editingStyle == UITableViewCellEditingStyleDelete) {
        // Delete the row from the data source
        [managedObjectContext deleteObject:[self.fetchedResultsController
                                    objectAtIndexPath:indexPath]];

        NSError *error;
        if (![managedObjectContext save:&error]) {
            UIAlertView *alert =
                [[UIAlertView alloc]
                    initWithTitle:NSLocalizedString(@"Error saving entity",
                                            @"Error saving entity")
                        message:
                            [NSString stringWithFormat:NSLocalizedString(@"Error was: %@, quitting.",
                                                    @"Error was: %@, quitting."),
                                                [error localizedDescription]]
                    delegate:self
                cancelButtonTitle:NSLocalizedString(@"Aw, Nuts", @"Aw, Nuts")
                otherButtonTitles:nil];
            [alert show];
        }
    }
}
```

## Sorting the Table View

Finally, you need to make the table view order change when you toggle the tab bar. You need to add the following code to `tabBar:didSelectItem:` delegate method:

```
- (void)tabBar:(UITabBar *)tabBar didSelectItem:(UITabBarItem *)item
{
    NSUserDefaults *defaults=[NSUserDefaults standardUserDefaults];
    NSUInteger tabIndex=[tabBar.items indexOfObject:item];
    [defaults setInteger:tabIndex forKey:kSelectedTabDefaultsKey];

    [NSFetchedResultsController deleteCacheWithName:@"Hero"];
    _fetchedResultsController.delegate=nil;
    _fetchedResultsController=nil;

    NSError *error;
    if (![self.fetchedResultsController performFetch:&error]) {
        NSLog(@"Error performing fetch: %@", [error localizedDescription]);
    }

    [self.heroTableView reloadData];
}
```

## Loading the Fetch Request At Launch

Add the following to the `HeroListController` `viewDidLoad` method:

```
// Fetch any existing entities
NSError *error = nil;
if (![[self fetchedResultsController] performFetch:&error]) {
    UIAlertView *alert =
      [[UIAlertView alloc]
          initWithTitle:NSLocalizedString(@"Error loading data",
                                          @"Error loading data")
                message:[NSString stringWithFormat:NSLocalizedString(@"Error was: %@, quitting.",
                                                                     @"Error was: %@, quitting."),
                                                    [error localizedDescription]]
               delegate:self
      cancelButtonTitle:NSLocalizedString(@"Aw, Nuts", @"Aw, Nuts")
      otherButtonTitles:nil];
    [alert show];
}
```

And that's pretty much everything.

## Let 'Er Rip

Well, what are you waiting for? That was a lot of work; you deserve to try it out. Make sure everything is saved, then build and run the app.

If everything went okay, when the application first launches, you should be presented with an empty table with a navigation bar at the top and a tab bar at the bottom (Figure 3-40). Pressing the right button in the navigation bar will add a new unnamed superhero to the database. Pressing the Edit button will allow you to delete heroes.

*Figure 3-40. The SuperDB application at launch time*

> **Note**   If your app crashed when you ran it, there's a couple of things to look for. First, make sure you saved all your source code and nib files before you ran your project. Also, make sure that you have defaults specified for your hero's name and secret identity in your data model editor. If you did that and your app still crashes, try resetting your simulator. Here's how: bring up the simulator, and from the iPhone Simulator menu, select Reset Contents and Settings. That should do it. In Chapter 5, we'll show you how to ensure that changes to your data model don't cause such problems.

Add a few unnamed superheroes to your application and try out the two tabs to make sure that the display changes when you select a new tab. When you select the By Name tab, it should look like Figure 3-1, but when you select the By Secret Identity tab, it should look like Figure 3-41.

*Figure 3-41. Pressing the By Secret Identity tab doesn't change the order of the rows yet, but it does change which value is displayed first*

# Done, but Not Done

In this chapter, you did a lot of work. You saw how to set up a navigation-based application that uses a tab bar, and you learned how to design a basic Core Data data model by creating an entity and giving it several attributes.

This application isn't done, but you've now laid a solid foundation upon which to move forward. When you're ready, turn the page and start creating a detail editing page to allow the user to edit their superheroes.

# Chapter 4

# The Devil in the Detail View

In Chapter 3, you built your application's main view controller. You set it up to display heroes ordered by their name or their secret identity, and you put in place the infrastructure needed to save, delete, and add new heroes. What you didn't do was give the user a way to edit the information about a particular hero, which means you're limited to creating and deleting superheroes named *Untitled Hero*. Guess you can't ship your application yet ;-).

That's okay. Application development is an iterative process, and the first several iterations of any application likely won't have enough functionality to stand on its own. In this chapter, you're going to create an editable detail view to let the user edit the data for a specific superhero.

The controller you're going to write will be a subclass of `UITableViewController`, and you're going to use an approach that is somewhat conceptually complex but one that will be easy to maintain and expand. This is important because you're going to be adding new attributes to the `Hero` managed object, as well as expanding it in other ways, so you'll need to keep changing the user interface to accommodate those changes.

After you've written your new detail view controller, you will then add functionality to allow the user to edit each attribute, *in place*.

## View Implementation Choices

In Chapters 3 and 4 of *Beginning iOS 6 Development*, by David Mark, Jack Nutting, and Jeff LaMarche (Apress), you learned how to build a user interface using Interface Builder. Building your editable detail views in Interface Builder is definitely one way to go. But another common approach is to implement your detail view as a grouped table. Take a look at your iPhone's Contacts application or the Contacts tab of the Phone application (Figure 4-1). The detail editing view in Apple's navigation applications is often implemented using a grouped table rather than using an interface designed in Interface Builder.

*Figure 4-1.* *The Contacts tab of the iPhone application uses a table-based detail editing view*

Since you've chosen to use storyboards for your SuperDB application, you'll be using the storyboard editor. For all intents and purposes, it's the same as building your interface with Interface Builder.

The iOS Human Interface Guidelines (http://developer.apple.com/library/ios/#documentation/ UserExperience/Conceptual/MobileHIG) do not give any real guidance as to when you should use a table-based detail view as opposed to a detail view designed in Interface Builder, so it comes down to a question of which feels right. Here's our take: if you're building a navigation-based application and the data can reasonably and efficiently be presented in a grouped table, it probably should be. Since your superhero data is structured much like the data displayed in the Contacts application, a table-based detail view seems the obvious choice.

The table view shown in Figure 4-2 displays data from a single hero, which means that everything in that table comes from a single managed object. Each row corresponds to a different attribute of the managed object. The first section's only row displays the hero's name, for example. When in editing mode, tapping a specific row will display the appropriate subview to modify that attribute. For a string, it will present a keyboard; for a date, a date picker.

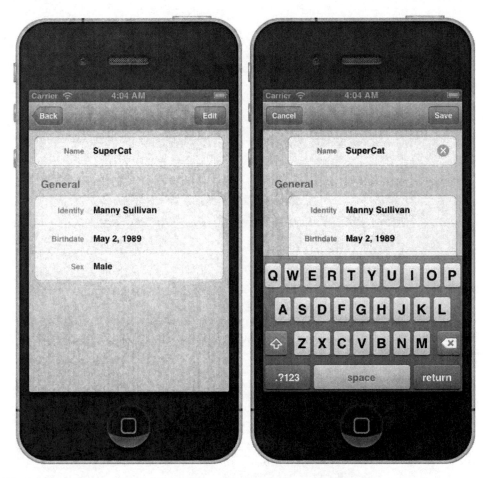

*Figure 4-2. The detail view that you'll be building in this application, in view and editing mode*

The organization of the table view into sections and rows are not determined by the managed object. Instead, they are the results of design decisions you, as the developer, must make by trying to anticipate what will make sense to your users. You could, for example, put the attributes in alphabetical order, which would put birthdate first. That wouldn't have been very intuitive because birthdate is not the most important or defining attribute of a hero. In our minds, the hero's name and secret identity are the most important attributes and thus should be the first two elements presented in your table view.

# Creating the Detail View Controller

Find your SuperDB project folder from Chapter 3 and make a copy of it. This way, if things go south when you add your new code for this chapter, you won't have to start at the very beginning. Open this new copy of your project in Xcode.

Next, create the detail view controller itself. Remember that you're creating a table-based editing view, so you want to subclass UITableViewController. Select SuperDB.storyboard and open the storyboard editor. Open the Utility pane, if it's not already open, and find the table view controller in the Object library. Drag it onto the storyboard editor, to the right of the HeroListController (Figure 4-3).

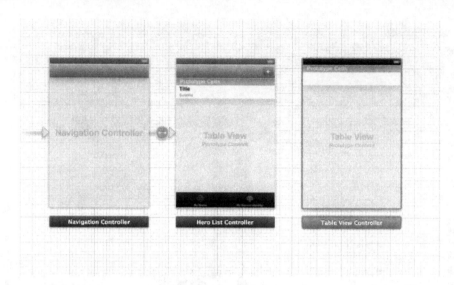

*Figure 4-3. The layout of your storyboard*

Make sure you're zoom level is such that you see the three icons on the table view's label. Single-click the table view (the grey area of the view), and switch the Utility pane to the Attribute Inspector (Figure 4-4).

*Figure 4-4. Table view's attributes*

Let's look at the Figure 4-2 again. Your detail view has two sections, so let's configure the table view that way. Change the Style field from Plain to Grouped. Once that's done, the Separator field should have changed itself to Single Line Etched. If not, make the change yourself. Next, you know the number of rows in each section; one and three, respectively. Since that number is fixed, you can change the Content field from Dynamic Prototypes to Static Cells. Again, the field right below the Content field automatically changed from Prototype Cells to Sections. You know the number of sections is two, so enter 2 in that field. Finally, you don't want to have the cells highlight on selection, so change the Selection field to No Selection. The Attribute Inspector for the table view should look like Figure 4-5.

*Figure 4-5. The final state of your table view attributes*

Your table view should have two sections of three cells each (Figure 4-6). Section one has too many cells. You only need one cell. Select the second cell in section one. It should highlight. Delete the cell (press the Delete key, or Edit ➤ Delete). Section one should now have two cells, with the bottom cell highlighted. Delete that cell, too.

*Figure 4-6. Table view*

Select the table view cell in the first section. Bring the Attribute Inspector up. Change the Style from Custom to Left Detail. Set the Identifier to HeroDetailCell. Finally, set the Selection to None. The Attribute Inspector should look like Figure 4-7. Repeat the settings for the three table view cells in the second section.

*Figure 4-7. Table view cell's attributes*

The second section needs a header label, General. Select the area right above or right below the three cells in the second section. The Attribute Inspector should change to table view section (Figure 4-8). In the Header field, enter General. Now the second section should have the correct header label.

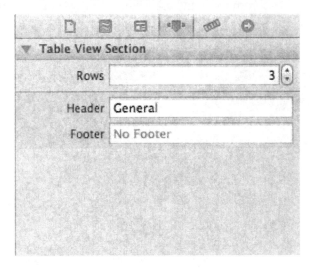

*Figure 4-8. Table view section's attributes*

By the way, notice that the first field in the table view section's Attribute Inspector is Rows. You could have used this to change the first section's row count from three to one.

So your table view should look like Figure 4-9. It looks like the layout is all set.

*Figure 4-9. Table view layout complete*

# Wiring Up the Segue

When the user taps on a cell in the HeroListController, you want the application to transition to your detail table view. Control-drag from the table view cell in the HeroListController to your detail table view (Figure 4-10). When the Segue pop-up appears (Figure 4-11), select push under the Selection Segue header.

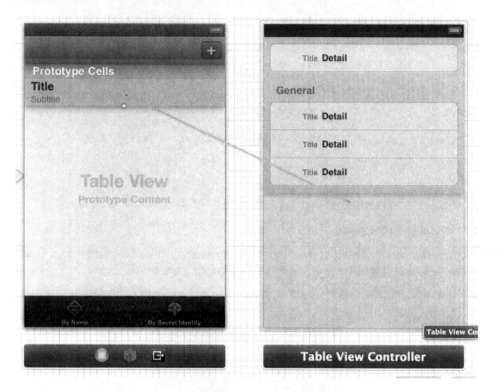

*Figure 4-10.  Control-drag to create the segue*

*Figure 4-11.  Segue pop-up selector*

Now you need to create your table view subclass in order to populate your detail table view cells.

# HeroDetailController

Single-click the SuperDB group in the Navigation pane. Create a new file. In the New File Assistant, select Objective-C subclass and click Next. On the next screen, name the class **HeroDetailController**, making it a subclass of UITableViewController. Make sure that both the "Targeted for iPad" and "With XIB for user interface" are both unchecked. Click Next. Create the file.

Moving on, select SuperDB.storyboard. In the storyboard editor, select your detail table view. Make sure the zoom level is set so you see three icons in the detail table view label. Select the table view controller icon, and bring up the Identity Inspector in the Utility pane. In the Custom Class section, change the Class field to HeroDetailController.

One more thing. When you subclassed UITableViewController, Xcode gave your HeroDetailController implementations of table view data source and delegate methods. You don't need them right now (but will later), so you'll comment them out. Find the following methods

```
- (NSInteger)numberOfSectionsInTableView:(UITableView *)tableView
- (NSInteger)tableView:(UITableView *)tableView numberOfRowsInSection:(NSInteger)section
- (UITableViewCell *)tableView:(UITableView *)tableView cellForRowAtIndexPath:(NSIndexPath *)indexPath
```

and comment them out (method bodies, too).

You've created your HeroDetailController and set your detail view controller in your storyboard to be an instance of HeroDetailController. Now you'll create the property list that will define the table sections.

# Detail View Challenges

The table view architecture was designed to efficiently present data stored in collections. For example, you might use a table view to display data in an NSArray or in a fetched results controller. When you're creating a detail view, however, you're typically presenting data from a single object, in this case an instance of NSManagedObject that represents a single superhero. A managed object uses key-value coding but has no mechanism to present its attributes in a meaningful order. For example, NSManagedObject has no idea that the name attribute is the most important one or that it should be in its own section the way it is in Figure 4-2.

Coming up with a good, maintainable way to specify the sections and rows in a detail editing view is a non-trivial task. The most obvious solution, and one you'll frequently see in online sample code, uses an enum to list the table sections, followed by additional enums for each section, containing constants and a count of rows for each section, like so:

```
enum HeroEditControllerSections {
    HeroEditControllerSectionName = 0,
    HeroEditControllerSectionGeneral,
    HeroEditControllerSectionCount
};

enum HeroEditControllerNameSection {
    HeroEditControllerNameRow = 0,
    HeroEditControllerNameSectionCount
};
```

```
enum HeroEditControllerGeneralSection {
    HeroEditControllerGeneralSectionSecretIdentityRow,
    HeroEditControllerGeneralSectionBirthdateRow,
    HeroEditControllerGeneralSectionSexRow,
    HeroEditControllerGeneralSectionCount
};
```

Then, in every method where you are provided with an index path, you can take the appropriate
action based on the row and section represented by the index path, using switch statements, like this:

```
- (void)tableView:(UITableView *)tableView didSelectRowAtIndexPath:(NSIndexPath *)indexPath
{
    NSUInteger section = [indexPath section];
    NSUInteger row = [indexPath row];

    switch (section) {
        case HeroEditControllerSectionName:
            switch (row)
        {
            case HeroEditControllerNameRow :
                // Create a controller to edit name
                // and push it on the stack
                ...
                break;
            default:
                break;
        }
            break;
        case HeroEditControllerSectionGeneral:
            switch (row) {
                case HeroEditControllerGeneralSectionSecretIdentityRow:
                    // Create a controller to edit secret identity
                    // and push it on the stack
                    ...
                    break;
                case HeroEditControllerGeneralSectionBirthdateRow:
                    // Create a controller to edit birthdate and
                    // push it on the stack
                    ...
                    break;
                case HeroEditControllerGeneralSectionSexRow:
                    // Create a controller to edit sex and push it
                    // on the stack
                    ...
                    break;
                default:
                    break;
            }
            break;
        default:
            break;
    }
}
```

The problem with this approach is that it doesn't scale very well at all. A nested set of switch statements like this will need to appear in almost every table view delegate or data source method that takes an index path, which means that adding or deleting rows or sections involves updating your code in multiple places.

Additionally, the code under each of the case statements is going to be relatively similar. In this particular case, you will have to create a new instance of a controller or use a pointer to an existing controller, set some properties to indicate which values need to get edited, then push the controller onto the navigation stack. If you discover a problem in your logic anywhere in these switch statements, chances are you're going to have to change that logic in several places, possibly even dozens.

# Controlling the Table Structure with Property Lists

As you can see, the most obvious solution isn't always the best one. You don't want to have very similar chunks of code scattered throughout your controller class, and you don't want to have to maintain multiple copies of a complex decision tree. There's a better way to do this.

You can use property lists to mirror the structure of your table. As the user navigates down the app, you can use the data stored in a property list to construct the appropriate table. Property lists are a simple, but powerful way to store information.

Chapter 10 of *Beginning iOS 6 Development* discussed property lists. Let's quickly review them here.

# Property Lists Explained

Property lists are a simple way to represent, store, and retrieve data. Both Mac OS X and iOS make extensive use of property lists. Within property lists, two kinds of data types can be used: primitive and collections. The primitive types available are strings, numbers, binary data, dates, and Boolean values. The available collection types are arrays and dictionaries. The collections types can contain both primitive types and additional collections. Property lists can be stored in two file types: XML and binary data. Xcode provides a property list editor to make management of property lists easier for you. We'll discuss that in a little bit.

Property lists start with a *root node*. Technically, the root node can be of any type, primitive or collection. However, a property list of a primitive type has limited usefulness as it would be a "list" of one value. More common is a root node of a collection type: an array or a dictionary. When you create a property list with the Xcode property list editor, the root node will be a dictionary.

> **Note**   To learn more detail about property lists, read Apple's documentation at
> `http://developer.apple.com/library/ios/#documentation/Cocoa/Conceptual/`
> `PropertyLists/Introduction/Introduction.html`.

# Modeling Table Structure with a Property List

So how can you use a property list to describe your table? Refer back to Figure 4-2. Looking at the table, you can see two sections. The first section has no header, but the second section has a header of General. Each section has a certain number of rows (one and three, respectively) where each row represents a specific attribute of your managed object. Additionally, each row also has a label, which tells you what value is being displayed.

To start, you represent the table as an array, with each item in the array representing a section of the table. Each section, in turn, will be represented by a dictionary. You have a header key in the section dictionary, which stores the string value of the header. Note that the first section of the table does not have a header; you just use an empty string to represent it.

> **Note**    If you recall, there are only five primitive data types in a property list: string, numbers, binary data, dates, and Booleans. That doesn't leave you with a way to represent nil values. So you must rely on an empty string to represent nil.

The second key of the section dictionary will be rows. The value for this key will be another array, where each item of the rows array will represent the data to render the row. To represent a row, you'll use another dictionary. This row dictionary will have a key of label, referencing a string that will be used as the row label plus a key of attribute, which will be a string of the managed object's attribute to render in the row.

Confused? Don't worry, it's very difficult to model things descriptively. Figure 4-12 tries to explain it graphically.

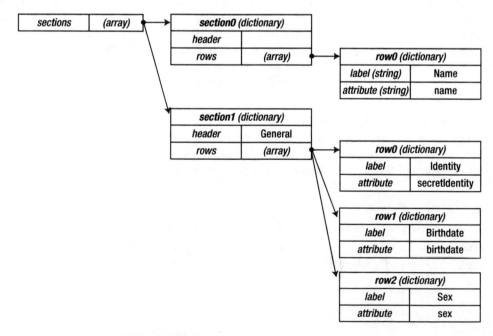

*Figure 4-12.* *Graphical representation of your property list*

That should be all the data structures you need to represent the table's structure to start. Fortunately, if you discover that you need additional information for each row, you can always add additional data later without impacting your existing design.

Let's begin building your detail view.

# Defining the Table View via Property List

In the Navigator pane, select the Supporting Files group so that it is highlighted. Now, create a new file. Once the new file template appears, select Resource under the iOS heading. Choose the Property List template (Figure 4-13), and click Next. Name the file **HeroDetailConfiguration. plist**, and click Create. A new file, named HeroDetailConfiguration.plist, should appear in the Supporting Files group. The file should be selected and the editor should switch to the property list editor (Figure 4-14).

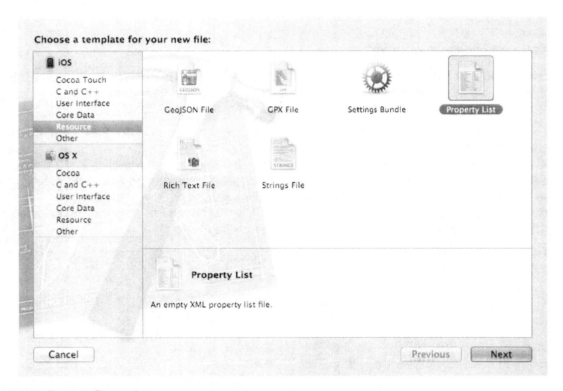

*Figure 4-13. Resource file templates*

*Figure 4-14. Xcode property list editor mode*

Earlier we stated that the root node of a property list is a dictionary. That means each node will be a key/value pair. You can treat the key as a string, and the value can be of any of the primitive (string, number, binary data, date, or Boolean) or collection (array or dictionary) data types.

You're going to start by creating the sections array, as we discussed earlier. To do so, you need to add a new item to the property list. There are two ways to do this. Both methods require you select the row with the name Root in the Key column. Using the first method, control-click in the blank area of the property list editor. When the pop-up menu appears, choose Add Row. Alternately, you can use the regular menu Editor ➤ Add Item option. Either way, a new row should appear in the property list editor (Figure 4-15). The item should have a key of New item, which will be selected and highlighted. Type **sections** and press Return to change the key name.

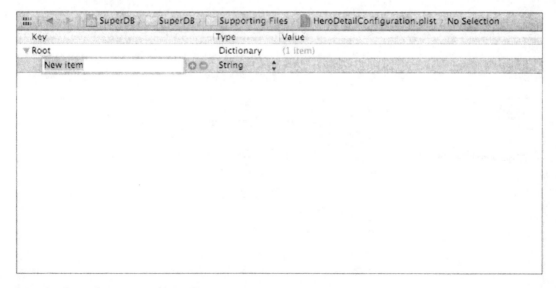

*Figure 4-15. Adding an item to the property list*

Next, click the arrows next to string under the Type column to expose the possible data types. Select array. The Value column should change to read (0 items). Adding items to the sections array is a little tricky, so make sure you follow the next steps carefully.

When you changed the type from string to array, a disclosure triangle was added to the left of the sections key (Figure 4-16). Click this triangle so it is pointed downward (Figure 4-17). Now click the + button to the right of the sections. This will insert a new row. Additionally, the Value column for sections will change to read (1 item). The key of the new row will be Item 0; the type will be string; the Value column will be selected. Don't type anything; select the sections row so it is highlighted and click the + next to sections again. This will insert another row with the key Item 1, of type string, with no value. The Value cell should be selected with a cursor. Change the type for Item 0 and Item 1 from string to dictionary (Figure 4-18).

*Figure 4-16. Changing the type from string to array*

*Figure 4-17. Click the disclosure triangle to open the array*

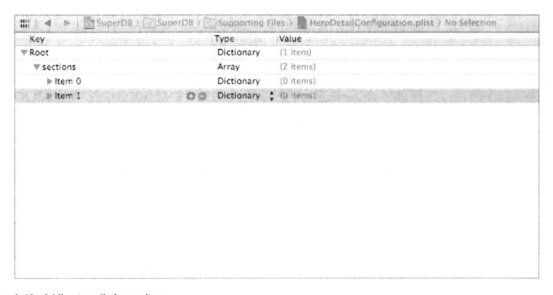

*Figure 4-18. Adding two dictionary items*

Remember that you were going to create an array where each item in the array represented a section of your table view? You've created those two items. Item 0 is the first section of `HeroDetailController` table view; Item 1 is the second.

Now you create the rows array under each section to hold the row information for each section. Next to Item0 there should be a disclosure triangle. Open it, and click the+next to Item0. This will create a new row with key New Item, of type string, under Item0. Change the key to rows, and change the type to array. Open the disclosure triangle next to rows, and click the+button. This will create another Item0, this time under rows. Change the type from string to dictionary. Repeat this procedure, adding a rows item under the Item1 header. This time, create three items under this second rows item. Your property list editor should look like Figure 4-19.

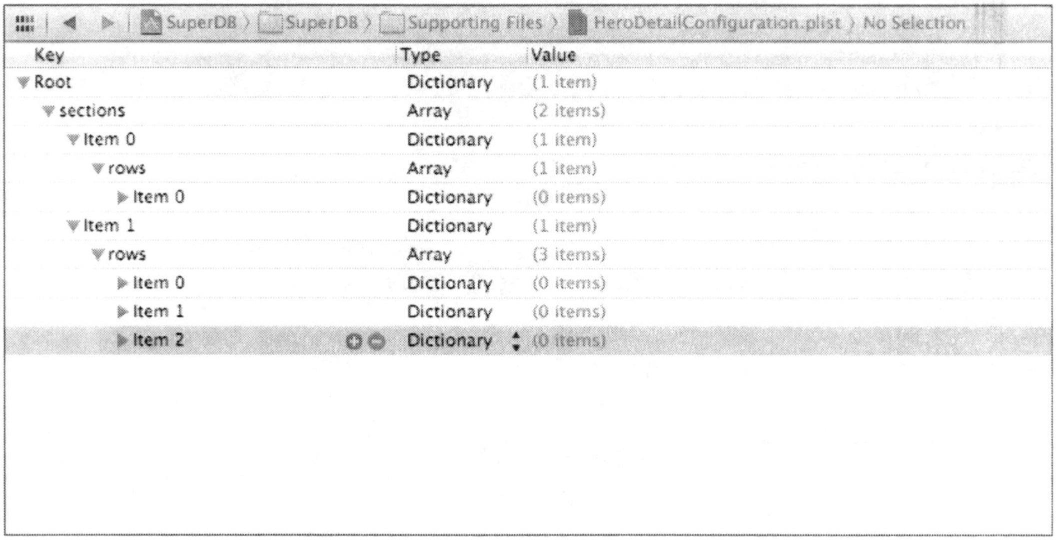

| Key | Type | Value |
| --- | --- | --- |
| ▼ Root | Dictionary | (1 item) |
| ▼ sections | Array | (2 items) |
| ▼ Item 0 | Dictionary | (1 item) |
| ▼ rows | Array | (1 item) |
| ▶ Item 0 | Dictionary | (0 items) |
| ▼ Item 1 | Dictionary | (1 item) |
| ▼ rows | Array | (3 items) |
| ▶ Item 0 | Dictionary | (0 items) |
| ▶ Item 1 | Dictionary | (0 items) |
| ▶ Item 2 | Dictionary | (0 items) |

*Figure 4-19. HeroDetailConfiguration.plist*

For each item in each rows array, you need to add two more entries. They should be of type string, and their keys should be key and label, respectively. For section ➤ Item 0 ➤ rows, the key value should be name and the label value should be set to Name. For section ➤ Item 1 ➤ rows, the values for key and label should be secretIdentity and Identity; birthdate and Birthdate; sex and Sex. When completed, the property list editor pane should look like Figure 4-20.

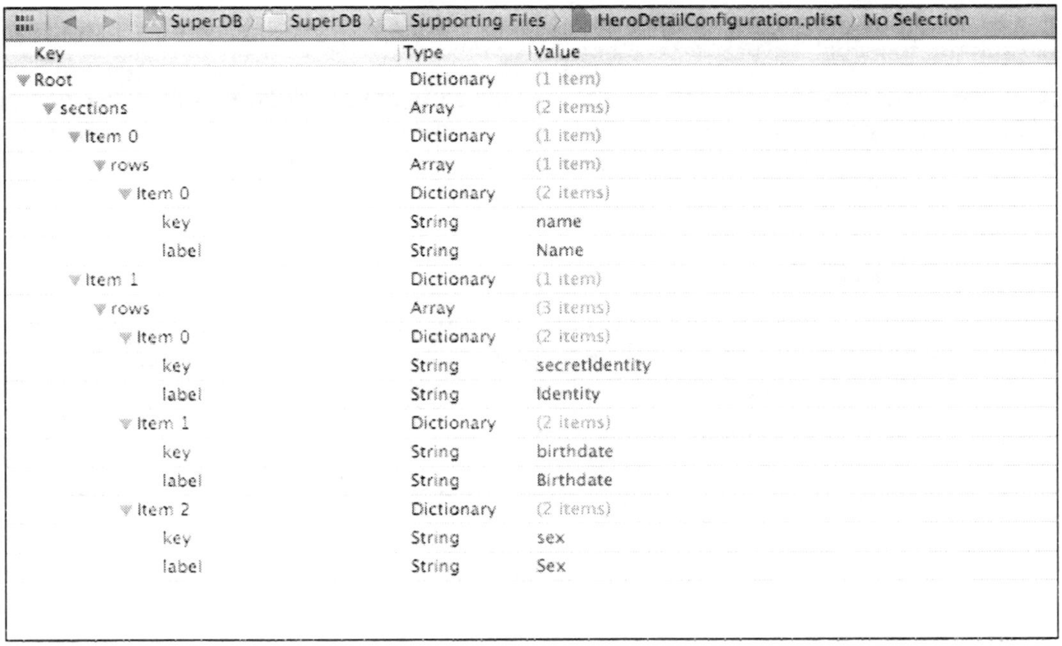

**Figure 4-20.** *The completed HeroDetailConfiguration.plist*

Now, you'll use this property list to set up the `HeroDetailController` table view.

# Parsing the Property List

You need to add a property to store the information from the property list you just created. Since this property only needs to be used by the `HeroDetailController` internally, you'll make it a private, via the category inside of `HeroDetailController.m`.

```
@interface HeroDetailController ()
@property (strong, nonatomic) NSArray *sections;
@end
```

Next, you need to load the property list and read the sections key. Before the end of `viewDidLoad`, add the following:

```
NSURL *plistURL = [[NSBundle mainBundle] URLForResource:@"HeroDetailConfiguration"
                                          withExtension:@"plist"];
NSDictionary *plist = [NSDictionary dictionaryWithContentsOfURL:plistURL];
self.sections = [plist valueForKey:@"sections"];
```

You declare a property, sections, of type NSArray, to hold the contents of the sections array in your `HeroDetailConfiguration.plist` property list. You read in the contents of the property list using the NSDictionary class method `dictionaryWithContentsOfURL:`. Since you know that this dictionary only has one key/value pair, with a key of sections, you read that value into sections property. You then use that property to layout the HeroDetailController table view.

You now have the metadata needed to populate your HeroDetailController's table view cells, but you don't have the data. The data should come from the HeroListController in one of two ways: when the user taps on a cell and when the user taps on the Add (+) button.

## Pushing the Details

Before you can send the data down from the HeroListController, you need something to receive it in the HeroDetailController. Add the following property to the HeroDetailController interface declaration in HeroDetailController.h:

```
@property (strong, nonatomic) NSManagedObject *hero;
```

Now edit the HeroListController.m. Find the addHero: method. Change the line that reads

```
[NSEntityDescription insertNewObjectForEntityForName:[entity name]
                        inManagedObjectContext:managedObjectContext];
```

to

```
NSManagedObject *newHero = [NSEntityDescription insertNewObjectForEntityForName:[entity name]
                                    inManagedObjectContext:managedObjectContext];
```

Then add the following to the end:

```
[self performSegueWithIdentifier:@"HeroDetailSegue" sender:newHero];
```

First, you assign your new Hero instance to the variable newHero. Then you told the HeroListController to execute the segue named HeroDetailSegue and pass newHero as the sender. Where did that segue name, HeroDetailSegue, come from? From you.

Remember the segue you created earlier for when a user taps on a cell in the HeroListController? Well, now you're going to get rid of it. Why? Because it doesn't give you the flexibility you need to transition from both a cell and the Add (+) button. You need to create a manual segue and invoke it from code.

Select the SuperDB.storyboard, and find the segue between the HeroListController and the HeroDetailController. Delete it. Control-drag from the HeroListController (the icon in the label) to the HeroDetailController (somewhere in the view). A pop-up with a header of Manual Segue should appear; choose the push menu item. A new segue should appear between the two view controllers, select it. In the Attributes Inspector, give it the identifier HeroDetailSegue (Figure 4-21).

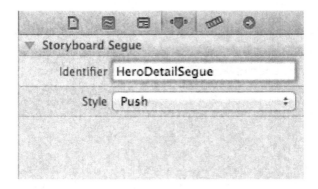

*Figure 4-21. Setting the segue identifier*

Now you need to reconnect the HeroListController cells to the HeroDetailSegue. Edit HeroListController.m. Find the method tableView:didSelectRowAtIndexPath: and replace the method body with

```
NSManagedObject *selectedHero = [self.fetchedResultsController objectAtIndexPath:indexPath];
[self performSegueWithIdentifier:@"HeroDetailSegue" sender:selectedHero];
```

You're essentially doing the same thing you did in addHero:, except that the Hero object is coming from the fetched results controller rather than being created. This looks good so far, but you still aren't sending data to the HeroDetailController. You handle that in the UIViewController method prepareForSegue:sender:. Add this method to the HeroListController (you can put it anywhere, but you put it after the setEditing:animated: method):

```
- (void)prepareForSegue:(UIStoryboardSegue *)segue sender:(id)sender
{
    if ([segue.identifier isEqualToString:@"HeroDetailSegue"])
    {
        if ([sender isKindOfClass:[NSManagedObject class]]) {
            HeroDetailController *detailController = segue.destinationViewController;
            detailController.hero = sender;
        }
        else {
            UIAlertView *alert =
                [[UIAlertView alloc] initWithTitle:NSLocalizedString(@"Hero Detail Error",
                                                            @"Hero Detail Error")
                                message:NSLocalizedString(@"Error trying to show Hero detail",
                                                            @"Error trying to show Hero detail")
                                delegate:self
                        cancelButtonTitle:NSLocalizedString(@"Aw, Nuts", @"Aw, Nuts")
                        otherButtonTitles:nil];
            [alert show];
        }
    }
}
```

Note that prepareForSegue:sender: is called by performSegueWithName:sender: internally. It's a hook Apple gives you to set things up correctly before showing the HeroDetailController.

By the way, Xcode should have complained about HeroDetailController and detailController.hero. Add the following #import at the top of HeroListViewController.m:

```
#import "HeroDetailController.h"
```

# Showing the Details

You're sending the Hero object down from the HeroListController to the HeroDetailController. Now you're ready to show the details. Edit HeroDetailController.m and find tableView:cellForRowAtIndexPath:. Remember you commented it out earlier, so it won't show up in the jump bar function menu. Uncomment it and replace the body with this:

```
static NSString *CellIdentifier = @"HeroDetailCell";
UITableViewCell *cell = [tableView dequeueReusableCellWithIdentifier:CellIdentifier];
if (cell == nil)
    cell = [[UITableViewCell alloc] initWithStyle:UITableViewCellStyleValue2
                                  reuseIdentifier:CellIdentifier];

// Configure the cell...
NSUInteger sectionIndex = [indexPath section];
NSUInteger rowIndex = [indexPath row];

NSDictionary *section = [self.sections objectAtIndex:sectionIndex];
NSArray *rows = [section objectForKey:@"rows"];
NSDictionary *row = [rows objectAtIndex:rowIndex];
cell.textLabel.text = [row objectForKey:@"label"];
cell.detailTextLabel.text = [self.hero valueForKey:[row objectForKey:@"key"]];

return cell;
```

Build and run the app. You get your list of heroes. Tap one to see the details.

It didn't work, did it? Why not? The problem is the birthdate attribute. If you recall, birthdate is an NSDate object. And cell.textLabel.text expects a string. You'll handle properly in a little bit, but for now change the assignment to read

```
cell.detailTextLabel.text = [[self.hero valueForKey:[row objectForKey:@"key"]] description];
```

Try running it again. View an existing hero and try adding a new one. After adding a hero, your detail view should look like Figure 4-22.

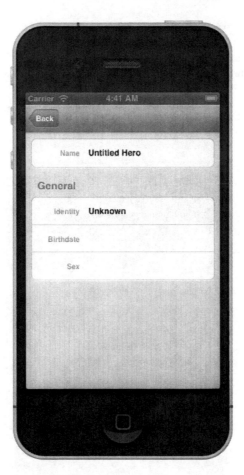

*Figure 4-22. Detail view for a new hero*

# Editing the Details

Look back at Figure 4-2 and compare it to Figure 4-22. Note that the left image in Figure 4-2 has an Edit button on the right side of the navigation bar. And Figure 4-2 specifies that you have an Edit mode for the detail view, as seen in the right image. Let's add the Edit button and implement the Edit mode in the HeroDetailController.

# Editing Mode in the Detail View

Compare the two images in Figure 4-2. How do they differ? First, the Edit button in the left image has been replaced with a Save button in the right image. Also, the Save button is highlighted. The Back button has been replaced with a Cancel button. The cells in the right image appear to be indented. While it appears to be a lot of changes, it's actually not that much effort to implement.

First, add the Edit button to the navigation bar. Select HeroDetailController.m and find the viewDidLoad method. Uncomment the following line:

```
self.navigationItem.rightBarButtonItem = self.editButtonItem;
```

Run the application and drill down to the detail view. There's the Edit button on the right side of the navigation bar. If you click it, the view should change to look like Figure 4-23.

*Figure 4-23.* *The detail view in editing mode*

Note that the Edit button has automatically changed into a Done button and is highlighted. If you click Done, it will revert back into the Edit button. This is fine, but you really want the Done button to read Save. That's a little more work.

As you've seen, the editButtonItem method gives you an instance of a UIBarButton that toggles between Edit and Done when pressed. It also toggles the editing property in your HeroDetailController (which inherits the property from UITableViewController) between NO and YES. The button also invokes the setEditing:animated: callback.

You want to replace the Done with Save. To accomplish this, you need to replace the Edit button with a Save button. While you're at it, add a specific method to handle the saving, which you'll use later. First, you need to add a property for the Save button and a callback method. Since you only access the Save button inside HeroDetailController, you can make it a private property. And since the callback is only used by the Save button you can make that a private declaration as well. Edit HeroDetailController.m and add it to the category.

```
@interface HeroDetailController ()
@property (strong, nonatomic) NSArray *sections;
@property (strong, nonatomic) UIBarButtonItem *saveButton;
- (void)save;
@end
```

Now you need to create an instance of a Save button and assign it to this variable. Add the following to viewDidLoad in HeroDetailController.m, right after the Edit button code you just uncommented.

```
self.saveButton = [[UIBarButtonItem alloc] initWithBarButtonSystemItem:UIBarButtonSystemItemSave
                                                target:self
                                                action:@selector(save)];
```

Now, you need to switch between the Edit and Save buttons. But where do you call this method? Remember, when the Edit button is pressed, it invokes the setEditing:animated: method. Override the default setEditing:animated: method, and have yours switch the buttons.

```
- (void)setEditing:(BOOL)editing animated:(BOOL)animated
{
        [super setEditing:editing animated:animated];
        self.navigationItem.rightBarButtonItem = (editing) ? self.saveButton : self.editButtonItem;
}
```

And you need to add the save method (put it at the bottom of the file, just before the @end).

```
#pragma mark - (Private) Instance Methods

- (void)save
{
        [self setEditing:NO animated:YES];
}
```

Save your work and run the application. Navigate down the detail view, and click the Edit button. It should toggle between Edit and Save as you toggle in and out of editing mode. Now, let's fix it so the Back button changes into a Cancel button.

The process is almost identical to what you did for the Edit/Save buttons: declare a property and callback method, and toggle the button in the navigation bar. However, you also need an property to store the Back button. Add the following to the HeroDetailController category:

```
@property (strong, nonatomic) UIBarButtonItem *backButton;
@property (strong, nonatomic) UIBarButtonItem *cancelButton;
- (void)cancel;
```

Assign the backButton to the left navigation bar button, and create an instance of the Cancel button in viewDidLoad.

```
self.backButton = self.navigationItem.leftBarButtonItem;
self.cancelButton = [[UIBarButtonItem alloc] initWithBarButtonSystemItem:UIBarButtonSystemItemCancel
                                                        target:self
                                                        action:@selector(cancel)];
```

Modify setEditing:animated: to toggle the Back and Cancel buttons.

```
self.navigationItem.leftBarButtonItem = (editing) ? self.cancelButton : self.backButton;
```

Finally, add the cancel callback method. For now, it's identical to the save method, but you'll be changing that soon.

```
- (void)cancel
{
    [self setEditing:NO animated:YES];
}
```

Run the application again. When you hit the Edit button in the detail view, the Back button should switch to Cancel. If you press the Cancel button, you should exit editing mode.

Now you want to eliminate those red buttons that appear to right of each cell in editing mode. When you click those buttons, they rotate and a Delete button will appear in the appropriate cell. This isn't really relevant for the detail view, you can't delete an attribute (you can, however, clear it, or set its value to nil). So you don't want this button to appear at all. Add this method to HeroDetailController.m (somewhere with the other table view delegate methods):

```
- (UITableViewCellEditingStyle)tableView:(UITableView *)tableView
            editingStyleForRowAtIndexPath:(NSIndexPath *)indexPath
{
        return UITableViewCellEditingStyleNone;
}
```

Running application shows that the red buttons are gone. You are able to toggle the detail view in and out of editing mode, but you still can't edit anything. There's still a bit of work ahead of you to add this functionality.

## Creating a Custom UITableViewCell Subclass

Let's look at the Contacts application. When you edit a contact's attributes, an accessory view appears, with a keyboard (Figure 4-24), allowing for inline editing. You're going to emulate this functionality in your SuperDB application. This is going to require you to develop a custom UITableViewCell subclass.

*Figure 4-24. Editing in the Contacts application*

Let's look at the current layout of the table view cell. Currently, you set two parts of the cell: the textLabel and the detailTextLabel (Figure 4-25). Both parts are static text; you can assign the values programmatically, but you are unable to interact with them via the user interface. The iOS SDK does not give you a class where you can assign the textLabel statically but edit the detailTextLabel portion. That's what you have to build.

*Figure 4-25. Current breakdown of the table view cell*

The key component is replacing the detailTextLabel property with a UITextField. This will give you the ability to edit within the table view cell. Since you replaced one portion of the table view cell, you have to replace the textLabel as well. Since that text is static, you'll use a UILabel. In principle, your custom table view cell should look like Figure 4-26.

*Figure 4-26. Breakdown of your custom table view cell*

Let's get started.

Single click the SuperDB group in the Navigator pane, and create a new file. Choose Objective-C class, under the iOS/Cocoa Touch templates. Make this class a subclass of `UITableViewCell`. Let's name the file `SuperDBEditCell.m`. Click Next, then Create.

You need a `UILabel` and a `UITextField`. Add those properties to `SuperDBEditCell.h`.

```
@interface SuperDBEditCell : UITableViewCell

@property (strong, nonatomic) UILabel *label;
@property (strong, nonatomic) UITextField *textField;

@end
```

Now add the appropriate initialization code. Edit `SuperDBEditCell.m` and find `initWithStyle:reuseIdentifier:`. Right after the Initialization Code comment, add

```
self.selectionStyle = UITableViewCellSelectionStyleNone;

self.label = [[UILabel alloc] initWithFrame:CGRectMake(12.0, 15.0, 67.0, 15.0)];
self.label.backgroundColor = [UIColor clearColor];
self.label.font = [UIFont boldSystemFontOfSize:[UIFont smallSystemFontSize]];
self.label.textAlignment = NSTextAlignmentRight;
self.label.textColor = kLabelTextColor;
self.label.text = @"label";
[self.contentView addSubview:self.label];

self.textField = [[UITextField alloc] initWithFrame:CGRectMake(93.0, 13.0, 170.0, 19.0)];
self.textField.backgroundColor = [UIColor clearColor];
self.textField.clearButtonMode = UITextFieldViewModeWhileEditing;
self.textField.enabled = NO;
self.textField.font = [UIFont boldSystemFontOfSize:[UIFont systemFontSize]];
self.textField.text = @"Title";
[self.contentView addSubview:self.textField];
```

Note that `kLabelTextColor` is a constant that you calculated so the label will have the same color as before. Add this #define before the @implementation directive:

```
#define kLabelTextColor [UIColor colorWithRed:0.321569f green:0.4f blue:0.568627f alpha:1.0f]
```

Now you need to adjust the `HeroDetailController` to use `SuperDBEditCell`. But before you do that, you need to fix the configuration in `SuperDB.storyboard`.

Open SuperDB.storyboard, and select the first table view cell in the HeroDetailController. Open the Identity Inspector and change the Class field to SuperDBEditCell. Switch to the Attributes Inspector, and change the Style to Custom. Repeat this for the three other table view cells.

Open HeroDetailController.m. Add this #import

```
#import "SuperDBEditCell.h"
```

as the second #import directive. Then find tableView:cellForRowAtIndexPath: and edit it to read

```
static NSString *CellIdentifier = @"SuperDBEditCell";
SuperDBEditCell *cell = [tableView dequeueReusableCellWithIdentifier:CellIdentifier];
if (cell == nil)
    cell = [[SuperDBEditCell alloc] initWithStyle:UITableViewCellStyleValue2
                               reuseIdentifier:CellIdentifier];

// Configure the cell...
NSUInteger sectionIndex = [indexPath section];
NSUInteger rowIndex = [indexPath row];

NSDictionary *section = [self.sections objectAtIndex:sectionIndex];
NSArray *rows = [section objectForKey:@"rows"];
NSDictionary *row = [rows objectAtIndex:rowIndex];
cell.label.text = [row objectForKey:@"label"];
cell.textField.text = [[self.hero valueForKey:[row objectForKey:@"key"]] description];

return cell;
```

Save and run the app. It should behave exactly as before you created your custom table view cell. Now you can turn on the ability to edit.

Override the setEditing: method in SuperDBEditCell.m.

```
- (void)setEditing:(BOOL)editing animated:(BOOL)animated
{
        [super setEditing:editing animated:animated];
        self.textField.enabled = editing;
}
```

Save and run the app again. Navigate to the detail view, and enter editing mode. Tap over the Unknown Hero of the Identity row. You should see the keyboard input view appear on the bottom of the screen, and a cursor should appear at the end of Unknown Hero. Click another row. The cursor should appear in that row.

Let's edit the Identity row. Tap over the Unknown Hero to activate the keyboard input view. Click the **x** button at the right end of the cell. This should erase Unknown Hero. Now type **Super Cat**, and tap Save. You should exit editing mode, and your hero's new identity should read Super Cat. Tap on Back to return to the list view.

Wait. What happened? You renamed your hero Super Cat, but the list view still shows Unknown Hero. If you click on the Unknown Hero row, the detail view also still shows Unknown Hero. Why weren't your changes saved?

Remember when you added the Save button to the detail view? You also added a callback, save, to be invoked when the Save button was pressed. Let's look at the callback again.

```
- (void)save
{
    [self setEditing:NO animated:YES];
}
```

Note that this method *doesn't save anything*! All it does is turn off editing mode. Let's figure out how to save your changes for real.

# Saving Your Changes

Let's review your detail view. The detail view is a table view managed by your HeroDetailController. The HeroDetailController also has a reference to your Hero object, which is an NSManagedObject. Each row in the table view is your custom table view cell class, SuperDBEditCell. Depending on which row you need, you assign a different hero attribute to display.

Now, to save the changes you make, the Save button invokes the save method. This is the point where you need to save the changes to your NSManagedObject. You will modify your SuperDBEditCell class to know what attribute it is displaying. In addition, you will define a property, value, to tell you the new data in the cell.

First, add your properties to SuperDBEditCell.h.

```
@property (strong, nonatomic) NSString *key;
@property (strong, nonatomic) id value;
```

Next, edit SuperDBEditCell.m to define an property override methods for the value property.

```
#pragma mark - Property Overrides

- (id)value
{
    return self.textField.text;
}

- (void)setValue:(id)aValue
{
    self.textField.text = aValue;
}
```

Finally, modify HeroDetailController.m to assign the key name to each cell inside tableView:cellForRowAtIndexPath.

```
cell.key = [row objectForKey:@"key"];
```

Then iterate over each cell on save to update the hero's attributes in the save method.

```
for (SuperDBEditCell *cell in [self.tableView visibleCells])
    [self.hero setValue:[cell value] forKey:[cell key]];

NSError *error;
if (![self.hero.managedObjectContext save:&error])
    NSLog(@"Error saving: %@", [error localizedDescription]);

[self.tableView reloadData];
```

Save and run the application. Navigate down to the detail view, and enter editing mode. Change the Identity to Super Cat and click Save. Click the Back button to return to the list view. You should see that the hero's identity is now displaying Super Cat.

Now you're going to work on specialized input views for the birthdate and sex attributes.

# Specialized Input Views

Note that when you click the Birthdate or Sex row in the detail view, the keyboard input view is displayed. You could allow the user to enter the birthdate or sex via the keyboard and validate the input, but there is a better way. You can create subclasses of SuperDBEditCell to handle those special cases.

## DatePicker SuperDBEditCell Subclass

Single-click the SuperDB group in the Navigator pane, and create a new file. Select Objective-C class, and make it a subclass of SuperDBEditCell. Name the class **SuperDBDateCell** and create the files. Edit SuperDBDateCell.m to read as follows:

```
#import "SuperDBDateCell.h"

static NSDateFormatter *__dateFormatter = nil;

@interface SuperDBDateCell ()
@property (strong, nonatomic) UIDatePicker *datePicker;
- (IBAction)datePickerChanged:(id)sender;
@end

@implementation SuperDBDateCell

+ (void)initialize
{
    __dateFormatter = [[NSDateFormatter alloc] init];
    [__dateFormatter setDateStyle:NSDateFormatterMediumStyle];
}
```

```objc
- (id)initWithStyle:(UITableViewCellStyle)style reuseIdentifier:(NSString *)reuseIdentifier
{
    self = [super initWithStyle:style reuseIdentifier:reuseIdentifier];
    if (self) {
        // Initialization code
        self.textField.clearButtonMode = UITextFieldViewModeNever;

        self.datePicker = [[UIDatePicker alloc] initWithFrame:CGRectZero];
        self.datePicker.datePickerMode = UIDatePickerModeDate;
        [self.datePicker addTarget:self
                            action:@selector(datePickerChanged:)
                  forControlEvents:UIControlEventValueChanged];
        self.textField.inputView = _datePicker;
    }

    return self;
}

#pragma mark - SuperDBEditCell Overrides

- (id)value
{
    if (self.textField.text == nil || [self.textField.text length] == 0)
        return nil;
    return self.datePicker.date;
}

- (void)setValue:(id)value
{
    if (value != nil && [value isKindOfClass:[NSDate class]]) {
        [self.datePicker setDate:value];
        self.textField.text = [__dateFormatter stringFromDate:value];
    }
    else {
        self.textField.text = nil;
    }
}

#pragma mark - (Private) Instance Methods

- (IBAction)datePickerChanged:(id)sender
{
    NSDate *date = [self.datePicker date];
    self.value = date;
    self.textField.text = [__dateFormatter stringFromDate:date];
}

@end
```

What have you done here? You defined a local static variable __dateFormatter of type NSDateFormatter. You're doing this because creating an NSDateFormatter is an expensive operation, and you don't want to have to create a new instance every time you want to format a an NSDate object. You could have made it a private property of SuperDBDateCell and lazily created it, but that would mean you would create a new one for every instance of SuperDBDateCell. By making it a local static variable, you only have to create one instance for the lifetime of the SuperDB application.

Next, you declared a private UIDatePicker property, datePicker, and a callback for datePicker, datePickerChanged.

In the SuperDBDateCell @implementation, you defined a class method, +initialize. This is a special class method inherited from NSObject. The SuperDB application will call SuperDBDateCell+initialize exactly one time, before any call to the SuperDBDateCell class or an instance. This is where you initialize the local static __dateFormatter to hold an NSDateFormatter instance.

You added some custom initialization code to initWithStyle:reuseIdentifier:. This is where you instantiate the datePicker property and assign it to the textField inputView property. Normally inputView is nil. This tells iOS to use the keyboard input view for the textField. By assigning it an alternate view, you're telling iOS to show the alternate view when editing the textField.

SuperDBDateCell overrides the value property to make sure you display and return an NSDate, rather than an NSString. This is where you use the __dateFormatter to convert the date to a string, then assign it to the textField text property.

Finally, you implement the datePicker's callback for when you change the date via the UI. Every time you change the date in the datePicker, you update the textField to reflect that change.

## Using the DatePicker SuperDBEditCell Subclass

Let's review how the table view cells are created. In the HeroDetailController, you created the cells in the tableView:cellForRowAtIndexPath: method. When you first wrote this method, you created an instance UITableViewCell. Later, you replaced this with an instance of your custom subclass, SuperDBEditCell. Now you've created another subclass for a specific IndexPath, the IndexPath displaying the birthdate attribute. How can you tell your application which custom subclass to use? That's right, you'll add that information to your property list: HeroDetailController.plist.

Single-click HeroDetailController.plist. Expand all the disclosure triangles, so you can see all the elements. Navigate down sections ➤ Item 0 ➤ rows ➤ Item 0 ➤ key. Single-click the key row so that it is highlighted. Click the+button next to key. Rename this row from New Item to **class**. In the value column, type **SuperDBEditCell**. Repeat this for all the key rows under sections ➤ Item 1. They should all have the value SuperDBEditCell, except for the class row below the birthdate key. That should have a value of SuperDBDateCell (Figure 4-27).

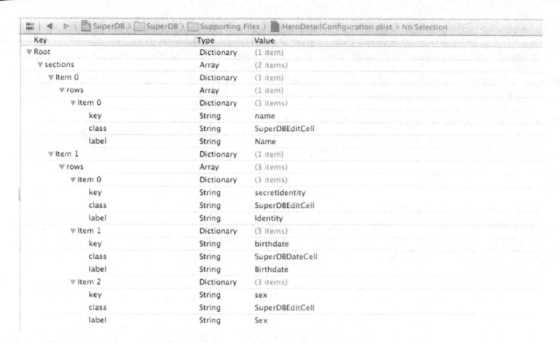

| Key | Type | Value |
|---|---|---|
| ▼ Root | Dictionary | (1 item) |
| ▼ sections | Array | (2 items) |
| ▼ Item 0 | Dictionary | (1 item) |
| ▼ rows | Array | (1 item) |
| ▼ Item 0 | Dictionary | (3 items) |
| key | String | name |
| class | String | SuperDBEditCell |
| label | String | Name |
| ▼ Item 1 | Dictionary | (1 item) |
| ▼ rows | Array | (3 items) |
| ▼ Item 0 | Dictionary | (3 items) |
| key | String | secretIdentity |
| class | String | SuperDBEditCell |
| label | String | Identity |
| ▼ Item 1 | Dictionary | (3 items) |
| key | String | birthdate |
| class | String | SuperDBDateCell |
| label | String | Birthdate |
| ▼ Item 2 | Dictionary | (3 items) |
| key | String | sex |
| class | String | SuperDBEditCell |
| label | String | Sex |

*Figure 4-27. HeroDetailController.plist after adding the table view cell class key*

You need to modify `tableView:cellForRowAtIndexPath:` to make use of the information you just placed in the property list. Open `HeroDetailController.m`, and edit `tableView:cellForRowAtIndexPath:` to appear like this:

```
- (UITableViewCell *)tableView:(UITableView *)tableView cellForRowAtIndexPath:(NSIndexPath *)indexPath
{
    NSUInteger sectionIndex = [indexPath section];
    NSUInteger rowIndex = [indexPath row];
    NSDictionary *section = [self.sections objectAtIndex:sectionIndex];
    NSArray *rows = [section objectForKey:@"rows"];
    NSDictionary *row = [rows objectAtIndex:rowIndex];

    NSString *cellClassname = [row valueForKey:@"class"];
    SuperDBEditCell *cell = [tableView dequeueReusableCellWithIdentifier:cellClassname];
    if (cell == nil) {
        Class cellClass = NSClassFromString(cellClassname);
        cell = [cellClass alloc];
        cell = [cell initWithStyle:UITableViewCellStyleValue2 reuseIdentifier:cellClassname];
    }

    // Configure the cell...
    cell.key = [row objectForKey:@"key"];
    cell.value = [self.hero valueForKey:[row objectForKey:@"key"]];
    cell.label.text = [row objectForKey:@"label"];

    return cell;
}
```

Save and run the application. Navigate down to the detail view, and enter editing mode. Click the Birthdate cell, next to the label. The accessory input view should appear and should be a date picker set to today's date. When you change the date in the date picker, the date should change in the table view cell.

There's one more input to take care of. This version of your application uses the string attribute editor to solicit the sex (sorry, we couldn't resist!) of the superhero. This means that there is no validation on the input other than that it's a valid string. A user could type M, Male, MALE, or Yes, Please, and they would all be happily accepted by the application. That means, later on, if you want to let the user sort or search their heroes by gender, you could have problems because the data won't be structured in a consistent manner. You'll tackle that problem next.

## Implementing a Selection Picker

As you saw earlier, you could have enforced a specific sex spelling by using a regular expression, putting up an alert if the user typed something besides Male or Female. This would have prevented values other than the ones you want from getting entered, but this approach is not all that user friendly. You don't want to annoy your user. Why make them type anything at all? There are only two possible choices here. Why not present a selection list and let the user just tap the one they want? Hey, that sounds like a great idea! You're glad you thought of it. Let's implement it now, shall you?

Again, create a new Objective-C class, and make it a subclass of SuperDBEditCell. Name the class **SuperDBPickerCell**, after that fact that you will be using a UIPickerView. Most of what you do will be similar to what you did for SuperDBDateCell, but there are some key differences.

Edit the interface definition in SuperDBPickerCell.h to read

```
@interface SuperDBPickerCell : SuperDBEditCell<UIPickerViewDataSource, UIPickerViewDelegate>

@property (strong, nonatomic) NSArray *values;

@end
```

The property is named pickerValues, which will hold the possible selections. You also added the UIPickerViewDataSource and UIPickerViewDelegate protocols to SuperDBPickerCell.

Now, let's edit the implementation of SuperDBPickerCell in SuperDBPickerCell.m.

```
@interface SuperDBPickerCell ()
@property (strong, nonatomic) UIPickerView *pickerView;
@end

@implementation SuperDBPickerCell

- (id)initWithStyle:(UITableViewCellStyle)style reuseIdentifier:(NSString *)reuseIdentifier
{
    self = [super initWithStyle:style reuseIdentifier:reuseIdentifier];
    if (self) {
        self.textField.clearButtonMode = UITextFieldViewModeNever;

        self.pickerView = [[UIPickerView alloc] initWithFrame:CGRectZero];
        self.pickerView.dataSource = self;
```

```objc
        self.pickerView.delegate = self;
        self.pickerView.showsSelectionIndicator = YES;
        self.textField.inputView = self.pickerView;
    }

    return self;
}

#pragma mark UIPickerViewDataSource Methods

- (NSInteger)numberOfComponentsInPickerView:(UIPickerView *)pickerView
{
    return 1;
}

- (NSInteger)pickerView:(UIPickerView *)pickerView numberOfRowsInComponent:(NSInteger)component
{
    return [self.values count];
}

#pragma mark - UIPickerViewDelegate Methods

- (NSString *)pickerView:(UIPickerView *)pickerView
             titleForRow:(NSInteger)row
           forComponent:(NSInteger)component
{
    return [self.values objectAtIndex:row];
}

- (void)pickerView:(UIPickerView *)pickerView
      didSelectRow:(NSInteger)row
       inComponent:(NSInteger)component
{
    self.value = [self.values objectAtIndex:row];
}

#pragma mark - SuperDBEditCell Overrides

- (void)setValue:(id)value
{

    if (value != nil) {
        NSInteger index = [self.values indexOfObject:value];
        if (index != NSNotFound) {
            self.textField.text = value;
        }
    }
    else {
        self.textField.text = nil;
    }
}

@end
```

SuperDBPickerCell is conceptually identical to SuperDBDateCell. Rather than using an NSDatePicker, you use a UIPickerView. In order to tell the pickerView what to display, you need to have SuperDBDateCell conform to the protocols UIPickerViewDataSource and UIPickerViewDelegate. Rather than having a callback on the pickerView to indicate when the picker value has changed, you use the delegate method pickerView:didSelectRow:. Since you're storing the value as a string, you don't need to override the implementation of the value accessor method. However, you do need to override the value mutator.

You need to tell the application to use this new class for the Sex attribute. Edit the class row in the property list, HeroDetailController.plist. Change the value from SuperDBEditableCell to SuperDBPickerCell. Make sure you are changing the right row. The label row should read Sex, and the attribute row should read sex.

If you run the application now and try to edit the Sex attribute, you should see the picker wheel appear on the bottom on of the screen. However, there are no values to choose from. If you look back at the code you just added, the picker wheel gets its information from the values property. But you never set this. Again, you could hardcode this in the SuperDBPickerCell object, but that would limit the usefulness of this object. Instead, you'll add a new item to the property list.

Just like you did earlier with the class item, you need to add a new key, which you'll call values. Unlike the class key, you'll only add it to the item with the sex key. Edit the HeroDetailController.plist and open all the nodes. For the last item, find the row with the key label. Click the + button on that row. Name the new item **values** and change its type to array. Add two string items to the values array and give them the values Male and Female. See Figure 4-28.

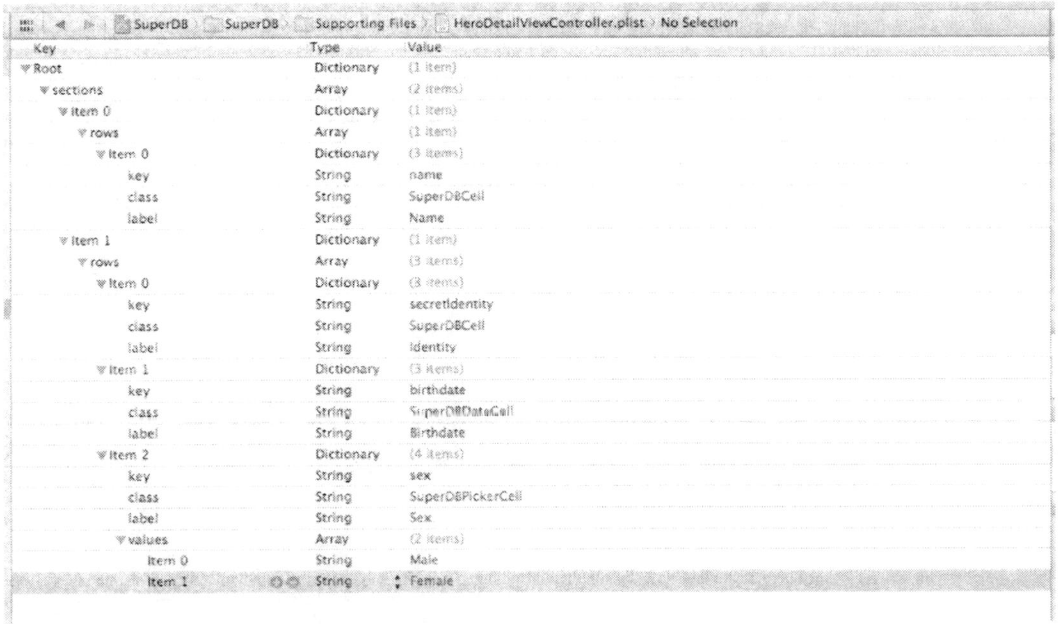

*Figure 4-28. HeroDetailController.plist with values for the sex item*

Now you need to pass the contents of values to table view cell when `tableView:cellForRowAtIndexPath:` is in the HeroDetailController. Open HeroDetailController.m, and add the following to `tableView:cellForRowAtIndexPath:` before the other cell configuration code:

```
NSArray *values = [row valueForKey:@"values"];
if (values != nil) {
    // TODO clean this up - ugh
    [cell performSelector:@selector(setValues:) withObject:values];
}
```

Build and run the app. Navigate down to the detail view and tap the Edit button. Tap on the Sex cell, and the picker view should appear with the choices Male and Female. Set the value, tap Save, and the Sex cell should be populated.

# Devil's End

Well, you're at the end of a long and conceptually difficult chapter. You should congratulate yourself on making it all the way through with us. Table-based detail editing view controllers are some of the hardest controller classes to write well, but now you have a handful of tools in your toolbox to help you create them. You've seen how to use a property list to define your table view's structure, you've seen how to create a custom `UITableViewCell` subclasses to edit different types of data, and you've also seen how to use Objective-C's dynamic nature to create instances of classes based on the name of the class stored in an `NSString` instance.

Ready to move on? Turn the page. Let's get going!

# Chapter 5

# Preparing for Change: Migrations and Versioning

By the end of Chapter 4 you had mastered a great deal of the Core Data architecture and functionality by building a fully functioning, albeit somewhat simple, Core Data application. You've now got enough Core Data chops to build a solid app, send it to your testers, and then on to the App Store.

But what happens if you change your data model and send a new version of your application out to testers who already have the previous version? Consider the SuperDB app. Let's say you decide to add a new attribute to the Hero entity; make one of the existing, currently optional attributes required; and then add a new entity. Can you just send the program out to your users or will this cause problems with their data?

As things stand right now, if you make changes to your data model, the existing data sitting in the user's persistent store on their iPhone will be unusable in the new version of your application. Your application will crash on launch. If you launch the new version from Xcode, you will see a big, scary error message like the following:

```
2012-07-17 17:33:56.641 SuperDB[11233:c07] Unresolved error Error Domain=NSCocoaErrorDomain
Code=134100 "The operation couldn't be completed. (Cocoa error 134100.)" UserInfo=0x80a3b30
{metadata={
    NSPersistenceFrameworkVersion = 409;
    NSStoreModelVersionHashes =     {
        Hero = <0fe30005 4578f63c 124e2af7 3798fb56 7a194f27 f9281223 bd2c5ee3 d985d2fc>;
    };
    NSStoreModelVersionHashesVersion = 3;
    NSStoreModelVersionIdentifiers =     (
        ""
    );
    NSStoreType = SQLite;
    NSStoreUUID = "719284D9-793C-48A7-8F3E-C633CD4F0402";
    "_NSAutoVacuumLevel" = 2;
```

```
}, reason=The model used to open the store is incompatible with the one used to create the store}, {
    metadata =        {
        NSPersistenceFrameworkVersion = 409;
        NSStoreModelVersionHashes =          {
            Hero = <0fe30005 4578f63c 124e2af7 3798fb56 7a194f27 f9281223 bd265ee3 d985d2fc>;
        };
        NSStoreModelVersionHashesVersion = 3;
        NSStoreModelVersionIdentifiers =         (
            ""
        );
        NSStoreType = SQLite;
        NSStoreUUID = "719284D9-793C-48A7-8F3E-C633CD4F0402";
        "_NSAutoVacuumLevel" = 2;
    };
    reason = "The model used to open the store is incompatible with the one used to create the store";
}
```

If this happens in development, it's not usually a big deal. If nobody else has a copy of your app and you don't have any irreplaceable data stored in it, you can just select **"Reset Content and Settings"** from the iPhone Simulator menu in the simulator or uninstall the application from your iPhone using Xcode's Organizer window, and Core Data will create a new persistent store based on the revised data model the next time you install and run your application.

If, however, you have given the application to others, they will be stuck with an unusable application on their iPhone unless they uninstall and re-install the application, thereby losing all of their existing data.

As you probably imagine, this is not something that makes for particularly happy customers. In this chapter, we're going to show you how to version your data model. Then we'll talk about Apple's mechanism for converting data between different data model versions, which are called migrations. We'll talk about the difference between the two types of migrations: lightweight migrations and standard migrations. Then you will set up the SuperDB Xcode project to use lightweight migrations so that the changes you make in the next few chapters won't cause problems for your (admittedly non-existent) users.

At the end of this chapter, the SuperDB application will be all set up and ready for new development, including changes to your data model, without having to worry about your users losing their data when you ship a new version.

# About Data Models

When you create a new Xcode project using a template that supports Core Data, you are provided with a single data model in the form of an .xcdatamodel file in your project. In Chapter 2, you saw how this file was loaded into an instance of NSManagedObjectModel at runtime in the application delegate's managedObjectModel method. In order to understand versioning and migrations, it's important to look a little deeper under the hood to see what's going on.

# Data Models Are Compiled

The .xcdatamodel class in your project does not get copied into your application's bundle the way other resources do. The data model file contains a lot of information that your application doesn't need. For example, it contains information about the layout of the objects in Xcode's model editor's diagram view (Figure 5-1), which is only there to make your life easier. Your application doesn't care about how those rounded rectangles are laid out, so there's no reason to include that information inside your application bundle.

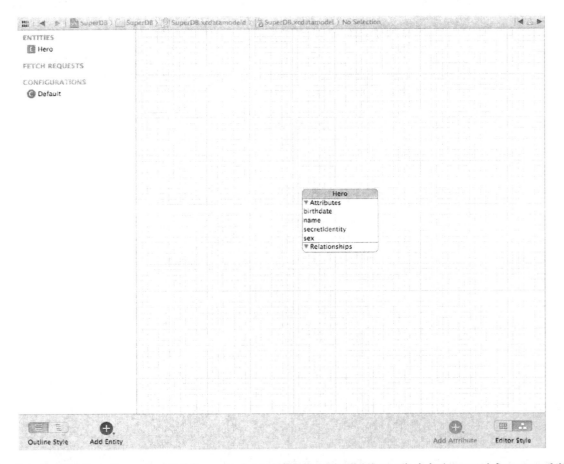

*Figure 5-1. Certain information, such as that the rounded rectangle representing the Hero entity is in the upper-left corner and that the disclosure triangles next to Attributes and Relationships are expanded, is stored in the .xcdatamodel file but not in the .mom file*

Instead, your .xcdatamodel files get compiled into a new type of file with an extension of .mom, which stands for managed object model (sorry, Mom). This is a much more compact binary file that contains just the information that your application needs. This .mom file is what is actually loaded to create instances of NSManagedObjectModel.

## Data Models Can Have Multiple Versions

You most likely understand what versioning means in a general sense. When a company releases a new version of a piece of software with new features, it typically has a new number or designation. For example, you are working on a specific version of Xcode (for us, it's 4.5) and a specific version of Mac OS X (for us it's 10.8, also known as Mountain Lion).

These are called *marketing version identifiers* or *numbers*, as they are primarily intended to tell customers  the difference between various released versions of the software. Marketing versions are incremented when a new version of the program is released to customers.

There are other, finer-grained forms of versioning used by developers, however. If you've ever used a concurrent versioning system such as cvs, svn, or git, you're probably aware of how this all works. Versioning software keeps track of the changes over time to all of the individual source code and resource files that make up your project (among other things).

> **Note**    We're not going to discuss regular version control, but it's a good thing to know about if you're a developer. Fortunately, there are a lot of resources on the Web for learning how to install and use different version-control software packages. A good place to start is the Wikipedia page on version control at http://en.wikipedia.org/wiki/Revision_control.

Xcode integrates with several version-control software packages, but it also has some built-in version-control mechanisms, including one that's intended for use with Core Data data models. Creating new versions of your data models is the key to keeping your users happy. Every time you release a version of your application to the public, you should create a new version of your data model. This will create a new copy so that the old version can be kept around to help the system figure out how to update the data from a persistent store made with one version to a newer version.

## Creating a New Data Model Version

Single-click SuperDB.xcdatamodeld in Xcode. Now click the Editor menu and select "Add Model Version." You will be asked to name this new version. The default values Xcode presents to you (Figure 5-2) are fine.  Just click Finish.

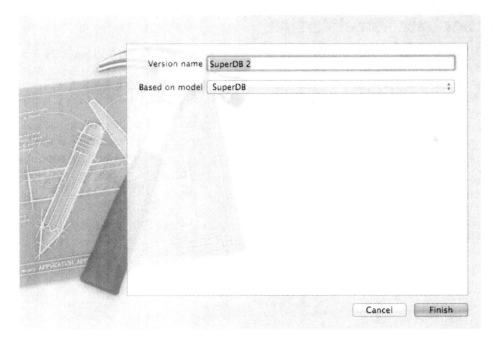

*Figure 5-2. Naming the new data model version*

You just added a new version of your data model. Once you click Finish, the SuperDB.xcdatamodeld file will gain a disclosure triangle next to it. It will be opened to reveal two different versions of your data model (Figure 5-3).

*Figure 5-3. A versioned data model contains the current version, marked with a green checkmark on its icon, along with every previous version*

The icon for one of the versions will have a green checkmark on it. This indicates the current version (in your case, SuperDB.xcdatamodel), which is the one that your application will use. By default, when you create a new version, you actually create a copy of the original. However, the new version keeps the *same file name* as the original, whereas the name of the copy is appended with an incrementally larger number. This file represents what your data model looked like when you created the new version and it should be left untouched.

The fact that the higher number is the older file might seem a little weird but, as more versions accumulate, the numbering will make more sense. The next time you create a new version, the old version will be named SuperDB 3.xcdatamodel, and so on. The numbering makes sense for all the non-current versions, since each version will have a number one higher than the previous one. By keeping the name of the current model the same, it's easy to tell which is the one you can change.

# The Current Data Model Version

In Figure 5-3, SuperDB.xcdatamodel is the current version of the data model and SuperDB 2.xcdatamodel is the previous version. You can now safely make changes to the current version, knowing that a copy of the previous version exists, frozen in time, which will give you the ability to migrate your users' data from the old version to the next version when you release it.

You can change which version is the current version. To do this, select SuperDB.xcdatamodeld, then open the File Inspector in the Utility pane (Figure 5-4). You should see a section named Version Core Data Model. Find a drop-down box labeled Current. Here you can select the data model you want to make current. You won't do this often, but you might do it if you need to revert to an older version of the application for some reason. You can use migrations to go back to an older version or move to a new version.

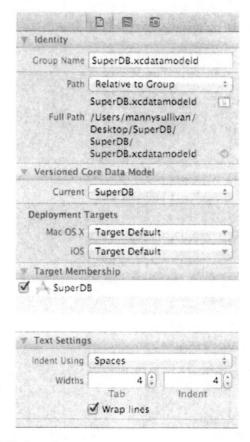

*Figure 5-4. The Core Data (Directory) File Inspector*

# Data Model Version Identifiers

Although you can assign version identifiers like 1.1 or Version A to data models by selecting the specific data model version in the Navigation pane and bringing up the File Inspector (Figure 5-5), this identifier is purely for your own use and is completely ignored by Core Data.

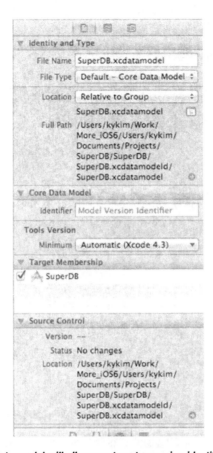

*Figure 5-5. The File Identity pane for a data model will allow you to set a version identifier*

Instead, Core Data performs a mathematical calculation called a hash on each entity in your data model file. The hash values are stored in your persistent store. When Core Data opens your persistent store, Core Data uses these hash values to ensure that the version of your data stored in the store is compatible with the current data model.

Since Core Data does its version validation using the stored hash values, you don't need to worry about incrementing version numbers for versioning to work. Core Data will just know which version a persistent store was created for by looking at the stored hash value and comparing it to the hash calculated on the current version of the data model.

# Migrations

As you saw at the beginning of the chapter, when Core Data detects that the persistent store in use is incompatible with the current data model, it throws an exception. The solution is to provide a migration to tell Core Data how to move data from the old persistent store to a new one that matches the current data model.

## Lightweight vs. Standard

There are two different types of migrations supported by Core Data. The first, called a lightweight migration, is only available in the case of relatively straightforward modifications to your data model. If you add or remove an attribute from an entity, or add or delete an entity from the data model, for example, Core Data is perfectly capable of figuring out how to migrate the existing data into the new model. In the case of a new attribute, it simply creates storage for that attribute, but doesn't populate it with data for the existing managed objects. In a lightweight migration, Core Data actually analyzes the two data models and creates the migration for you.

If you make a change that's not straightforward and thus can't be resolved by the lightweight migration mechanism, then you have to use a standard migration. A standard migration involves creating a mapping model and possibly writing some code to tell Core Data how to move the data from the old persistent store to the new one.

## Standard Migrations

The changes you will be making to the SuperDB application in this book are all pretty straightforward, and an in-depth discussion of standard migrations is beyond the scope of this book. Apple has documented the process fairly thoroughly in the developer documentation, though, so you can read more about standard migrations at http://developer.apple.com/library/ ios/#documentation/Cocoa/Conceptual/CoreDataVersioning/Articles/Introduction.html.

# Setting Up Your App to Use Lightweight Migrations

On the other hand, you will be using lightweight migrations a lot through the rest of the book. In every remaining Core Data chapter, you will create a new version of your data model and let lightweight migrations handle moving the data. However, lightweight migrations are not turned on by default, so you need to make some changes to your application delegate to enable them.

Edit AppDelegate.m and find the persistentStoreCoordinator method. Replace this line

```
if (![_persistentStoreCoordinator addPersistentStoreWithType:NSSQLiteStoreType
                          configuration:nil
                          URL:storeURL
                          options:nil
                          error:&error]) {
```

with these lines

```
NSDictionary *options = @{NSMigratePersistentStoresAutomaticallyOption:@YES,
                          NSInferMappingModelAutomaticallyOption:@YES};
if (![_persistentStoreCoordinator addPersistentStoreWithType:NSSQLiteStoreType
                          configuration:nil
                          URL:storeURL
                          options:options
                          error:&error]) {
```

The way to turn on lightweight migrations is to pass a dictionary into the options argument when you call the addPersistentStoreWithType:configuration:URL:options:error: method to add your newly created persistent store to the persistent store coordinator. In that dictionary, you use two system-defined constants, NSMigratePersistentStoresAutomaticallyOption and NSInferMappingModelAutomaticallyOption, as keys in the dictionary, and store an NSNumber under both of those keys that holds an Objective-C BOOL value of YES. By passing a dictionary with these two values in when you add the persistent store to the persistent store coordinator, you indicate to Core Data that you want it to attempt to automatically create migrations if it detects a change in the data model version, and if it's able to create the migrations, to automatically use those migrations to migrate the data to a new persistent store based on the current data model.

And that's it. With these changes, you are ready to start making changes to your data model without fear. (Well, maybe not completely without fear.) By using lightweight migrations, you limit the complexity of the changes you're able to make. For example, you won't be able to split an entity up into two different entities or move attributes from one entity to another, but the majority of changes you'll need to make outside of major refactoring can be handled by lightweight migrations. Plus, once you set your project up the way you've done in this chapter, that functionality is basically free.

# Time to Migrate On

After a couple of long, conceptually difficult chapters, taking a break to set up your project to use migrations gave you a nice breather, but don't underestimate the importance of migrations. The people who use your applications are trusting you to take a certain amount of care with their data. Putting some effort into making sure that your changes don't cause major problems for your users is important.

Any time you put out a new release of your application with a new data model version, make sure you test the migration thoroughly. This is true regardless of whether you're using the lightweight migrations you set up in this chapter or the heavier-duty standard migrations.

Migrations, especially lightweight migrations, are relatively easy to use, but they hold the potential for causing your users significant inconvenience, so don't get lulled into a false sense of security by how easy they are to use. Test every migration thoroughly with as much realistic data as you can.

And with that warning out of the way, let's continue adding functionality to the SuperDB application. Up next? Custom managed objects for fun and profit.

# Chapter 6

# Custom Managed Objects

At the moment, the Hero entity is represented by instances of the class NSManagedObject. Thanks to key-value coding, you have the ability to create entire data models without ever having to create a class specifically designed just to hold your application's data.

There are some drawbacks to this approach, however. For one thing, when using key-value coding with managed objects, you use NSString constants to represent your attributes in code, but these constants are not checked in any way by the compiler. If you mistype the name of an attribute, the compiler won't catch it. It can also be a little tedious having to use valueForKey: and setValue:forKey: all over the place instead of just using properties and dot notation.

Although you can set default values for some types of data model attributes, you can't, for example, set conditional defaults such as defaulting a date attribute to today's date. For some types of attributes, there's no way at all to set a default in the data model. Validation is similarly limited. Although you can control certain elements of some attributes, like the length of a string or max value of a number, there's no way to do complex or conditional validation, or to do validation that depends on the values in multiple attributes.

Fortunately, NSManagedObject can be subclassed, just like other Objective-C classes, and that's the key to doing more advanced defaulting and validation. It also opens the door to adding additional functionality to your entity by adding methods. You can, for example, create a method to return a value calculated from one or more of the entity's attributes.

In this chapter, you're going to create a custom subclass of NSManagedObject for your Hero entity. Then, you're going to use that subclass to add some additional functionality. You're also going to add two new attributes to Hero. One is the hero's age. Instead of storing the age, you're going to calculate it based on their birthdate. As a result, you won't need Core Data to create space in the persistent store for the hero's age, so you're going to use the transient attribute type and then write an accessor method to calculate and return the hero's age. The transient attribute type tells Core Data not to create storage for that attribute. In your case, you'll calculate the hero's age as needed at runtime.

The second attribute you're going to add is the hero's favorite color. Now, there is no attribute type for colors, so you're going to implement something called a transformable attribute. Transformable attributes use a special object called a *value transformer* to convert custom objects to instances of NSData so they can be stored in the persistent store. You'll write a value transformer that will let you save UIColor instances this way. In Figure 6-1, you can see what the detail editing view will look like at the end of the chapter with the two new attributes in place.

*Figure 6-1.* *The Hero detail view as it will look at the end of the chapter*

Of course, you don't have an attribute editor for colors, so you'll have to write one to let the user select the hero's favorite color. You're just going to create a simple, slider-based color chooser (Figure 6-2).

*Figure 6-2. The simple, slider-based color attribute editor*

Because there's no way to set a default color in the data model, you're going to write code to default the favorite color attribute to white. If you don't do that, then the color will be nil when the user goes to edit it the first time, which will cause problems.

Finally, you'll add validation to the date field to prevent the user from selecting a birthdate that occurs in the future and you're also going to tweak your attribute editors so that they notify the user when an entered attribute has failed validation. You'll give the user the option to go back and fix the attribute or to just cancel the changes they made (Figure 6-3).

**Figure 6-3.** *When attempting to save an attribute that fails validation, the user will have the option of fixing the problem or canceling their changes*

Although you're only going to be adding validation to the Birthdate field, the reporting mechanism you're going to write will be generic and reusable if you add validation to another field. You can see an example of the generic error alert in Figure 6-4.

*Figure 6-4. Since your goal is generally to write reusable code, your validation mechanism will also enforce validations done on the data model, such as minimum length*

There's a fair amount of work to do, so let's get started. You're going to continue working with the same SuperDB application from last chapter. Make sure that you created a new version of your data model and that you turned on lightweight migrations, as shown in the last chapter.

# Updating the Data Model

The first order of business is to add your two new attributes to the data model. Make sure that the disclosure triangle next to SuperDB.xcdatamodeld in the SuperDB folder in the Navigator pane is expanded, and single-click on the current version of the data model, the one with the green check mark icon on it.

Once the model editor comes up, first make sure you are in table view mode. Then, select the Hero entity in the component pane (Figure 6-5).

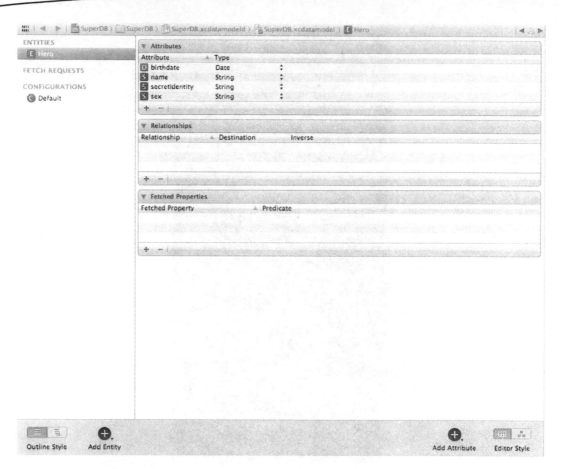

*Figure 6-5.  Back in the model editor*

# Adding the Age Attribute

Click the plus icon labeled Add Attribute in the lower right of the data model. Change the new attribute's name to **age**. In the model editor, uncheck Optional and check the Transient. That will let Core Data know that you don't need to store a value for this attribute. In your case, since you're using SQLite for your persistent store, this will tell Core Data not to add a column for age to the database table used to store hero data. Change the attribute type to Integer 16; you're going to calculate age as a whole number. That's all you have to do for now for the age attribute. Of course, as things stand, you can't do anything meaningful with this particular attribute because it can't store anything, and you don't yet have any way to tell it how to calculate the age. That will change in a few minutes, when you create a custom subclass of NSManagedObject.

# Adding the Favorite Color Attribute

Add another attribute. This time, call the new attribute **favoriteColor** and set the attribute type to Transformable. Once you've changed the Type pop-up to Transformable, you should notice a new text field labeled Name, with a greyed value of value transformer name (Figure 6-6).

*Figure 6-6.* *Making the favoriteColor attribute a transformable attribute*

The value transformer name is the key to using transformable attributes. We'll discuss value transformers in more depth in just a few minutes, but you'll populate this field now to save yourself a trip back to the model editor later. This field is where you need to put the name of the value transformer class that will be used to convert whatever object represents this attribute into an NSData instance for saving in the persistent store and vice versa. If you leave the field blank, CoreData will use the default value transformer, NSKeyedUnarchiveFromDataTransformerName. The default value transformer will work with a great many objects by using NSKeyedArchiver and NSKeyedUnarchiver to convert any object that conforms to the NSCoding protocol into an instance of NSData.

## Adding a Minimum Length to the Name Attribute

Next, let's add some validation to ensure that your name attribute is at least one character long. Single-click the name attribute to select it. In the model editor, enter **1** in the text field next to the Validation label to specify that the value entered into this attribute must to be at least one character long. The Min. Length checkbox should automatically check itself. This may seem like a redundant validation, since you already unchecked Optional in a previous chapter for this attribute, but the two do not do exactly the same thing. Because the Optional check box is unchecked, the user will be prevented from saving if name is nil. However, your application takes pains to ensure that name is never nil. For example, you give name a default value. If the user deletes that value, the text field will still return an empty string instead of nil. Therefore, to ensure that an actual name is entered, you're going to add this validation.

Save the data model.

# Creating the Hero Class

It's now time to create your custom subclass of NSManagedObject. This will give you the flexibility to add custom validation and defaulting as well as the ability to use properties instead of key-value coding, which will make your code easier to read and give you additional checks at compile time.

Single-click the SuperDB group in the Navigator pane of Xcode. Create a new file. When the New File Assistant appears, select Core Data from under the iOS heading in the left pane, then look for an icon in the upper-right pane that you've probably never seen before: NSManagedObject subclass (Figure 6-7). Select it, and click the Next button.

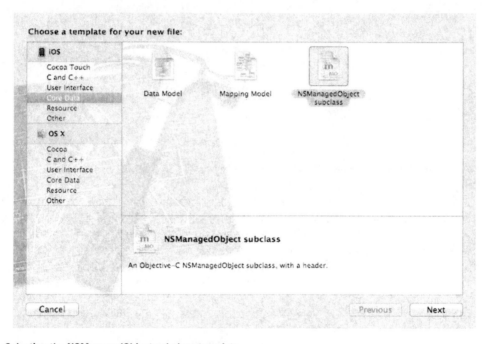

*Figure 6-7. Selecting the NSManagedObject subclass template*

Next, you will be prompted to select the entities you want to manage (Figure 6-8). Check Hero and click Next.

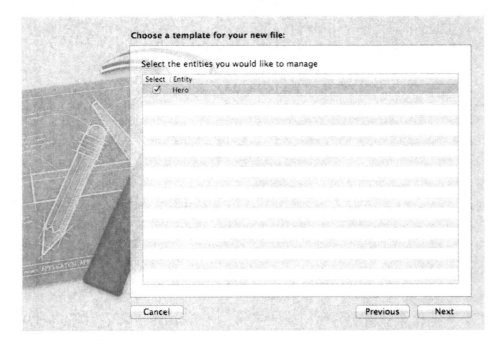

**Figure 6-8.** *Select the Hero entity*

Finally, you will be prompted where to save the generated class files (Figure 6-9). Leave the "Use scalar properties for primitive data types" box unchecked. The default location should be fine, so just click Create.

*Figure 6-9.* *Select the location to put the class files*

## Tweaking the Hero Header

You should now have a pair of files called Hero.h and Hero.m in your project folder. Xcode also tweaked your data model so that the Hero entity uses this class rather than NSManagedObject at runtime. Single-click on the new Hero.h file now. It should look something look like this, though the exact order of your property declarations may not be exactly the same as ours:

```
#import <Foundation/Foundation.h>
#import <CoreData/CoreData.h>

@interface Hero : NSManagedObject

@property (nonatomic, retain) NSDate * birthdate;
@property (nonatomic, retain) NSString * name;
@property (nonatomic, retain) NSString * secretIdentity;
@property (nonatomic, retain) NSString * sex;
```

```
@property (nonatomic, retain) NSNumber * age;
@property (nonatomic, retain) id favoriteColor;

@end
```

> **Caution**   If your Hero.h file does not include declarations of age and favoriteColor, chances are
> you did not save properly somewhere along the way. If so, select Hero.h and Hero.m in your project file
> and press Delete, being sure the files are moved to the trash. Then go back, make sure your attributes
> were properly created in your data model, make sure the data model was saved, then recreate Hero.h
> and Hero.m.

You need to make two quick changes here. First, you want to make age read-only. You're not going to allow people to set a hero's age; you're just going to calculate it based on the birthdate. You also want to change favoriteColor from the generic ID to UIColor to indicate that your favoriteColor attribute is, in fact, an instance of UIColor. This will give you some additional type safety by letting the compiler know what type of object represents the favoriteColor attribute. You also need to add a couple of constants that will be used in your validation methods.

Add the following after the #imports but before the @interface declaration:

```
#define kHeroValidationDomain @"com.AppOrchard.SuperDB.HeroValidationDomain"
#define kHeroValidationBirthdateCode 1000
#define kHeroValidationNameOrSecretIdentityCode 1001
```

Then change the age and favoriteColor property declarations.

```
@property (nonatomic, retain, readonly) NSNumber * age;
@property (nonatomic, retain) UIColor * favoriteColor;
```

Don't worry too much about the constants. We'll explain error domains and error codes in a few moments. Switch over to Hero.m. You've got a bit more work to do in the implementation file. Before you do that, let's talk about what you're going to do.

# Defaulting

One of the most common Core Data tasks that requires you to subclass NSManagedObject is setting conditional default values for attributes, or setting the default value for attribute types that can't be set in the data model, such as default values for transformable attributes.

The NSManagedObject method awakeFromInsert is designed to be overridden by subclasses for the purpose of setting default values. It gets called immediately after a new instance of an object is inserted into a managed object context and before any code has a chance to make changes to or use the object.

In your case, you have a transformable attribute called favoriteColor that you want to default to white. To accomplish that, add the following method before the @end declaration in Hero.m:

```
- (void)awakeFromInsert
{
    self.favoriteColor = [UIColor colorWithRed:1.0 green:1.0 blue:1.0 alpha:1.0];
    [super awakeFromInsert];
}
```

Notice the use of the @dynamic keyword in Hero.m. This tells the compiler not to generate accessors and mutators for the property that follows. The idea here is that the accessors and mutators will be provided by the superclass at runtime. Don't worry too much about the specifics, just know that this bit of complexity is required in order for Core Data to work properly.

> **Tip**  Notice that you didn't use [UIColor whiteColor] for the default. The reason you used the colorWithRed:green:blue:alpha: factory method is because it always creates an RGBA color. UIColor supports several different color models. Later, you're going to be breaking the UIColor down into its separate components (one each for red, green, blue, and alpha) in order to save it in the persistent store. You're also going to let the user select a new color by manipulating sliders for each of these components. The whiteColor method, however, doesn't create a color using the RGBA color space. Instead, it creates a color using the grayscale color model, which represents colors with only two components, gray and alpha.

Simple enough. You just create a new instance of UIColor and assign it to favoriteColor. Another common usage of awakeFromInsert is for defaulting date attributes to the current date. You could, for example, default the birthdate attribute to the current date by adding the following line of code to awakeFromInsert:

```
self.birthdate = [NSDate date];
```

# Validation

Core Data offers two mechanisms for doing attribute validation in code, one that's intended to be used for single-attribute validations and one that's intended to be used when a validation depends on the value of more than one attribute. Single attribute validations are relatively straightforward. You might want to make sure that a date is valid, a field is not nil, or that a number attribute is not negative. Multi-field validations are a little more complex. Let's say that you have a Person entity, and it has a string attribute called legalGuardian where you keep track of the person who is legally responsible and able to make decisions for a person if they are a minor. You might want to make sure this attribute is populated, but you only want to do that for minors, not for adults. Multi-attribute validation will let you make the attribute required if the person's age attribute is less than 18, but not otherwise.

# Single-Attribute Validations

NSManagedObject provides a method for validating single attributes called validateValue:forKey:error:. This method takes a value, key, and an NSError handle. You could override this method and perform validation by returning YES or NO based on whether the value is valid. If it doesn't pass, you would also be able to create an NSError instance to hold specific information about what is not valid and why. You could do that. But don't. As a matter of fact, Apple specifically states you *shouldn't* do this. You never actually need to override this method because the default implementation uses a very cool mechanism to dynamically dispatch error handling to special validation methods that aren't defined in the class.

For example, let's say you have a field called birthdate. NSManagedObject will, during validation, automatically look for a method on your subclass called validateBirthdate:error:. It will do this for every attribute, so if you want to validate a single attribute, all you have to do is declare a method that follows the naming convention of validateXXX:error: (where XXX is the name of the attribute to be validated), returning a BOOL that indicates whether the new value passed validation.

Let's use this mechanism to prevent the user from entering birthdates that occur in the future. Above the @end declaration in Hero.m, add the following method:

```
- (BOOL)validateBirthdate:(id *)ioValue error:(NSError **)outError
{
    NSDate *date = *ioValue;
    if ([date compare:[NSDate date]] == NSOrderedDescending) {
        if (outError != NULL) {
            NSString *errorStr = NSLocalizedString(@"Birthdate cannot be in the future",
                                                   @"Birthdate cannot be in the future");
            NSDictionary *userInfoDict = [NSDictionary dictionaryWithObject:errorStr
                                                        forKey:NSLocalizedDescriptionKey];
            NSError *error = [[NSError alloc] initWithDomain:kHeroValidationDomain
                                                code:kHeroValidationBirthdateCode
                                              userInfo:userInfoDict];

            *outError = error;
        }
        return NO;
    }
    return YES;
}
```

> **Tip**  Are you wondering why you're passing a pointer to a pointer to an NSError rather than just a pointer? Pointers to pointers allow a pointer to be passed by reference. In Objective-C methods, arguments, including object pointers, are passed by value, which means that the called method gets its own copy of the pointer that was passed in. So if the called method wants to change the pointer, as opposed to the data the pointer points to, you need another level of indirection. Thus, the pointer to the pointer.

As you can see from the preceding method, you return NO if the date is in the future and YES if the date is in the past. If you return NO, you also take some additional steps. You create a dictionary and store an error string under the key NSLocalizedDescriptionKey, which is a system constant that exists for this purpose. You then create a new instance of NSError and pass that newly created dictionary as the NSError's userInfo dictionary. This is the standard way to pass back information in validation methods and pretty much every other method that takes a handle to an NSError as an argument.

Notice that when you create the NSError instance, you use the two constants you defined earlier, kHeroValidationDomain and kHeroValidationBirthdateCode:

```
NSError *error = [[NSError alloc] initWithDomain:kHeroValidationDomain
                                            code:kHeroValidationBirthdateCode
                                        userInfo:userInfoDict];
```

> **Tip**    Notice that you don't call super in the single-attribute validation methods. It's not that these methods are defined as abstract, it's that they simply don't exist. These methods are created dynamically at runtime, so not only is there no point in calling super, there's actually no method on super to call.

Every NSError requires an error domain and an error code. Error codes are integers that uniquely identify a specific type of error. An error domain defines the application or framework that generated the error. For example, there's an error domain called NSCocoaErrorDomain that identifies errors created by code in Apple's Cocoa frameworks. You defined your own error domain for your application using a reverse DNS-style string and assigned that to the constant kHeroValidationDomain. You'll use that domain for any error created as a result of validating the Hero object. You could also have chosen to create a single domain for the entire SuperDB application, but by being more specific, your application will be easier to debug.

By creating your own error domains, you can be as specific as you want to be. You also avoid the problem of searching through long lists of system-defined constants, looking for just the right code that covers a specific error. kHeroValidationBirthdateCode is the first code you've created in your domain, and the value of 1000 is arbitrary; it would have been perfectly valid to choose 0, 1, 10000, or 34848 for this error code. It's your domain; you can do what you want.

# nil vs. NULL

In your validation methods, you may have noticed that you're comparing outError to NULL to see if you've been provided a valid pointer, rather than comparing to nil as you typically do. Both nil and NULL serve the same purpose (to represent empty pointers) and, in fact, they are defined to the same thing: the number zero. In terms of your code functioning, nil and NULL are 100% interchangeable.

That being said, you should endeavor to use the right one at the right time. The one you use will be a clue to your future self, as well as any other developers who work with your code, as to what you are doing.

When you are checking an Objective-C object pointer, compare to nil. With any other C pointers, use NULL. In this case, you're dealing with a pointer to a pointer, so you use NULL. If a pointer doesn't directly reference an Objective-C object, NULL is the appropriate comparison value, even if the pointer it references points to an object.

# Multiple-Attribute Validations

When you need to validate a managed object based on the values of multiple fields, the approach is a little different. After all the single-field validation methods have fired, another method will be called to let you do more complex validations. There are actually two such methods, one that is called when an object is first inserted into the context, and another when you save changes to an existing managed object.

When inserting a new managed object into a context, the multiple-attribute method you use is called validateForInsert:. When updating an existing object, the validation method you implement is called validateForUpdate:. In both cases, you return YES if the object passes validation and NO if there's a problem. As with single-field validation, if you return NO, you should also create an NSError instance that identifies the specifics of the problem encountered.

In many instances, the validation you want to do at insert and at update are identical. In those cases, do not copy the code from one and paste it into the other. Instead, create a new validation method and have both validateForInsert: and validateForUpdate: call that new validation method.

In your application, you don't have a need for any multiple-attribute validations (yet!), but let's say, hypothetically, that instead of making both name and secretIdentity required, you only wanted to require one of the two. You could accomplish that by making both name and secretIdentity optional in the data model, then using the multiple-attribute validation methods to enforce it. To do that, you would add the following three methods to your Hero class:

```
- (BOOL)validateNameOrSecretIdentity:(NSError **)outError
{
    if ((0 == [self.name length]) && (0 == [self.secretIdentity length])) {
        if (outError != NULL) {
            NSString *errorStr = NSLocalizedString(@"Must provide name or secret identity.",
                                                   @"Must provide name or secret identity.");
            NSDictionary *userInfoDict =
                [NSDictionary dictionaryWithObject:errorStr
                                           forKey:NSLocalizedDescriptionKey];
            NSError *error = [[NSError alloc] initWithDomain:kHeroValidationDomain
                                                       code:kHeroValidationNameOrSecretIdentityCode
                                                   userInfo:userInfoDict];

            *outError = error;
        }
    }
    return YES;
}
```

```
- (BOOL)validateForInsert:(NSError **)outError
{
    return [self validateNameOrSecretIdentity:outError];
}

- (BOOL)validateForUpdate:(NSError **)outError
{
    return [self validateNameOrSecretIdentity:outError];
}
```

# Virtual Accessors

At the beginning of the chapter, you added a new attribute called age to your data model. You don't need to store the hero's age, however, because you can calculate it based on the hero's birthdate. Calculated attributes like this are often referred to as virtual accessors. They look like accessors, and as far as other objects are concerned, they can be treated just like the other attributes. The fact that you're calculating the value at runtime rather than retrieving it from the persistent store is simply an implementation detail.

As your Hero object stands right now, the age accessor will always return nil because you've told your data model not to create storage space for it in the persistent store and have made it read only. In order to make it behave correctly, you must implement the logic to calculate age in a method that looks like an accessor (hence, the name "virtual accessor"). To do that, add the following method to Hero.m, just before @end:

```
- (NSNumber *)age
{
    if (self.birthdate == nil)
        return nil;

    NSCalendar *gregorian = [[NSCalendar alloc] initWithCalendarIdentifier:NSGregorianCalendar];
    NSDateComponents *components = [gregorian components:NSYearCalendarUnit
                                               fromDate:self.birthdate
                                                 toDate:[NSDate date]
                                                options:0];
    NSInteger years = [components year];
    return [NSNumber numberWithInteger:years];
}
```

Note the check you put in the beginning in the method. If you haven't set your hero's birthdate, you don't want to calculate the age.

Now any code that uses the age property accessor will be returned an NSNumber instance with the calculated age of the superhero.

# Adding Validation Feedback

In Chapter 4, you created a class named SuperDBEditCell that encapsulates the common functionality shared by the various table view cells. The SuperDBEditCell class does not include code designed to save the managed object; it just concerns itself with the display. You did store the attribute that each SuperDBEditCell instance displays. But now you want to add validation feedback when the edited attribute fails validation, and you don't want to duplicate functionality across subclasses.

What you want to do is have each instance of SuperDBEditCell (or subclass) validate the attribute it is handling. You want to perform the validation when the table view cell loses focus (i.e., you move to another cell), and when the user attempts to save. If the edited value does not pass validation, you should pop up an alert window telling your user the validation error and present two buttons: Cancel, reverting the value, or Fix, letting the user edit the cell. To handle this, you need to have SuperDBEditCell respond to the UITextFieldDelegate and UIAlertViewDelegate protocols. Finally, if the user clicks the Cancel button on the navigation bar, you will undo all the changes they've made.

First, edit SuperDBEditCell.h, and change the @interface declaration to read

```
@interface SuperDBEditCell : UITableViewCell <UITextFieldDelegate, UIAlertViewDelegate>
```

Next, you need to add a property to your NSManagedObject.

```
@property (strong, nonatomic) NSManagedObject *hero;
```

Finally, you need a validate method to invoke when you want the validation to occur.

```
- (IBAction)validate;
```

Switch over to SuperDBEditCell.m, and add the validate method you just declared.

```
#pragma mark - Instance Methods

- (IBAction)validate
{
    id val = self.value;
    NSError *error;
    if (![self.hero validateValue:&val forKey:self.key error:&error]) {
        NSString *message = nil;
        if ([[error domain] isEqualToString:@"NSCocoaErrorDomain"]) {
            NSDictionary *userInfo = [error userInfo];
            message =
                [NSString stringWithFormat:NSLocalizedString(@"Validation error on:
                                                   %@\rFailure Reason: %@",
                                            @"Validation error on: %@,
                                            Failure Reason: %@)"),
                                [userInfo valueForKey:@"NSValidationErrorKey"],
                                [error localizedFailureReason]];
        }
```

```
        else
            message = [error localizedDescription];
        UIAlertView *alert = [[UIAlertView alloc] initWithTitle:NSLocalizedString(@"Validation Error",
                                                                           @"Validation Error")
                                              message:message
                                             delegate:self
                                    cancelButtonTitle:NSLocalizedString(@"Cancel", @"Cancel")
                                    otherButtonTitles:NSLocalizedString(@"Fix", @"Fix"), nil];
        [alert show];
    }
}
```

In order for the Alert View to work correctly, you need to implement its delegate method.

```
#pragma mark Alert View Delegate

- (void)alertView:(UIAlertView *)alertView clickedButtonAtIndex:(NSInteger)buttonIndex
{
    if (buttonIndex == [alertView cancelButtonIndex])
        [self setValue:[self.hero valueForKey:self.key]];
    else
        [self.textField becomeFirstResponder];
}
```

You need the textField delegate method textField:didEndEditing: to call your validate method.

```
#pragma mark UITextFieldDelegate methods

- (void)textFieldDidEndEditing:(UITextField *)textField
{
    [self validate];
}
```

Finally, you need out cell's textField to know about its new delegate. In SuperDB's initWithStyle:reuseIdentifier: method, just before the textField is added to the cell's contentView, add this:

```
self.textField.delegate = self;
```

What have you done here? First, you made sure the NSTextField delegate was set to self in initWithStyle:reuseIdentifier:. Then, you added the validate method. Basically, you validate calls validateValue:forKey:error: on your NSManagedObject. If this validation fails, you parse the NSError object and create a UIAlertView. Next, you defined a textFieldDidEndEditing: delegate method. This method gets invoked when the NSTextField in your SuperDBEditCell class exits editing mode. This happens when you click from cell to another or when you click Save or Back on the navigation bar. Finally, you added alertView:clickedButtonAtIndex:. This delegate method gets called when the user clicks a button on the UIAlertView you display on validation error. Depending on which button was clicked, Cancel or Fix, you either revert the value or move the focus to the table view cell.

Now you just need to pass your Hero object down from the HeroDetailController to the SuperDBEditCell. Edit HeroDetailController.m and find the tableView:cellForRowAtIndexPath:. Just before all the other cell configurations, add this:

```
cell.hero = self.hero;
```

## Updating the Detail View

Looking at Figure 6-2, you see that you need two more cells in the General section of the table view. Before you go any further, let's update the detail view.

Open SuperDB.storyboard, and find the HeroDetailController. Select the second table view section by clicking in an area outside the table view cells (next to the General label is a good place). Open the Attributes Inspector in the Utility pane, and change the Rows field from 3 to 5. The second section of the table view should now show five rows. That's all you need to do in the storyboard editor. Easy, right?

Now let's take a look at Figure 6-2 again. The order of the labels in the second section are: Identity, Birthdate, Age, Sex, and Favorite Color. When you last ran the application, the section labels were Identity, Birthdate, and Sex. Not only do you need to add Age and Favorite Color, you need to reorder things so that Age comes before Sex. Fortunately, since your cells are configured from a property list, this should be (relatively) simple.

Open HeroDetailController.plist. Navigate down to Root ➤ Sections ➤ Item 1 ➤ rows ➤ Item 1. If the disclosure triangle next to the last Item 1 is open, close it. Item 1 and Item 2 should be right next to each other. If the Item 2 disclosure triangle is open, close it as well. Now select the last Item 1 row, and click the (+) button next to the Item 1 label. A new row should have been inserted between Item 1 and Item 2. Item 2 is renamed to Item 3. The new Item 2 has a type of string with no value.

Change the new Item 2's type to Dictionary, and open its disclosure triangle. This is the configuration for your Age cell. Click the (+) button next to the new Item 2 three times to add three rows. Keep all three rows as type string and give them the following key/value pairs: key/age, class/ SuperDBEditCell, label/Age.

Now add a row after Item 3, repeat the process, adding three rows with type string to the new Item 4. The key/value pairs will be: key/favoriteColor, class/SuperDBEditCell, label/Color.

Build and run the app. Navigate down to the detail view.

The app should have crashed. Why?

Well, you're assigning the age attribute to the textField's text property. Age will be an instance of NSNumber, and textField.text will expect an NSString. You could subclass SuperDBEditCell to handle NSNumbers, but you probably won't need it. It's far easier to change this method in SuperDBEditCell.m.

```
- (void)setValue:(id)aValue
{
    if ([newValue isKindOfClass:[NSString class]])
        self.textField.text = aValue;
    else
        self.textField.text = [aValue description];
}
```

If you were showing a lot of NSNumbers, you probably wouldn't do this, but this works for now.

Try building and running the app again. If you add a new hero, you should see something like Figure 6-10.

*Figure 6-10. The Hero detail view*

There's a problem with the Age cell. For one, in Edit mode, you can tap inside the Age cell and it will get focus and show the keyboard input. Second, when you try to save from Edit mode, the app will crash. Let's fix this.

# Refactoring SuperDBEditCell

The Age cell is editable by default. There is a table view data source method, tableView:canEditRowAtIndexPath:, that determines if a specific table view cell is editable. By default, this method is provided in the UITableViewController template, but commented out. As a result, the table view assumes all cells are editable. Clearly, you need this method to return NO for the Age cell index path. Unfortunately, by specifing a cell as uneditable, the cell won't indent in Edit mode. That may be okay, but you'd like your Age cell to indent even if you can't edit it.

The app crash is due to these lines of code in the HeroDetailController save method:

```
for (SuperDBEditCell *cell in [self.tableView visibleCells])
    [self.hero setValue:[cell value] forKey:[cell key]];
```

When you try to set the value in the Hero entity's attribute of age, you'll get an exception crash. Remember, you declared age to be transient in your data model. That means the value of age is calculated, and there's no way to set it. You need a way to check if you should save the value in the cell.

First, you need to define an uneditable version of SuperDBEditCell. But rather than do that, let's make a superclass of SuperDBEditCell, called SuperDBCell, that uses a textField, but doesn't allow it to be enabled for editing. This seems like a good time to try out Xcode's refactoring capabilities.

# Xcode Refactoring Options

Open Edit ➤ Refactor in Xcode. You should see the submenu in Figure 6-11.

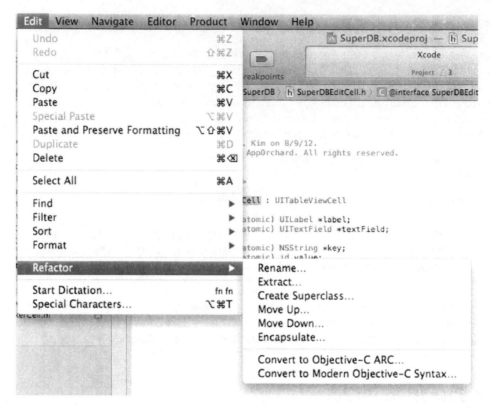

*Figure 6-11. Xcode Refactor menu*

Before you continue, let's quickly review what refactoring is and what each menu item does. Refactoring is restructuring code without changing its external behavior. Typically, you refactor some code (usually a method) to improve some nonfunctional attribute (i.e., reduce complexity, improve readability). This is not undertaken as a random "rewrite" of the code. Rather, it's a disciplined approach of small changes.

> **Note**    An excellent resource on refactoring patterns is Martin Fowler's *Refactoring: Improving the Design of Existing Code* (Addison-Wesley, 1999). Not only does it explain the process behind refactoring, but it outlines several refactoring techniques.

Xcode's refactoring options are

- *Rename*: Rename symbols so they indicate more clearly their purpose and make the source easier to read. Examples of symbols are the name of a class, method, or function. Unfortunately, methods declared in a protocol cannot be renamed.

- *Extract*: Extracts code you select in Xcode into a new method or function.

- *Create Superclass*: Defines a superclass for the class currently selected in Xcode.

- *Move Up*: Moves the selected method, property, or instance variable from a class to the superclass, provided both are defined in your project.

- *Move Down*: The opposite of Move Up, it moves the selected symbol from a class to a subclass, provided both are defined in your project.

- *Encapsulate*: Encapsulates an instance variable and create the appropriate accessors.

- *Convert to Objective-C ARC*: A tool to assist in converting legacy projects to use Automatic Reference Counting.

- *Convert to Modern Objective-C Syntax*: A tool to update code to use more modern Objective-C features like new Literals syntax (arrays, dictionaries, Booleans).

This a just a brief introduction to the Refactor menu items to familiarize yourself with what's available in Xcode for future projects. Let's get back to the SuperDB app.

You're going to use the Create Superclass option. Open SuperDBEditCell.h, and highlight the class name, SuperDBEditCell, after the @interface declaration. Select Edit ➤ Refactor ➤ Create Superclass. Xcode should present a pop-up on what to call the superclass (Figure 6-12). Name the class SuperDBCell, select the "Create files for new superclass" option, and click Preview. You should see a File Merge pop-up that shows all the changes it will make to create the super class SuperDBCell (Figure 6-13).

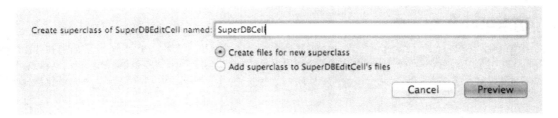

Create superclass of SuperDBEditCell named: SuperDBCell

⦿ Create files for new superclass
◯ Add superclass to SuperDBEditCell's files

Cancel    Preview

*Figure 6-12. Create Superclass pop-up*

*Figure 6-13. Refactoring file merge preview*

This particular preview doesn't show much, other that the creation of the SuperDBCell interface and implementation files. Click Save. Xcode may ask if it should take a snapshot. Whether you use snapshots or not are up to you. We use them occasionally, but we prefer using a revision control system like Git.

# Moving Code Around

Now, Xcode didn't do everything you wanted. It did create the files for SuperDBCell, and it did make SuperDBEditCell a subclass of SuperDBCell, but it didn't do much else. Remember you wanted to make SuperDBCell the same as SuperDBEditCell, but the textField wasn't going to ever been enabled.

Let's start with the SuperDBCell interface file. You're going to move most of SuperDBEditCell into SuperDBCell.

```
#import <UIKit/UIKit.h>

@interface SuperDBCell : UITableViewCell

@property (strong, nonatomic) UILabel *label;
@property (strong, nonatomic) UITextField *textField;

@property (strong, nonatomic) NSString *key;
@property (strong, nonatomic) id value;

@property (strong, nonatomic) NSManagedObject *hero;

@end
```

As a result, SuperDBEditCell.h will change as well.

```
#import <UIKit/UIKit.h>
#import "SuperDBCell.h"

@interface SuperDBEditCell : SuperDBCell <UITextFieldDelegate, UIAlertViewDelegate>

- (IBAction)validate;

@end
```

Next, you adjust the SuperDBCell implementation.

```
#import "SuperDBCell.h"

#define kLabelTextColor [UIColor colorWithRed:0.321569f green:0.4f blue:0.568627f alpha:1.0f]

@implementation SuperDBCell

- (id)initWithStyle:(UITableViewCellStyle)style reuseIdentifier:(NSString *)reuseIdentifier
{
    self = [super initWithStyle:style reuseIdentifier:reuseIdentifier];
    if (self) {
        // Initialization code
        self.selectionStyle = UITableViewCellSelectionStyleNone;

        // TODO - use Auto Layout to adjust sizes
        self.label = [[UILabel alloc] initWithFrame:CGRectMake(12.0, 15.0, 67.0, 15.0)];
        self.label.backgroundColor = [UIColor clearColor];
        self.label.font = [UIFont boldSystemFontOfSize:[UIFont smallSystemFontSize]];
        self.label.textAlignment = NSTextAlignmentRight;
        self.label.textColor = kLabelTextColor;
        self.label.text = @"label";
        [self.contentView addSubview:self.label];

        self.textField = [[UITextField alloc] initWithFrame:CGRectMake(93.0, 13.0, 170.0, 19.0)];
        self.textField.backgroundColor = [UIColor clearColor];
        self.textField.clearButtonMode = UITextFieldViewModeWhileEditing;
        self.textField.enabled = NO;
        self.textField.font = [UIFont boldSystemFontOfSize:[UIFont systemFontSize]];
        self.textField.text = @"Title";
        [self.contentView addSubview:self.textField];
    }
    return self;
}

#pragma mark - Property Overrides
```

```
- (id)value
{
    return self.textField.text;
}

- (void)setValue:(id)newValue
{
    if ([newValue isKindOfClass:[NSString class]])
        self.textField.text = newValue;
    else
        self.textField.text = [newValue description];
}

@end
```

You moved most of the initWithStyle:reuseIdentifier: code from SuperDBEditCell to SuperDBCell. Note that you disabled the textField.

```
self.textField.enabled = NO;
```

Also, you did not declare SuperDBCell to be the textField delegate. SuperDBCell does not have a setEditing:animated: method; it doesn't need one. The only reason SuperDBEditCell had one was to enable and disable the textField.

As a result of the SuperDBCell implementation, you need to change SuperDBEditCell.m. First, you update initWithStyle:reuseIdentifier:.

```
- (id)initWithStyle:(UITableViewCellStyle)style reuseIdentifier:(NSString *)reuseIdentifier
{
    self = [super initWithStyle:style reuseIdentifier:reuseIdentifier];
    if (self) {
        // Initialization code
        self.textField.delegate = self;
    }
    return self;
}
```

Next, you delete the value property accessor and mutator. While you're at it, you can delete the #define at the top of the file, since you moved it to SuperDBCell.m.

Your "refactoring" is complete, but you still need to make some changes.

# Editable Property

The SuperDB app crashes when you try to save an edited Hero since it tries to save the value in the Age cell. You want the HeroDetailController's save method to skip the Age cell when updating its Hero instance.

You could weave some Core Data wizardry and ask the Hero instance to check if the cell's attribute key is transient or not. That seems a lot work just to know something you can infer pretty reliably.

Remember, you created the SuperDBCell class to handle those fields that are uneditable (and probably don't need to be updated). So what you want is for SuperDBCell to return YES on some query and SuperDBEditCell to return NO (or vice-versa). Let's just define a method, isEditable, in SuperDBCell to return NO. You'll override the method in SuperDBEditCell to return YES.

Add this to SuperDBCell.h:

```
- (BOOL)isEditable;
```

And its implementation to SuperDBCell.m:

```
#pragma mark - Instance Methods

- (BOOL)isEditable
{
    return NO;
}
```

Override the method in SuperDBEditCell.m.

```
#pragma mark - SuperDBCell Overrides

- (BOOL)isEditable
{
    return YES;
}
```

Now you need to use this method in HeroDetailController.m. Update the appropriate code in the save method.

```
for (SuperDBEditCell *cell in [self.tableView visibleCells]) {
    if ([cell isEditable])
        [self.hero setValue:[cell value] forKey:[cell key]];
}
```

Finally, you need to update your HeroDetailConfiguration.plist to have the Age cell use SuperDBCell. Open HeroDetailConfiguration.plist and navigate to Root ➤ sections ➤ Item 1 ➤ rows ➤ Item 2 ➤ class, and change its value to SuperDBCell.

Build and run the app. Navigate to the detail view and enter Edit mode. Try to tap on the Age cell. You can't because it's not editable.

# Creating a Color Table View Cell

Now that you've completed your color value transformer, let's think about how you can enter your hero's favorite color. Look back at Figure 6-1. You have a table view cell that displays a band of your hero's favorite color. When the user chooses the favorite color cell in Edit mode, you want to display a color picker (Figure 6-2). The color picker is not available via the iOS SDK, like the date and value pickers you used in Chapter 4. You're going to have to build one from scratch.

# Custom Color Editor

Single-click the SuperDB folder in the navigation pane, and create a new Objective-C class. When prompted, name the class UIColorPicker and make it a subclass of UIControl. UIControl is the base class for control objects like buttons and sliders. Here you define a subclass of UIControl that encapsulates four sliders. The only property you need UIColorPicker to declare is its color.

```
@property (strong, nonatomic) UIColor *color;
```

Every other property can be declared privately in a category in the implementation file, UIColorPicker.m.

```
@interface UIColorPicker ()
@property (strong, nonatomic) UISlider *redSlider;
@property (strong, nonatomic) UISlider *greenSlider;
@property (strong, nonatomic) UISlider *blueSlider;
@property (strong, nonatomic) UISlider *alphaSlider;
- (IBAction)sliderChanged:(id)sender;
- (UILabel *)labelWithFrame:(CGRect)frame text:(NSString *)text;
@end
```

You also declared two (private) methods. One is the callback for when the sliders change (siderChanged:). The other is a convenience method for creating the picker view.

Xcode should have created an initWithFrame: method for your UIColorPicker class. Add the following initialization code:

```
self.autoresizingMask = UIViewAutoresizingFlexibleHeight | UIViewAutoresizingFlexibleWidth;

[self addSubview:[self labelWithFrame:CGRectMake(20.0, 40.0,  60, 24) text:@"Red"]];
[self addSubview:[self labelWithFrame:CGRectMake(20.0, 80.0,  60, 24) text:@"Green"]];
[self addSubview:[self labelWithFrame:CGRectMake(20.0, 120.0, 60, 24) text:@"Blue"]];
[self addSubview:[self labelWithFrame:CGRectMake(20.0, 160.0, 60, 24) text:@"Alpha"]];

_redSlider   = [[UISlider alloc] initWithFrame:CGRectMake(100.0, 40.0,  190, 24)];
_greenSlider = [[UISlider alloc] initWithFrame:CGRectMake(100.0, 80.0,  190, 24)];
_blueSlider  = [[UISlider alloc] initWithFrame:CGRectMake(100.0, 120.0, 190, 24)];
_alphaSlider = [[UISlider alloc] initWithFrame:CGRectMake(100.0, 160.0, 190, 24)];

[_redSlider addTarget:self
                action:@selector(sliderChanged:)
      forControlEvents:UIControlEventValueChanged];
[_greenSlider addTarget:self
                action:@selector(sliderChanged:)
        forControlEvents:UIControlEventValueChanged];
[_blueSlider addTarget:self
                action:@selector(sliderChanged:)
        forControlEvents:UIControlEventValueChanged];
[_alphaSlider addTarget:self
                action:@selector(sliderChanged:)
        forControlEvents:UIControlEventValueChanged];
```

```
[self addSubview:_redSlider];
[self addSubview:_greenSlider];
[self addSubview:_blueSlider];
[self addSubview:_alphaSlider];
```

Here you are laying out the appearance of your color picker. You place the sliders in the view with the initWithFrame: method.

You need to override the color property mutator in order to set the slider values correctly:

```
#pragma mark - Property Overrides

- (void)setColor:(UIColor *)color
{
    _color = color;
    const CGFloat *components = CGColorGetComponents(color.CGColor);
    [_redSlider setValue:components[0]];
    [_greenSlider setValue:components[1]];
    [_blueSlider setValue:components[2]];
    [_alphaSlider setValue:components[3]];
}
```

Now you can implement your (private) instance methods. First, sliderChanged:

```
#pragma mark - (Private) Instance Methods

- (IBAction)sliderChanged:(id)sender
{
    _color = [UIColor colorWithRed:_redSlider.value
                             green:_greenSlider.value
                              blue:_blueSlider.value
                             alpha:_alphaSlider.value];

    [self sendActionsForControlEvents:UIControlEventValueChanged];
}
```

Next, labelWithFrame:text:

```
- (UILabel *)labelWithFrame:(CGRect)frame text:(NSString *)text
{
    UILabel *label = [[UILabel alloc] initWithFrame:frame];
    label.userInteractionEnabled = NO;
    label.backgroundColor = [UIColor clearColor];
    label.font = [UIFont boldSystemFontOfSize:[UIFont systemFontSize]];
    label.textAlignment = NSTextAlignmentRight;
    label.textColor = [UIColor darkTextColor];
    label.text = text;
    return label;
}
```

Now that you've created your custom color picker, you need to add a custom table view cell class to use it.

# Custom Color Table View Cell

Since you have a custom picker view, you're going to need to subclass SuperDBEditCell, like you did for SuperDBDateCell and SuperDBPickerCell. But how are you going to display a UIColor value in your SuperDBEditableCell class? You could create a string that displays the four values of the color (red, green, blue and alpha). For most end users, those numbers are meaningless. Your users are going to expect to see the actual color when they're viewing the hero detail. You don't have a mechanism to display colors in table view cell.

If you build a complicated table view cell subclass to display the color, are you going to use it elsewhere in the application? The likely answer is no. So, while you could spend time and effort building this class, don't. Here's a simpler solution: populate the text field with an NSString with a special Unicode character that displays as a solid rectangle. Then add code to change the font color of the text to make it appear in your hero's favorite color.

Create a new Objective-C subclass. Make it a subclass of SuperDBEditCell, and name it SuperDBColorCell. Add the Color Picker class the (private) property to SuperDBColorCell.m.

```
#import "UIColorPicker.h"

@interface SuperDBColorCell ()
@property (strong, nonatomic) UIColorPicker *colorPicker;
- (void)colorPickerChanged:(id)sender;
- (NSAttributedString *)attributedColorString;
@end
```

You also add a (private) instance method, attributedColorString, that returns an NSAttributedString. An attributed string is a string that also has information on how to format itself. Prior to iOS 6, attributed strings were extremely limited. Now, you're able to use them with UIKit objects. You'll see why you want this method soon.

Define the initWithStyle:reuseIdentifier: method as follows:

```
- (id)initWithStyle:(UITableViewCellStyle)style reuseIdentifier:(NSString *)reuseIdentifier
{
    self = [super initWithStyle:style reuseIdentifier:reuseIdentifier];
    if (self) {
        // Initialization code
        self.colorPicker = [[UIColorPicker alloc] initWithFrame:CGRectMake(0, 0, 320, 216)];
        [self.colorPicker addTarget:self
                             action:@selector(colorPickerChanged:)
                   forControlEvents:UIControlEventValueChanged];
        self.textField.inputView = self.colorPicker;
    }
    return self;
}
```

This should be pretty straightforward. Like the other SuperDBEditCell subclasses, you've instantiated your picker object and set it as the textField's inputView.

Next, override SuperDBEditCell's value accessor and mutator.

```
#pragma mark - SuperDBEditCell Overrides

- (id)value
{
    return self.colorPicker.color;
}

- (void)setValue:(id)value
{
    if (value != nil && [value isKindOfClass:[UIColor class]]) {
        [super setValue:value];
        self.colorPicker.color = value;
    }
    else {
        self.colorPicker.color = [UIColor colorWithRed:1.0 green:1.0 blue:1.0 alpha:1.0];
    }
    self.textField.attributedText = self.attributedColorString;
}
```

Make note of this line

```
self.textField.attributedText = self.attributedColorString;
```

in setValue:. Rather than setting the textField's text property, you using the new attributedText property. This tells the textView that you're using an attributed string and to use the attributes you've defined to format the string. You also set the Color Picker to white if the Hero has no color attribute defined.

Add the colorPicker callback method.

```
#pragma mark - (Private) Instance Methods

- (void)colorPickerChanged:(id)sender
{
    self.textField.attributedText = self.attributedColorString;
}
```

Again, you're telling the textField to update itself. But with what?

Finally, add the following code:

```
- (NSAttributedString *)attributedColorString
{
    NSString *block = [NSString
stringWithUTF8String:"\u2588\u2588\u2588\u2588\u2588\u2588\u2588\u2588\u2588\u2588\u2588"];
    UIColor *color = self.colorPicker.color;
    NSDictionary *attrs = @{NSForegroundColorAttributeName:color,
                            NSFontAttributeName:[UIFont boldSystemFontOfSize:[UIFont systemFontSize]]};
    NSAttributedString *attributedString =
        [[NSAttributedString alloc] initWithString:block attributes:attrs];
    return attributedString;
}
```

First, you define a string with a bunch of Unicode characters in it. \u2588 is the Unicode character for a block character. All you've done is is made a string of 10 block characters. Next, you ask the colorPicker to tell us its color. Then you use that color, and the system bold font (15pt) to define a dictionary. The keys you use are NSForegroundColorAttributeName and NSFontAttributeName. These keys are specifically defined for UIKit attributed string support. As you can infer from their names, NSForegroundColorAttributeName sets the foreground (or text) color of the string and NSFontAttributeName allows you to define the font you want for the string. Finally, you instantiate the attributed string with the Unicode string block and the attributes dictionary.

You could have use the textField's regular text property and just set the textColor as needed, but we thought this brief demonstration of attributed strings might pique your curiosity. Attributed strings are extremely flexible and powerful, and are worth your time to investigate.

> **Note**    To learn more about attributed strings, check out Apple's Attributed String Programming Guide
> at http://developer.apple.com/library/mac/#documentation/Cocoa/Conceptual/
> AttributedStrings/AttributedStrings.html.

## Cleaning up the Picker

You've got one more step before you can use your new Color Picker. First, you need to update the configuration property list to use the SuperDBColorCell. Open the HeroDetailController.plist and drill down to Root ➤ sections ➤ Item 1 ➤ rows ➤ Item 4 ➤ class. Change its value from SuperDBEditCell to SuperDBColorCell.

All set? Let's build and run. Navigate down the detail view. Tap the Edit button, and tap on the Color cell.

That's weird. You didn't get the Color Picker to appear at all. But the Color cell has a cursor and clear text button (Figure 6-14).

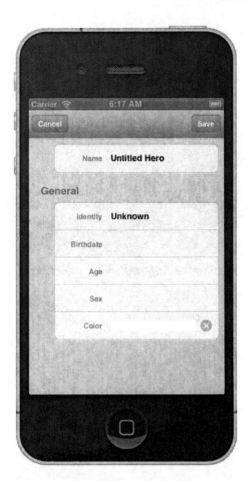

*Figure 6-14. Weird Color cell appearance*

You're probably getting tired of us having you build and run the app when we know things won't work. Think of it as an exercise in actual development. Many times you'll think you've gotten everything right, only to find things don't work when you run the app. That's when you've got to (unit) test, debug, or think your way through to a solution.

Anyway, there's a reason why the Color Picker didn't appear. Edit SuperDBColorCell.m and find the initWithStyle:reuseIdentifier:. In the initializer code, you created the Color Picker like this:

```
self.colorPicker = [[UIColorPicker alloc] initWithFrame:CGRectZero];
```

You made the size of the Color Picker a zero-sized CGRect. For all you know, it could be appearing. But since its size is zero, there's nothing to see. Didn't you do this with the Date Picker and Picker View? Yes, you did, but those classes have hooks inside of them to resize themselves according. Since you built the Color Picker from scratch, you've got to call those hooks manually.

First, you need to initialize the Color Picker with a non-zero CGRect. Use a default size to start.

```
self.colorPicker = [[UIColorPicker alloc] initWithFrame:CGRectMake(0, 0, 320, 216)];
```

Switch to UIColorPicker.m, and add this method after the initWithFrame: method:

```
- (void)willMoveToSuperview:(UIView *)newSuperview
{
    self.frame = newSuperview.bounds;
}
```

Now when you run it and try to edit the Color cell, you should see something like Figure 6-15.

***Figure 6-15.*** *The Color Picker*

Well, it works, but it doesn't look very pretty. You can fix that with some graphical magic. You should still be editing UIColorPicker.m. Add the following #import:

```
#import "QuartzCore/CAGradientLayer.h"
```

Now add the following #defines:

```
#define kTopBackgroundColor    [UIColor colorWithRed:0.98 green:0.98 blue:0.98 alpha:1.0]
#define kBottomBackgroundColor [UIColor colorWithRed:0.79 green:0.79 blue:0.79 alpha:1.0]
```

Look for a commented out drawRect: method and uncomment it. If you deleted it, don't worry, just make it look like this:

```
- (void)drawRect:(CGRect)rect
{
    CAGradientLayer *gradient = [CAGradientLayer layer];
    gradient.frame = self.bounds;
    gradient.colors = [NSArray arrayWithObjects:(__bridge id)[kTopBackgroundColor CGColor],
                                                 (__bridge id)[kBottomBackgroundColor CGColor], nil];
    [self.layer insertSublayer:gradient atIndex:0];
}
```

We want to point out the drawRect: method. This method is used to set the background color of the Color Picker and give it a smooth color transition. You're able to do this thanks to the QuartzCore framework. You need to add this framework to your project.

Single-click the SuperDB project in the Navigator pane. In the Project Editor view, select the SuperDB target, then navigate to the Build Phases pane. Expand the "Link Binary With Libraries" build phase (Figure 6-16). Click the + on the lower left of the build phase. Scroll down the chooser dialog and select the QuartzCore.framework (Figure 6-17). Click Add.

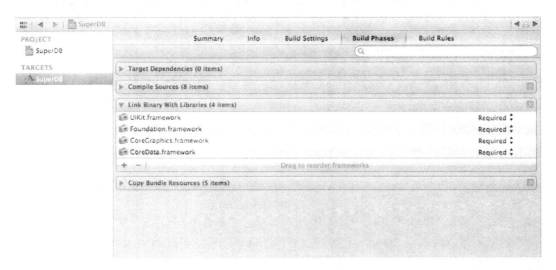

**Figure 6-16.** *The Link Libraries build phase*

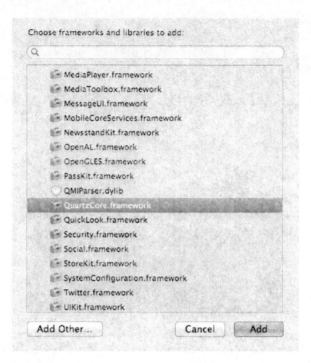

*Figure 6-17. Add the QuartzCore.framework*

One last thing: you want to turn off the Clear Text button in the Color Cell. It's pretty simple. In SuperDBColorCell.m, add this line to the initialization code in initWithStyle:reuseIdentifier:

```
self.textField.clearButtonMode = UITextFieldViewModeNever;
```

Build and run the app. Navigate down and edit the Color cell. Much better (Figure 6-18)!

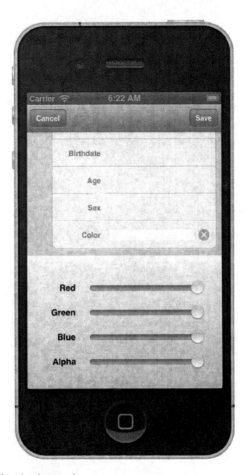

*Figure 6-18. Color Picker with a gradient background*

# One More Thing

Run the app, and add a new hero. Enter Edit mode and clear out the Name field. Now tap on the Identity field. As expected, the validation alert dialog will appear. However, it will not display the proper failure reason (Figure 6-19).

*Figure 6-19. Validation dialog without a failure reason*

Looking back at the `validate` method in `SuperDBCell.m`, you see the message is populated like this:

```
message =
    [NSString stringWithFormat:NSLocalizedString(@"Validation error on: %@\rFailure Reason: %@",
                                    @"Validation error on: %@, Failure Reason: %@)"),
                    [userInfo valueForKey:@"NSValidationErrorKey"],
                    [error localizedFailureReason]];
```

The method call to the `NSError` instance

```
[error localizedFailureReason]
```

is returning nil. Prior to iOS 4, Core Data use to populate the `localizedFailureReason`. Since then, it doesn't. You need to provide a simple fix for this that you can customize.

`NSError` provides a method, `code`, that will return an integer error code. The value of this code is defined depending on the origination of the error.

> **Note**   To learn more about how NSError and error codes work, read The Error Handling Programming Guide at https://developer.apple.com/library/ios/#documentation/Cocoa/Conceptual/ ErrorHandlingCocoa/ErrorHandling/ErrorHandling.html. Specifically, read the chapter entitled "Error Objects, Domains, and Codes."

The error code you get here is defined in the Core Data header file, CoreDataErrors.h.

> **Note**   CoreDataError.h is documented by Apple at https://developer.apple.com/library/ ios/#documentation/Cocoa/Reference/CoreDataFramework/Miscellaneous/CoreData_ Constants/Reference/reference.html.

You happen to know that the error code value you're getting is 1670. This is assigned the enumeration of NSValidationStringTooShortError. You could put some logic to handle this specific error code, and you'd be set, but we did a little more work for you.

Find the file CoreDataErrors.plist in the Book Downloads package. This is a simple plist file we've created that maps the Core Data error code to a simple error message. Add this file to the SuperDB project, making sure to make a copy.

You could make a CoreDataError class to handle the loading of this plist, but you'll take an easier route for expediency's sake. First, declare a static dictionary at the top of SuperDBEditCell.m, right before the @implementation declaration.

```
static NSDictionary *__CoreDataErrors;
```

Populate this dictionary in the class initializer. This will go right after the @implementation declaration.

```
+ (void)initialize
{
    NSURL *plistURL = [[NSBundle mainBundle] URLForResource:@"CoreDataErrors"
                                              withExtension:@"plist"];
    __CoreDataErrors = [NSDictionary dictionaryWithContentsOfURL:plistURL];
}
```

Now, you need to edit the validate method to use this dictionary. Find the line that begins with

```
if ([[error domain] isEqualToString:@"NSCocoaErrorDomain"]) {
```

and edit the if block to read

```
if ([[error domain] isEqualToString:@"NSCocoaErrorDomain"]) {
        NSString *errorCodeStr = [NSString stringWithFormat:@"%d", [error code]];
        NSString *errorMessage = [__CoreDataErrors valueForKey:errorCodeStr];
        NSDictionary *userInfo = [error userInfo];
```

```
message =
    [NSString stringWithFormat:NSLocalizedString(@"Validation error on: %@\rFailure Reason: %@",
                                    @"Validation error on: %@, Failure Reason: %@)"),
                        [userInfo valueForKey:@"NSValidationErrorKey"],
                        errorMessage];
}
```

Build and run the app. Erase the Hero's name and try to move to another field. The validation alert dialog should look like Figure 6-4.

You can edit the string values in CoreDataErrors.plist to customize the error message however you like. Let's hope Apple restores this functionality soon.

# Color Us Gone

By now, you should have a good grasp on just how much power you gain from subclassing, and subclassing NSManagedObject specifically. You saw how to use it to do conditional defaulting and both single-field and multi-field validation. You also saw how to use custom managed objects to create virtual accessors. You saw how to politely inform your user when they've entered an invalid attribute that causes a managed object to fail validation, and you saw how to use transformable attributes and value transformers to store custom objects in Core Data.

This was a dense chapter, but you should really be starting to get a feel for just how flexible and powerful Core Data can be. You've got one more chapter on Core Data before you move on to other parts of the iOS 6 SDK. When you're ready, turn the page to learn about relationships and fetched properties.

# Chapter 7

# Relationships, Fetched Properties and Expressions

Welcome to the final chapter on Core Data. So far, your application includes only a single entity, Hero. In this chapter, we're going to show you how managed objects can incorporate and reference other managed objects through the use of relationships and fetched properties. This will give you the ability to make applications of much greater complexity than your current SuperDB application.

That's not the only thing you're going to do in this chapter, however. You're also going turn your HeroDetailController into a generic managed object controller. By making the controller code even more generic, you'll make the controller subclasses smaller and easier to maintain. You'll extend the configuration property list to allow you to define additional entity views.

You have a lot to do in this chapter, so no dallying. Let's get started.

## Expanding Your Application: Superpowers and Reports

Before we talk about the nitty-gritty, let's quickly look at the changes you're going to make to the SuperDB application in this chapter. On the surface, the changes look relatively simple. You'll add the ability to specify any number of superpowers for each hero, and also add a number of reports that show other superheroes that meet certain criteria, including heroes who are either younger or older than this hero, or who are the same sex or the opposite sex (Figure 7-1).

**Figure 7-1.** *At the end of this chapter, you'll have added the ability to specify any number of superpowers for each hero, as well as provided a number of reports that let you find other heroes based on how they relate to this hero*

The powers will be represented by a new entity that you'll create and imaginatively call Power. When users add or edit a power, they will be presented with a new view (Figure 7-2), but in reality, under the hood, it will be a new instance of the same object used to edit and display heroes.

*Figure 7-2.* *The new view for editing powers is actually an instance of the same object used to edit heroes*

When users drill down into one of the reports, they will get a list of the other heroes that meet the selected criteria (Figure 7-3).

*Figure 7-3. The Reports section on your hero will let you find other heroes who meet certain criteria in relation to the hero you're currently editing. Here, for example, you're seeing all the heroes who were born after Super Cat*

Tapping any of the rows will take you to another view where you can edit that hero, using another instance of the same generic controller class. Your users will be able to drill down an infinite number of times (limited only by memory), all courtesy of a single class.

Before you start implementing these changes, you need to understand a few concepts and then make some changes to your data model.

# Relationships

We introduced the concept of Core Data relationships back in Chapter 2. Now we will go into more detail, and show how they can be used in applications. The relationship is one of the most important concepts in Core Data. Without relationships, entities would be isolated. There would be no way to have one entity contain another entity or reference another entity. Let's look at a hypothetical header file for a simple example of an old-fashioned data model class to give you a familiar point of reference:

```
#import <UIKit/UIKit.h>

@class Address;

@interface Person : NSObject

@property (strong, nonatomic) NSString *firstName;
@property (strong, nonatomic) NSString *lastName;
@property (strong, nonatomic) NSDate *birthdate;
@property (strong, nonatomic) UIImage *image;
@property (strong, nonatomic) Address *address;
@property (strong, nonatomic) Person *mother;
@property (strong, nonatomic) Person *father;
@property (strong, nonatomic) NSMutableArray *children;

@end
```

Here you have a class that represents a single person. You have instance variables to store a variety of information about that person and properties to expose that information to other objects. There's nothing earth-shattering here. Now, let's think about how you could re-create this object in Core Data.

The first four instance variables—firstName, lastName, birthDate, and image—can all be handled by built-in Core Data attribute types, so you could use attributes to store that information on the entity. The two NSString instances would become String attributes, the NSDate instance would become a Date attribute, and the UIImage instance would become a Transformable attribute, handled in the same way as UIColor in the previous chapter.

After that, you have an instance of an Address object. This object probably stores information like street address, city, state or province, and postal code. That's followed by two Person instance variables and a mutable array designed to hold pointers to this person's children. Most likely, these arrays are intended to hold pointers to more Person objects.

In object-oriented programming, including a pointer to another object as an instance variable is called *composition*. Composition is an incredibly handy device because it lets you create much smaller classes and reuse objects, rather than have data duplicated.

In Core Data, you don't have composition per se, but you do have relationships, which essentially serve the same purpose. Relationships allow managed objects to include references to other managed objects of a specific entity, known as *destination entities*, or sometimes just destinations. Relationships are Core Data properties, just as attributes are. As such, they have an assigned name, which serves as the key value used to set and retrieve the object or objects represented by the relationship. Relationships are added to entities in Xcode's data model editor in the same way attributes are added. You'll see how to do this in a few minutes. There are two basic types of relationships: to-one relationships and to-many relationships.

# To-One Relationships

When you create a to-one relationship, you are saying that one object can contain a pointer to a single managed object of a specific entity. In your example, the Person entity has a single to-one relationship to the Address entity.

Once you've added a to-one relationship to an object, you can assign a managed object to the relationship using key-value coding (KVC). For example, you might set the Address entity of a Person managed object like so:

```
NSManagedObject *address = [NSEntityDescription insertNewObjectForEntityForName:@"Address"
                                    inManagedObjectContext:thePerson.managedObjectContext];
[thePerson setValue:address forKey:@"address"];
```

Retrieving the object can also be accomplished using KVC, just with attributes:

```
NSManagedObject *address = [thePerson valueForKey:@"address"];
```

When you create a custom subclass of NSManagedObject, as you did in the previous chapter, you can use Objective-C properties and dot notation to get and set those properties. The property that represents a to-one relationship is an instance of NSManagedObject or a subclass of NSManagedObject, so setting the address looks just like setting attributes:

```
NSManagedObject *address = [NSEntityDescription insertNewObjectForEntityForName:@"Address"
                                    inManagedObjectContext:thePerson.managedObjectContext];
thePerson.address = address;
```

And retrieving a to-one relationship becomes as follows:

```
NSManagedObject *address = thePerson.address;
```

In almost every respect, the way you deal with a to-one relationship in code is identical to the way you've been dealing with Core Data attributes. You use KVC to get and set the values using Objective-C objects. Instead of using Foundation classes that correspond to different attribute types, you use NSManagedObject or a subclass of NSManagedObject that represents the entity.

# To-Many Relationships

To-many relationships allow you to use a relationship to associate multiple managed objects to a particular managed object. This is equivalent to using composition with a collection class such as NSMutableArray or NSMutableSet in Objective-C, as with the children instance variable in the Person class you looked at earlier. In that example, you used an NSMutableArray, which is an editable, ordered collection of objects. That array allows you to add and remove objects at will. If you want to indicate that the person represented by an instance of Person has children, you just add the instance of Person that represents that person's children to the children array.

In Core Data, it works a little differently. To-many relationships are unordered. They are represented by instances of NSSet, which is an unordered, immutable collection that you can't change, or by NSMutableSet, an unordered collection that you can change. Here's how getting a to-many relationship and iterating over its contents might look with an NSSet:

```
NSSet *children = [thePerson valueForKey:@"children"];
for (NSManagedObject *oneChild in children) {
    // do something
}
```

> **Note**    Do you spot a potential problem from the fact that to-many relationships are returned as an unordered NSSet? When displaying them in a table view, it's important that the objects in the relationship are ordered consistently. If the collection is unordered, you have no guarantee that the row you tap will bring up the object you expect. You'll see how to deal with that a little later in the chapter.

On the other hand, if you wish to add or remove managed objects from a to-many relationship, you must ask Core Data to give you an instance of NSMutableSet by calling mutableSetValueForKey: instead of valueForKey:, like so:

```
NSManagedObject *child = [NSEntityDescription insertNewObjectForEntityForName:@"Person"
                                  inManagedObjectContext:thePerson.managedObjectContext];
NSMutableSet *children = [thePerson mutableSetValueForKey:@"children"];
[children addObject:child];
[children removeObject:child];
```

If you don't need to change which objects a particular relationship contains, use valueForKey:, just as with to-one arrays. Don't call mutableSetValueForKey: if you don't need to change which objects make up the relationship, as it incurs slightly more overhead than just calling valueForKey:.

In addition to using valueForKey: and mutableSetValueForKey:, Core Data also provides special methods, created dynamically at runtime, that let you add and delete managed objects from a to-many relationship. There are four of these methods per relationship. Each method name incorporates the name of the relationship. The first allows you to add a single object to a relationship

```
- (void)addXXXObject:(NSManagedObject *)value;
```

where XXX is the capitalized name of the relationship and value is either an NSManagedObject or a specific subclass of NSManagedObject. In the Person example you've been working with, the method to add a child to the children relationship looks like this:

```
- (void)addChildrenObject:(Person *)value;
```

The method for deleting a single object follows a similar form.

```
- (void)removeXXXObject:(NSManagedObject *)value;
```

The dynamically generated method for adding multiple objects to a relationship takes the following form:

```
- (void)addXXX:(NSSet *)values;
```

The method takes an instance of NSSet containing the managed objects to be added. So, the dynamically created method for adding multiple children to your Person managed object is as follows:

```
- (void)addChildren:(NSSet *)values;
```

Finally, here's the method used to remove multiple managed objects from a relationship:

```
- (void)removeXXX:(NSSet *)values;
```

Remember that these methods are generated for you when you declare a custom NSManagedObject subclass. When Xcode encounters your NSManagedObject subclass declaration, it creates a category on the subclass that declares the four dynamic methods using the relationship name to construct the method names. Since the methods are generated at runtime, you won't find any source code in your project that implements the methods. If you never call the methods, you'll never see the methods. As long as you've already created the to-many relationship in your model editor, you don't need to do anything extra to access these methods. They are created for you and ready to be called.

> **Note**    There's one tricky point associated with the methods generated for to-many relationships. Xcode declares the four dynamic methods when you first generate the NSManagedObject subclass files from the template. If you have an existing data model with a to-many relationship and a subclass of NSManagedObject, what happens if you decide to add a new to-many relationship to that data model? If you add the to-many relationship to an existing NSManagedObject subclass, you need to add the category containing the dynamic methods yourself, which is what you'll do a little later in the chapter.

There is absolutely no difference between using these four methods and using mutableSetValueForKey:. The dynamic methods are just a little more convenient and make your code easier to read.

## Inverse Relationships

In Core Data, every relationship can have an inverse relationship. A relationship and its inverse are two sides of the same coin. In your Person object example, the inverse relationship for the children relationship might be a relationship called parent. A relationship does not need to be the same kind as its inverse. A to-one relationship, for example, can have an inverse relationship that is to-many. In fact, this is pretty common. If you think about it in real-world terms, a person can have many children. The inverse is that a child can have only one biological mother and one biological father, but the child can have multiple parents and guardians. So, depending on your needs and the way you modeled the relationship, you might choose to use either a to-one or a to-many relationship for the inverse.

If you add an object to a relationship, Core Data will automatically take care of adding the correct object to the inverse relationship. So, if you had a person named Steve and added a child to Steve, Core Data would automatically make the child's parent Steve.

Although relationships are not required to have an inverse, Apple generally recommends that you always create and specify the inverse, even if you won't need to use the inverse relationship in your application. In fact, the compiler will actually warn you if you fail to provide an inverse. There are some exceptions to this general rule, specifically when the inverse relationship will contain an extremely large number of objects, since removing the object from a relationship triggers its removal from the inverse relationship. Removing the inverse will require iterating over the set that represents the inverse, and if that's a very large set, there could be performance implications. But unless you have a specific reason not to do so, you should model the inverse, as it helps Core Data ensure data integrity. If you have performance issues as a result, it's relatively easy to remove the inverse relationship later.

> **Note**   You can read more about how the absence of inverse relationships can cause integrity problems at `https://developer.apple.com/library/mac/#documentation/Cocoa/Conceptual/CoreData/Articles/cdRelationships.html`.

# Fetched Properties

Relationships allow you to associate managed objects with specific other managed objects. In a way, relationships are sort of like iTunes playlists where you can put specific songs into a list and then play them later. If you're an iTunes user, you know that there are things called Smart Playlists, which allow you to create playlists based on criteria rather than a list of specific songs. You can create a Smart Playlist, for example, that includes all the songs by a specific artist. Later on, when you buy new songs from that artist, they are added to that Smart Playlist automatically because the playlist is based on criteria and the new songs meet those criteria.

Core Data has something similar. There's another type of attribute you can add to an entity that will associate a managed object with other managed objects based on criteria, rather than associating specific objects. Instead of adding and removing objects, fetched properties work by creating a predicate that defines which objects should be returned. Predicates, as you may recall, are objects that represent selection criteria. They are primarily used to sort collections and fetch results.

> **Tip**   If you're rusty on predicates, *Learn Objective-C on the Mac, 2nd Edition*, by Scott Knaster, Waqar Maliq, and Mark Dalrymple (Apress, 2012) devotes an entire chapter to the little beasties.

Fetched properties are always immutable. You can't change their contents at runtime. The criteria are usually specified in the data model (a process that you'll look at shortly), and then you access the objects that meet that criteria using properties or KVC.

Unlike to-many relationships, fetched properties are ordered collections and can have a specified sort order. Oddly enough, the data model editor doesn't allow you to specify how fetched properties are sorted. If you care about the order of the objects in a fetched property, you must actually write code to do that, which you'll look at later in this chapter.

Once you've created a fetched property, working with it is pretty straightforward. You just use valueForKey: to retrieve the objects that meet the fetched property's criteria in an instance of NSArray.

```
NSArray *olderPeople = [person valueForKey:@"olderPeople"];
```

If you use a custom NSManagedObject subclass and define a property for the fetched property, you can also use dot notation to retrieve objects that meet the fetched property's criteria in an NSArray instance, like so:

```
NSArray *olderPeople = person.olderPeople;
```

# Creating Relationships and Fetched Properties in the Data Model Editor

The first step in using relationships or fetched properties is to add them to your data model. Let's add the relationship and fetched properties you'll need in your SuperDB application now. If you look back at Figure 7-1, you can probably guess that you're going to need a new entity to represent the heroes' powers, as well as a relationship from your existing Hero entity to the new Power entity you're going to create. You'll also need four fetched properties to represent the four different reports.

# Delete Rules

Every relationship, regardless of its type, has something called a delete rule, which specifies what happens when one object in the relationship is deleted. There are four possible delete rules:

- **Nullify:** This is the default delete rule. With this delete rule, when one object is deleted, the inverse relationship is just updated so that it doesn't point to anything. If the inverse relationship is a to-one relationship, it is set to nil. If the inverse relationship is a to-many relationship, the deleted object will be removed from the inverse relationship. This option ensures that there are no references to the object being deleted, but does nothing more.

- **No Action:** If you specify a delete rule of No Action, when you delete one object from a relationship, nothing happens to the other object. Instances where you would use this particular rule are extremely rare and are generally limited to one-way relationships with no inverse. This action is rarely used because the other object's inverse relationship would end up pointing to an object that no longer exists.

- **Cascade:** If you set the delete rule to Cascade, when you delete a managed object, all the objects in the relationship are also removed. This is a more dangerous option than Nullify, in that deleting one object can result in the deletion of other objects. You would typically choose Cascade when a relationship's inverse relationship is to-one and the related object is not used in any other relationships. If the object or objects in the relationship are used only for this relationship and not for any other reason, then you probably do want a Cascade rule, so that you don't leave orphaned objects sitting in the persistent store taking up space.

- **Deny:** This delete rule option will actually prevent an object from being deleted if there are any objects in this association, making it the safest option in terms of data integrity. The Deny option is not used frequently, but if you have situations where an object shouldn't be deleted as long as it has any objects in a specific relationship, this is the one you would choose.

# Expressions and Aggregates

Another use of expressions is to aggregate attributes without loading them all into memory. If you want to get the average, median, minimum, or maximum for a specific attribute, such as the average age of your heroes or count of female heroes, you can do that (and more) with an expression. In fact, that's how you should do it. To understand why, you need to know a little about the way Core Data works under the hood.

The fetched results controller you're using in `HeroListController` contains objects for all of the heroes in your database, but it doesn't have all of them fully loaded into memory as managed objects. Core Data has a concept of a fault. A fault is sort of like a stand-in for a managed object. A fault object knows a bit about the managed object it's standing in for, such as its unique ID and perhaps the value of one attribute being displayed, but it's not a fully managed object.

A fault turns into a full-fledged managed object when something triggers the fault. Triggering a fault usually happens when you access an attribute or key that the fault doesn't know about. Core Data is smart enough to turn a fault into a managed object when necessary, so your code usually doesn't need to worry about whether it's dealing with a fault or a managed object. However, it's important to know about this behavior so you don't unintentionally cause performance problems by triggering faults unnecessarily.

Most likely, the faults in your fetched results controller don't know anything about the sex attribute of `Hero`. So, if you were to loop through the heroes in your fetched results controller to get a count of the female heroes, you would be triggering every fault to become a managed object. That's inefficient because it uses a lot more memory and processing power than necessary. Instead, you can use expressions to retrieve aggregate values from Core Data without triggering faults.

Here's an example of how to use an expression to retrieve the average birth date calculated for all female heroes in your application (you can't use age in a fetch request because it's a transient attribute that isn't stored).

```
NSExpression *ex = [NSExpression expressionForFunction:@"average:"
                              arguments:@[[NSExpression expressionForKeyPath:@"birthdate"]]];
NSPredicate *pred = [NSPredicate predicateWithFormat:@"sex == 'Female'"];

NSExpressionDescription *ed = [[NSExpressionDescription alloc] init];
[ed setName:@"averageBirthdate"];
[ed setExpression:ex];
[ed setExpressionResultType:NSDateAttributeType];

NSArray *properties = [NSArray arrayWithObject:ed];

NSFetchRequest *request = [[NSFetchRequest alloc] init];
[request setPredicate:pred];
[request setPropertiesToFetch:properties];
[request setResultType:NSDictionaryResultType];

NSEntityDescription *entity = [NSEntityDescription entityForName:@"Hero"
                              inManagedObjectContext:context];
[request setEntity:entity];

NSArray *results = [context executeFetchRequest:request error:nil];
NSDate *date = [results objectAtIndex:0];
NSLog(@"Average birthdate for female heroes: %@", date);
```

Aggregate expressions are relatively new to Core Data. As of this writing, the process of using expressions to obtain aggregates is not thoroughly documented, but the preceding code sample, along with the API documentation for NSExpression and NSExpressionDescription, should get you pointed in the right direction for working with aggregates.

# Adding the Power Entity

Before you start making changes, create a new version of your data model by single-clicking the current version in the Groups & Files pane (the one with the green check mark), and then selecting "Add Model Version" from the Data Model submenu of the Design menu. This ensures that the data you collected using the previous data models migrate properly to the new version you'll be creating in this chapter.

Click the current data model to bring up the model editor. Using the plus icon in the lower-left corner of the model editor's entity pane, add a new entity and call it **Power**. You can leave all the other fields at their default values (Figure 7-4).

*Figure 7-4. Rename the new entity Power and leave the other fields at their default values*

If you look back at Figure 7-2, you can see that the Power object has two fields: one for the name of the power and another that identifies the source of this particular power. In the interest of keeping things simple, the two attributes will just hold string values.

With Power still selected in the property pane, add two attributes using the property pane. Call one of them **name**, uncheck the Optional check box, set its Type to String, and give it a Default value of New Power. Give the second one a name of **source**, and set its Type to String as well. Leave Optional checked. There is no need for a default value. Once you're finished, you should have two rounded rectangles in the model editor's diagram view (Figure 7-5).

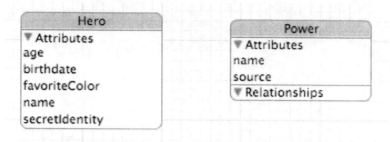

*Figure 7-5.  You now have two entities, but they are not related in any way*

# Creating the Powers Relationship

Right now, the Power entity is selected. Single-click the rounded rectangle that represents the Hero entity or select Hero in the entity pane to select it. Now, in the properties pane, click and hold the plus button and select Add Relationship. In the model editor's detail pane, change the name of the new relationship to powers and the Destination to Power. The Destination field specifies which entity's managed objects can be added to this relationship, so by selecting Power, you are indicating that this relationship stores powers.

You can't specify the inverse relationship yet, but you do want to check the To-Many Relationship box to indicate that each hero can have more than one power. Also, change the delete rule to Cascade. In your application, every hero will have his or her own set of powers—no sharing of powers between heroes. When a hero is deleted, you want to make sure that hero's powers are deleted as well, so you don't leave orphaned data in the persistent store. Once you're finished, the detail pane should look like Figure 7-6, and the diagram view should have a line drawn between the Hero and Power entities to represent the new relationship (Figure 7-7).

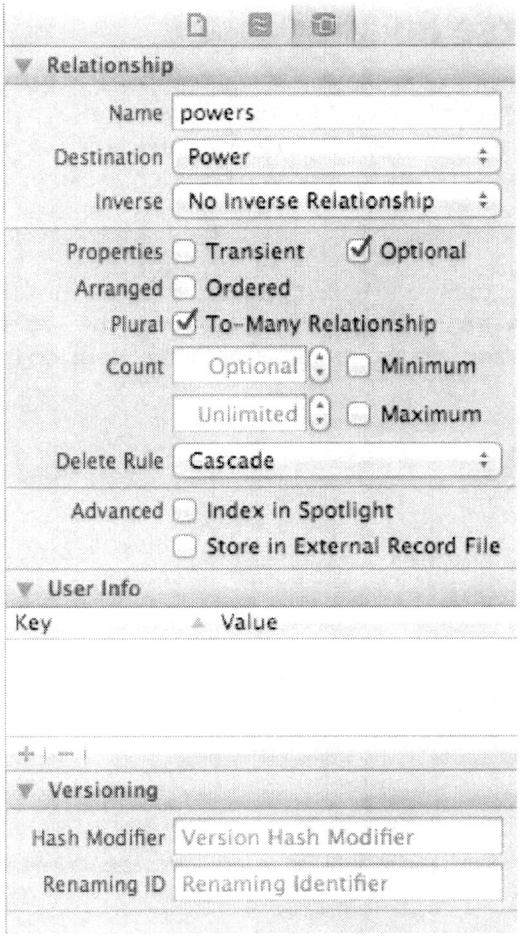

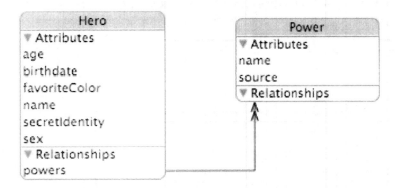

*Figure 7-6.* *The detail pane view of the powers relationship*

*Figure 7-7.* *Relationships are represented in the diagram view by lines drawn between rounded rectangles. A single arrowhead represents a to-one relationship and a double arrowhead (as shown here) represents a to-many relationship*

# Creating the Inverse Relationship

You won't actually need the inverse relationship in your application, but you're going to follow Apple's recommendation and specify one. Since the inverse relationship will be to-one, it doesn't present any performance implications. Select the Power entity again, and add a relationship to it using the property pane. Name this new relationship **hero**, and select a Destination entity of Hero. If you look at your diagram view now, you should see two lines representing the two different relationships you've created.

Next, click the Inverse pop-up menu and select powers. This indicates that the relationship is the inverse of the one you created earlier. Once you've selected it, the two relationship lines in the diagram view will merge together into a single line with arrowheads on both sides (Figure 7-8).

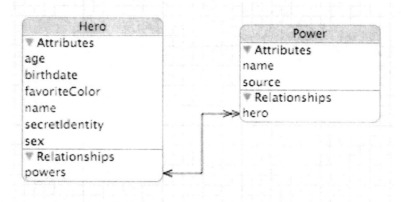

**Figure 7-8.** *Inverse relationships are represented as a single line with arrowheads on both sides, rather than two separate lines*

# Creating the olderHeroes Fetched Property

Select the Hero entity again so that you can add some fetched properties to it. In the property pane, click and hold the plus button and choose Add Fetched Property. Call the new fetched property olderHeroes. Notice that there is only one other field that can be set on the detail pane: a big white box called Predicate (Figure 7-9).

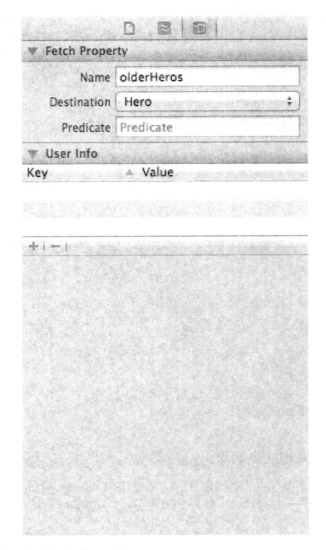

*Figure 7-9. The detail pane showing a fetched property*

**Tip**    Both relationships and fetched properties can use their own entity as the Destination.

## What is a Predicate?

A predicate is a statement that returns a Boolean value. Think of them as like a conditional statement within an `if` or `while`. They are intended to be used against a set of objects, whether Cocoa or Core Data. Predicates are not dependent on the specific data being searched, but rather provide an abstract way of defining a query to filter data. At its simplest, a predicate compares two values using an operator. An example operator would be '==' to test if two values are equal. There are more sophisticated operators that allow for string comparison (using LIKE or CONTAINS). Predicates can be joined to format a compound predicated. Typically, predicates are joined with an AND or an OR operator.

There are two special variables you can use in the predicate of a fetched property: $FETCH_SOURCE and $FETCHED_PROPERTY. $FETCH_SOURCE refers to the specific instance of a managed object. $FETCHED_PROPERTY is a description of the entity property being fetched.

You can read more detail in Apple's Predicate Programming Guide (https://developer.apple.com/library/ios/#documentation/Cocoa/Conceptual/Predicates/predicates.html).

> **Tip**  Both relationships and fetched properties can use their own entity as the Destination.

So you need to define a predicate that finds all the heroes who are older (i.e. have an earlier birthdate) than the Hero in the detail view. You need to compare your Hero's birthdate against all the other Hero entities. If $FETCH_SOURCE is your Hero entity, your predicate will be

```
$FETCH_SOURCE.birthdate > birthdate
```

Enter this formula into the Predicate field in the attribute inspector. Remember, a date is really just an integer; the later the date, the greater the value.

# Creating the youngerHeroes Fetched Property

Add another fetched property named **youngerHeroes**. The Destination will be Hero again, and the predicate should be the same as the previous one, except the operator will be < instead of >. Type the following for the youngerHeroes predicate in the attribute inspector:

```
$FETCH_SOURCE.birthdate < birthdate
```

One thing to be aware of is that a fetched property retrieves all matching objects, potentially including the object on which the fetch is being performed. This means it is possible to create a result set that, when executed on Super Cat, returns Super Cat.

Both the youngerHeroes and olderHeroes fetched properties automatically exclude the hero being evaluated. Heroes cannot be older or younger than themselves; their birth date will always exactly equal their own birth date, and so no hero will ever meet the two criteria you just created.

Let's now add a fetched property that has slightly more complex criteria.

## Creating the sameSexHeroes Fetched Property

The next fetched property you're going to create is called sameSexHeroes and it returns all heroes who are the same sex as this hero. You can't just specify to return all heroes of the same sex, however, because you don't want this hero to be included in the fetched property. Super Cat is the same sex as Super Cat, but users will not expect to see Super Cat when they look at a list of the heroes who are the same sex as Super Cat.

Create another fetched property, naming it **sameSexHeroes**. Open the model editor. Make sure the Destination is set to Hero. For the Predicate field, type

```
($FETCH_SOURCE.sex == sex) AND ($FETCH_SOURCE != SELF)
```

It's pretty clear what the left side of this compound predicate is doing. But what are you doing on the right side? Remember, a fetched property predicate will return all matching objects, including the object that owns the fetched property. In this case, you asked for all heroes of a certain sex, and your hero in the detail view will match that criteria. You need to exclude that specific hero.

You could just compare names and exclude heroes with the same name as yours. That might work, except for the fact that two heroes might have the same name. Maybe using name isn't the best idea. But what value is there that uniquely identifies a single hero? There isn't one, really.

Fortunately, predicates recognize a special value called SELF, which returns the object being compared. The $FETCH_SOURCE variable represent the object where the fetch request is happening. Therefore, to exclude the object where the fetch request is firing, you just need to require it to return only objects where $FETCH_SOURCE != SELF.

## Creating the oppositeSexHeroes Fetched Property

Create a new fetched property called **oppositeSexHeroes** and enter the predicate of

```
$FETCH_SOURCE.sex != sex
```

Make sure you save your data model before continuing.

## Adding Relationships and Fetched Properties to the Hero Class

Since you created a custom subclass of NSManagedObject, you need to update that class to include the new relationship and fetched properties. If you had not made any changes to the Hero class, you could just regenerate the class definition from your data model, and the newly generated version would include properties and methods for the relationships and fetched properties you just added to your data model. Since you have added validation code, you need to update it manually. Single-click Hero.h and add the following code:

(Before @interface)

```
@class Power;
```

(After other properties)

```
@property (nonatomic, retain) NSSet *powers;

@property (nonatomic, readonly) NSArray *olderHeroes;
@property (nonatomic, readonly) NSArray *youngerHeroes;
@property (nonatomic, readonly) NSArray *sameSexHeroes;
@property (nonatomic, readonly) NSArray *oppositeSexHeroes;
```

(After @end)

```
@interface Hero (PowerAccessors)
- (void)addPowersObject:(Power *)value;
- (void)removePowersObject:(Power *)value;
- (void)addPowers:(NSSet *)value;
- (void)removePowers:(NSSet *)value;
@end
```

Save the file. Switch over to Hero.m and make the following changes (after the other @dynamic declarations):

```
@dynamic powers;
@dynamic olderHeroes, youngerHeroes, sameSexHeroes, oppositeSexHeroes;
```

## Updating the Detail View

Looking at Figure 7-1, you have two new table view sections to add to your detail view: Powers and Reports. Unfortunately, it won't be as easy as adding new cells to the General section was in Chapter 6. It turns out that you can't use the storyboard editor to set things up for you. The reason is that the Powers section is dynamically data driven. You don't know how many rows are in the Powers section until you have a Hero entity to inspect. All the other sections have a fixed set of rows.

You start by converting HeroDetailController to be more data-driven in its current configuration. Open SuperDB.storyboard and find the HeroDetailController. Select the table view and open the attribute inspector. Change the table view's Content field from Static Cells to Dynamic Prototypes. The detail view should change to a single table view cell with a section header of Prototype Cells (Figure 7-10).

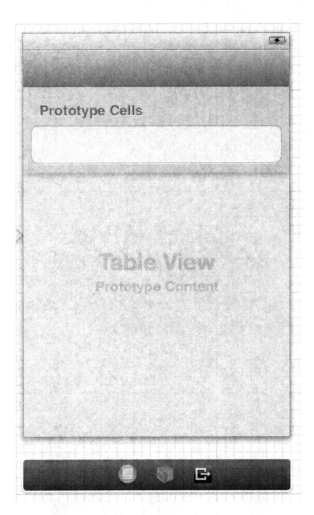

*Figure 7-10. Changing the table view content to dynamic prototypes*

Select the one table view cell that remains and change the Utility pane to the attribute inspector. In the Identifier field, delete it so that it is empty.

Now open HeroDetailController.m. Look for the methods numberOfSectionsInTableView: and tableView:numberOfRowsInSection:. You can't use the jump bar to find them because you commented them out, but if you look for the label "Table view data source," it should place you near the right place. Uncomment the methods, and change their bodies to read

```
- (NSInteger)numberOfSectionsInTableView:(UITableView *)tableView
{
    return self.sections.count;
}
```

```
- (NSInteger)tableView:(UITableView *)tableView numberOfRowsInSection:(NSInteger)section
{
    NSDictionary *sectionDict = [self.sections objectAtIndex:section];
    NSArray *rows = [sectionDict objectForKey:@"rows"];
    return rows.count;
}
```

You're simply using your configuration information to determine how many sections your table view has and how many rows are in each section.

Now, your configuration information doesn't contain the Header value. If you ran the app now, the detail view would look like Figure 7-11.

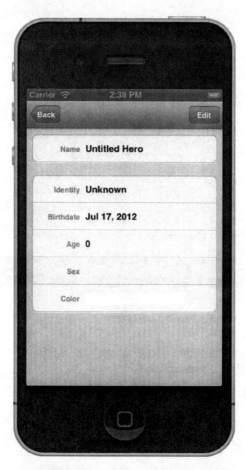

*Figure 7-11. Detail view with no general section header*

Add the header information to your configuration plist. Edit HeroDetailController.plist and navigate to Root ➤ Section ➤ Item 1. Open Item 1, select the Item 1 row, and add a new item. Give the item a key of header and a value of General. Keep the type as String (Figure 7-12).

**Figure 7-12.** *Adding the general section header to the property list*

Now head back over the HeroDetailController.m. And add the following method (we put it after tableView:numberOfRowsInSection:):

```
- (NSString *)tableView:(UITableView *)tableView titleForHeaderInSection:(NSInteger)section
{
    NSDictionary *sectionDict = [self.sections objectAtIndex:section];
    return [sectionDict objectForKey:@"header"];
}
```

The General label should be there. Since you didn't put the header item in the first section, objectForKey: will return nil, which the table view interprets as no header label.

Now you're ready to add the new Powers and Reports sections.

Head back to the HeroDetailController.plist property list and select the Sections item. Open the Sections item, then make sure Item 0 and Item 1 are both closed. Hover the pointer over Item 1 until the (+) and (–) buttons appear next to Item 1. Click the (+) button. A new Item 2 should appear. Set Item 2's type to Dictionary and open it. Add an to Item 2. Name it **header** with a value of Powers.

# Rethinking Configuration

Before you go further, take a step back and think about your detail configuration property list. You just added a new section to represent the Powers section. You added a header item to contain the Section Header string. Now you need to add the rows item, right?

Probably not.

Remember that the rows item is an array that tells you how to configure each cell in the section plus what label, cell class, and property key to use. The number of cells is determined by the number of array items. The situation with the Powers section is almost the opposite. You don't know how many rows you need; that's coming from the Powers relationship of the Hero entity. And the configuration of each cell should be identical.

There are a couple of approaches you can take. Let's discuss two ideas.

For the Powers section, you'll make the rows item a dictionary. The dictionary will contain three String items. The keys will be key, class, and label. These are the same keys you are using for each item when rows is an Array. You can infer that when the rows item is a dictionary, the section is data-driven; but when the rows item is an Array, the section is configuration-driven.

Here's another approach. For each section, along with the header item, you define an item titled **dynamic** which will be a Boolean type, If YES, then the section is data-driven; if NO, the section is configuration-driven. For all cases, rows will be an array, but for dynamic sections, it will contain only one entry. If there is no dynamic item, it is the same as dynamic being set to NO.

Either approach will work. There are probably many more ideas we could toss around, but that's not where we're heading with this. Regardless of the approach you take, it's going to require adding a lot of code to handle this logic—code that, so far, you've put inside the HeroDetailController class. Adding this parsing logic may belong inside the HeroDetailController, but as it gets more complicated, will only muddy your code. You're going to refactor your application to pull the property list handling code out of HeroDetailController into a new class, HeroDetailConfiguration. Then you'll choose which approach to take to handle the data-driven Powers section.

Create a new Objective-C class. Make it a subclass of NSObject and name it **HeroDetailConfiguration**.

Looking at HeroDetailController, you see that you put the sections array inside a private category. You'll do the same for HeroDetailConfiguration. Open HeroDetailConfiguration.m and add the following above the @implmentation:

```
@interface HeroDetailConfiguration ()
@property (strong, nonatomic) NSArray *sections;
@end
```

Next you need to create your initializer. You want it to open the property list and parse the contents into the sections array.

```
- (id)init
{
    self = [super init];
    if (self) {
        // Initialization Code
        NSURL *plistURL = [[NSBundle mainBundle] URLForResource:@"HeroDetailConfiguration"
                                                  withExtension:@"plist"];
        NSDictionary *plist = [NSDictionary dictionaryWithContentsOfURL:plistURL];
        self.sections = [plist valueForKey:@"sections"];
    }
    return self;
}
```

Now let's go back to HeroDetailController.m and see where to use the sections array. The following methods access the HeroDetailController sections array:

```
numberOfSectionsInTableView:
tableView:numberOfRowsInSection:
tableView:titleForHeaderInSection:
tableView:cellForRowAtIndexPath:
```

You can use this to design your methods for HeroDetailConfiguration. Right off the bat, you can see the three methods needed:

```
numberOfSections
numberOfRowsInSection:
headerInSection:
```

Define the methods in HeroDetailConfiguration.h.

```
- (NSInteger)numberOfSections;
- (NSInteger)numberOfRowsInSection:(NSInteger)section;
- (NSString *)headerInSection:(NSInteger)section;
```

Now let's implement them in HeroDetailConfiguration.m. It should be pretty straightforward.

```
- (NSInteger)numberOfSections
{
    return self.sections.count;
}

- (NSInteger)numberOfRowsInSection:(NSInteger)section
{
    NSDictionary *sectionDict = [self.sections objectAtIndex:section];
    NSArray *rows = [sectionDict objectForKey:@"rows"];
    return rows.count;
}

- (NSString *)headerInSection:(NSInteger)section
{
    NSDictionary *sectionDict = [self.sections objectAtIndex:section];
    return [sectionDict objectForKey:@"header"];
}
```

The implementations are should be pretty much the same as what you implemented before in the HeroDetailController.

Now you need to look at what you're doing in HeroDetailController tableView:cellForRowAtIndexPath:. The heart of the what's needed is at the beginning of the method.

```
    NSUInteger sectionIndex = [indexPath section];
    NSUInteger rowIndex = [indexPath row];
    NSDictionary *section = [self.sections objectAtIndex:sectionIndex];
    NSArray *rows = [section objectForKey:@"rows"];
    NSDictionary *row = [rows objectAtIndex:rowIndex];
```

Essentially, you get the row dictionary for a specific index path. And that's what you need your HeroDetailConfiguration object to do for you: give you a row dictionary for an index path. So the method you want would be something like

```
- (NSDictionary *)rowForIndexPath:(NSIndexPath *)indexPath;
```

Let's add it to HeroDetailConfiguration.h. And let's stub the body in HeroDetailConfiguration.m.

Before you worry about handling the issue of implementing the Powers section, just replicate the functionality you already have in place. In this case, you just add that the five lines of code from the beginning of HeroDetailController tableView:cellForRowAtIndexPath: and put it in your new method.

```
- (NSDictionary *)rowForIndexPath:(NSIndexPath *)indexPath
{
    NSUInteger sectionIndex = [indexPath section];
    NSUInteger rowIndex = [indexPath row];
    NSDictionary *section = [self.sections objectAtIndex:sectionIndex];
    NSArray *rows = [section objectForKey:@"rows"];
    NSDictionary *row = [rows objectAtIndex:rowIndex];
    return row;
}
```

Now let's edit HeroDetailController.m to use your new HeroDetailConfiguration class. First, add the #import at the top (right below the SuperDBEditCell #import).

```
#import "HeroDetailConfiguration.h"
```

Replace the sections Property declaration with one for HeroDetailConfiguration.

```
@property (strong, nonatomic) NSArray *sections;
@property (strong, nonatomic) HeroDetailConfiguration *config;
```

Replace the sections initialization code in viewDidLoad with config initialization.

```
    NSURL *plistURL = [[NSBundle mainBundle] URLForResource:@"HeroDetailController"
withExtension:@"plist"];
    NSDictionary *plist = [NSDictionary dictionaryWithContentsOfURL:plistURL];
    self.sections = [plist valueForKey:@"sections"];
    self.config = [[HeroDetailConfiguration alloc] init];
```

Replace the code in numberOfSectionsInTableView.

```
- (NSInteger)numberOfSectionsInTableView:(UITableView *)tableView
{
    return self.sections.count;
    return [self.config numberOfSections];
}
```

Replace the code in tableView:numberOfRowsInSection:.

```
- (NSInteger)tableView:(UITableView *)tableView numberOfRowsInSection:(NSInteger)section
{
    NSDictionary *sectionDict = [self.sections objectAtIndex:section];
    NSArray *rows = [sectionDict objectForKey:@"rows"];
    return row.count;
        return [self.config numberOfRowsInSection:section];
}
```

Replace the code in `tableView:titleForHeaderInSection:`.

```
- (NSString *)tableView:(UITableView *)tableView titleForHeaderInSection:(NSInteger)section
{
    NSDictionary *sectionDict = [self.sections objectAtIndex:section];
    return [sectionDict objectForKey:@"header"];
    return [self.config headerInSection:section];
}
```

Finally, replace the code in `tableView:cellForRowAtIndexPath:`.

```
    NSUInteger sectionIndex = [indexPath section];
    NSUInteger rowIndex = [indexPath row];
    NSDictionary *section = [self.sections objectAtIndex:sectionIndex];
    NSArray *rows = [section objectForKey:@"rows"];
    NSDictionary *row = [rows objectAtIndex:rowIndex];
    NSDictionary *row = [self.config rowForIndexPath:indexPath];
```

At this point, your app should behave just like it did before you started this refactoring.

# Encapsulation and Information Hiding

Before you move on to handling the Power section (you'll get there soon, promise!), let's look at HeroDetailController `tableView:cellForRowAtIndexPath:` once more. Your HeroDetailConfiguration is returning a row dictionary. In turn, you are using that information throughout the remainder of the method.

```
    NSDictionary *row = [self.config rowForIndexPath:indexPath];
    NSString *cellClassname = [row objectForKey:@"class"];
       ...
    NSArray *values = [row valueForKey:@"values"];
       ...
    cell.key = [row objectForKey:@"key"];
    cell.value = [self.hero valueForKey:[row objectForKey:@"key"]];
    cell.label.text = [row objectForKey:@"label"];
```

While it's probably fine to keep things this way, you probably want replace these calls with a method in HeroDetailConfiguration. Why? In short, because of two concepts: encapsulation and information hiding. Information hiding is the idea of hiding the implementation details. Imagine that you change how you store your configuration information. In that case, you'd have to change the way you populate your table view cell. By putting the specific access calls inside HeroDetailConfiguration, you don't have to worry if your configuration storage mechanism changes. You can freely change the internal implementation without having to worry about your table view cell code. Encapsulation is the idea that you placed all the configuration access code into a single object, HeroDetailConfiguration, rather peppering the access code all over your view controllers.

Looking at the calls to objectForKey: on the row dictionary, you probably want methods like

```
- (NSString *)cellClassnameForIndexPath:(NSIndexPath *)indexPath;
- (NSArray *)valuesForIndexPath:(NSIndexPath *)indexPath;
- (NSString *)attributeKeyForIndexPath:(NSIndexPath *)indexPath;
- (NSString *)labelForIndexPath:(NSIndexPath *)indexPath;
```

Add them to HeroDetailConfiguration.h and then add their implementations to HeroDetailConfiguration.m.

```
- (NSString *)cellClassnameForIndexPath:(NSIndexPath *)indexPath
{
    NSDictionary *row = [self rowForIndexPath:indexPath];
    return [row objectForKey:@"class"];
}

- (NSArray *)valuesForIndexPath:(NSIndexPath *)indexPath
{
    NSDictionary *row = [self rowForIndexPath:indexPath];
    return [row objectForKey:@"values"];
}

- (NSString *)attributeKeyForIndexPath:(NSIndexPath *)indexPath
{
    NSDictionary *row = [self rowForIndexPath:indexPath];
    return [row objectForKey:@"key"];
}

- (NSString *)labelForIndexPath:(NSIndexPath *)indexPath
{
    NSDictionary *row = [self rowForIndexPath:indexPath];
    return [row objectForKey:@"label"];
}
```

Finally, replace the code in HeroDetailController tableView:cellForRowAtIndexPath: with the new methods.

```
    NSDictionary *row = [self.config rowForIndexPath:indexPath];
    NSString *cellClassname = [row objectForKey:@"class"];
    NSString *cellClassname = [self.config cellClassnameForIndexPath:indexPath];
        ...
    NSArray *values = [row valueForKey:@"values"];
    NSArray *values = [self.config valuesForIndexPath:indexPath];
        ...
    cell.key = [row objectForKey:@"key"];
    cell.value = [self.hero valueForKey:[row objectForKey:@"key"]];
    cell.label.text = [row objectForKey:@"label"];
    cell.key = [self.config attributeKeyForIndexPath:indexPath];
    cell.value = [self.hero valueForKey:[self.config attributeKeyForIndexPath:indexPath]];
    cell.label.text = [self.config labelForIndexPath:indexPath];
```

If you wanted to, you could keep refactoring your code, but this is a good point to move on.

# Data-Driven Configuration

Okay, now you're ready to tackle the whole point of this refactoring. It's time to set up the property list to handle the data-driven Powers section. We detailed two possible approaches earlier. You're going to take the approach that has you add a dynamic Boolean item and keeps the row item as an array. For items where dynamic is YES, the row item array will have only one element. If there are more, you're going to ignore them.

Open HeroDetailConfiguration.plist, and navigate to Root ➤ sections ➤ Item 2. If the disclosure triangle is closed, open it. Select the item named header, and add an two items after it. Name the first item **dynamic**, set its type to Boolean, and give it a value of YES. Name the second item **rows**, and set its type to Array. Add a dictionary to the rows Array and give the dictionary three items. Give the three Dictionary items the names of **key**, **class**, and **label**. Leave the type of all three items as String. Set the key value to powers; class to SuperDBCell. Leave the label value blank.

Your property list editor should look something like Figure 7-13.

| Key | | Type | Value |
|---|---|---|---|
| ▼ Root | | Dictionary | (1 item) |
| ▼ sections | | Array | (3 items) |
| ▷ Item 0 | | Dictionary | (1 item) |
| ▷ Item 1 | | Dictionary | (2 items) |
| ▼ Item 2 | | Dictionary | (3 items) |
| header | | String | Powers |
| dynamic | | Boolean | YES |
| ▼ rows | | Array | (1 item) |
| ▼ Item 0 | | Dictionary | (3 items) |
| key | ○ ○ | String | powers |
| class | | String | SuperDBCell |
| label | ○ ○ | String | |

*Figure 7-13.  The Power section property list configuration*

Now you need the HeroDetailConfiguration to use this new dynamic item.

First, you need to define a method to check if the section you are looking at is dynamic or not. Let's add that method declaration to HeroDetailConfiguration.h.

```
- (BOOL)isDynamicSection:(NSInteger)section;
```

Let's add the implementation to HeroDetailConfiguration.m.

```
- (BOOL)isDynamicSection:(NSInteger)section
{
    BOOL dynamic = NO;
```

```objc
    NSDictionary *sectionDict = [self.sections objectAtIndex:section];
    NSNumber *dynamicNumber = [sectionDict objectForKey:@"dynamic"];
    if (dynamicNumber != nil)
        dynamic = [dynamicNumber boolValue];

    return dynamic;
}
```

By default, you'll assume that a section is not dynamic if there's no dynamic entry in the configuration property list section.

Now, you need to update the `rowForIndexPath:` method to handle dynamic sections. You just need to change one line.

```objc
    NSUInteger rowIndex = [indexPath row];
    NSUInteger rowIndex = ([self isDynamicSection:sectionIndex]) ? 0 : [indexPath row];
```

While you're here, add the following method declaration to `HeroDetailConfiguration.h`:

```objc
- (NSString *)dynamicAttributeKeyForSection:(NSInteger)section;
```

(You're cheating a little here because you know that this method will make your life easier in a little bit.) The implementation in `HeroDetailConfiguration.m` will look like this:

```objc
- (NSString *)dynamicAttributeKeyForSection:(NSInteger)section
{
    if (![self isDynamicSection:section])
        return nil;

    NSIndexPath *indexPath = [NSIndexPath indexPathForRow:0 inSection:section];
    return [self attributeKeyForIndexPath:indexPath];
}
```

If the section is not dynamic, you'll return nil. Otherwise, you create an index path and use the existing functionality.

# Adding Powers

Now you can move on to updating the `HeroDetailController` to use this new configuration setup. In `HeroDetailController.m`, edit `tableView:numberOfRowsInSection:` like so:

```objc
- (NSInteger)tableView:(UITableView *)tableView numberOfRowsInSection:(NSInteger)section
{
    NSInteger rowCount = [self.config numberOfRowsInSection:section];
    if ([self.config isDynamicSection:section]) {
        NSString *key = [self.config dynamicAttributeKeyForSection:section];
```

```
        NSSet *attributeSet = [self.hero mutableSetValueForKey:key];
        rowCount = attributeSet.count;
    }

    return rowCount;
}
```

You ask the HeroDetailConfiguration to tell you the number of rows in the section. If the section is dynamic, you read the row configuration to determine what property to use from your Hero entity. That property will be a Set, so you need to convert it to an Array to get its size.

Well, you still don't have any powers in your Hero entity. So you need a way to add new powers to your Hero. Clearly, you should do that when you're editing the Hero's details. If you run the app, navigate to the detail view and tap the Edit button, the Powers section is still blank. Go back to the Address Book application: when you need a new address, a cell appears with a green (+) button to add a new address (Figure 7-14). You need to mimic that behavior.

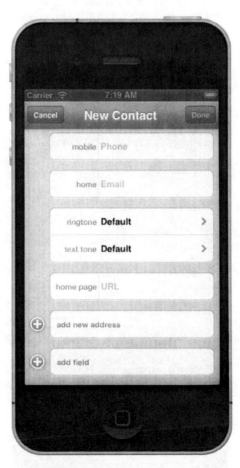

*Figure 7-14. Adding a new address in the Address Book app*

Open HeroDetailController.m and find the tableView:numberOfRowsInSection: method you just modified. Change this line

```
rowCount = attributeSet.count;
```

to this

```
rowCount = (self.editing) ? attributeSet.count+1 : attributeSet.count;
```

However, this is not enough. You need to have the table view refresh when you enter Edit mode. In setEditing:animated:, add this line

```
[self.tableView reloadData];
```

after the call to super.

If you run the app now and edit your Hero's details (Figure 7-15), there are two issues. First, the new cell in the Powers section has a strange value. Second, if you watch closely while entering and exiting Edit mode, the transition no longer seems smooth. The cells seem to jump. Everything works but it isn't a good user experience.

*Figure 7-15.* First step to adding new powers

Let's take a look at fetched results controller delegate methods in the HeroListController. When the updates begin, you call the beginUpdates method on the table view. Then you insert or delete rows with insertRowsAtIndexPath:withRowAnimation: and deleteRowsAtIndexPath:withRowAnimation:. Finally, when the updates are complete, you call endUpdates on the table view. You need to do something similar with the Powers section when entering and leaving Edit mode.

In the private category at the top of HeroDetailController.m, add the new method declaration

```
- (void)updateDynamicSections:(BOOL)editing;
```

and call it from setEditing:animated:.

```
- (void)setEditing:(BOOL)editing animated:(BOOL)animated
{
    [self.tableView beginUpdates];
    [self updateDynamicSections:editing];
    [super setEditing:editing animated:animated];
    [self.tableView endUpdates];

    self.navigationItem.rightBarButtonItem = (editing) ? self.saveButton : self.editButtonItem;
    self.navigationItem.leftBarButtonItem = (editing) ? self.cancelButton : self.backButton;
}
```

Here's the implementation:

```
- (void)updateDynamicSections:(BOOL)editing
{
    for (NSInteger section = 0; section < [self.config numberOfSections]; section++) {
        if ([self.config isDynamicSection:section]) {
            NSIndexPath *indexPath;
            NSInteger row = [self tableView:self.tableView numberOfRowsInSection:section];
            if (editing) {
                indexPath = [NSIndexPath indexPathForRow:row inSection:section];
                [self.tableView insertRowsAtIndexPaths:@[indexPath]
                                withRowAnimation:UITableViewRowAnimationAutomatic];
            }
            else {
                indexPath = [NSIndexPath indexPathForRow:row-1 inSection:section];
                [self.tableView deleteRowsAtIndexPaths:@[indexPath]
                                withRowAnimation:UITableViewRowAnimationAutomatic];
            }
        }
    }
}
```

Now the addition and removal of a cell to Powers section when entering and exiting Edit mode looks much smoother.

Way back in Chapter 4 when you first wrote the HeroDetailController, you implemented the table view delegate method of tableView:editingStyleForRowAtIndexPath:.

```objc
- (UITableViewCellEditingStyle)tableView:(UITableView *)tableView
        editingStyleForRowAtIndexPath:(NSIndexPath *)indexPath
{
    return UITableViewCellEditingStyleNone;
}
```

If you recall, this turns off the appearance of the Delete button next to table view cell when the detail view enters Edit mode. Now you want it to show the appropriate button next to the Power section cells.

```objc
- (UITableViewCellEditingStyle)tableView:(UITableView *)tableView
        editingStyleForRowAtIndexPath:(NSIndexPath *)indexPath
{
    UITableViewCellEditingStyle editStyle = UITableViewCellEditingStyleNone;
    NSInteger section = [indexPath section];
    if ([self.config isDynamicSection:section]) {
        NSInteger rowCount = [self tableView:self.tableView numberOfRowsInSection:section];
        if ([indexPath row] == rowCount-1)
            editStyle = UITableViewCellEditingStyleInsert;
        else
            editStyle = UITableViewCellEditingStyleDelete;
    }
    return editStyle;
}
```

For the Insert button to work, you need to implement the table view data source method tableView:commitEditingStyle:forRowAtIndexPath: method. This method already exists in HeroDetailController.m, but is commented it out. You can find it in the table view data source section of the jump bar. Uncomment it, and modify it so it looks like this:

```objc
- (void)tableView:(UITableView *)tableView
        commitEditingStyle:(UITableViewCellEditingStyle)editingStyle
        forRowAtIndexPath:(NSIndexPath *)indexPath
{
    NSString *key = [self.config attributeKeyForIndexPath:indexPath];
    NSMutableSet *relationshipSet = [self.hero mutableSetValueForKey:key];
    NSManagedObjectContext *managedObjectContext = [self.hero managedObjectContext];

    if (editingStyle == UITableViewCellEditingStyleDelete) {
        // Delete the row from the data source
        NSManagedObject *relationshipObject =
            [[relationshipSet allObjects] objectAtIndex:[indexPath row]];
        [relationshipSet removeObject:relationshipObject];
    }
    else if (editingStyle == UITableViewCellEditingStyleInsert) {
        NSEntityDescription *entity = [self.hero entity];
        NSDictionary *relationships = [entity relationshipsByName];
        NSRelationshipDescription *destRelationship = [relationships objectForKey:key];
        NSEntityDescription *destEntity = [destRelationship destinationEntity];
```

```objc
    NSManagedObject *relationshipObject =
        [NSEntityDescription insertNewObjectForEntityForName:[destEntity name]
                                  inManagedObjectContext:managedObjectContext];
    [relationshipSet addObject:relationshipObject];
}

NSError *error = nil;
if (![managedObjectContext save:&error]) {
    // need to make HeroDetailController a UIAlertViewDelegate
    UIAlertView *alert =
        [[UIAlertView alloc] initWithTitle:NSLocalizedString(@"Error saving entity",
                                                @"Error saving entity")
                    message:[NSString stringWithFormat:NSLocalizedString(@"Error was: %@, quitting.",
                                                @"Error was: %@, quitting."),
                                            [error localizedDescription]]
                    delegate:self
              cancelButtonTitle:NSLocalizedString(@"Aw, Nuts", @"Aw, Nuts")
              otherButtonTitles:nil];
    [alert show];
}

if (editingStyle == UITableViewCellEditingStyleDelete) {
    // Delete the row from the data source
    [tableView deleteRowsAtIndexPaths:@[indexPath]
                    withRowAnimation:UITableViewRowAnimationFade];
}
else if (editingStyle == UITableViewCellEditingStyleInsert) {
    // Create a new instance of the appropriate class, insert it into the array,
    // and add a new row to the table view
     [tableView insertRowsAtIndexPaths:@[indexPath]
                    withRowAnimation:UITableViewRowAnimationAutomatic];
}
}
}
```

Every time you get a new Powers cell, it displays some strange String, Relationship 'powers'...
That's because it's displaying the results of a valueForKey: call on the Hero entity, with a key
of powers. You need to update your tableView:cellForRowAtIndexPath: to handle dynamic
sections. Replace

```objc
    cell.value = [self.hero valueForKey:[self.config attributeKeyForIndexPath:indexPath]];
```

with

```objc
    if ([self.config isDynamicSection:[indexPath section]]) {
        NSString *key = [self.config attributeKeyForIndexPath:indexPath];
        NSMutableSet *relationshipSet = [self.hero mutableSetValueForKey:key];
        NSArray *relationshipArray = [relationshipSet allObjects];
        if ([indexPath row] != [relationshipArray count]) {
            NSManagedObject *relationshipObject = [relationshipArray objectAtIndex:[indexPath row]];
            cell.value = [relationshipObject valueForKey:@"name"];
```

```
                cell.accessoryType = UITableViewCellAccessoryDetailDisclosureButton;
                cell.editingAccessoryType = UITableViewCellAccessoryDetailDisclosureButton;
            }
            else {
                cell.label.text = nil;
                cell.textField.text = @"Add New Power...";
            }
        }
        else {
            cell.value = [self.hero valueForKey:[self.config attributeKeyForIndexPath:indexPath]];
        }
```

Notice that for a dynamic cell, you set the `accessoryType` and `editingAccessoryType`. This is the blue arrow button on the cell's right edge. Also, you handle the case for when you add an additional cell in Edit mode.

Now you need to add a power view so that you can edit the name and source of your Hero's new powers.

# Refactoring the Detail View Controller

You have a new managed object that you want to display and edit. You could make a new table view controller class specifically to handle displaying a `Power` entity. It would a pretty simple class, and you could implement it very quickly. Sometimes when developing, you might do that. It's not necessarily the most elegant solution, but it might the most expedient. And sometimes you just need to get it working.

But since this a book and you're working through this example, it makes sense to refactor your `HeroDetailController` into a more generic `ManagedObjectController`. Later you can use this refactored controller to implement the views for the fetched properties of the Hero entity. You laid the foundation for this work when you moved the view controller configuration into a property list. Since then, you've tried to implement generic solutions in the `HeroDetailController`. Hopefully, that work paid off.

First, you're going to rename the `HeroDetailConfiguration` class to `ManagedObjectConfiguration`. You won't change the name of the property list because that's still specific for displaying the Hero entity. Next, you'll create the `ManagedObjectController` class. You'll move most of the logic from the `HeroDetailController` to the `ManagedObjectController`. The only `HeroDetailController` will be a very thin subclass that knows the name of the configuration property list to load.

Let's get started.

# Renaming the Configuration Class

The `HeroDetailConfiguration` class name worked because it was used by the `HeroDetailController`. Now that you're renaming the `Controller` class, you should rename the configuration class. Open `HeroDetailConfiguration.h`, and highlight the class name in the Editor. Select the Edit ➤ Refactor ➤ Rename menu, and rename the class to `ManagedObjectConfiguration` (Figure 7-16). Click Preview and review the changes Xcode made. It should change the interface and implementation files, as well as the references in `HeroDetailController`. When you're ready, click Save.

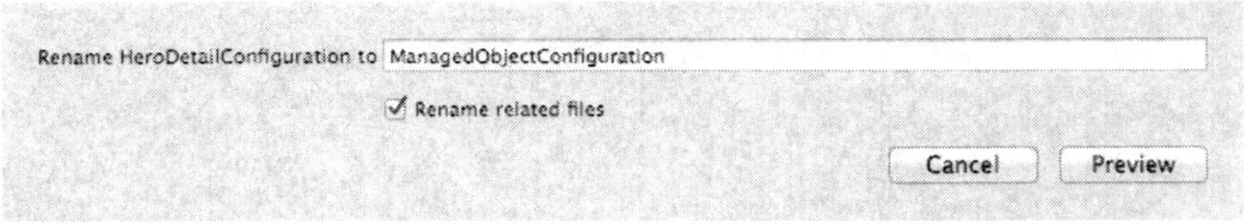

*Figure 7-16. The Rename refactoring pane*

There's a code change you need to make. In the `ManagedObjectConfiguration` init method, the configuration property list is loaded like this:

```
NSURL *plistURL = [[NSBundle mainBundle] URLForResource:@"ManagedObjectConfiguration"
                                    withExtension:@"plist"];
```

Remember, you're keeping the current configuration property list name as `HeroDetailController.plist`. If you hardcode that name, you won't have really done anything useful. You need to change the initializer from a simple `init` method to something like

```
- (id)initWithResource:(NSString *)resource;
```

Add that declaration to the `ManagedObjectController.h` file, inside the `@interface`. Then you can change the `init` method to

```
- (id)init
- (id)initWithResource:(NSString *)resource
{
    self = [super init];
    if (self) {
        // Initialization Code
        NSURL *plistURL = [[NSBundle mainBundle] URLForResource:@"ManagedObjectConfiguration"
                                            withExtension:@"plist"];
        NSURL *plistURL = [[NSBundle mainBundle] URLForResource:resource withExtension:@"plist"];
        NSDictionary *plist = [NSDictionary dictionaryWithContentsOfURL:plistURL];
        self.sections = [plist valueForKey:@"sections"];
    }
    return self;
}
```

Now you need to change this line in the `HeroDetailController` `viewDidLoad` method

```
self.config = [[ManagedObjectConfiguration alloc] init];
```

to

```
self.config = [[ManagedObjectConfiguration alloc] initWithResource:@"HeroDetailConfiguration"];
```

> **Note**    Why make this change if you're just going to refactor `HeroDetailController`? Well, one of the big
> keys with refactoring is making small changes and checking things still work. You wouldn't want to make a
> lot of changes, just to find things don't work. Another key to successful refactoring is writing unit tests. Then
> you have a repeatable set of tests that will help ensure you haven't make drastic changes you don't expect.
> You'll learn about unit tests in Chapter 15.

At this point your app should still be working, but you've only made a very minor change. The big
one is coming up next.

## Refactoring the Detail Controller

You could just create a new class named `ManagedObjectController` and move most of the code from
`HeroDetailController` to your new class. But this is adding a layer of complexity (moving code), that
could lead to a mistake being made. It's easier to rename the `HeroDetailController`, clean up the
code to be more generic, and then implement a new `HeroDetailController` class.

Open `HeroDetailController.h` and rename the class to `ManagedObjectController`, using Edit ➤
Refactor ➤ Rename. Review the proposed changes by Xcode. You'll notice that Xcode is changing
`SuperDB.storyboard`, which is just an XML file internally. You'll just have to have faith that Xcode knows
what it's doing. Click Save. You may want to build and run the app, just to check it's still working.

## Refactoring the Hero Instance Variable

In your `ManagedObjectEditor` class, you have an instance variable called `hero`. That variable
name is no longer representative of what that variable holds, so let's refactor it as well. Open
`ManagedObjectEditor.h`, and rename the `hero` property to `managedObject`. Now you must make the
changes in the rest of the app.

> **Note**    Why not use the Xcode refactor option? You could have, but it's not so good at renaming instance
> variables. When we tried it, it wanted to make changes to both the data model and storyboard. That's just
> wrong. We could have unchecked those changes in the File Preview pane, and saved the changes. But Xcode
> doesn't rename the other occurrences, so you have to do it manually anyway.

Open `ManagedObjectEditor.m`, and find all occurrences of

`self.hero`

and change them to

`self.managedObject`

Lastly, edit `HeroListContoller.m`, and change this line in `prepareForSegue:sender`

```
detailController.hero = sender;
```

to

```
detailController.managedObject = sender;
```

Save your work, and check the app.

# A Little More Abstraction

While you're working on `ManagedObjectController`, take this opportunity to add some discrete functionality. Specifically, when you add or remove powers, you put the code to do this in `tableView:commitEditingStyle:forRowAtIndexPath:`. Let's split this code into specific methods to add and remove Relationship objects. Add the following method declarations to `ManagedObjectController.h`:

```
- (NSManagedObject *)addRelationshipObjectForSection:(NSInteger)section;
- (void)removeRelationshipObjectInIndexPath:(NSIndexPath *)indexPath;
```

Before you implement these methods, add a new private method. Find the private category in `ManagedObjectController.m`, and add this line:

```
- (void)saveManagedObjectContext;
```

Then, add the implementation:

```
- (void)saveManagedObjectContext
{
    NSError *error;
    if (![self.managedObject.managedObjectContext save:&error]) {
        // need to make HeroDetailController a UIAlertViewDelegate
        UIAlertView *alert =
            [[UIAlertView alloc] initWithTitle:NSLocalizedString(@"Error saving entity",
                                                                 @"Error saving entity")
                        message:[NSString stringWithFormat:NSLocalizedString(@"Error was: %@, quitting.",
                                                                             @"Error was: %@, quitting."),
                                                            [error localizedDescription]]
                        delegate:self
                cancelButtonTitle:NSLocalizedString(@"Aw, Nuts", @"Aw, Nuts")
                otherButtonTitles:nil];
        [alert show];
    }
}
```

Does this look familiar? It should; it's essentially the code in the save method. So update the following lines in the save method from

```
    NSError *error;
    if (![self.managedObject.managedObjectContext save:&error])
        NSLog(@"Error saving: %@", [error localizedDescription]);
```

into

```
    [self saveManagedObjectContext];
```

Now you can add the new method implementations (we added them just for the @end in
ManagedObjectController.m).

```
#pragma mark - Instance Methods

- (NSManagedObject *)addRelationshipObjectForSection:(NSInteger)section
{
    NSString *key = [self.config dynamicAttributeKeyForSection:section];
    NSMutableSet *relationshipSet = [self.managedObject mutableSetValueForKey:key];

    NSEntityDescription *entity = [self.managedObject entity];
    NSDictionary *relationships = [entity relationshipsByName];
    NSRelationshipDescription *destRelationship = [relationships objectForKey:key];
    NSEntityDescription *destEntity = [destRelationship destinationEntity];

    NSManagedObject *relationshipObject =
        [NSEntityDescription insertNewObjectForEntityForName:[destEntity name]
                                      inManagedObjectContext:self.managedObject.managedObjectContext];
    [relationshipSet addObject:relationshipObject];
    [self saveManagedObjectContext];
    return relationshipObject;
}


- (void)removeRelationshipObjectInIndexPath:(NSIndexPath *)indexPath
{
    NSString *key = [self.config dynamicAttributeKeyForSection:[indexPath section]];
    NSMutableSet *relationshipSet = [self.managedObject mutableSetValueForKey:key];
    NSManagedObject *relationshipObject =
        [[relationshipSet allObjects] objectAtIndex:[indexPath row]];
    [relationshipSet removeObject:relationshipObject];
    [self saveManagedObjectContext];
}
```

Finally, change tableView:commitEditingStyle:forRowAtIndexPath:.

```
- (void)tableView:(UITableView *)tableView
        commitEditingStyle:(UITableViewCellEditingStyle)editingStyle
        forRowAtIndexPath:(NSIndexPath *)indexPath
{
    if (editingStyle == UITableViewCellEditingStyleDelete) {
        // Delete the row from the data source
        [tableView deleteRowsAtIndexPaths:@[indexPath] withRowAnimation:UITableViewRowAnimationFade];
    }
    else if (editingStyle == UITableViewCellEditingStyleInsert) {
```

```
        // Create a new instance of the appropriate class, insert it into the array,
        // and add a new row to the table view
        [tableView insertRowsAtIndexPaths:@[indexPath]
                        withRowAnimation:UITableViewRowAnimationAutomatic];
    }
}
```

You're not adding or removing the Relationship object anymore. All you're doing is adding or removing table view cells. You'll see why soon.

# A New HeroDetailController

Now you want to create a new HeroDetailController to replace the one you renamed to the ManagedObjectController. Create a new Objective-C class, name it HeroDetailController, and make it a subclass of ManagedObjectController. Before you modify the HeroDetailController, you need to make some changes to the ManagedObjectController. You need to move the property that holds the configuration information from the private category to the @interface declaration. Edit ManagedObjectController.h, and declare the configuration property (you also need to declare the ManagedObjectConfiguration).

```
#import <UIKit/UIKit.h>

@class ManagedObjectConfiguration;

@interface ManagedObjectController : UITableViewController

@property (strong, nonatomic) ManagedObjectConfiguration *config;
@property (strong, nonatomic) NSManagedObject *managedObject;

- (NSManagedObject *)addRelationshipObjectForSection:(NSInteger)section;
- (void)removeRelationshipObjectInIndexPath:(NSIndexPath *)indexPath;

@end
```

Since you moved the configuration, you need to delete the declaration in ManagedObjectController.m.

```
@interface ManagedObjectController ()
@property (strong, nonatomic) ManagedObjectConfiguration *config;
@property (nonatomic, strong) UIBarButtonItem *saveButton;
```

You also need to delete the assignment in viewDidLoad.

```
- (void)viewDidLoad
{
    [super viewDidLoad];
        ...
    self.config = [[ManagedObjectConfiguration alloc] initWithResource:@"HeroDetailConfiguration"];
}
```

Now you can update HeroDetailController. All you need to do is load your configuration property list. Your HeroDetailController.m should look like this:

```
#import "HeroDetailController.h"
#import "ManagedObjectConfiguration.h"

@implementation HeroDetailController

- (void)viewDidLoad
{
    [super viewDidLoad];
    // Do any additional setup after loading the view.
    self.config = [[ManagedObjectConfiguration alloc] initWithResource:@"HeroDetailConfiguration"];
}

@end
```

Now you need to tell your storyboard to use this HeroDetailController. Open SuperDB.storyboard, and select the ManagedObjectController scene. Set the zoom level so that you see the View Controller icon in the scene's label. Select the View Controller icon and open the identity inspector. Change the class from ManagedObjectController to HeroDetailController.

> **Note** How did this change? It happened when you used the rename refactoring. When Xcode showed you the change in SuperDB.storyboard, this was the change it was making.

And that should do it. You're ready to create a power view.

# The Power View Controller

You'll start by creating the new power view controller in SuperDB.storyboard. Open SuperDB.storyboard and add a new table view controller to the right of the hero detail controller. If you zoom out in the storyboard editor, your storyboard should look like Figure 7-17.

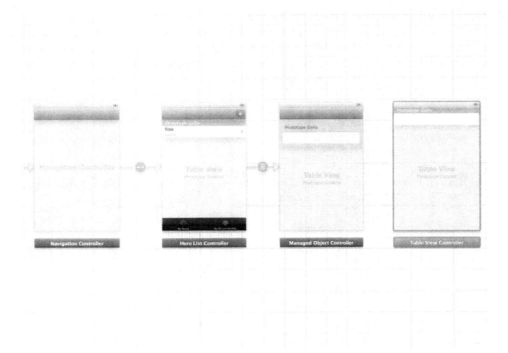

*Figure 7-17. Adding a table view controller to SuperDB.storyboard*

Zoom in so the icons are visible in the table view controller label. Select the table view controller and in the identity inspector, change the class to PowerViewController. Next select the table view in the scene and in the attribute inspector, change the style from Single to Grouped.

The last thing you need to do is define the segue between the HeroDetailController to your new PowerViewController. Control-drag from the HeroDetailController icon (in the label bar) to the PowerViewController scene. When the Manual Segue pop-up appears, select Push. Select the segue, and give it the name **PowerViewSegue** in the attribute inspector.

Now you need to create the PowerViewController class and configuration. Create a new Objective-C class, named PowerViewController, subclass of ManagedObjectController. Edit PowerViewController.m.

```
#import "PowerViewController.h"
#import "ManagedObjectConfiguration.h"

@implementation PowerViewController

- (void)viewDidLoad
{
    [super viewDidLoad];
    // Do any additional setup after loading the view.
    self.config = [[ManagedObjectConfiguration alloc] initWithResource:@"PowerViewConfiguration"];
}

@end
```

Essentially, this is the same as the HeroDetailController.m. Instead of loading the HeroDetailConfiguration property list, you load the PowerViewConfiguration property list. Let's create this property list. Create a new property list file and name it PowerViewConfiguration.plist. You need a configuration property list with two sections. Each section has no header label and one row each. In the end, your property list should look like Figure 7-18.

*Figure 7-18. Power view configuration*

# Navigating to the PowerViewController

Your PowerViewController is defined and configured. You've defined the segue to transition from the HeroDetailController to PowerViewController. Now you need to execute the PowerViewSegue when the user adds a new power or selects a power in Edit mode. Open HeroDetailController.m, and add the following table view data source method:

```
#pragma mark - Table view data source

- (void)tableView:(UITableView *)tableView
      commitEditingStyle:(UITableViewCellEditingStyle)editingStyle
      forRowAtIndexPath:(NSIndexPath *)indexPath
{
    if (editingStyle == UITableViewCellEditingStyleDelete)
        [self removeRelationshipObjectInIndexPath:indexPath];
    else if (editingStyle == UITableViewCellEditingStyleInsert) {
        NSManagedObject *newObject = [self addRelationshipObjectForSection:[indexPath section]];
        [self performSegueWithIdentifier:@"PowerViewSegue" sender:newObject];
    }

    [super tableView:tableView commitEditingStyle:editingStyle forRowAtIndexPath:indexPath];
}
```

Since you added this method, you added the logic to remove a power as well. Remember when you changed this method in `ManagedObjectController`? You only added and removed the table view cells. We said you were going to handle adding and removing powers to the `Hero` entity later. Well, here it is. Pretty simple, right? Finally, you call the super method (which is in the `ManagedObjectController`).

One last thing you need to do is handle when you want to view an existing power. Below the `HeroDetailController` `tableView:commitEditingStyle:forRowAtIndexPath:`, add this table view delegate method:

```
#pragma mark - Table view delegate

- (void)tableView:(UITableView *)tableView
        accessoryButtonTappedForRowWithIndexPath:(NSIndexPath *)indexPath
{
    NSString *key = [self.config attributeKeyForIndexPath:indexPath];
    NSMutableSet *relationshipSet = [self.managedObject mutableSetValueForKey:key];
    NSManagedObject *relationshipObject =
        [[relationshipSet allObjects] objectAtIndex:[indexPath row]];
    [self performSegueWithIdentifier:@"PowerViewSegue" sender:relationshipObject];
}
```

When the user taps the blue disclosure button in the Power cell, it will push the `PowerViewController` onto the `NavigationController` stack. In order to pass the power managed object to the `PowerViewController`, you need to implement the `prepareForSegue:sender:` method in `HeroDetailController.m`.

```
- (void)prepareForSegue:(UIStoryboardSegue *)segue sender:(id)sender
{
    if ([segue.identifier isEqualToString:@"PowerViewSegue"]) {
        if ([sender isKindOfClass:[NSManagedObject class]]) {
            ManagedObjectController *detailController = segue.destinationViewController;
            detailController.managedObject = sender;
        }
    }
    else {
        UIAlertView *alert = [[UIAlertView alloc] initWithTitle:NSLocalizedString(@"Power Error",
                                                                                  @"Power Error")
                                    message:NSLocalizedString(@"Error trying to show Power detail",
                                                              @"Error trying to show Power detail")
                                    delegate:self
                          cancelButtonTitle:NSLocalizedString(@"Aw, Nuts", @"Aw, Nuts")
                          otherButtonTitles:nil];
        [alert show];
    }
}
```

That's it. The Power section and view are all set. Now let's look into displaying fetched properties.

# Fetch Properties

Look back at Figure 7-1. Below the Powers section is another section titled Reports that shows four cells. Each cell holds a fetched property and accessory disclosure button. Tapping on the disclosure button will show the results of the fetched property (Figure 7-3). Let's get this working.

Looking at Figure 7-3, you can see that it's a simple table view that displays the hero's name and secret identity. You need to create a new table view controller for the report display. Create a new Objective-C class named HeroReportController; make it a subclass of UITableViewController. Select HeroReportController.h, and add new property to hold the list of heroes you wish to display.

```
@property (strong, nonatomic) NSArray *heroes;
```

Switch over to HeroReportController.m. You need to import your Hero header at the top of the file.

```
#import "Hero.h"
```

Next, adjust the table view data source methods.

```
- (NSInteger)numberOfSectionsInTableView:(UITableView *)tableView
{
    // Return the number of sections.
    return 1;
}

- (NSInteger)tableView:(UITableView *)tableView numberOfRowsInSection:(NSInteger)section
{
    // Return the number of rows in the section.
    return self.heroes.count;
}

- (UITableViewCell *)tableView:(UITableView *)tableView
         cellForRowAtIndexPath:(NSIndexPath *)indexPath
{
    static NSString *CellIdentifier = @"HeroReportCell";
    UITableViewCell *cell = [tableView dequeueReusableCellWithIdentifier:CellIdentifier
                                                           forIndexPath:indexPath];

    // Configure the cell...
    Hero *hero = [self.heroes objectAtIndex:[indexPath row]];
    cell.textLabel.text = hero.name;
    cell.detailTextLabel.text = hero.secretIdentity;

    return cell;
}
```

Let's lay out your `HeroReportController` in your storyboard. Open `SuperDB.storyboard`. Select a table view controller from the Object Library in the Utility pane, and drop it below the `PowerViewController`. Select this new table view controller and open the identity inspector. Change the class to `HeroReportController`. Next, select the table view in the new table view controller, and open the attribute inspector. Change the Selection field from Single Selection to No Selection. Finally, select the table view cell. In the attribute inspector, change the Style to Subtitle; enter `HeroReportCell` for the Identifier; and change the Selection field to None.

Now control-drag from the `HeroDetailController` view controller to the new table view controller. When the Manual Segue pop-up appears, select Push. Select the new segue, and in the attribute inspector, name it `ReportViewSegue`.

Next, you need to edit `HeroDetailConfiguration` property list to add the Reports section. Navigate to Root ➤ sections ➤ Item 2. Make sure the Item 2 disclosure triangle is closed. Select the Item 2 row, and add an new item. Item 3 should appear. Change Item 3 from String to Dictionary. Open the Item 3 disclosure triangle and add two sub items. Name the first one **header**, and give it a value of Reports. Name the second **rows** and make it an Array. You're going to add four items to the rows Array, each one representing the report you wish to view. By the time you're done, it should look like Figure 7-19.

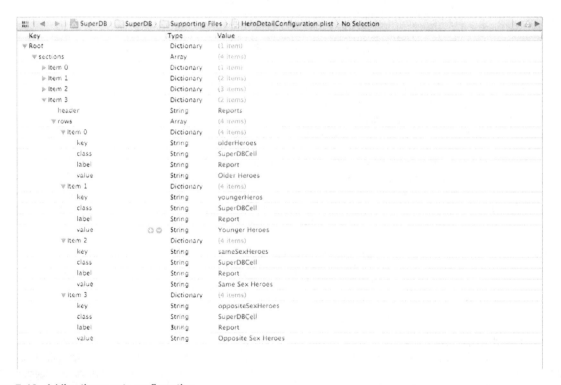

***Figure 7-19.** Adding the reports configuration*

Notice that you've added a new item for these row items: value. You're going to use this to use a static value for your report section cells. Open ManagedObjectController.m, and navigate to tableView:cellForRowAtIndexPath:. Replace the non-dynamic table view cell configuration code.

```
else {
    cell.value =
        [self.managedObject valueForKey:[self.config attributeKeyForIndexPath:indexPath]];
    NSString *value = [[self.config rowForIndexPath:indexPath] objectForKey:@"value"];
    if (value != nil) {
        cell.value = value;
        cell.accessoryType = UITableViewCellAccessoryDetailDisclosureButton;
        cell.editingAccessoryType = UITableViewCellAccessoryDetailDisclosureButton;
    }
    else
        cell.value =
            [self.managedObject valueForKey:[self.config attributeKeyForIndexPath:indexPath]];
}
```

You've added the disclosure button for the Report section cells as well, so you need to handle that in the HeroDetailController. Edit HeroDetailController.m, and modify tableView:accessoryButtonTappedForRowWithIndexPath:.

```
- (void)tableView:(UITableView *)tableView accessoryButtonTappedForRowWithIndexPath:(NSIndexPath *)
indexPath
{
    NSString *key = [self.config attributeKeyForIndexPath:indexPath];
    NSEntityDescription *entity = [self.managedObject entity];
    NSDictionary *properties = [entity propertiesByName];
    NSPropertyDescription *property = [properties objectForKey:key];

    if ([property isKindOfClass:[NSAttributeDescription class]]) {
        NSMutableSet *relationshipSet = [self.managedObject mutableSetValueForKey:key];
        NSManagedObject *relationshipObject =
            [[relationshipSet allObjects] objectAtIndex:[indexPath row]];
        [self performSegueWithIdentifier:@"PowerViewSegue" sender:relationshipObject];
    }
    else if ([property isKindOfClass:[NSFetchedPropertyDescription class]]) {
        NSArray *fetchedProperties = [self.managedObject valueForKey:key];
        [self performSegueWithIdentifier:@"ReportViewSegue" sender:fetchedProperties];
    }
}
```

Now you need to check if you've tapped a relationship cell (the Powers section) or a fetched property cell (the Reports section). You're calling the segue, ReportViewSegue, when tapping on a fetched property cell. You haven't defined that segue yet, but you will in a just a second. Before you do that, let's update prepareForSegue:sender: to handle the ReportViewSegue. After the PowerViewSegue check, add this

```
    else if ([segue.identifier isEqualToString:@"ReportViewSegue"]) {
        if ([sender isKindOfClass:[NSArray class]]) {
            HeroReportController *reportController = segue.destinationViewController;
            reportController.heroes = sender;
        }
        else {
            UIAlertView *alert = [[UIAlertView alloc] initWithTitle:NSLocalizedString(@"Power Error",
                                                                          @"Power Error")
                                    message:NSLocalizedString (@"Error trying to show Power detail",
                                                                @"Error trying to show Power detail")
                                    delegate:self
                              cancelButtonTitle:NSLocalizedString(@"Aw, Nuts", @"Aw, Nuts")
                              otherButtonTitles:nil];
            [alert show];
        }
    }
}
```

Finally, since you're using the `HeroReportController`, you need to import its header file at the top of `HeroDetailController.m`.

```
#import "HeroReportController.h"
```

Build and run SuperDB. Add a few different heroes with different birthdays and of different sex. Drill down the report and see the results when looking for older, younger, same sex, and opposite sex heroes. Create a new hero, but don't set the sex. See what happens. The sexless hero will appear on the opposite sex report, but not on the same sex report. We'll leave it you to reason out why, and how you might fix this ;-).

# Wonderful to the Core

This chapter and the previous chapters have given you a solid foundation in the use of Core Data. Along the way, we provided some information about how to design complex iPhone applications so that they can be maintained and expanded without writing unnecessary code or repeating the same logic in multiple places. We demonstrated just how much benefit you can get from taking the time to write code generically. We showed you how to look for opportunities to refactor your code to make it smaller, more efficient, easier to maintain, and just generally more pleasant to be around.

We could go on for several more chapters about Core Data and not exhaust the topic. But Core Data is not the only new framework introduced since iOS SDK 3. At this point, you should have a solid enough understanding of Core Data to be able to, armed with Apple's documentation, take your explorations even further.

Now it's time to leave our friend Core Data behind and explore some of the other aspects of iOS SDK.

# Chapter 8

# Behind Every iCloud

With iOS 5, Apple introduced iCloud, the latest in its line of Internet-based tools and services. To the end user, iCloud extends Apple's previous MobileMe offerings of e-mail, contact management, and Find My iPhone, with iOS backup and restore, iTunes Match, Photo Stream, and Back to My Mac.

For all the bells and whistles that Apple has built, at its heart iCloud is a cloud-based storage and synchronization service. Its main purpose is to allow users to access their content across all their devices: iPhone, iPad, or Mac. Best of all, Apple has given iOS developers a set of APIs for accessing iCloud. This lets you build apps that can take advantage of the same iCloud features as Apple without having to invest in building an extensive server infrastructure. Even better, you don't have to learn a new complicated SDK. Rather than providing a new iCloud framework, Apple added new classes to existing frameworks, primarily Foundation and UIKit, and extended existing classes to enable iCloud access.

The basic idea behind iCloud is to have a single place where apps can store and access data. Changes made by one instance of your app on one device can be instantly propagated to another instance of the app running on another device. At the same time, iCloud provides an authoritative copy of your application's data. This data can be used to restore your application's state on a new device, providing a seamless user experience as well as backup data.

## Data Storage with iCloud

There are a few different ways to store your data in iCloud.

- *iOS Backup*: This is a global device configuration that backs up your iOS device to iCloud.

- *Key-Value Data Storage*: Used for storing small amounts of infrequently changing data used by your application.

- *Document Storage*: Used for storing user documents and application data.

- *Core Data with iCloud*: Puts your application's persistent backing store on iCloud.

Before we discuss these storage mechanisms in detail, let's review how iCloud and iOS work together.

# iCloud Basics

Inside your iCloud application there is a ubiquity container. Depending on the storage type used, you may explicitly define the URL for this container or iOS will create one for you. The ubiquity container is where iCloud data is stored by your application. iOS will synchronize the data between your device and iCloud. This means that any changes your application makes to data in the ubiquity container will be sent to iCloud. Conversely, any changes in iCloud will be sent to your application's ubiquity container on your device.

Now, iOS doesn't send the entire data file back and forth from iCloud for every change. Internally, iOS and iCloud break up your application's data into smaller chunks of data. When changes occur, only the chunks that have changed are synchronized with iCloud. On iCloud, your application data is versioned, keeping track of each set of changes.

In addition to breaking up your application's data into chunks, iOS and iCloud will send the data file's metadata. Since the metadata is relatively small and important, the metadata is sent all the time. In fact, iCloud will know a data file's metadata before the actual data is synchronized. This is especially important with iOS. Since an iOS device may be space and bandwidth constrained, iOS won't necessarily automatically download data from iCloud until it needs it. But since iOS has the metadata, it knows when its copy is out of date with iCloud.

> **Note**    Interestingly, if iOS detects another iOS device on the same WiFi network, rather than sending data up to iCloud and down to the other device, iOS will simply transfer the data from one device to the other.

# iCloud Backup

Backup is an iOS system service offered by iCloud. It automatically backs up your iOS device daily over WiFi. Everything in your application's home directory is backed up. The application bundle, caches directory, and temp directory are ignored by iOS. Since the data is transmitted over WiFi and sent to Apple's iCloud data center, you should try to keep your application's data as small as possible. The more data, the longer the backup time and the more iCloud storage your users will consume.

> **Note**    If you've used up your iCloud storage capacity (at the time of this writing, 5GB by default), iOS will ask you if you want to buy more storage. Regardless, you'll need to figure out how your application will handle the case if iCloud is full.

When designing your application's data storage policy, keep the following in mind:

- User-generated data, or data that cannot be recreated by your application, should be stored in the Documents directory. From there it will be automatically backed up to iCloud

- Data that can be downloaded or recreated by your application should live in Library/Caches.

- Data that is temporary should be stored in the tmp directory. Remember to delete these files when they are no longer needed.

- Data that your application needs to persist, even in low storage situations, should be flagged with the NSURLIsExcludedFromBackupKey attribute. Regardless of where you put these files, they will not be deleted by Backup. It's your application's responsibility to manage these files.

You can set NSURLIsExcludedFromBackupKey via the setResource:forKey:error: method in NSURL.

```
NSURL *url = [[NSBundle mainBundle] URLForResource:@"NoBackup" withExtension:@"txt"];
NSError *error = nil;
BOOL success = [URL setResourceValue:@YES
                         forKey:NSURLIsExcludedFromBackupKey
                           error:&error];
```

# Enabling iCloud in Your Application

In order to use iCloud data storage within your application, you need to perform two tasks. First, you need to enable the application's entitlements and enable them for iCloud. Second, you need to create an iCloud-enabled provisioning profile. This is done via the iOS Provisioning Portal that you access via the Apple Developer Center web site. We'll go over the specifics of enabling your application later in this chapter, when you extend your SuperDB application to use iCloud.

When entitlements are enabled in your application, Xcode expects to find a .entitlements file within your project directory. This .entitlements file is simply a property list of key-values pairs. These key-value pairs configure additional capabilities or security features of your application. For iCloud access, the .entitlements file specifies the keys to define ubiquity identifiers for the iCloud key-value and document ubiquity containers.

# Key-Value Data Storage

As the name suggests, iCloud key-value data storage is a simple key-value storage mechanism integrated with iCloud. Conceptually, it's similar to NSUserDefaults. Like NSUserDefaults, the only allowable data types are those supported by property lists. It is best to use it for data with values that are infrequently updated. Placing your application's preferences or settings would be  a good use case. You shouldn't use key-value data storage in place of NSUserDefaults. You should keep writing configuration information to NSUserDefault and write shared data to key-value data storage. This way your application still has configuration information if iCloud is unavailable.

There are a number of limitations on the key-value data storage that you need to keep in mind. First, there is a 1MB maximum storage limit per value. Keys have a separate 1MB per-key limit.

Furthermore, each application is allowed a maximum of 1024 separate keys. As a result, you will need to be judicious about what you put in key-value data storage.

Key-value data is synced with iCloud at periodic intervals. The frequency of these intervals is determined by iCloud, so you don't have much control over this. As a result, you shouldn't use the key-value data storage for time-sensitive data.

Key-value data storage handles data conflicts by always choosing the latest value for each key.

To use key-value data storage, you use the default NSUbiquitousKeyValueStore. You access values using the appropriate *ForKey: and set*ForKey: methods, similar to NSUserDefaults. You will also need to register for notifications about changes to the store via iCloud. To synchronize data changes, you call the synchronize method. You can also use the synchronize method as a check to see if iCloud is available. You might initialize your application to use key-value data storage like this:

```
NSUbiquitousKeyValueStore *kv_store = [NSUbiquitousKeyValueStore defaultStore];

// register for KV Data Storage changes from iCloud
[[NSNotificationCenter defaultCenter] addObserver:self
                             selector:@selector (storeDidChange:)
                             name:NSUbiquitousKeyValueStoreDidChangeExternallyNotification
                             object:self.kv_store];
BOOL avail = [self.kv_store synchronize];
if (avail) {
    // iCloud is available
    ...
}
else {
    // iCloud is NOT available
}
```

The synchronize method does not push data to iCloud. It simply notifies iCloud that new data is available. iCloud will determine when to retrieve the data from your device.

# Document Storage

For iCloud document storage, a document is a custom subclass of UIDocument. UIDocument is an abstract class that is used to store your application's data, either as a single file or as a file bundle. A file bundle is a directory that behaves as a single file. To manage a file bundle, use the NSFileWrapper class.

Before we describe iCloud Document Storage, let's look at UIDocument.

## UIDocument

UIDocument eases the development of document-based applications by giving a number of features for "free."

- *Background reading and writing of data*: Keeps your application's UI responsive.
- *Conflict detection*: Helps you resolve differences between document versions.

- *Safe-saving*: Makes sure your document is never in a corrupted state.

- *Automated saves*: Makes life easier for your users.

- *Automatic iCloud integration*: Handles all interchanges between your document and iCloud.

If you want to build a single file document, you would create a simple UIDocument subclass.

```
@interface MyDocument : UIDocument

@property (strong, nonatomic) NSString *text;

@end
```

There are a number of methods you need to implement in your UIDocument subclass. First, you need to be able to load the document data. To do this, you override the loadFromContents:ofType:error: method.

```
- (BOOL)loadFromContents:(id)contents ofType:(NSString *)typeName error:(NSError **)error
{
    if ([contents length] > 0) {
        self.text = [[NSString alloc] initWithData:(NSData *)contents
                                      encoding:NSUTF8StringEncoding];
    }
    else {
        self.text = @"";
    }

    // update view here

    return YES;
}
```

The contents parameter is defined as id. If your document is a file bundle, the content will be of type NSFileWrapper. For your single document file case, the content is an NSData object. This is a simple implementation; it never fails. If you implemented a failure case and returned NO, you should create an error object and give it a meaningful error message. You also want to put code in place to update the UI once the data is successfully loaded. You also never check the content type. Your application could support multiple data types, and you have to use the typeName parameter to handle the different data loading scenarios.

When you close your application or when auto-save is invoked, the UIDocument method contentForType:error: is called. You need to override this method as well.

```
- (id)contentsForType:(NSString *)typeName error:(NSError **)error
{
    if (!self.text) {
        self.text = @"";
    }
```

```
    NSData *data = [self.documentText dataUsingEncoding:NSUTF8StringEncoding
                              allowLossyConversion:NO];
    return data;
}
```

If your document is stored as a file bundle, you return an instance of `NSFileWrapper` rather than the `NSData` object for a single file. That's all you need to do to ensure your data gets saved; `UIDocument` will handle the rest.

`UIDocument` needs a file URL to determine where to read and write data. The URL will define the document directory, filename, and possibly file extension. The directory can either be a local (application sandbox) directory or a location in the iCloud ubiquity container. The filename should be generated by your application, optionally allowing the user to override the default value. While using a file extension might be optional, it's probably a good idea to define one (or more) for your application. You pass this URL to the `initWithFileURL:` method of your `UIDocument` subclass to create a document instance.

```
MyDocument *doc = [[MyDocument alloc] initWithFileURL:aURL]];
...

[doc saveToURL:doc.fileURL forSaveOperation:UIDocumentSaveForCreating
        completionHandler:^(BOOL success){
    if (success) {
        // handle successful save
    }
    else {
        // handle failed save
    }
}];
```

Once you have created a `UIDocument` instance, you create the file using the `saveToURL:forSaveOperation:` `completionHandler:` method. You use the value `UIDocumentSaveForCreating` to indicate that you are saving the file for the first time. The `completionHandler:` parameter takes a block. The block takes a BOOL parameter to tell you if the save operation was successful or not.

You don't just need to create documents; your application may need to open and close existing documents. You still need to call `initWithFileURL:` to create a document instance, but then you call `openWithCompletionHandler:` and `closeWithCompletionHandler:` to open and close your document.

```
MyDocument *doc = [[MyDocument alloc] initWithFileURL:aURL]];
...
[doc openWithCompletionHandler:^(BOOL success){
    if (success) {
        // handle successful open
    }
    else {
        // handle failed open
    }
}];
...
// work on document
...
[doc closeWithCompletionHandler:nil];
```

Both methods take a block to execute on completion. Like the saveToURL:forSaveOperation:
completionHandler: method, the block has a BOOL parameter to tell you if the open/close
succeeded or failed. You're not required to pass a block. In the example code above, you pass
nil to closeWithCompletionHandler: to indicate you don't do anything after the document is closed.

To delete a document, you could simply use the NSFileManager removeItemAtURL: and pass in the
document file URL. However, you should do what UIDocument does for reading and writing, and
perform the delete operation in the background.

```
MyDocument *doc = [[MyDocument alloc] initWithFileURL:aURL]];

...

// close the document

...

dispatch_async(dispatch_get_global_queue(DISPATCH_QUEUE_PRIORITY_DEFAULT, 0), ^(void){

    NSFileCoordinator *fileCoordinator = [[NSFileCoordinator alloc] initWithFilePresenter:nil];

    [fileCoordinator coordinateWritingItemAtURL:aURL
                    options:NSFileCoordinatorWritingForDeleting
                    error:nil
                    byAccessor:^(NSURL *writingURL){
                        NSFileManager *fileManager = [[NSFileManager alloc] init];
                        [fileManager removeItemAtURL:writingURL error:nil];
                    }];
});
```

First, you dispatch the entire delete operation to a background queue via the dispatch_async function.
Inside the background queue, you create an NSFileCoordinator instance. NSFileCoordinator
coordinates file operations between processes and objects. Before any file operation is performed, it
sends messages to all the NSFilePresenter protocol objects that have registered themselves with the
file coordinator. Delete the document file by invoking the NSFileCoordinator method coordinateWrit
ingItemAtURL:options:error:byAccessor:. The accessor is a block operation that defines the actual
file operation you want performed. It's passed an NSURL parameter, representing the location of the
file. Always use the block parameter NSURL, not the NSURL passed to coordinateWritingItemAtURL:.

Before performing an operation on your UIDocument subclass, you probably want to check the
documentState property. The possible states are defined as

- UIDocumentStateNormal: The document is open and has no issues.

- UIDocumentStateClosed: The document is closed. If the document is in this state
  after opening, it indicates there may be a problem with the document.

- UIDocumentStateInConflict: There are versions of this document in conflict. You
  may need to write code to allow your user to resolve these conflicts.

- UIDocumentStateSavingError: The document could not be saved due to some error.

- UIDocumentStateEditingDisabled: The document cannot be edited; either your application or iOS will not permit it.

You can check the document state using a simple bitwise operator.

```
MyDocument *doc = [[MyDocument alloc] initWithFileURL:aURL]];
...
if (doc.documentState & UIDocumentStateClosed) {
    // documentState == UIDocumentStateClosed
}
```

UIDocument also provides a notification named UIDocumentStateChangedNotification that you can use to register an observer.

```
MyDocument *doc = [[MyDocument alloc] initWithFileURL:aURL]];
...
[[NSNotificationCenter defaultCenter] addObserver:anObserver
                            selector:@selector(documentStateChanged:)
                                name:UIDocumentStateChangedNotification
                              object:doc]
```

Your observer class would implement the method documentStateChanged: to check the document state and handle each state accordingly.

In order to perform automated saves, UIDocument periodically invokes the method hasUnsavedChanges, which returns a BOOL depending on whether or not your document has changed since the last save. The frequency of these calls is determined by UIDocument and cannot be adjusted. Generally, you don't override hasUnsavedChanges. Rather, you do one of two things: register the NSUndoManager via the UIDocument undoManager property to register for undo/redo operations; or call the updateChangeCount: method every time a trackable change is made to your document. For your document to work with iCloud, you must enable the automated saves feature.

## UIDocument with iCloud

Using iCloud document storage requires an adjustment to the normal UIDocument process to use a Documents subdirectory of your application's ubiquity container. In order to get the ubiquity container URL, you pass the document identifier into the NSFileManager method URLForUbiquityContainerIdentifer:, passing nil as the argument.

```
id iCloudToken = [[NSFileManager defaultManager] ubiquityIdentityToken];
if (iCloudToken) {
    // Have iCloud Access
    NSURL *ubiquityURL = [[NSFileManager defaultManager] URLForUbiquityContainerIdentifier:nil];
    NSURL *ubiquityDocURL = [ubiquityURL URLByAppendingPathComponent:@"Documents"];
}
else {
    // No iCloud Access
}
```

By using nil in `URLForUbiquityContainerIdentifer:`, `NSFileManager` will use the ubiquity container ID defined in the application's entitlements file. We'll cover this in the "Entitlements" section later on, but for now, just try to follow along. If you want to use the ubiquity container identifier explicitly, it's a combination of your ADC Team ID and App ID.

```
NSString *ubiquityContainer = @"SA4AKF8Z52.com.apporchard.iCloudAppID";
NSURL *ubiquityURL = [[NSFileManager defaultManager]
                              URLForUbiquityContainerIdentifier:ubiquityContainer];
```

Notice the use of the `NSFileManager` method `ubiquityIdentityToken` to check for iCloud availability. This method returns a unique token tied to the user's iCloud account. Depending on your application, if iCloud access is unavailable, you should inform the user and either work with local storage or exit the application.

# NSMetadataQuery

Earlier, we stated that iCloud and iOS don't automatically sync documents in an application's ubiquity container. However, a document's metadata is synced. For an iCloud document storage application, you can't simple use the file contents of the `Documents` directory in your ubiquity container to know what documents are available for your application. Rather, you have to perform a metadata query using the `NSMetadataQuery` class.

Early in your application lifecycle you need to instantiate an `NSMetadataQuery` and configure it to look for the appropriate documents in the `Documents` subdirectory of the ubiquity container.

```
self.query = [[NSMetadataQuery alloc] init];
[self.query setSearchScopes:@[NSMetadataQueryUbiquitousDocumentsScope]];
NSString* filePattern = @"*.txt";
[self.query setPredicate:[NSPredicate predicateWithFormat:@"%K LIKE %@",
                                    NSMetadataItemFSNameKey, filePattern]];
```

This example assumes that you have a query property and it's configured to look for all files with the `.txt` extension.

After creating the `NSMetadataQuery` object, you need to register for its notifications.

```
[[NSNotificationCenter defaultCenter] addObserver:self
                                    selector:@selector(processFiles:)
                                        name:NSMetadataQueryDidFinishGatheringNotification
                                      object:nil];

[[NSNotificationCenter defaultCenter] addObserver:self
                                    selector:@selector(processFiles:)
                                        name:NSMetadataQueryDidUpdateNotification
                                      object:nil];

[self.query startQuery];
```

`NSMetadataQueryDidFinishGatheringNotification` is sent when the query object has finished its initial information loading query. `NSMetadataQueryDidUpdateNotification` is sent when the contents of the Documents subdirectory have changed and affect the results of the query. Finally, you start the query.

When a notification is sent, the processFiles: method is invoked. It might look something like this:

```objc
- (void)processFiles:(NSNotification*)aNotification
{
    NSMutableArray *files = [NSMutableArray array];

    // disable query during processing
    [self.query disableUpdates];

    NSArray *queryResults = [self.query results];
    for (NSMetadataItem *result in queryResults) {
        NSURL *fileURL = [result valueForAttribute:NSMetadataItemURLKey];
        NSNumber *aBool = nil;

        // exclude hidden files
        [fileURL getResourceValue:&aBool forKey:NSURLIsHiddenKey error:nil];

        if (aBool && ![aBool boolValue])
            [files addObject:fileURL];
    }

    // do something with the files array
    ...

    // reenable query
    [self.query enableUpdates];
}
```

First, you disable the query updates to prevent notifications from being sent while you're processing. In this example, you simply get a list of files in the Documents subdirectory and add them to an array. You make sure to exclude any hidden files in the directory. Once you have the array of files, you use them in your application (perhaps to update a table view of file names). Finally, you re-enable the query to receive updates.

You've only skimmed the surface of how to use iCloud document storage. There are a lot of document life-cycle issues that your document-based application should handle to be effective.

> **Note**    For more information, read Apple's documentation. Check the iCloud chapter of the iOS App Programming Guide first (https://developer.apple.com/library/ios/#documentation/iPhone/ Conceptual/iPhoneOSProgrammingGuide/AppArchitecture/AppArchitecture.html#//apple_ ref/doc/uid/TP40007072-CH3-SW21). Then read the iCloud Design Guild (https://developer. apple.com/library/ios/#documentation/General/Conceptual/iCloudDesignGuide) and the document-based App Programming Guide for iOS (https://developer.apple.com/library/ ios/#documentation/General/Conceptual/iCloudDesignGuide).

# Core Data with iCloud

Using Core Data with iCloud is a fairly simple process. You place your persistent store in your application's ubiquity container. However, you don't want your persistent store to be synchronized with iCloud. That would create unnecessary overhead. Rather, you want to synchronize the transactions between applications. When another instance of your application receives the transaction data from iCloud, it reapplies every operation performed on the persistent store. This helps ensure that the different instances are updated with the same set of operations.

Even though you don't want to synchronize the persistent store with iCloud, Apple recommends that you place the data file in the ubiquity container within a folder with the extension .nosync. This tells iOS not to synchronize the contents of this folder but will keep the data associated with the correct iCloud account.

```
// Assume we have an instance of NSPersistentStoreCoordinator *persistentStoreCoordinator

NSString *dataFileName = @"iCloudCoreDataApp.sqlite";
NSString *dataDirectoryName = @"Data.nosync";
NSString *logsDirectoryName = @"Logs";

__block NSPersistentStoreCoordinator *psc = persistentStoreCoordinator;
dispatch_async(dispatch_get_global_queue(DISPATCH_QUEUE_PRIORITY_DEFAULT, 0), ^{
    NSError *error = nil;

    // Get Ubiquity Identity Token to check of iCloud access
    NSFileManager *fileManager = [NSFileManager defaultManager];
    id ubiquityToken = [fileManager ubiquityIdentityToken];
    NSURL *ubiquityURL = [fileManager URLForUbiquityContainerIdentifier:nil];
    if (ubiquityToken && ubiquityURL) {
        // Have iCloud Access
        NSString *dataDir = [[ubiquityURL path] stringByAppendingPathComponent:dataDirectoryName];
        if([fileManager fileExistsAtPath:dataDir] == NO) {
            NSError *fileSystemError;
            [fileManager createDirectoryAtPath:dataDir
                    withIntermediateDirectories:YES
                                     attributes:nil
                                          error:&fileSystemError];
            if (fileSystemError != nil) {
                NSLog(@"Error creating database directory %@", fileSystemError);
                // handle the error
            }
        }

        NSString *ubiquityContainer = [ubiquityURL lastPathComponent];
        NSURL *logsPath = [NSURL fileURLWithPath:[[ubiquityURL path]
                                          stringByAppendingPathComponent:logsDirectoryName]];

        NSDictionary *options = @{ NSMigratePersistentStoresAutomaticallyOption : @YES,
                                   NSInferMappingModelAutomaticallyOption : @YES,
                                   NSPersistentStoreUbiquitousContentNameKey : ubiquityContainer,
                                   NSPersistentStoreUbiquitousContentURLKey : logsPath };
```

```
        NSString *dataPath = [dataDir stringByAppendingPathComponent:dataFileName];
        [psc lock];
        [psc addPersistentStoreWithType:NSSQLiteStoreType
                configuration:nil
                URL:[NSURL fileURLWithPath:dataPath]
                options:options
                error:&error];
        [psc unlock];
    }
    else {
        // No iCloud Access
    }
});
```

Notice that you perform your persistent store operations in a background queue so that your iCloud access does not block your application UI. Most of the example here defines your data directory path, Data.nosync, and the log directory path, Logs. The actually persistent store creation is similar to what you've done earlier. You added two key-value pairs to the options dictionary: NSPersistentStoreUbiquitousContentNameKey with your ubiquity container ID and NSPersistentStoreUbiquityContentURLKey with the transaction log directory path. Core Data and iCloud will use NSPersistentStoreUbiquityContentURLKey to synchronize the transaction logs.

Now you need to register to observe a notification when changes are received from iCloud. Generally, you don't want to put this when you create the persistent store coordinator; rather, you do it when creating the managed object context.

```
[[NSNotificationCenter defaultCenter]
                    addObserver:self
                    selector:@selector(mergeChangesFromUbiquitousContent:)
                    name:NSPersistentStoreDidImportUbiquitousContentChangesNotification
                    object:coordinator];
```

The implementation of mergeChangesFromUbiquitousContent: will have to handle the merging of content between iCloud and local persistent store. Fortunately, for all but the most complicated models, Core Data makes this relatively painless.

```
- (void)mergeChangesFromUbiquitousContent:(NSNotification *)notification
{
    NSManagedObjectContext *context = [self managedObjectContext];
    [context performBlock:^{
        [context mergeChangesFromContextDidSaveNotification:notification];
            // Send a notification to refresh the UI, if necessary
    }];
}
```

# Enhancing SuperDB

You're going to enhance the Core Data SuperDB application and place the persistent store in iCloud. Based on your review of the iCloud APIs, this should be a fairly straightforward process. Remember, you can't run iCloud apps on the simulator (yet), so you need to tether your device to your development machine. Additionally, since you need a provisioning profile, you need an Apple Developer Center account.

Make a copy of the SuperDB project from Chapter 6. If you haven't completed Chapter 6, that's okay. You can copy the project from this book's download archive and start from there.

# Entitlements

First, you need to enable entitlements for your application. Once you've opened the project in Xcode, select the project in the Navigator pane to open the Project Editor. Select the SuperDB target, and open the target Summary Editor. Scroll down to the section labeled Entitlements. Check the checkbox in the first subsection labeled Entitlements (Figure 8-1).

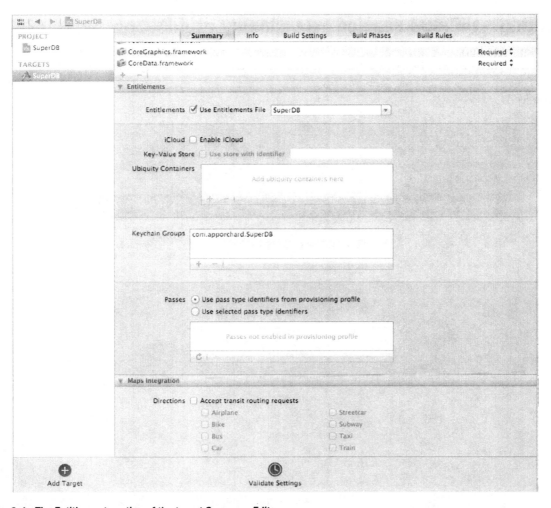

*Figure 8-1. The Entitlement section of the target Summary Editor*

Notice, next to the checkbox, that the dropbox labeled "Use Entitlements File" is automatically populated with the value of SuperDB. Earlier we said that Xcode expects a .entitlements file in your project when entitlements are enabled. Look at the Navigator pane. There should be a new file called SuperDB.entitlements in the SuperDB group. Xcode automatically created this file for you. Further down, the subsection labeled Keychain Groups is also automatically populated as well. For us, the value is com.apporchard.SuperDB.

Now that entitlements are enabled, you need to enable iCloud for your application. The second subsection of the Entitlement section should start with a checkbox to enable iCloud. Check it. The next checkbox activates the key-value data storage for your application. You won't be using the key-value store, so you can leave it unchecked. You do need to populate the next section, the ubiquity containers. At the bottom of the list box, click the + button. Xcode will automatically add a row with a default value. Again, for us, this value is com.apporchard.SuperDB. The default value works for us, so we'll leave it.

## Creating an iCloud enabled Provisioning Profile

Now that you have your application iCloud entitlements enabled, you need to create an iCloud-enabled provisioning profile. Set your web browser to the Apple Developer Center at http://developer.apple.com. Sign into your ADC account, and go to the iOS Developer Center (Figure 8-2).

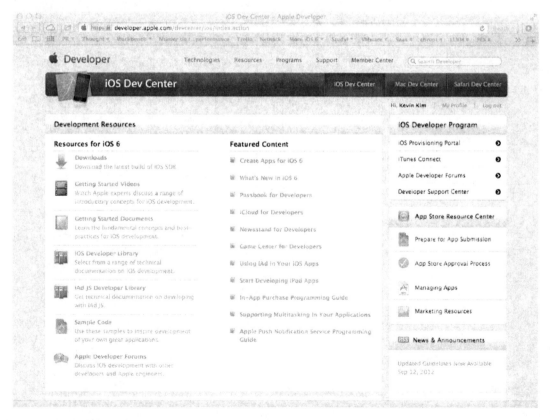

*Figure 8-2. The iOS Developer Center*

On the right of the web page is a section labelled iOS Developer Program. The first choice is iOS Provisioning Portal. Enter the Provisioning Portal (Figure 8-3).

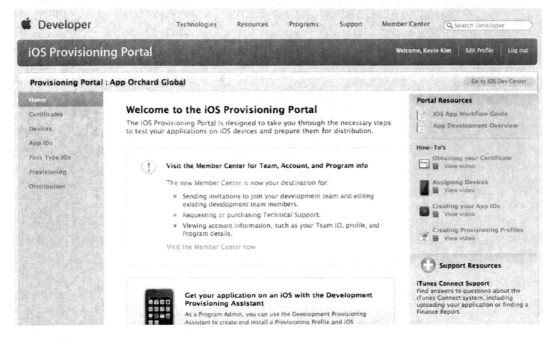

*Figure 8-3. The iOS Provisioning Portal*

Once in the Provisioning Portal, you first need to create an App ID. On the left of the provisioning profile, click on the App IDs link. You should be taken to the App ID Manage page of the provisioning profile (Figure 8-4).

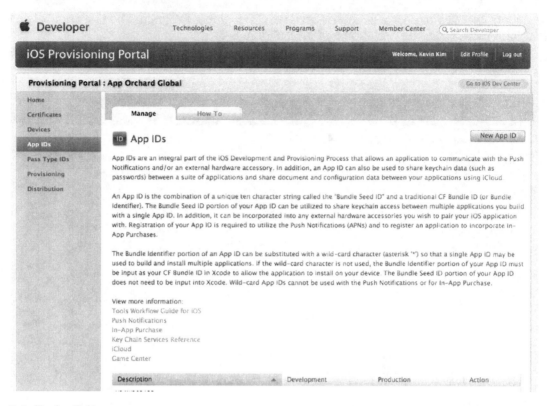

*Figure 8-4. The App ID Manage page*

If you have created other App IDs, you will see a list of them. Since you need to (hopefully) create a new App ID, click the New App ID button near the upper right of the page. This will open a form to create a new App ID. The first field is the description, or common name, of your application. Since you're entering this data for SuperDB, that's what you'll enter here. The Bundle Seed ID should be automatically selected to be your Team ID. It is possible that you may be given a choice here if you're part of many ADC development teams. If so, you should pick the Team ID that's appropriate here. Finally, you need to give your Bundle ID suffix. The convention is the reverse-domain name style. It's important to note the value here should match your Bundle Identifier in Xcode. You can find this value at the top of the target Summary Editor in Xcode (Figure 8-5). Our completed form looks like Figure 8-6. Click the Create button to submit the form and create your App ID.

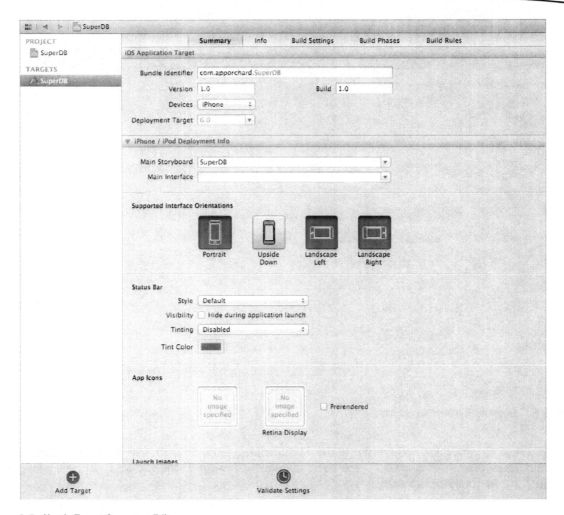

*Figure 8-5.  Xcode Target Summary Editor*

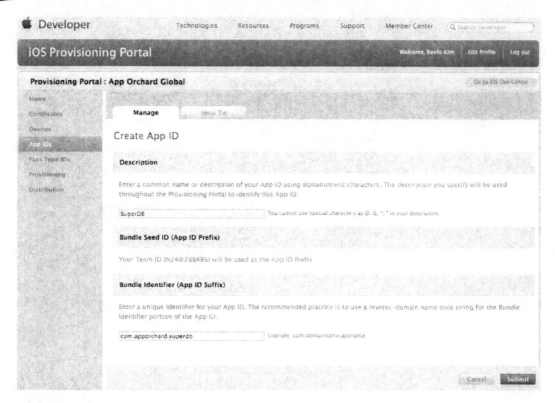

**Figure 8-6.** *The completed New App ID form*

Once the App ID is created, you return to the App ID management page, where the SuperDB App ID should have an entry (Figure 8-7). You need to enable the App ID for iCloud. Start by clicking the Configure link in your App ID entry.

| Description | Development | Production | Action |
| --- | --- | --- | --- |
| N24W28B485.com.apporchard... SuperDB | | | |
| Passes: | Configurable | Configurable | |
| Data Protection: | Configurable | Configurable | |
| iCloud: | Configurable | Configurable | Configure |
| In–App Purchase: | Configurable | Configurable | |
| Game Center: | Configurable | Configurable | |
| Push Notification: | Configurable | Configurable | |

**Figure 8-7.** *SuperDB has been added the App IDs list*

The App ID Configuration page should present a series of checkboxes for your SuperDB application (Figure 8-8).

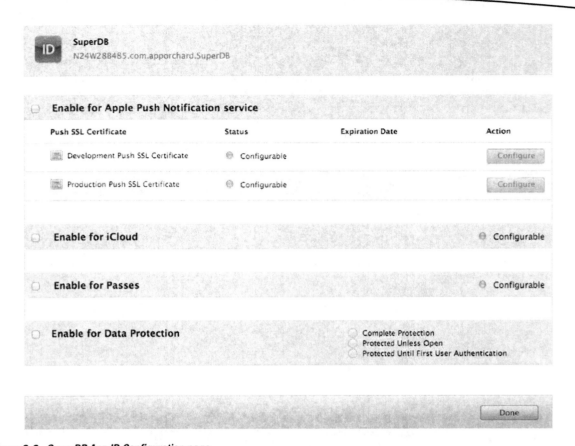

*Figure 8-8. SuperDB App ID Configuration page*

Click the checkbox labeled "Enable for iCloud." You should receive a dialog like the one in Figure 8-9. This is a warning to tell you that all new provisioning profiles for this App ID will be enabled for iCloud, but any existing profile is not enabled. Click OK. When you return to the App ID management page, your SuperDB application should be enabled for iCloud. You're done creating the App ID for SuperDB, so now you can move on to the provisioning profile.

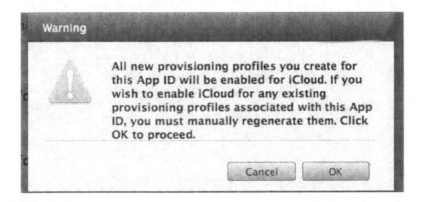

*Figure 8-9. Enabling iCloud warning dialog*

Select the Provisioning link in the provisioning navigation column on the left of the Provisioning Portal page. Like the App IDs page, if you have existing profiles, they'll be listed here. There are Development and Deployment tabs at the top of the page. Depending on which tab is selected, you'll create a profile appropriate for development or deployment. For your purposes, a development profile is sufficient. Make sure that the Development tab is selected, and click the New Profile button. Again, as with the App IDs, you're taken to a form to create a new profile (Figure 8-10).

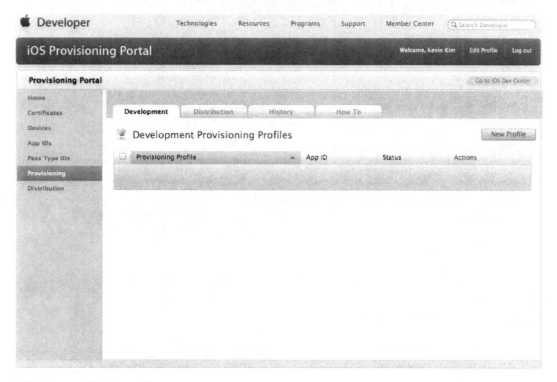

*Figure 8-10. New provisioning profile page*

Give the profile a unique, descriptive name. Check the Certificates checkbox (if you're given more than one choice, select the appropriate one). Pick the SuperDB application from the App ID drop-down. Finally, check the devices you wish this profile to be enabled on. When finished, click Submit to create your profile. The completed form looks like Figure 8-11.

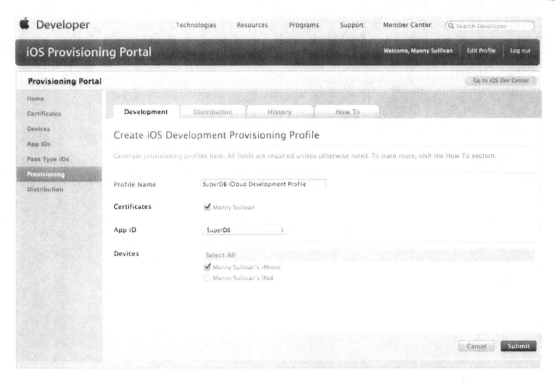

*Figure 8-11. Our completed new Provisioning Profile form*

You should be redirected back to the provisioning profile Manage page, where your new profile will be listed with a status of Pending (Figure 8-12). Wait a few moments, and refresh the page. The status should change to Active, and you can now download or edit the profile (Figure 8-13).

| | Provisioning Profile | App ID | Status | Actions |
|---|---|---|---|---|
| | SuperDB iCloud Development Pro... | S444KF8Z53.com.apporchard.com | Pending | |
| | | | | Remove Selected |

*Figure 8-12. The provisioning profile is pending*

| | Provisioning Profile | App ID | Status | Actions |
|---|---|---|---|---|
| | SuperDB iCloud Development Pro... | S444KF8Z53.com.apporchard.com | Active | Download  Edit |
| | | | | Remove Selected |

*Figure 8-13. The provisioning profile is active*

At this point, there are two ways of loading your provisioning profile into Xcode. You can click the Download button, which will download a `.mobileprovision` file. Then, you can open the Xcode Organizer and select Devices in the toolbar. Once the Devices organizer is open, select the

Provisioning Profiles under the Library section in the left side of the organizer (Figure 8-14). Click the Import button on the bottom of the Profiles pane and open the `.mobileprovision` file you just downloaded. The provisioning profile you just created should appear in the list.

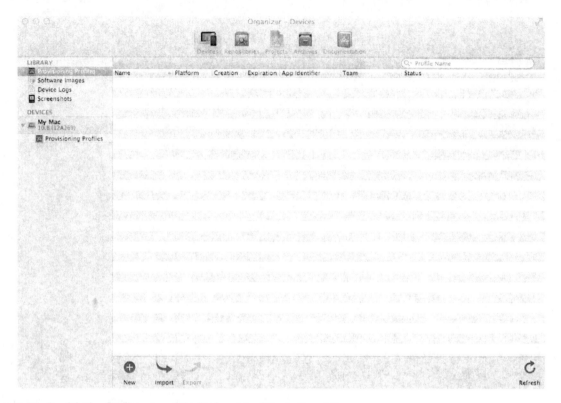

**Figure 8-14.** *Provisioning Profiles pane of the Devices tab of Xcode Organizer*

Alternatively, you can simply click the Refresh button on the bottom right of the Profiles pane. Xcode will ask for your ADC login information. Once you enter that information and click the Log In button, Xcode should automatically download and install the provisioning profile.

On that note, let us also mention that Apple provides an alternative method of creating a provisioning profile via the Xcode Organizer. In many ways, it's much easier than using the ADC iOS Provisioning Portal. In Figure 8-14, you can see a New button on the bottom left of the Profiles pane. You may be asked for your ADC login information. Once you're logged in, you should be presented with a New Profile Assistant (Figure 8-15).

*Figure 8-15.  Xcode Organizer New Profile Assistant*

In essence, this information is identical to the new profile form from the ADC iOS Provisioning Portal (Figure 8-10). You enter a unique, descriptive name for the profile. Select the appropriate App ID, devices, and certificates. Then click Finish. If successful, Xcode will create and install the new provisioning profile.

That was a lot of work just to get iCloud activated for your application. The upside is that the amount of code that you need to implement should be pretty easy to write.

# Updating the Persistent Store

In the SuperDB Xcode project window, open AppDelegate.m and find the persistentStoreCoordinator method. You need to rewrite it to check and use an iCloud persistent store if possible, or else fall back to a local persistent store. The beginning of the method remains the same: you check if you've already created an Instance of your persistent store coordinator; if not, you instantiate one.

```
- (NSPersistentStoreCoordinator *)persistentStoreCoordinator
{
    if (_persistentStoreCoordinator != nil) {
        return _persistentStoreCoordinator;
    }

    _persistentStoreCoordinator = [[NSPersistentStoreCoordinator alloc]
                            initWithManagedObjectModel:[self managedObjectModel]];
```

You dispatch the following code to a background queue so as not to block the main thread. The following code is similar to the example provided in the "Core Data with iCloud" section earlier. Review that section for a detailed explanation.

```
__block NSPersistentStoreCoordinator *psc = _persistentStoreCoordinator;
dispatch_async(dispatch_get_global_queue(DISPATCH_QUEUE_PRIORITY_DEFAULT, 0), ^{
    NSPersistentStore *newStore = nil;
    NSError *error = nil;

    NSString *dataFile = @"SuperDB.sqlite";
    NSString *dataDir = @"Data.nosync";
    NSString *logsDir = @"Logs";

    NSFileManager *fileManager = [NSFileManager defaultManager];
    id ubiquityToken = [fileManager ubiquityIdentityToken];
    NSURL *ubiquityURL = [fileManager URLForUbiquityContainerIdentifier:nil];
    if (ubiquityToken && ubiquityURL) {
        NSString *dataDirPath = [[ubiquityURL path] stringByAppendingPathComponent:dataDir];
        if([fileManager fileExistsAtPath:dataDirPath] == NO) {
            NSError *fileSystemError;
            [fileManager createDirectoryAtPath:dataDirPath
                    withIntermediateDirectories:YES
                                     attributes:nil
                                          error:&fileSystemError];
            if(fileSystemError != nil) {
                NSLog(@"Error creating database directory %@", fileSystemError);
            }
        }

        NSURL *logsURL = [NSURL fileURLWithPath:[[ubiquityURL path]
                                                    stringByAppendingPathComponent:logsDir]];
        NSDictionary *options =
            @{ NSMigratePersistentStoresAutomaticallyOption : @YES,
                      NSInferMappingModelAutomaticallyOption : @YES,
                   NSPersistentStoreUbiquitousContentNameKey : [ubiquityURL lastPathComponent],
                    NSPersistentStoreUbiquitousContentURLKey : logsURL };
        [psc lock];
        NSURL *dataFileURL =
            [NSURL fileURLWithPath:[dataDirPath stringByAppendingPathComponent:dataFile]];

        newStore = [psc addPersistentStoreWithType:NSSQLiteStoreType
                                     configuration:nil
                                               URL:[NSURL fileURLWithPath:dataFileURL]
                                           options:options
                                             error:&error];
        [psc unlock];
    }
```

If for some reason you don't have access to iCloud, you can fall back to using the local persistent store coordinator.

```
    else {
        NSURL *storeURL = [[self applicationDocumentsDirectory]
                                URLByAppendingPathComponent:dataFile];
        NSDictionary *options = @{ NSMigratePersistentStoresAutomaticallyOption : @YES,
                                   NSInferMappingModelAutomaticallyOption : @YES };
        [psc lock];
        newStore = [psc addPersistentStoreWithType:NSSQLiteStoreType
                                     configuration:nil
                                               URL:storeURL
                                           options:options
                                             error:&error];
        [psc unlock];
    }
```

You need to check if you actually have a new persistent store coordinator.

```
    if (!newStore) {
        /*
         Replace this implementation with code to handle the error appropriately.

         abort() causes the application to generate a crash log and terminate.
                 You should not use this function in a shipping application,
                 although it may be useful during development.

         */
        NSLog(@"Unresolved error %@, %@", error, [error userInfo]);
        abort();
    }
```

Once complete, you send a notification on the main thread that you've loaded the persistent store coordinator. You use this notification to update the UI, if necessary.

```
    dispatch_async(dispatch_get_main_queue(), ^{
        [[NSNotificationCenter defaultCenter] postNotificationName:@"DataChanged"
                                             object:self
                                             userInfo:nil];
    });
});

    return _persistentStoreCoordinator;
}
```

# Updating the Managed Object Context

You need to register to receive notifications when the data in the ubiquity container changes. You do that in the managedObjectContext method of the AppDelegate. The additions are in bold.

```
- (NSManagedObjectContext *)managedObjectContext
{
    if (_managedObjectContext != nil) {
        return _managedObjectContext;
    }
```

```
NSPersistentStoreCoordinator *coordinator = [self persistentStoreCoordinator];
if (coordinator != nil) {
    _managedObjectContext = [[NSManagedObjectContext alloc] init];
    [_managedObjectContext setPersistentStoreCoordinator:coordinator];
    [[NSNotificationCenter defaultCenter]
            addObserver:self
            selector:@selector(mergeChangesFromUbiquitousContent:)
            name:NSPersistentStoreDidImportUbiquitousContentChangesNotification
            object:coordinator];
}
return _managedObjectContext;
}
```

You've told the Notification Center to invoke the AppDelegate method mergeChangesFromUbiquitousContent: so you need to implement that method. First, add the method declaration to the interface file, AppDelegate.h, before the @end declaration.

```
- (void)mergeChangesFromUbiquitousContent:(NSNotification *)notification;
```

Then add the implementation to the bottom of AppDelegate.m, just before the @end.

```
#pragma mark - Handle Changes from iCloud to Ubiquitous Container

- (void)mergeChangesFromUbiquitousContent:(NSNotification *)notification
{
    NSManagedObjectContext* moc = [self managedObjectContext];
    [moc performBlock:^{
        [moc mergeChangesFromContextDidSaveNotification:notification];
        NSNotification* refreshNotification = [NSNotification notificationWithName:@"DataChanged"
                                                    object:self
                                                    userInfo:[notification
userInfo]];
        [[NSNotificationCenter defaultCenter] postNotification:refreshNotification];
    }];
}
```

This method first merges the changes into your managed object context. Then it sends a DataChanged notification. You used that notification earlier when you created the persistent store coordinator. It's intended to notify you when the UI should be updated. Let's do that.

## Updating the UI on DataChanged

Open HeroListController.m in the Xcode Editor and find the viewDidLoad method. Just before the end of the method, register for the DataChanged notification.

```
[[NSNotificationCenter defaultCenter] addObserver:self
                                selector:@selector(updateReceived:)
                                name:@"DataChanged"
                                object:nil];
```

While you're at it, be a good iOS programmer and unregister in the `didReceiveMemoryWarning` method.

```
[[NSNotificationCenter defaultCenter] removeObserver:self];
```

When the `DataChanged` notification is received, the `updateReceived:` method will be invoked. So you need to declare and implement it. First, add the method declaration to `HeroListController.h`, before the @end.

```
- (void)updateReceived:(NSNotification *)notification;
```

Now, add the implementation to `HeroListController.m`, again before the @end.

```
- (void)updateReceived:(NSNotification *)notification
{
    NSError *error;
    if (![self.fetchedResultsController performFetch:&error]) {
        NSLog(@"Error performing fetch: %@", [error localizedDescription]);
    }
    [self.heroTableView reloadData];
}
```

Essentially, it just refreshes the data and table view.

## Testing the Data Store

You can't use iCloud on the simulator, so you need to run it on your device. Build and run the app. Since you're starting with a new persistent store, there should be no entries. Add a new hero, edit the details, and save. Now quit the application (and/or stop it in Xcode). On your device, tap and hold the SuperDB app icon until it begins to shake. Delete the app. You should receive an alert dialog to tell you that the local data will be lost, but the iCloud data will be kept. Tap Delete.

Now run the app again. Wait a few moments, and the Hero list should update to include the hero you added earlier. Even though you deleted the app (and its local data), iCloud was able to synchronize and restore the persistent store.

## Keep Your Feet on the Ground

While developing an application for iCloud, there may be times when you want to view or even delete the data in iCloud. There are a few ways you can view and/or manage the data your application is putting in iCloud.

- *Via Mac*: Open the System Preference, and choose iCloud. Click the Manage button on the lower right.

- *Via iOS*: Use the Settings app, and navigate to iCloud ➤ Storage & Backup ➤ Manage Storage.

- *Via the Web (view only)*: Navigate to http://developer.icloud.com/ and log in. Click the Documents icon.

These are just the basics of building an iCloud-enabled application for iOS. For any application, there are many things to keep in mind, but here are some key things to remember:

- How will your app behave if iCloud is not available?

- If you allow "offline" use, how will your application synchronize with iCloud?

- How will your application handle conflicts? This will be highly dependent on your data model.

- Try to design your data/document model to minimize the data transfer between your device and iCloud.

Hopefully, you've gotten a good taste of what it means to enable iCloud in your app. Let's head back to Earth and have some fun building a game.

# Chapter 9

# Peer-to-Peer Over Bluetooth Using Game Kit

Game Kit has to be one of the coolest frameworks available for people interested in developing games on the iOS SDK. Game Kit classes provide three different technologies: GameCenter, Peer-to-Peer Connectivity, and In Game Voice. While this chapter will focus on Peer-to-Peer Connectivity, we'll briefly cover the other two components of Game Kit so that you're familiar with them.

## Game Center

Game Center is a centralized, social-networking gaming service provided by Apple. Game Center provides the services so that users of your game can share information and join other players, if your game is multiplayer. Game Center has three components:

- Game Center App built into iOS (Figure 9-1).
- Game Center Service that Apple manages "in the cloud."
- Game Center APIs provided in the Game Kit framework.

*Figure 9-1. Game Center on your iOS device*

Game Center provides the following basic services:

- **Authentication:** This is simply an account on the Game Center service that identifies your user on Game Center.

- **Leaderboards:** This is the "high score" of your application. If you decide to implement a leaderboard, it's up to your application what constitutes a "high score." For example, it could be a simple point system or it could be time played. Your app can also download leaderboard information and store it locally.

- **Achievements:** Another measure of game activity. These are usually specific milestones a player has reached (i.e. "Level 2") as opposed to a score, which would be measured in the leaderboard.

- **Multiplayer:** Allows players to find other players (of the same game) to compete against. You can use Game Center to connect all players of a game where everyone plays together or deliver a list of players to compete against. This may require you to implement a service of your own.

All Game Center games must start by authenticating a player. All other features depend on the user being authenticated against the Game Center Service. Authentication with Game Center is system-wide, meaning if you authenticate one game with Game Center, any other Game Center-enabled game will use that authentication as well. If there isn't an authenticated player, Game Center features will be disabled. Whether your game still works or not is up to you.

If you do use the other Game Center features in your game, you need to have at least one view controller in place. This view controller is used as the "root" for Game Center to work off. For example, the leaderboard is a Game Kit view controller class that provides a standard way for your game to display leaderboard information. Your game needs to provide a view controller to modally display the leaderboard.

Since Game Center is a network-based service, you need to put guards in place to handle the loss of network.

> **Note** For more information on Game Center, and Game Kit in general, you can read *Beginning iOS Game Center and Game Kit* (www.apress.com/9781430235279) by Kyle Richter (Apress, 2011) and Apple's Game Kit Programming Guide (https://developer.apple.com/library/ios/#documentation/ NetworkingInternet/Conceptual/GameKit_Guide/Introduction/Introduction.html).

# Peer-to-Peer Connectivity

Game Kit makes it easy to wirelessly connect multiple iOS devices, either via Bluetooth or WiFi. Bluetooth is a wireless networking option built into all but the first-generation iPhone and iPod touch. Game Kit allows any supported devices to communicate with any other supported devices that are within range. For Bluetooth, this is roughly 30 feet (about 10 meters) of each other. Though the name implies differently, Game Kit is useful for non-gaming apps, too. For example, you might build a social networking app that allows people to easily transfer contact information over Bluetooth.

> **Caution** The code in this chapter will not run in the Simulator because the Simulator does not support Bluetooth. The only way to build and debug apps on a device attached to your machine is by joining the paid iPhone Developer Program. So you'll need to do that if you want to fully experience this chapter's chewy goodness.
>
> In addition, as of this writing, you cannot play Game Kit games between a device and the Simulator. If you have only one device, you will not be able to try out the game in this chapter.

Peer-to-Peer Connectivity relies on two components:

- The *session* allows iPhone OS devices running the same application to easily send information back and forth over Bluetooth without writing any networking code.
- The *peer picker* provides an easy way to find other devices without writing any networking or discovery (Bonjour) code.

Under the hood, Game Kit sessions leverage Bonjour, Apple's technology for zero-configuration networking and device discovery. As a result, devices using Game Kit are capable of finding each other on the network without the user needing to enter an IP address or domain name.

# In Game Voice

In Game Voice allows you to add voice chat to your game, allowing players to communicate with each other. This can be done with either through the Game Center Service or Peer-to-Peer Connectivity.

Each Game Kit client gets assigned a unique identifier. Game Kit does not provide a mechanism to generate this identifier; it's up to you to provide one. Once you have an identifier, you need a way to discover other game instances to initiate a voice chat. That discovery can be handled in a number of ways. For Peer-to-Peer Connectivity, you could use the session to find another player. With Game Center, you can use Game Center's multiplayer mechanism to find other players.

Once another player is found, In Game Voice makes it easy to start and stop voice chats between players.

# This Chapter's Application

In this chapter, you're going to explore Game Kit by writing a simple networked game. You'll write a two-player version of tic-tac-toe (Figure 9-2) that will use Game Kit to let people on two different iPhones or iPod touches play against each other over Bluetooth. You won't be implementing online play over the Internet or local area network in this chapter.

*Figure 9-2. You'll use a simple game of tic-tac-toe to learn the basics of Game Kit*

When users launch your application, they will be presented with an empty tic-tac-toe board and a single button labeled **New Game**. (For the sake of simplicity, you're not going to implement a single-device mode to let two players play on the same device.) When the user presses the New Game button, the application will start looking for Bluetooth peers using the peer picker (Figure 9-3).

*Figure 9-3.* *When the user presses the New Game button, it will launch the peer picker to look for other devices running the tic-tac-toe game*

If another device within range runs the TicTacToe application and the user also presses the New Game button, the two devices will find each other and the peer pickerwill present a dialog to the users, letting them choose among the available peers (Figure 9-4).

**Figure 9-4.** *When another device within range starts a game, the two devices will show up in each other's peer picker dialog*

After one player selects a peer, the iPhone will attempt to make a connection (Figure 9-5). Once the connection is established, the other person will be asked to accept or refuse the connection (Figure 9-6). If the connection is accepted, the two applications will negotiate to see who goes first. Each side will randomly select a number, the numbers will be compared, and the highest number will go first. Once that decision is made, play will commence (Figure 9-7) until someone wins (Figure 9-8).

*Figure 9-5.  Establishing the connection*

*Figure 9-6.* *Asking the other player to accept the connection*

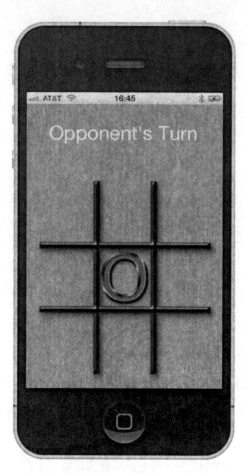

*Figure 9-7.* *The user whose turn it is can tap any available space. That space will get an X or an O on both users' devices*

*Figure 9-8. We have a winner!*

If the connection is lost for whatever reason, the iPhone will report the lost connection to the user (Figure 9-9).

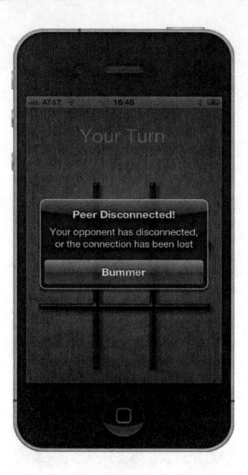

*Figure 9-9. Lost connection alert*

# Network Communication Models

Before we look at how Game Kit and the peer picker work, let's talk generally about communication models used in networked programs so that we're all on the same page in terms of terminology.

## Client–server Model

You're probably familiar with the client–server model, as it is the model used by the World Wide Web. Machines called *servers* listen for connections from other machines, referred to as *clients*. The server then takes actions based on the requests received from the clients. In the context of the Web, the client is usually a web browser, and there can be any number of clients attaching to a single server. The clients never communicate with each other directly, but direct all communications through the server. Most massively multiplayer online role-playing games (MMORPGs) like World of Warcraft also use this model. Figure 9-10 represents a client–server scenario.

*Figure 9-10.* *The client–server model features one machine acting as a server with all communications—even communications between clients—going through the server*

In the context of an iPhone application, a client–server setup is where one phone acts as a server and listens for other iPhones running the same program. The other phones can then connect to that server. If you've ever played a game where one machine "hosts" a game and others then join the game, that game is almost certainly using a client–server model.

A drawback with the client–server model is that everything depends on the server, which means that the game cannot continue if anything happens to the server. If the user whose phone is acting as the server quits, crashes, or moves out of range, the entire game is ended. Since all the other machines communicate through the central server, they lose the ability to communicate if the server is unavailable. This is generally not an issue with client–server games where the client is a hefty server farm connected to the Internet by redundant high-speed lines, but it certainly can be an issue with mobile games.

# Peer-to-Peer Model

In the peer-to-peer model, all the individual devices (called *peers*) can communicate with each other directly. A central server may be used to initiate the connection or to facilitate certain operations, but the main distinguishing feature of the peer-to-peer model is that peers can talk to each other directly and can continue to do so even in the absence of a server (Figure 9-11).

*Figure 9-11.* *In the peer-to-peer model, peers can talk to each other directly and can continue to do so even in the absence of a server*

The peer-to-peer model was popularized by file-sharing services like BitTorrent. A centralized server is used to find other peers that have the file you are looking for, but once the connection is made to those other peers, they can continue, even if the server goes offline.

The simplest and probably the most common implementation of the peer-to-peer model on the iPhone is when you have two devices connected to each other. This is the model used in head-to-head games, for example. Game Kit makes this kind of peer-to-peer network exceedingly simple to set up and configure, as you'll see in this chapter.

## Hybrid Client–server/Peer-to-Peer

The client–server and peer-to-peer models of network communication are not mutually exclusive, and it is possible to create programs that utilize a hybrid of both. For example, a client–server game might allow certain communications to go directly from client to client without going through the server. In a game that had a chat window, it might allow messages intended for only one recipient to go directly from the machine of the sender to the machine of the intended recipient, while any other kind of chat would go to the server to be distributed to all clients.

You should keep these different networking models in mind as we discuss the mechanics of making connections and transferring data between application nodes. *Node* is a generic term that refers to any computer connected to an application's network. A client, server, or peer is a node. The game you will be writing in this chapter will use a simple, two-machine, peer-to-peer model.

## The Game Kit Session

The key to Game Kit is the session, represented by the class GKSession. The session represents your end of a network connection with one or more other iPhones. Regardless of whether you are acting as a client, a server, or a peer, an instance of GKSession will represent the connections you have with other phones. You will use GKSession whether you employ the peer picker or write your own code to find machines to connect to and let the user select from them.

> **Note** As you make your way through the next few pages, don't worry too much about where each of these elements is implemented. This will all come together in the project you create in this chapter.

You will also use GKSession to send data to connected peers. You will implement session delegate methods to get notified of changes to the session, such as when another node connects or disconnects, as well as to receive data sent by other nodes.

# Creating the Session

To use a session, you must first create allocate and initialize a GKSession object, like so:

```
GKSession *theSession = [[GKSession alloc] initWithSessionID:@"com.apporchard.game"
                                          displayName:nil
                                          sessionMode:GKSessionModePeer];
```

There are three arguments you pass in when initializing a session.

The first argument is a *session identifier*, which is a string that is unique to your application. This is used to prevent your application's sessions from accidentally connecting to sessions from another program. Since the session identifier is a string, it can be anything, though the convention is to use a reverse DNS-style name, such as com.apporchard.game. By assigning session identifiers in this manner, rather than by just randomly picking a word or phrase, you are less likely to accidentally choose a session identifier that is used by another application on the App Store.

The second argument is the *display name*. This is a name that will be provided to the other nodes to uniquely identify your phone. If you pass in nil, the display name will default to the device's name as set in iTunes. If multiple devices are connected, this will allow the other users to see which devices are available and connect to the correct one. In Figure 9-3, you can see an example of where the unique identifier is used. In that example, one other device is advertising itself with the same session identifier as us, using a display name of Manny Sullivan's iPhone.

The last argument is the *session mode*. Session modes determine how the session will behave once it's all set up and ready to make connections. There are three options:

- If you specify GKSessionModeServer, your session will advertise itself on the network so that other devices can see it and connect to it, but it won't look for other sessions being advertised.

- If you specify GKSessionModeClient, the session will not advertise itself on the network, but will look for other sessions that are advertising themselves.

- If you specify GKSessionModePeer, your session will both advertise its availability on the network and also look for other sessions.

> **Note**    Although you will generally use GKSessionModePeer when establishing a peer-to-peer network
> and GKSessionModeServer and GKSessionModeClient when setting up a client–server
> network, these constants dictate only whether an individual session will advertise its availability on
> the network using Bonjour or look for other available nodes. They are not necessarily indicative of which
> of the network models is being used by the application.

Regardless of the type of session you create, it won't actually start advertising its availability or looking for other available nodes until you tell it to do so. You do that by setting the session property available to YES. Alternatively, you can have the node stop advertising its availability and/or stop looking for other available nodes by setting available to NO.

## Finding and Connecting to Other Sessions

When a session that was created using GKSessionModeClient or GKSessionModePeer finds another node advertising its availability, it will call the method session:peer:didChangeState: and pass in a state of GKPeerStateAvailable. This same method will be called every time a peer becomes available or unavailable, as well as when a peer connects or disconnects. The second argument will tell you which peer's state changed, and the last argument will tell you its new state.

If you find one or more other sessions that are available, you can choose to connect the session to one of the available sessions by calling connectToPeer:withTimeout:. Here's an example of session:peer:didChangeState: that connects to the first available peer it finds:

```
- (void)session:(GKSession *)session peer:(NSString *)peerID
                   didChangeState:(GKPeerConnectionState)inState
{
    if (inState == GKPeerStateAvailable) {
        [session connectToPeer:peerID withTimeout:60];
        session.available = NO;
    }
}
```

This isn't a very realistic example, as you would normally allow the user to choose the node to which they connect. It's a good example, though, because it shows both of the basic functions of a client node. In this example, you've set available to NO after you connect. This will cause your session to stop looking for additional sessions. Since a session can connect to multiple peers, you won't always want to do this. If your application supports multiple connections, you will want to leave it at YES.

## Listening for Other Sessions

When a session is specified with a session mode of GKSessionModeServer or GKSessionModePeer, it will be notified when another node attempts to connect. When this happens, the session will call the method session:didReceiveConnectionRequestFromPeer:. You can choose to accept the connection by calling acceptConnectionFromPeer:error: or you can reject it by calling denyConnectionFromPeer:. The following is an example that assumes the presence of a Boolean instance variable called amAcceptingConnections. If it's set to YES, it accepts the connection, and if it's set to NO, it rejects the connection.

```
- (void)session:(GKSession *)session didReceiveConnectionRequestFromPeer:(NSString *)peerID
{
    if (amAcceptingConnections) {
        NSError *error;
        if (![session acceptConnectionFromPeer:peerID error:&error]) {
            // Handle error
        }
    }
    else {
        [session denyConnectionFromPeer:peerID];
    }
}
```

## Sending Data to a Peer

Once you have a session that is connected to another node, it's very easy to send data to that node. All you need to do is call one of two methods. Which method you call depends on whether you want to send the information to all connected sessions or to just specific ones. To send data to just specified peers, use the method sendData:toPeers:withDataMode:error:. To send data to every connected peer, use the method sendDataToAllPeers:withDataMode:error:.

In both cases, you need to specify a *data mode* for the connection. The data mode tells the session how it should try to send the data. There are two options:

- GKSendDataReliable: This option ensures that the information will arrive at the other session. It will send the data in chunks if it's over a certain size and wait for an acknowledgment from the other peer for every chunk.

- GKSendDataUnreliable: This mode sends the data immediately and does not wait for acknowledgment. It's much faster than GKSendDataReliable, but there is a small chance of the complete message not arriving at the other node.

Usually, the GKSendDataReliable data mode is the one you'll want to use, though if you have a program where speed of transmission matters more than accuracy, then you should consider GKSendDataUnreliable.

Here is what it looks like when you send data to a single peer:

```
NSError *error = nil;
if (![session sendData:theData
                toPeers:[NSArray arrayWithObject:thePeerID]
          withDataMode:GKSendDataReliable error:&error]) {
        // Do error handling
}
```

And here's what it looks like to send data to all connected peers:

```
NSError *error = nil;
if (![session sendDataToAllPeers:data
                withDataMode:GKSendDataReliable
          error:&error]) {
      // Do error handling
}
```

## Packaging Up Information to Send

Any information that you can get into an instance of NSData can be sent to other peers. There are two basic approaches to doing this for use in Game Kit. The first is to use archiving and unarchiving, just as we did in the archiving section of Chapter 11 of *Beginning iOS 6 Development* (Apress, 2012).

With the archiving/unarchiving method, you define a class to hold a single packet of data to be sent. That class will contain instance variables to hold whatever types of data you might need to send. When it's time to send a packet, you create and initialize an instance of the packet object, and then you use NSKeyedArchiver to archive the instance of that object into an instance of NSData, which can be passed to sendData:toPeers:withDataMode:error: or to sendDataToAllPeers:withDataMode:error:. You'll use this approach in this chapter's example. However, this approach incurs a small amount of overhead, since it requires the creation of objects to be passed, along with archiving and unarchiving those objects.

Although archiving objects is the best approach in many cases, because it is easy to implement and it fits well with the design of Cocoa Touch, there may be some cases where applications need to constantly send a lot of data to their peers, and this overhead might be unacceptable. In those situations, a faster option is to just use a static array (a regular old C array, not an NSArray) as a local variable in the method that sends the data.

You can copy any data you need to send to the peer into this static array, and then create an NSData instance from that static array. There's still some object creation involved in creating the NSData instance, but it's one object instead of two, and you don't have the overhead of archiving. Here's a simple example of sending data using this faster technique:

```
NSUInteger packetData[2];
packet[0] = foo;
packet[1] = bar;
NSData *packet = [NSData dataWithBytes:packetData length:2 * sizeof(packetData)];
NSError *error = nil;
if (![session sendDataToAllPeers:packet withDataMode:GKSendDataReliable error:&error]) {
    // Handle error
}
```

## Receiving Data from a Peer

When a session receives data from a peer, the session passes the data to a method on an object known as a *data receive handler*. The method is receiveData:fromPeer:inSession:context:. By default, the data receive handler is the session's delegate, but it doesn't have to be. You can specify another object to handle the task by calling setDataReceiveHandler:withContext: on the session and passing in the object you want to receive data from the session.

Whichever object is specified as the data receive handler must implement receiveData:fromPeer: inSession:context: and that method will be called any time new data comes in from a peer. There's no need to acknowledge receipt of the data or worry about waiting for the entire packet. You can just use the provided data as is appropriate for your program. All the gnarly aspects of network data transmission are handled for you. Every call to sendDataToAllPeers:withDataMode:error: made by other peers, and every call to sendData:toPeers:withDataMode:error: made by other peers who specify your peer identifier, will result in one call of the data receive handler.

Here's an example of a data receive handler method that would be the counterpart to the earlier send example:

```
- (void)receiveData:(NSData *)data
          fromPeer:(NSString *)peer
          inSession: (GKSession *)theSession
            context:(void *)context
{
    NSUInteger *packet = [data bytes];
    NSUInteger foo = packet[0];
    NSUInteger bar = packet[0];
    // Do something with foo and bar
}
```

You'll look at receiving archived objects when you build this chapter's example.

# Closing Connections

When you're finished with a session, before you release the session object, it's important to do a little cleanup. Before releasing the session object, you must make the session unavailable, disconnect it from all of its peers, set the data receive handler to nil, and set the session delegate to nil. Here's what the code in your dealloc method (or any other time your need to close the connections) might look like:

```
session.available = NO;
[session disconnectFromAllPeers];
[session setDataReceiveHandler: nil withContext: nil];
session.delegate = nil;
```

If, instead, you just want to disconnect from one specific peer, you can call disconnectPeerFromAllPeers:, which will disconnect the remote peer from all the peers to which it was connected. Use this method with caution, as it will cause the peer on which it was called to disconnect from all remote peers, not just your application. Here's what using it might look like:

```
[session disconnectPeerFromAllPeers:thePeer];
```

# The Peer Picker

Although Game Kit does not need to be used only for games, network games are clearly the primary motivator behind the technology—at least if the name Apple chose is any clue. The most common type of network model for mobile games is the head-to-head or simple peer-to-peer model, where one player plays a game against one other player. Because this scenario is so common, Apple has provided a mechanism called the *peer picker* for easily setting up this simple type of peer-to-peer network.

## Creating the Peer Picker

The peer picker was designed specifically to connect one device to a single other device using Bluetooth. Though limited in this way, the peer picker is incredibly simple to use and is a great choice if it meets your needs. To create and show the peer picker, you just create an instance of GKPeerPickerController, set its delegate, and then call its show method, like so:

```
GKPeerPickerController *picker;
picker = [[GKPeerPickerController alloc] init];
picker.delegate = self;
[picker show];
```

## Handling a Peer Connection

When the user has selected a peer and the sessions have been connected to each other, the delegate method peerPickerController:didConnectPeer:toSession: will be called. In your implementation of that method, you need to do a few things. First, you might want to store the *peer identifier*, which is a string that identifies the device to which you're connected. The peer identifier defaults to the iPhone's device name, though you can specify other values. You also need to save a reference to the session so you can use it to send data and to disconnect the session later.

```
- (void)peerPickerController:(GKPeerPickerController *)picker
            didConnectPeer:(NSString *)thePeerID
                 toSession:(GKSession *)theSession
{
    self.peerID = thePeerID;
    self.session = theSession;
    self.session.delegate = self;
    [self.session setDataReceiveHandler:self withContext:NULL];
    [picker dismiss];
    picker.delegate = nil;
}
```

## Creating the Session

There's one last delegate task that you must handle when using the peer picker, which is to create the session when the picker asks for a session. You don't need to worry about most of the other tasks related to finding and connecting to other peers when using the peer picker, but you are responsible for creating the session for the picker to use. Here's what that method typically looks like:

```
- (GKSession *)peerPickerController:(GKPeerPickerController *)picker
            sessionForConnectionType:(GKPeerPickerConnectionType)type
{
    GKSession *theSession;
    theSession = [[GKSession alloc] initWithSessionID:@"a session id"
                                          displayName:nil
                                          sessionMode:GKSessionModePeer];
    return theSession;
}
```

**GKPeerPickerConnectionType** can be one of two types: **GKPeerPickerConnectionOnline** (network/Internet) and **GKPeerPickerConnectionNearby** (Bluetooth). You can configure the allowable types by using the **connectionTypesMask** property on your **GKPeerPickerController** instance. By default, it assumes only a Bluetooth connection.

We've already talked about the session, so there shouldn't be anything in this method that's confusing.

---

**Note**   There's actually another peer picker delegate method that you need to implement if you want to support online play over the WiFi with the peer picker: **peerPickerController:didSelect ConnectionType:**. Check the Apple documentation or *Beginning iOS Game Center and Game Kit*.

---

Well, that's enough discussion. Let's start building the application.

# Creating the Project

Okay, you know the drill. Fire up Xcode if it's not already open and create a new project. Use the Single View Application template and call the project **TicTacToe**. You're not going to use storyboards, so only the "Use Automatic Reference Counting" box should be checked. Once the project is open, look in the project archives that accompany this book, in the folder 09 - TicTacToe. Find the image files called wood_button.png, board.png, O.png, and X.png, and copy them into the Supporting Files group of your project. There's also an icon file called icon.png, which you can copy into your project if you want to use it.

# Turning Off the Idle Timer

The first thing you want to do is to turn off the *idle timer*. The idle timer is what tells your iPhone to go to sleep if the user has not interacted with it in a while. Because the user won't be tapping the screen during the opponent's turn, you need to turn this off to prevent the phone from going to sleep if the other user takes a while to make a move. Generally speaking, you don't want networked applications to go to sleep, because sleeping breaks the network connection. Most of the time, with networked iPhone games, disabling the idle timer is the best approach.

Expand the TicTacToe group in the Navigator pane in Xcode and single-click AppDelegate.m. Add the following line of code to applicationDidFinishLaunchingWithOptions:, before the method returns, to disable the idle timer.

```
[[UIApplication sharedApplication] setIdleTimerDisabled:YES];
```

> **Note**    There may be rare times when you want to leave the idle timer functioning and just close your sessions when the app goes to sleep, but closing sessions on sleep is not quite as straightforward as it would seem. The application delegate method applicationWillResignActive: is called before the phone goes to sleep, but unfortunately, it's also called at other times. In fact, it's called any time that your application loses the ability to respond to touch events. That makes it close to impossible to differentiate between when the user has been presented a system alert, such as from a push notification or a low-battery warning (which won't result in broken connections), and when the phone is actually going to sleep. So, until Apple provides a way to differentiate between these scenarios, your best bet is to simply disallow sleep while a networked program is running.

## Importing the Game Kit Framework

Game Kit is not one of the frameworks that is automatically linked by the Xcode project template, so you need to manually link it yourself in order to access the session and peer picker methods. Select the TicTacToe project at the top of the Navigator pane. Next, select the TicTacToe target in the Project Editor. Select the Build Phases tab and expand the Link Binary With Libraries (3 items) section. Click the + button on the lower left. Select GameKit.framework from the dialog that appears, then click Add.

GameKit.framework will appear in the Navigator pane, at the top of the project groups. Let's clean it up by dragging it into the Frameworks group.

## Designing the Interface

Now you're going to design your game's user interface. Since tic-tac-toe is a relatively simple game, you'll design your user interface in Interface Builder, rather than by using OpenGL ES.

Each space on the board will be a button. When the user taps a button that hasn't already been selected (which you determine by seeing if the button has an image assigned), you set the image to either X.png or O.png (which you added to your project a few minutes ago). You then send that information to the other device. You're also going to use the button's tag value to differentiate the buttons and make it easier to determine when someone has won. You assign each of the buttons that represents a space on the board with a sequential tag, starting in the upper-left corner. You can see which space will have which tag value by looking at Figure 9-12. This way, you can identify which button was pressed without having a separate action method for each button.

*Figure 9-12. Assign each game space button a tag value*

# Defining Application Constants

When referring to specific buttons on the tic-tac-toe board, you could use the tag values you defined in Figure 9-12 (and will have to in Interface Builder), but it would be better to use a set of mnemonic constants. You'll also define some constants for the current game state and whether the user is an X or an O.

You could stick these constant definitions in various header and implementation files throughout the application, but it might be easier to stick them in a single file. Let's do that.

Select the TicTacToe group in the Navigator pane, and create a new file. Select the C and C++ section under iOS in the template chooser dialog. Choose Header File and click Next. Save the file as TicTacToe.h. Select TicTacToe.h; it should look like this:

```
#ifndef TicTacToe_TicTacToe_h
#define TicTacToe_TicTacToe_h

#endif
```

Those macros (#ifndef, #define, #endif), are C language hooks to make sure you only include TicTacToe.h once. You don't really need to worry about that in Objective-C, as the #import macro takes care of that for you. You can delete those lines.

Now, you need to define some constants of your own. First, you defined a constant to represent the Game Kit session ID.

```
#define kTicTacToeSessionID  @"com.apporchard.TicTacToe.session"
```

Next, we defined a constant for use with encoding and decoding data packets through Game Kit.

```
#define kTicTacToeArchiveKey @"com.apporchard.TicTacToe"
```

When the application connects to another device, you have the application decide which player goes first by generating a random number and having the higher number go first. You define the number generator with the macro dieRoll(), which will generate a number between 0 and 999,999. You're using a large number here so that the chance of both devices rolling the same value (which would require a re-roll) will be extremely low.

```
#define dieRoll() (arc4random() % 1000000)
```

You also define a constant, kDiceNotRolled, that will identify when the die has not yet been rolled. Remember that you're storing both your die roll and your opponent's die roll in NSInteger instance variables. On the iPhone, NSInteger is the same as an int. You use the value INT_MAX to identify when those values have not yet been determined. INT_MAX is the largest value that an int can hold on the platform. Since the largest number the dieRoll() macro will generate is 999,999, you can safely use INT_MAX to identify when a die hasn't been rolled, because INT_MAX currently equals 2,147,483,647 on iOS. If INT_MAX ever changes, it will likely get bigger, not smaller.

```
#define kDiceNotRolled INT_MAX
```

You need some enumerations. GameState will be your definition to an enumerated list of the different game states.

```
typedef enum GameStates {
    kGameStateBeginning,
    kGameStateRollingDice,
    kGameStateMyTurn,
    kGameStateYourTurn,
    kGameStateInterrupted,
    kGameStateDone
} GameState;
```

BoardSpace is the enumerated list that you defined in Figure 9-12. Note that you defined the first enumeration, kUpperLeft, to 1000. Each subsequent enumeration is incremented up from there.

```
typedef enum BoardSpaces {
    kUpperLeft = 1000,
    kUpperMiddle,
    kUpperRight,
    kMiddleLeft,
    kMiddleMiddle,
    kMiddleRight,
    kLowerLeft,
    kLowerMiddle,
    kLowerRight
} BoardSpace;
```

PlayerPiece is a simple enumeration to let you know what piece the player is assigned.

```
typedef enum PlayerPieces {
    kPlayerPieceUndecided,
    kPlayerPieceO,
    kPlayerPieceX
} PlayerPiece;
```

Finally, you define an enumerated list to list the different kind of packet types the application will exchange via Game Kit.

```
typedef enum PacketTypes {
    kPacketTypeDieRoll,
    kPacketTypeAck,
    kPacketTypeMove,
    kPacketTypeReset,
} PacketType;
```

Now that you've defined these constants, you can start by working on the application view.

## Designing the Game Board

Select ViewController.xib in the Navigator. Xcode will open it in Interface Builder. There will be one view in Interface Builder. Find the Image View in the Object Library and drag it into the view. Because it's the first object you're adding to the view, it should resize to take up the full view. Place it so that it fills the entire view, and then bring up the attribute inspector in the Utility pane. At the top of the attribute inspector, set the Image field to board.png, which is one of the images you added to your project earlier.

Next, drag a round rect button from the library over to the top of the view. The exact placement doesn't matter yet. After it's placed, use the attribute inspector to change the button type from rounded rect to custom. Delete the button label text, "Button", either in Interface Builder or via the attribute inspector. In the Image field of the attributes inspector, select wood_button.png, and then select Editor ➤ Size to Fit Content (or type ⌘=) to change the button's size to match the image you assigned to it. Now use the blue guidelines to center the button in the view and place it against the top blue margin so it looks like Figure 9-13.

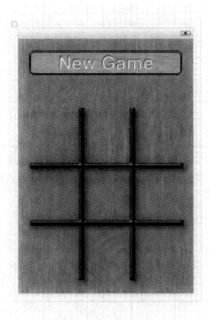

*Figure 9-13. Your interface after sizing and placing the button*

Look again in the library for a label, and drag it to the view. Center the label on top gameButton. Resize the label so it runs from the left blue margin to the right blue margin horizontally, and from the top blue margin down to just above the tic-tac-toe board. It will overlap the button you just added, and that's okay, because the label will display text only when the button isn't visible. Use the attribute inspector to center the text and to increase the size of the font to 60 points. Feel free to also set the text to a nice bright color if you want. Once you have the label the way you want it, delete the label text, "Label," so that it doesn't display anything at application start.

Now, you need to add a button for each of the nine game spaces and assign them each a tag value so that your code will have a way to identify which space on the board each button represents. Drag nine round rect buttons to the view, and use the attribute inspector to change their type to Custom. Use the size inspector to place them in the locations specified in Table 9-1, and use the attribute inspector to assign them the listed tag value. Here's one shortcut to consider: Create one, set its size and attributes, and then start making copies.

*Table 9-1. Game Space Locations, Sizes, and Tags*

| Game Space | X | Y | Width | Height | Tag |
|------------|-----|-----|-------|--------|------|
| Upper Left | 24 | 122 | 86 | 98 | 1000 |
| Upper Middle | 120 | 122 | 86 | 98 | 1001 |
| Upper Right | 217 | 122 | 86 | 98 | 1002 |
| Middle Left | 24 | 230 | 86 | 98 | 1003 |
| Middle | 120 | 230 | 86 | 98 | 1004 |
| Middle Right | 217 | 230 | 86 | 98 | 1005 |
| Lower Left | 24 | 336 | 86 | 98 | 1006 |
| Lower Middle | 120 | 336 | 86 | 98 | 1007 |
| Lower Right | 217 | 336 | 86 | 98 | 1008 |

Okay, you've defined your interface, now let's connect it to your controller. While still in Interface Builder, change the Editor from Standard to Assistant view in the Toolbar. The Editor pane should split horizontally, with Interface Builder on the left, and the Source Code Editor, open to ViewController.h, on the right. You want to add Outlets for the New Game button and Label you placed on top of it. If you control-drag from the middle of the New Game button, the Outlet pop-up should automatically set the Type field to UILabel. That means you're adding an Outlet for the Label. Name it **feedbackLabel** and click Connect.

You need to add an Outlet for the New Game button you created as well, but it's essentially blocked by the feedbackLabel. Open the disclosure triangle on the bottom left of the Interface Builder Editor pane, and expand the Object Dock on the left (Figure 9-14). In the Objects group, underneath the View (if it's not open, open it), find the New Game button object named Button. Control-drag from Button to just below the feedbackLabel Outlet and create a new Outlet. Name it **gameButton** and click Connect.

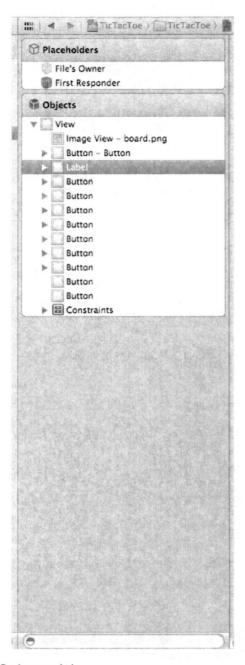

*Figure 9-14. Interface Builder Object Dock, expanded*

You need to connect an Action when the New Game button is pressed. Control-drag from the Button in the Object Dock to just above the @end in ViewController.h. Create a new Action named **gameButtonPressed** (Figure 9-15).

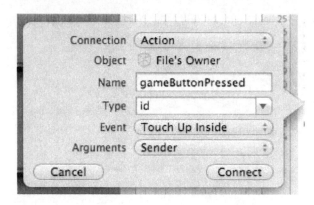

*Figure 9-15. Creating the gameButtonPressed Action*

Now you need to connect an Action to the nine game space buttons. You don't need to define Outlets for them though, just the actions. Control-drag from the upper-left button to the just below the Action, gameButtonPressed, you just created. Create a new Action named **gameSpacePressed**. Now, control-drag from every other game space button to the gameSpacePressed method declaration. The whole method declaration should highlight, and a pop-up label should appear called Connect Action. Make the connections.

Return to Standard Editor Mode and save the XIB.

# Creating the Packet Object

You need to define how you're going to have your game communicate with other instances of itself. You could use something simple like an array, where you know what each element represents; or a dictionary, and know what keys to use. Rather than doing that, you're going to define a specific class, Packet, that will be used to send information back and forth between the two nodes, via Game Kit. We alluded to this earlier when you created the enum PacketType in TicTacToe.h.

Select the TicTacToe group in the Navigator pane, and create a new Objective-C class with a class name of Packet, as a subclass of NSObject.

Once the files are created, select Packet.h and open it in the Editor. First, you need to add the TicTacToe.h header file.

```
#import "TicTacToe.h"
```

You need Packet to conform to the NSCoding protocol so that you can archive it into an NSData instance to send through the Game Kit session.

```
@interface Packet : NSObject <NSCoding>
```

The Packet class will have only three properties: one to identify the type of packet and two others to hold information that might need to be sent as part of that packet. The only other pieces of information you ever need to send are the results of a die roll and which space on the game board a player placed an X or O.

```objc
@property (nonatomic) PacketType type;
@property (nonatomic) NSUInteger dieRoll;
@property (nonatomic) BoardSpace space;
```

Then you need a handful of `init` methods for creating the different types of packets you will send.

```objc
- (id)initWithType:(PacketType)aPacketType dieRoll:(NSUInteger)aDieRoll space:(BoardSpace)
aBoardSpace;
- (id)initDieRollPacket;
- (id)initDieRollPacketWithRoll:(NSUInteger)aDieRoll;
- (id)initMovePacketWithSpace:(BoardSpace)aBoardSpace;
- (id)initAckPacketWithDieRoll:(NSUInteger)aDieRoll;
- (id)initResetPacket;
```

That's it. Save `Packet.h` and move over to `Packet.m`.

First, you implement the `init` methods you declared in the interface file.

```objc
- (id)initWithType:(PacketType)aPacketType dieRoll:(NSUInteger)aDieRoll space:(BoardSpace)
aBoardSpace
{
    self = [super init];
    if (self) {
        self.type = aPacketType;
        self.dieRoll = aDieRoll;
        self.space = aBoardSpace;
    }
    return self;
}

- (id)initDieRollPacket
{
    int roll = dieRoll();
    return [self initWithType:kPacketTypeDieRoll dieRoll:roll space:0];
}

- (id)initDieRollPacketWithRoll:(NSUInteger)aDieRoll
{
    return [self initWithType:kPacketTypeDieRoll dieRoll:aDieRoll space:0];
}

- (id)initMovePacketWithSpace:(BoardSpace)aBoardSpace
{
    return [self initWithType:kPacketTypeMove dieRoll:0 space:aBoardSpace];
}

- (id)initAckPacketWithDieRoll:(NSUInteger)aDieRoll
{
    return [self initWithType:kPacketTypeAck dieRoll:aDieRoll space:0];
}
```

```
- (id)initResetPacket
{
    return [self initWithType:kPacketTypeReset dieRoll:0 space:0];
}
```

Every other initializer is just a wrapped call to initWithType:dieRoll:space: with the BoardSpace being zero (undefined).

You also need to make Packet conform the NSCoding protocol, adding an encodeWithCoder: and initWithCoder: methods.

```
#pragma mark - NSCoder (Archiving) Methods

- (void)encodeWithCoder:(NSCoder *)coder
{
    [coder encodeInt:[self type] forKey:@"type"];
    [coder encodeInteger:[self dieRoll] forKey:@"dieRoll"];
    [coder encodeInt:[self space] forKey:@"space"];
}

- (id)initWithCoder:(NSCoder *)coder
{
    if (self = [super init]) {
        [self setType:[coder decodeIntForKey:@"type"]];
        [self setDieRoll:[coder decodeIntegerForKey:@"dieRoll"]];
        [self setSpace:[coder decodeIntForKey:@"space"]];
    }
    return self;
}
```

Packet is a fairly straightforward class. There shouldn't be anything in its implementation that you haven't seen before. Save Packet.m. Next, you'll write your view controller and finish up your application.

## Setting Up the View Controller Header

You declared two Outlets and two Actions to your view controller via Interface Builder. Now you'll complete your implementation of your view controller, including making it work with Game Kit. Open ViewController.h in the Editor.

The first thing you need to do is import the Game Kit and TicTacToe headers so that the compiler knows about the objects and methods from Game Kit and the constants you defined earlier.

```
#import <GameKit/GameKit.h>
#import "TicTacToe.h"
```

After that, you tell the compiler that there is a class called Packet. A @class declaration doesn't cause the compiler to look for the class header file—it's just a promise that a class really exists, so it's okay to declare it this way.

```
@class Packet;
```

Your controller class needs to conform to a few protocols. Your controller will be the delegate of the Game Kit peer picker and session. You'll also be using alert views to inform the user when there's a problem, so you conform your class to the three protocols used to define the delegate methods for each of these jobs.

```
@interface ViewController : UIViewController <GKPeerPickerControllerDelegate, GKSessionDelegate,
                                              UIAlertViewDelegate>
```

You need to add some instance variables (ivars). First, you'll add the braces

```
{
}
```

right after the `@interface` declaration. You need an ivar to keep track of the current game state.

```
GameState _state;
```

Because you don't know whether you will roll the die or receive your opponent's die roll first, you need variables to hold them both. Once you have both, you can compare them and start the game.

```
NSInteger _myDieRoll;
NSInteger _opponentDieRoll;
```

Once you know who goes first, you can store whether you're O or X in this instance variable.

```
PlayerPiece _playerPiece;
```

Finally, you have two more Booleans to keep track of whether you've received the opponent's die roll and whether your opponent has acknowledged receipt of yours. You don't want to begin the game until you have both die rolls and you know your opponent has both as well. When both of these are YES, you'll know it's time to start the actual game play.

```
BOOL _dieRollReceived;
BOOL _dieRollAcknowledged;
```

You already have two Outlet properties, `feedbackLabel` and `gameButton`, that you created via Interface Builder. You also need properties for the Game Kit session and to hold the peer identifier of the one connected node.

```
@property (nonatomic, strong) GKSession *session;
@property (nonatomic, strong) NSString *peerID;
```

You load both of the images representing the two game pieces when your view is loaded and keep a reference to them.

```
@property (nonatomic, strong) UIImage *xPieceImage;
@property (nonatomic, strong) UIImage *oPieceImage;
```

Finally, you declare a bunch of methods that you need in your game. We'll discuss the specific methods in more detail when you implement them in your controller. You add them before the two Actions, `gameButtonPressed:` and `gameSpacePressed:`, that you added via Interface Builder.

```
- (void)resetBoard;
- (void)startNewGame;
- (void)resetDieState;
- (void)startGame;
- (void)sendPacket:(Packet *)packet;
- (void)sendDieRoll;
- (void)checkForGameEnd;
```

That's all you need in this file. Save it and open ViewController.m.

### Implementing the Tic-Tac-Toe View Controller

There's a lot of code to add to ViewController.m, so let's get started.

First, you need to import the header file Packet.h.

```
#import "Packet.h"
```

Initialize the piece images and set your current die roll to kDiceNotRolled in viewDidLoad (after the call to super).

```
_myDieRoll = kDiceNotRolled;
self.oPieceImage = [UIImage imageNamed:@"O.png"];
self.xPieceImage = [UIImage imageNamed:@"X.png"];
```

At the bottom of your implementation file are the two Action methods. You need to implement them. First, edit gameButtonPressed:.

```
#pragma mark - Game-Specific Actions

- (IBAction)gameButtonPressed:(id)sender
{
    _dieRollReceived = NO;
    _dieRollAcknowledged = NO;

    _gameButton.hidden = YES;
    GKPeerPickerController *picker = [[GKPeerPickerController alloc] init];
    picker.delegate = self;
    [picker show];
}
```

This is the callback for when the user presses the New Game button. You set _dieRollReceived and _dieRollAcknowledged to NO, because you know neither of these things has happened yet for the new game. Next, you hide the button because you don't want your player to request a new game while you're looking for peers or playing the game. Then you create an instance of GKPeerPickerController, set self as the delegate, and show the peer picker controller. That's all you need to do to kick off the process of letting the user select another device to play against. The peer picker will handle everything, and then call delegate methods when you need to take some action.

Now, add the callback for when the user presses one of the game space buttons.

```
- (IBAction)gameSpacePressed:(id)sender
{
    UIButton *buttonPressed = sender;
    if (_state == kGameStateMyTurn && [buttonPressed imageForState:UIControlStateNormal] == nil) {
        [buttonPressed setImage:((_playerPiece == kPlayerPieceO) ? self.oPieceImage
                                                                 : self.xPieceImage)
                       forState:UIControlStateNormal];
        _feedbackLabel.text = NSLocalizedString(@"Opponent's Turn", @"Opponent's Turn");
        _state = kGameStateYourTurn;

        Packet *packet = [[Packet alloc] initMovePacketWithSpace:buttonPressed.tag];
        [self sendPacket:packet];

        [self checkForGameEnd];
    }
}
```

The first thing you do is cast sender to a UIButton. You know sender will always be an instance of UIButton, and doing this will prevent you from needing to cast sender every time you use it. Next, you check the game state. You don't want to let the user select a space if it's not that player's turn. You also check to make sure that the button pressed has no image already assigned. If it has an image assigned to it, then there's already either an X or an O in the space this button represents, and the user is not allowed to select it. If the space has no image assigned and it is your turn, you set the image to whichever image is appropriate for your player, based on whether you went first or second. The piece variable will get set later when you compare die rolls. You set the feedback label to inform the users that it's no longer their turn, and change the state to reflect that as well. You must inform the other device that you've made your move, so you create an instance of Packet, passing the tag value from the button that was pressed to identify which space the player selected. You use the method called sendPacket:, which you'll look at in a moment, to send the instance of Packet to the other node. At the last step, you check to see if the game is over. The method checkForGameEnd determines if either player won or if there are no spaces on the board, which would mean it's a tie.

Before you implement the methods you defined your interface file, you need think about the Protocol declarations you made. You defined ViewController to conform to the protocols GKPeerPickerControllerDelegate, GKSessionDelegate, and UIAlertViewDelegate. Let's tackle them in order, starting with GKPeerPickerControllerDelegate.

## Game Kit Peer-To-Peer Delegate Methods

When the Game Kit Peer-To-Peer Picker displays itself, it attempts to create a Game Kit session using the peerPickerController:sessionForConnectionType: method. So, you implement that first. Add this method to ViewController.m, before the @end.

```
#pragma mark - GameKit Peer Picker Delegate Methods

- (GKSession *)peerPickerController:(GKPeerPickerController *)picker
            sessionForConnectionType:(GKPeerPickerConnectionType)type
```

```
{
    GKSession *theSession;
    if (type == GKPeerPickerConnectionTypeNearby)
        theSession = [[GKSession alloc] initWithSessionID:kTicTacToeSessionID
                                              displayName:nil
                                              sessionMode:GKSessionModePeer];
    return theSession;
}
```

This is where the picker asks you to provide a session. Because you want all devices to both advertise and look for other devices on the network, you specify GKSessionModePeer for the session mode. Notice that you also use your constant kTicTacToeSessionID, which you defined in the TicTacToe.h header file to make sure that you connect only to other instances of TicTacToe. We discussed this earlier, so flip back a few pages if you need to review the code.

Add the method to handle the connection to the peer.

```
- (void)peerPickerController:(GKPeerPickerController *)picker
               didConnectPeer:(NSString *)thePeerID
                    toSession:(GKSession *)theSession
{
    self.peerID = thePeerID;
    self.session = theSession;
    self.session.delegate = self;
    [self.session setDataReceiveHandler:self withContext:NULL];
    [picker dismiss];
    picker.delegate = nil;
    [self startNewGame];
}
```

Because the peer picker is only for simple peer-to-peer games, once you're notified of a connection, you store the session and the peer identifier, and then dismiss the picker. After you've dismissed it, you call startNewGame to get things going.

Next, you add this delegate method to handle user cancels.

```
- (void)peerPickerControllerDidCancel:(GKPeerPickerController *)picker
{
    self.gameButton.hidden = NO;
}
```

You just unhide the New Game button.

## Game Kit Session Delegate Methods

Now, you need to implement the Game Kit session delegate methods. Start with the session:didFailWithError:.

```
#pragma mark - GameKit Session Delegate Methods

- (void)session:(GKSession *)theSession didFailWithError:(NSError *)error
```

```
{
    UIAlertView *alert = [[UIAlertView alloc]
                            initWithTitle:NSLocalizedString(@"Error Connecting!",
                                                            @"Error Connecting!")
                                  message:NSLocalizedString(@"Unable to establish the connection.",
                                                            @"Unable to establish the connection.")
                                 delegate:self
                        cancelButtonTitle:NSLocalizedString(@"Bummer", @"Bummer")
                        otherButtonTitles:nil];
    [alert show];
    theSession.available = NO;
    [theSession disconnectFromAllPeers];
    theSession.delegate = nil;
    [theSession setDataReceiveHandler:nil withContext:nil];
    self.session = nil;
}
```

When you get an error from the Game Kit session, you will display an alert view. Then you clean up the Game Kit session and close any connections. At the last step, you set the session property to nil.

Because you're using the peer picker, you don't need to handle choosing another node or connecting to it. But you must make sure that if the opponent disconnects, you don't keep trying to play that game. The following method is called any time a peer's state changes. If you're notified that another node has disconnected, you again inform the users through an alert view, and when they dismiss it, your alert view delegate method will reset the board.

```
- (void)session:(GKSession *)theSession peer:(NSString *)peerID
                            didChangeState:(GKPeerConnectionState)inState
{
    if (inState == GKPeerStateDisconnected) {
        _state = kGameStateInterrupted;
        UIAlertView *alert =
            [[UIAlertView alloc] initWithTitle:NSLocalizedString(@"Peer Disconnected!",
                                                                 @"Peer Disconnected!")
                message:NSLocalizedString(@"Your opponent has disconnected, or the connection has been lost",
                                          @"Your opponent has disconnected, or the connection has been lost")
                delegate:self
                cancelButtonTitle:NSLocalizedString(@"Bummer", @"Bummer")
                otherButtonTitles:nil];
        [alert show];
        theSession.available = NO;
        [theSession disconnectFromAllPeers];
        theSession.delegate = nil;
        [theSession setDataReceiveHandler:nil withContext:nil];
        self.session = nil;
    }
}
```

## Game Kit Data Receive Handler

Before you go on, there is one more method you need to implement: receiveData:fromPeer:
inSession:context:. This method is neither a Game Kit Peer Picker Controller delegate method
nor a Game Kit session delegate method. This method is invoked because you called the Game Kit
session method setDataReceiveHandler:withContext: when you created the session in
peerPickerController:didConnectPeer:toSession:.

```objc
- (void)receiveData:(NSData *)data
           fromPeer:(NSString *)peer
          inSession:(GKSession *)theSession
            context:(void *)context
{
    NSKeyedUnarchiver *unarchiver = [[NSKeyedUnarchiver alloc] initForReadingWithData:data];
    Packet *packet = [unarchiver decodeObjectForKey:kTicTacToeArchiveKey];

    switch (packet.type) {
        case kPacketTypeDieRoll: {
            _opponentDieRoll = packet.dieRoll;
            Packet *ack = [[Packet alloc] initAckPacketWithDieRoll:_opponentDieRoll];
            [self sendPacket:ack];
            _dieRollReceived = YES;
            break;
        }
        case kPacketTypeAck: {
            if (packet.dieRoll != _myDieRoll) {
                NSLog(@"Ack packet doesn't match yourDieRoll (mine: %d, send: %d",
                        packet.dieRoll, _myDieRoll);
            }
            _dieRollAcknowledged = YES;
            break;
        }
        case kPacketTypeMove: {
            UIButton *aButton = (UIButton *)[self.view viewWithTag:[packet space]];
            [aButton setImage:((_playerPiece == kPlayerPieceO) ? self.xPieceImage
                                                               : self.oPieceImage)
                     forState:UIControlStateNormal];
            _state = kGameStateMyTurn;
            _feedbackLabel.text = NSLocalizedString(@"Your Turn", @"Your Turn");
            [self checkForGameEnd];
            break;
        }
        case kPacketTypeReset: {
            if (_state == kGameStateDone)
                [self resetDieState];
            break;
        }
        default: {
            break;
        }
    }
}
```

```
    if (_dieRollReceived == YES && _dieRollAcknowledged == YES)
        [self startGame];
}
```

This is your data receive handler. This method is called whenever you receive a packet from the other node. The first thing you do is unarchive the data into a copy of the original Packet instance that was sent. Then you use a switch statement to take different actions based on the type of packet you received. If it's a die roll, you store your opponent's value, send back an acknowledgment of the value, and set dieRollReceived to YES. If you've received an acknowledgment, make sure the number returned is the same as the one you sent. This is just a consistency check. It shouldn't ever happen that the number is not the same. If it did, it might be an indication of a problem with your code, or it could mean that someone is cheating. Although we doubt that anyone would bother cheating at tic-tac-toe, people have been known to cheat in some networked games, so you might want to consider validating any information exchanged with peers. Here, you're just logging the inconsistency and moving on. In your real-world applications, you might want to take more serious action if you detect a data inconsistency of this nature.

If the packet is a move packet, which denotes that the other player chose a space, you update the appropriate space with an X or O image, and change the state and label to reflect the fact that it's now your player's turn. You also check to see if the other player's move resulted in the game being over. When you receive a reset packet, all you do is change the game state to kGameStateDone so that if a die roll comes in before you've realized the game is over, you don't discard it. If you received a packet, and both dieRollReceived and dieRollAcknowledged are now YES, you know it's time to start the game.

Finally, you add the alert view delegate method.

```
#pragma mark - UIAlertView Delegate Method

- (void)alertView:(UIAlertView *)alertView willDismissWithButtonIndex:(NSInteger)buttonIndex
{
    [self resetBoard];
    self.gameButton.hidden = NO;
}
```

You reset the game board and unhide the New Game button.

## Implementing Tic-Tac-Toe Methods

The method startNewGame is very simple. It just calls a method to reset the board, and then calls another method to roll the die and send the result to the other node. Both of these actions can happen at times other than game start. For example, you reset the board if the connection is lost, and you send the die roll if both nodes roll the same number.

```
#pragma mark - Instance Methods

- (void) startNewGame
{
    [self resetBoard];
    [self sendDieRoll];
}
```

Resetting the board involves removing the images from all of the buttons that represent spaces on the game board. Rather than declare nine outlets—one to point at each button—you just loop through the nine tag values and retrieve the buttons from your content view using viewWithTag:. You also blank out the feedback label. And you send a packet to the other node telling it that you're resetting. This is done just to make sure that if you follow up with another die roll, the other machine knows not to overwrite it. The fact that network communication happens asynchronously means you can't rely on things always happening in a specific order, as you can with a program running on only one device. It's possible that you'll send the die roll before the other device has finished determining who won. By sending a reset packet, you tell the other node that there may be another die roll coming for a new game, so make sure it's in the right state to accept that new roll. If you didn't do something like this, it might store your die roll, and then overwrite the rolled value when it resets its own board, which would cause a hang because the other device would then be waiting for a die roll that would never arrive. You also need to reset the player's game piece. Because the game is over, you don't know if the player will be X or O for the next game.

```
- (void)resetBoard
{
    for (int i = kUpperLeft; i <= kLowerRight; i++) {
        UIButton *aButton = (UIButton *)[self.view viewWithTag:i];
        [aButton setImage:nil forState:UIControlStateNormal];
    }
    self.feedbackLabel.text = @"";
    Packet *packet = [[Packet alloc] initResetPacket];
    [self sendPacket:packet];
    _playerPiece = kPlayerPieceUndecided;
}
```

Resetting the die state is nothing more than setting dieRollReceived and dieRollAcknowledged to NO, and setting both your die roll and the opponent's die roll to kDiceNotRolled.

```
- (void)resetDieState
{
    _dieRollReceived = NO;
    _dieRollAcknowledged = NO;
    _myDieRoll = kDiceNotRolled;
    _opponentDieRoll = kDiceNotRolled;
}
```

startGame is called once you have received your opponent's die roll and have also gotten an acknowledgment that it has received yours. First, you make sure that you don't have a tie. If you do have a tie, you kick off the die-rolling process again. Otherwise, you set state, piece, and the feedbackLabel's text based on whether it's your turn or the opponent's turn to go first. Then you reset the die state. It may seem odd to do it here, but at this point, you're finished with the die rolling for this game, and because you may receive your opponent's die roll before your code has realized the game is over, you reset now to ensure that the die rolls are not accidentally reused in the next game.

```
- (void)startGame
{
    if (_myDieRoll == _opponentDieRoll) {
        _myDieRoll = kDiceNotRolled;
```

```
        _opponentDieRoll = kDiceNotRolled;
        [self sendDieRoll];
        _playerPiece = kPlayerPieceUndecided;
    }
    else if (_myDieRoll < _opponentDieRoll) {
        _state = kGameStateYourTurn;
        _playerPiece = kPlayerPieceX;
        self.feedbackLabel.text = NSLocalizedString(@"Opponent's Turn", @"Opponent's Turn");

    }
    else {
        _state = kGameStateMyTurn;
        _playerPiece = kPlayerPieceO;
        self.feedbackLabel.text = NSLocalizedString(@"Your Turn", @"Your Turn");
    }
    [self resetDieState];
}
```

sendDieRoll: checks your die roll property. If you haven't rolled yet, it initializes a Packet that rolls the die for you and sets your die roll to the value of the packet's die roll. If you have a die roll, you initialize a Packer with that die roll value. Finally, you send the die roll Packet off to your opponent.

```
- (void)sendDieRoll
{
    Packet *rollPacket;
    _state = kGameStateRollingDice;
    if (_myDieRoll == kDiceNotRolled) {
        rollPacket = [[Packet alloc] initDieRollPacket];
        _myDieRoll = rollPacket.dieRoll;
    }
    else {
        rollPacket = [[Packet alloc] initDieRollPacketWithRoll:_myDieRoll];
    }
    [self sendPacket:rollPacket];

}
```

sendPacket: sends a packet to the other device (duh!). It takes an instance of Packet and archives it into an instance of NSData. It then uses the session's sendDataToAllPeers:withDataMode:error: method to send it across the wire—well, across the wireless, in this case.

```
- (void)sendPacket:(Packet *)packet
{
    NSMutableData *data = [[NSMutableData alloc] init];
    NSKeyedArchiver *archiver = [[NSKeyedArchiver alloc] initForWritingWithMutableData:data];
    [archiver encodeObject:packet forKey:kTicTacToeArchiveKey];
    [archiver finishEncoding];
```

```
    NSError *error = nil;
    if (![self.session sendDataToAllPeers:data withDataMode:GKSendDataReliable error:&error]) {
        // You would some do real error handling
        NSLog(@"Error sending data: %@", [error localizedDescription]);
    }
}
```

The checkForGameEnd method just checks all nine spaces to see whether they have X or O in them, and then looks for three in a row. It does this by first declaring a variable called moves to keep track of how many moves have happened. This is how it will tell if there's a tie. If there have been nine moves, and no one has won, then there are no available spaces left on the board, so it's a tie. Next, you declare an array of nine UIImage pointers. You're going to pull the images out of the nine buttons representing spaces on the board and put them in this array to make it easier to check if a player won. If you find three in a row, you'll store one of the three images in this variable so you know which player won the game. Next, you loop through the buttons by tag, as you did in the resetBoard method earlier, storing the images from the buttons in the array you declared earlier. The next big chunk of code just checks to see if there are three of the same images in a row anywhere. If it finds three in a row, it stores one of the three images in winningImage. When it completes the check, it will know which player, if any, has won. If there wasn't a winner, then you check to see if any spaces are left on the board by looking at moves. If no spaces remain, then you know the game is over, and the cat won.

> **Note**    In tic-tac-toe, a tie is also called a "cat's game." The expression "the cat won" refers to a tie.

If any of the preceding code set the state to kGameStateDone, then you use performSelector:withObject:afterDelay: to start a new game after the user has had time to read who won.

```
- (void)checkForGameEnd
{
    NSInteger moves = 0;

    UIImage     *currentButtonImages[9];
    UIImage     *winningImage = nil;

    for (int i = kUpperLeft; i <= kLowerRight; i++) {
        UIButton *oneButton = (UIButton *)[self.view viewWithTag:i];
        if ([oneButton imageForState:UIControlStateNormal])
            moves++;
        currentButtonImages[i - kUpperLeft] = [oneButton imageForState:UIControlStateNormal];
    }

    // Top Row
    if (currentButtonImages[0] == currentButtonImages[1]
        && currentButtonImages[0] == currentButtonImages[2]
        && currentButtonImages[0] != nil)
        winningImage = currentButtonImages[0];
```

```
// Middle Row
else if (currentButtonImages[3] == currentButtonImages[4]
        && currentButtonImages[3] == currentButtonImages[5]
        && currentButtonImages[3] != nil)
    winningImage = currentButtonImages[3];

// Bottom Row
else if (currentButtonImages[6] == currentButtonImages[7]
        && currentButtonImages[6] == currentButtonImages[8]
        && currentButtonImages[6] != nil)
    winningImage = currentButtonImages[6];

// Left Column
else if (currentButtonImages[0] == currentButtonImages[3]
        && currentButtonImages[0] == currentButtonImages[6]
        && currentButtonImages[0] != nil)
    winningImage = currentButtonImages[0];

// Middle Column
else if (currentButtonImages[1] == currentButtonImages[4]
        && currentButtonImages[1] == currentButtonImages[7]
        && currentButtonImages[1] != nil)
    winningImage = currentButtonImages[1];

// Right Column
else if (currentButtonImages[2] == currentButtonImages[5]
        && currentButtonImages[2] == currentButtonImages[8]
        && currentButtonImages[2] != nil)
    winningImage = currentButtonImages[2];

// Diagonal starting top left
else if (currentButtonImages[0] == currentButtonImages[4]
        && currentButtonImages[0] == currentButtonImages[8]
        && currentButtonImages[0] != nil)
    winningImage = currentButtonImages[0];

// Diagonal starting top right
else if (currentButtonImages[2] == currentButtonImages[4]
        && currentButtonImages[2] == currentButtonImages[6]
        && currentButtonImages[2] != nil)
    winningImage = currentButtonImages[2];

if (winningImage == self.xPieceImage) {
    if (_playerPiece == kPlayerPieceX) {
        self.feedbackLabel.text = NSLocalizedString(@"You Won!", @"You Won!");
        _state = kGameStateDone;
    }
    else {
        self.feedbackLabel.text = NSLocalizedString(@"Opponent Won!", @"Opponent Won!");
        _state = kGameStateDone;
    }
}
```

```
    else if (winningImage == self.oPieceImage) {
        if (_playerPiece == kPlayerPieceO){
            self.feedbackLabel.text = NSLocalizedString(@"You Won!", @"You Won!");
            _state = kGameStateDone;
        }
        else {
            self.feedbackLabel.text = NSLocalizedString(@"Opponent Won!", @"Opponent Won!");
            _state = kGameStateDone;
        }

    }
    else {
        if (moves >= 9) {
            self.feedbackLabel.text = NSLocalizedString(@"Cat Wins!", @"Cat Wins!");
            _state = kGameStateDone;
        }
    }

    if (_state == kGameStateDone)
        [self performSelector:@selector(startNewGame) withObject:nil afterDelay:3.0];
}
```

Hold on. You're not done yet. You need to back up and adjust the didReceiveMemoryWarning method. You need to disconnect from your peers.

```
self.session.available = NO;
[self.session disconnectFromAllPeers];
[self.session setDataReceiveHandler: nil withContext: nil];
self.session.delegate = nil;
```

# Trying It Out

Unlike most of the applications we've written together, this tic-tac-toe game can't be used in the Simulator. It will run there, but the Simulator does not support Bluetooth connections. This app currently relies on Bluetooth connections to work, since you're using Game Kit and the peer picker. As a result, you need to have two physical devices, and neither of them can be a first-generation device, because the original iPhone and the first-generation iPod touch do not work with Game Kit's peer picker. It also means that you need to have two devices provisioned for development. You should be able to connect to iOS devices to your computer at the same time. Xcode will display a drop-down menu in the Debug area to select which device to view.

If you do experience problems running Xcode with two devices, you need to build and run on one device, quit, unplug that device, and then plug in the other device and do the same thing. Once you've done that, you will have the application on both devices. You can run it on both devices, or you can launch it from Xcode on one device, so you can debug and read the console feedback

> **Note** Detailed instructions for installing applications on a device are available at http://developer. apple.com/ios in the developer portal, which is available only to paid iPhone SDK members.

You should be aware that debugging—or even running from Xcode without debugging—will slow down the program running on the connected iOS device, and this can have an effect on network communications. Underneath the hood, all of the data transmissions back and forth between the two devices check for acknowledgments and have a timeout period. If they don't receive a response in a certain amount of time, they will disconnect. So, if you set a breakpoint, chances are that you will break the connection between the two devices when it reaches the breakpoint. This can make figuring out problems in your Game Kit application tedious. You often will need to use alternatives to breakpoints, like `NSLog()` or breakpoint actions, so you don't break the network connection between the devices. We'll talk more about debugging in Chapter 15.

# Game On!

Another long chapter under your belt, and you should now have a pretty firm understanding of Game Kit networking. You saw how to use the peer picker to let your user select another iPhone or iPod touch to which to connect. You saw how to send data by archiving objects, and you got a little taste of the complexity that is introduced to your application when you start adding in network multiuser functionality.

# Chapter 10

# Map Kit

iPhones have always had a way to determine where in the world they are. Even though the original iPhone didn't have GPS, it did have a Maps application and was able to represent its approximate location on the map using cell phone triangulation or by looking up its WiFi IP address in a database of known locations. In the beginning of iOS development, there was no way to leverage this functionality within your own applications. It was possible to launch the Maps application to show a specific location or route, but it wasn't possible, using only Apple-provided APIs, to show map data without leaving your application.

That changed with the Map Kit. Applications now have the ability to show maps, including the user's current location, and even drop pins and show annotations on those maps. Map Kit's functionality isn't limited to just showing maps, either. It includes a feature called *reverse geocoding*, which allows you to take a set of specific coordinates and turn them into a physical address. Your application can use those coordinates to find out not just where the person is located but, frequently, the actual address associated with that location. You can't always get down to the street address, but you can almost always get the city and state or province no matter where in the world your user is. In this chapter, we're going to look at the basics of adding Map Kit functionality to any application.

> **Note** The application you build in this chapter will run just fine in the iPhone Simulator; however, the Simulator won't report your actual location. Instead, it returns the address of Apple's San Francisco Store at Stockton Street in San Francisco, California. You can change the location the Simulator uses via the Location Simulator on the Debug pane jump bar in Xcode.

## This Chapter's Application

This chapter's application will start by showing a map of North America (Figure 10-1). Other than the map, your interface will be empty except for a single button with the imaginative title of Go. When the button is pressed, the application will determine your current location, zoom the map to show that location, and drop a pin to mark the location (Figure 10-2).

*Figure 10-1. The MapMe application will start out showing a map of the United States*

*Figure 10-2. After determining the current location, the map will zoom in to that location and annotate it*

You will then use Map Kit's reverse geocoder to determine the address of your current location and you'll add an annotation to the map to display the specifics of that location.

Despite its simplicity, this application leverages most of the basic Map Kit functionality. Before you start building your project, let's explore Map Kit and see what makes it tick.

# Overview and Terminology

Although Map Kit is not particularly complex, it can be a bit confusing. Let's start with a high-level view and nail down the terminology, then you can dig down into the individual components.

To display map-related data, you add a map view to one of your application's views. Map views can have a delegate, and that delegate is usually the controller class responsible for the view in which the map view resides. That's the approach you'll use for this chapter's application. Your application will have a single view and a single view controller. That single view will contain a map view, along with a few other items, and your single view controller will be the map view's delegate.

Map views keep track of locations of interest using a collection of *annotations*. Any time you see an icon on a map, whether it's a pin, a dot, or anything else, it's an annotation. When an annotation is in the part of the map that's being shown, the map view asks its delegate to provide a view for that annotation (called an *annotation view*) that the map view will draw at the specific location on the map.

Annotations are selectable, and a selected annotation will display a *callout*, which is a small view that floats above the map like the You are Here! view shown in Figure 10-2. If the user taps an annotation view and that annotation view is selectable, the map view will display the callout associated with that view.

# The Map View

The core element of the Map Kit framework is the *map view* represented by the class `MKMapView`. The map view takes care of drawing the maps and responding to user input. Users can use all the gestures they're accustomed to, including a pinch in or out to do a controlled zoom, a double-tap to zoom in, or a two-finger double tap to zoom out. You can add a map view to your interface and configure it using Interface Builder. Like many iOS controls, much of the work of managing the map view is done by the map view's delegate.

# Map Types

Map views are capable of displaying maps in several different ways. They can display the map as a series of lines and symbols that represent the roadways and other landmarks in the area being shown. This is the default display, and it's known as the *standard map type*. You can also display the map using satellite images by specifying the *satellite map type*, or you can use what's called the *hybrid map type* where the lines representing roadways and landmarks from the standard type are superimposed on top of the satellite imagery of the satellite type. You can see an example of the default map type in Figure 10-2. Figure 10-3 shows the satellite map type and Figure 10-4 shows the hybrid map type.

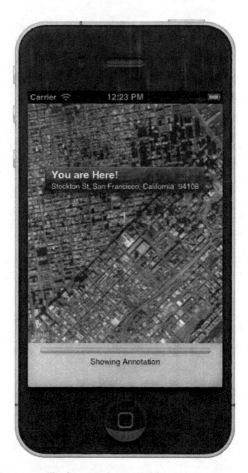

*Figure 10-3.* *The satellite map type shows satellite imagery instead of lines and symbols*

*Figure 10-4. The hybrid type overlays the lines and symbols of the default type on top of the imagery from the satellite type*

You can set the map type in Interface Builder or by setting the map view's `mapType` property to one of the following:

```
mapView.mapType = MKMapTypeStandard;
mapView.mapType = MKMapTypeSatellite;
mapView.mapType = MKMapTypeHybrid;
```

## User Location

Map views will, if configured to do so, use Core Location to keep track of the user's location and display it on the map using a blue dot, much like the way the Maps application does. You won't be using that functionality in this chapter's application, but you can turn it on by setting the map view's `showsUserLocation` property to YES, like so:

```
mapView.showsUserLocation = YES;
```

If the map is tracking the user's location, you can determine if their present location is visible in the map view by using the read-only property userLocationVisible. If the user's current location is being displayed in the map view, userLocationVisible will return YES.

You can get the specific coordinates of the user's present location from the map view by first setting showsUserLocation to YES and then accessing the userLocation property. This property returns an instance of MKUserLocation. MKUserLocation is an object and has a property called location, which itself is a CLLocation object. A CLLocation contains a property called coordinate that points to a set of coordinates. All this means you can get the actual coordinates from the MKUserLocation object, like so:

```
CLLocationCoordinate2D coords = mapView.userLocation.location.coordinate;
```

## Coordinate Regions

A map view wouldn't be much good if you couldn't tell it what to display or find out what part of the world it's currently showing. With map views, the key to being able to do those tasks is the MKCoordinateRegion, a struct that contains two pieces of data that together define the portion of the map to be shown in a map view.

The first member of MKCoordinateRegion is called center. This is another struct of type CLLocationCoordinate2D, which you may remember from the chapter on Core Location in *Beginning iOS 6 Development* by Jack Nutting, David Mark, and Jeff LaMarche (Apress, 2013). A CLLocationCoordinate2D contains two floating point values, a latitude and longitude, and is used to represent a single spot on the globe. In the context of a coordinate region, that spot on the globe is the spot that represents the center of the map view.

The second member of MKCoordinateRegion is called span, and it's a struct of type MKCoordinateSpan. The MKCoordinateSpan struct has two members called latitudeDelta and longitudeDelta. These two numbers are used to set the zoom level of the map by identifying how much of the area around center should be displayed. These values represent that distance in degrees latitude and longitude. If latitudeDelta and longitudeDelta are small numbers, the map will be zoomed in very close; if they are large, the map will be zoomed out and show a much larger area.

Figure 10-5 shows the makeup of the MKCoordinateRegion struct.

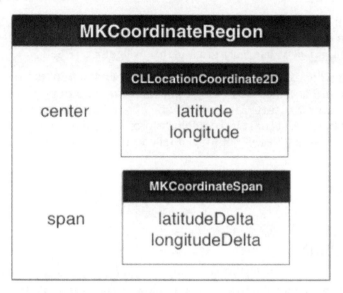

*Figure 10-5.  The MKCoordinateRegion represented graphically. It contains two members, both of which are, in turn, structs that own two members*

If you look back at Figure 10-2, the point of the pin you can see is at the coordinates that were passed in `MKCoordinateRegion.center`. The distance from the top of the map to the bottom of the map was passed in, represented as degrees latitude, using the `MKCoordinateRegion.span.latitudeDelta`. Similarly, the distance from the left side of the map to the right side of the map was passed in, represented as degrees longitude, as the `MKCoordinateRegion.span.longitudeDelta`.

**Tip**   If you have trouble remembering which lines are latitude and which are longitude, here's a tip from our third grade geography teacher, Mrs. Krabappel (pronounced kruh-bopple). Latitude sounds like altitude, so latitude tells you how high on the globe you are. The equator is a line of latitude. And the Prime Meridian is a line of longitude. Thanks, Mrs. Krabappel!

There are two challenges that this approach presents to the programmer. First, who thinks in degrees latitude or longitude? Although degrees latitude represent roughly the same distance everywhere in the world, degrees longitude vary greatly in the amount of distance they represent as you move from the pole to the equator, so calculating the degrees longitude isn't as straightforward.

The second challenge is that a map view has a specific width-to-height ratio (called an *aspect ratio*), and the `latitudeDelta` and `longitudeDelta` you specify must represent an area with that same aspect ratio. Fortunately, Apple provides tools for dealing with both of these issues.

## Converting Degrees to Distance

Each degree of latitude represents approximately 69 miles, or about 111 kilometers, no matter where you are. This makes determining the number to pass in as the latitudeDelta of an MKCoordinateSpan fairly easy to calculate. You can just divide the lateral distance you want to display by 69 if you're using miles or 111 if you're using kilometers.

> **Note**  Since the Earth isn't a perfect sphere (technically speaking, it's close to being an oblate spheroid), there actually is some variation between the amount of distance that one degree latitude represents, but it's not enough variation to bother factoring into this calculation, since it's only about a one degree variation from pole to equator. At the equator, one degree of latitude equals 69.046767 miles or 111.12 kilometers, and the number gets a little smaller as you move toward the poles. We chose 69 and 111 because they're nice round numbers that are within 1% of the actual distance pretty much everywhere.

The distance represented by one degree longitude, however, is not quite so easy to calculate. To do the same calculation for longitude, you have to take the latitude into account, because the distance represented by one degree longitude depends on where you are in relation to the equator. To calculate the distance represented by degrees longitude, you have to perform some gnarly math. Fortunately, Apple has done the gnarly math for you and provides a method called MKCoordinateRegionMakeWithDistance() that you can use to create a region. You provide coordinates to act as the center, along with the distance in meters for the latitudinal and longitudinal span. The function will look at the latitude in the coordinates provided and calculate both delta values for you in degrees. Here is how you might create a region to show one kilometer on each side of a specific location represented by a CLLocationCoordinate2D called center:

```
MKCoordinateRegion viewRegion = MKCoordinateRegionMakeWithDistance(center, 2000, 2000);
```

To show a kilometer on each side of center, you must specify 2000 meters total for each span: 1000 to the left plus 1000 to the right and 1000 to the top plus 1000 to the bottom. After this call, viewRegion will contain a properly formatted MKCoordinateRegion that's almost ready for use. All that's left is taking care of the aspect ratio problem.

---

### THE GNARLY MATH

The math to calculate the distance of one degree longitude really isn't that gnarly, so we thought we'd show those of you who are interested what the man behind the curtain is doing. To calculate the distance for one degree longitude at a given latitude, the calculation is

$$\frac{\pi}{180°} \times \text{radius of the Earth} \times \cos(\text{lat}°)$$

If Apple didn't provide a function for us, you could create a couple of macros that would accomplish the same thing just by following this formula. The radius of the earth is roughly 3963.1676 miles, or 6378.1 kilometers. So, to calculate the distance for one degree of longitude at a specific latitude contained in the variable lat, you would do this:

```
double longitudeMiles = ((M_PI/180.0) × 3963.1676 × cos(latitude));
```

You can do the same calculation to determine the distance of one degree longitude in kilometers, like so:

```
double longitudeKilometers = ((M_PI/180.0) × 6378.1 × cos(latitude));
```

## Accommodating Aspect Ratio

In the previous section we showed how to create a span that showed one kilometer on each side of a given location. However, unless the map view is perfectly square, there's no way that the view can show exactly one kilometer on each of the four sides of center. If the map view is wider than it is tall, the longitudeDelta will need to be larger than the latitudeDelta. If the map view is taller than it is wide, the opposite is true.

The MKMapView class has an instance method that will adjust a coordinate region to match the map view's aspect ratio. That method is called regionThatFits:. To use it, you just pass in the coordinate region you created, and it will return a new coordinate region that is adjusted to the map view's aspect ratio. Here's how to use it:

```
MKCoordinateRegion adjustedRegion = [mapView regionThatFits:viewRegion];
```

## Setting the Region to Display

Once you've created a coordinate region, you can tell a map view to display that region by calling the method setRegion:animated:. If you pass YES for the second parameter, the map view will zoom, shift, or otherwise animate the view from its current location to its new location. Here is an example that creates a coordinate region, adjusts it to the map views's aspect ratio, and then tells the map view to display that region:

```
MKCoordinateRegion viewRegion = MKCoordinateRegionMakeWithDistance(center, 2000, 2000);
MKCoordinateRegion adjustedRegion = [mapView regionThatFits:viewRegion];
[mapView setRegion:adjustedRegion animated:YES];
```

## The Map View Delegate

As mentioned earlier, map views can have delegates. Map views, unlike table views and pickers, can function without a delegate. On a map view delegate, there are a number of methods you can implement if you need to be notified about certain map-related tasks. They allow you, for example, to get notified when the user changes the part of the map they're looking at, either by dragging to reveal a new section of the map or by zooming to reveal a smaller or larger area. You can also get notified when the map view loads new map data from the server or when the map view fails to do so. The map view delegate methods are contained in the MKMapViewDelegate protocol, and any class that is used as a map view delegate should conform to that protocol.

## Map Loading Delegate Methods

With iOS 6, the Map Kit framework switched from Google Maps to an Apple-provided service to do its job. It doesn't store any map data locally except for temporary caches. Whenever the map view needs to go to Apple's servers to retrieve new map data, it will call the delegate method `mapViewWillStartLoadingMap:`, and when it has successfully retrieved the map data it needs, it will call the delegate method `mapViewDidFinishLoadingMap:`. If you have any application-specific processing that needs to happen at either time, you can implement the appropriate method on the map view's delegate.

If Map Kit encounters an error loading map data from the server, it will call the method `mapViewDidFailLoadingMap:withError:` on its delegate. At the very least, you should implement this delegate method and inform your user of the problem so they aren't sitting there waiting for an update that will never come. Here's a very simple implementation of that method that just shows an alert and lets the user know that something went wrong:

```
- (void)mapViewDidFailLoadingMap:(MKMapView *)mapView
                        withError:(NSError *)error
{
    UIAlertView *alert = [[UIAlertView alloc]
        initWithTitle:NSLocalizedString(@"Error loading map",
            @"Error loading map")
        message:[error localizedDescription]
        delegate:nil
        cancelButtonTitle:NSLocalizedString(@"Okay", @"Okay")
        otherButtonTitles:nil];
    [alert show];
}
```

## Region Change Delegate Methods

If your map view is enabled, the user will be able to interact with it using the standard iPhone gestures, like drag, pinch in, pinch out, and double-tap. Doing so will change the region being displayed in the view. There are two delegate methods that will get called whenever this happens, if the map view's delegate implements those methods. As the gesture starts, the delegate method `mapView:regionWillChangeAnimated:` gets called. When the gesture stops, the method `mapView:regionDidChangeAnimated:` gets called. You would implement these if you had functionality that needed to happen while the view region was changing or after it had finished changing.

---

### DETERMINING IF COORDINATES ARE VISIBLE

---

One task that you may need to do quite often in the region change delegate methods is to determine if a particular set of coordinates are currently visible on screen. For annotations, and for the user's current location (if it is being tracked), the map view will take care of figuring that out for you. There will still be times, however, when you need to know if a particular set of coordinates is currently within the map view's displayed region.

Here's how you can determine that:

```
CLLocationDegrees leftDegrees = mapView.region.center.longitude -
                                (mapView.region.span.longitudeDelta / 2.0);
CLLocationDegrees rightDegrees = mapView.region.center.longitude +
                                (mapView.region.span.longitudeDelta / 2.0);
CLLocationDegrees bottomDegrees = mapView.region.center.latitude -
                                (mapView.region.span.latitudeDelta / 2.0);
CLLocationDegrees topDegrees = self.region.center.latitude +
                                (mapView.region.span.latitudeDelta / 2.0);

if (leftDegrees > rightDegrees) { // Int'l Date Line in View
    leftDegrees = -180.0 - leftDegrees;
    if (coords.longitude > 0) // coords to West of Date Line
        coords.longitude = -180.0 - coords.longitude;
}

If (leftDegrees <= coords.longitude && coords.longitude <= rightDegrees &&
    bottomDegrees <= coords.latitude && coords.latitude <= topDegrees) {
    // Coordinates are being displayed
}
```

Before moving on to the rest of the map view delegate methods, we need to discuss the topic of annotations.

# Annotations

Map views offer the ability to tag a specific location with a set of supplementary information. That information, along with its graphic representation on the map, is called an *annotation*. The pin you drop in the application you're going to write (see Figure 10-2) is a form of annotation. The annotation is composed of two components, the *annotation object* and an *annotation view*. The map view will keep track of its annotations and will call out to its delegate when it needs to display any of its annotations.

## The Annotation Object

Every annotation must have an annotation object, which is almost always going to be a custom class that you write and that conforms to the protocol MKAnnotation. An annotation object is typically a fairly standard data model object whose job it is to hold whatever data is relevant to the annotation in question. The annotation object has to respond to two methods and implement a single property. The two methods that an annotation object must implement are called title and subtitle, and they are the information that will be displayed in the annotation's callout, the little floating view that pops up when the annotation is selected. Back in Figure 10-4, you can see the title and subtitle displayed in the callout. In that instance, the annotation object returned a title of You are Here! and a subtitle of Stockton St, San Francisco, CA  94108.

An annotation object must also have a property called coordinate that returns a CLLocationCoordinate2D specifying where in the world (geographically speaking) the annotation should be placed. The map view will use that location to determine where to draw the annotation.

# The Annotation View

As we said before, when a map view needs to display any of its annotations, it will call out to its delegate to retrieve an annotation view for that annotation. It does this using the method mapView:viewForAnnotation:, which needs to return an MKAnnotationView or a subclass of MKAnnotationView. The annotation view is the object that gets displayed on the map, not the floating window that gets displayed when the annotation is selected. In Figure 10-4, the annotation view is the pin in the center of the window. It's a pin because you're using a provided subclass of MKAnnotationView called MKPinAnnotationView, which is designed to draw a red, green, or purple pushpin. It includes some additional functionality that MKAnnotationView doesn't have, such as the pin drop animation.

You can subclass MKAnnotationView and implement your own drawRect: method if you have advanced drawing needs for your annotation view. Subclassing MKAnnotationView is often unnecessary, however, because you can create an instance of MKAnnotationView and set its image property to whatever image you want. This opens up a whole world of possibilities without having to ever subclass or add subviews to MKAnnotationView (see Figure 10-6).

*Figure 10-6. By setting the image property of an MKAnnotationView, you can display just about anything on the map. In this example, we've replaced the pin with a surprised cat because that's the way we roll*

# Adding and Removing Annotations

The map view keeps track of all of its annotations, so adding an annotation to the map is simply a matter of calling the map view's addAnnotation: method and providing an object that conforms to the MKAnnotation protocol.

```
[mapView addAnnotation:annotation];
```

You can also add multiple annotations by providing an array of annotations, using the method addAnnotations:.

```
[mapView addAnnotations:[NSArray arrayWithObjects:annotation1, annotation2, nil]];
```

You can remove annotations by using either the removeAnnotation: method and passing in a single annotation to be removed or by calling removeAnnotations: and passing in an array containing multiple annotations to be removed. All the map view's annotations are accessible using a property called annotations, so if you wanted to remove all annotations from the view, you could to this:

```
[mapView removeAnnotations:mapView.annotations];
```

# Selecting Annotations

At any given time, one and only one annotation can be selected. The selected annotation will usually display a *callout*, which is that floating bubble or other view that gives more detailed information about the annotation. The default callout shows the title and subtitle from the annotation. However, you can actually customize the callout, which is just an instance of UIView. We won't be providing custom callout views in this chapter's application, but the process is very similar to customizing table view cells the way we did in Chapter 8 of *Beginning iOS 6 Development*. For more information on customizing a callout, check the documentation for MKAnnotationView.

> **Note**  Although only a single annotation can currently be selected, MKMapView actually uses an instance of NSArray to keep track of the selected annotations. This may be an indication that at some point in the future map views will support selecting multiple annotations at once. Currently, if you provide a selectedAnnotations array with more than one annotation, only the first object in that array will be selected.

If the user taps an annotation's image (the push pin in Figure 10-4 or the shocked cat in Figure 10-6), it selects that annotation. You can also select an annotation programmatically using the method selectAnnotation:animated: and deselect an annotation programmatically using deselectAnnotation:animated:, passing in the annotation you want to select or deselect. If you pass YES to the second parameter, it will animate the appearance or disappearance of the callout.

# Providing the Map View with Annotation Views

Map views ask their delegate for the annotation view that corresponds to a particular annotation using a delegate method called `mapView:viewForAnnotation:`. This method is called anytime an annotation moves into the map view's displayed region.

Very much like the way table view cells work, annotation views are dequeued but not deallocated when they scroll off of the screen. Implementations of `mapView:viewForAnnotation:` should ask the map view if there are any dequeued annotation views before allocating a new one. That means that `mapView:viewForAnnotation:` is going to look a fair amount like the many `tableView:cellForRow AtIndexPath:` methods you've written. Here's an example that creates an annotation view, sets its image property to display a custom image, and returns it:

```
- (MKAnnotationView *) mapView:(MKMapView *)theMapView viewForAnnotation:(id <MKAnnotation>)
annotation
{
    static NSString *placemarkIdentifier = @"my annotation identifier";
    if ([annotation isKindOfClass:[MyAnnotation class]]) {
        MKAnnotationView *annotationView =
            [theMapView dequeueReusableAnnotationViewWithIdentifier:placemarkIdentifier];
        if (annotationView == nil)  {
            annotationView = [[MKAnnotationView alloc] initWithAnnotation:annotation
                reuseIdentifier:placemarkIdentifier];
            annotationView.image = [UIImage imageNamed:@"shocked_cat.png"];
        }
        else
            annotationView.annotation = annotation;
        return annotationView;
    }
    return nil;
}
```

A few things to notice here. First, notice that you check the `annotation` class to make sure it's an annotation you know about. The Map View delegate gets notified about all annotations, not just the custom one. Earlier, we talked about the `MKUserLocation` object that encapsulated the user's location. Well, that's an annotation also, and when you turn on user tracking for a map, your delegate method gets called whenever the user location needs to be displayed. You could provide your own annotation view for that, but if you return nil, the map view will use the default annotation view for it. Generally speaking, for any annotation you don't recognize, your method should return nil and the map view will probably handle it correctly.

Notice there is an identifier value called `placemarkIdentifier`. This allows you to make sure you're dequeing the right kind of annotation view. You're not limited to using only one type of annotation view for all of your map's annotations, and the identifier is the way you tell which ones are used for what.

If you did dequeue an annotation view, it's important that you set its annotation property to the annotation that was passed in (annotation in the preceding example). The dequeued annotation view is almost certainly linked to some annotation, and not necessarily the one it should be linked to.

# Geocoding and Reverse Geocoding

A big feature of Core Location is *geocoding*. Geocoding is the ability to convert from a coordinate (specified as longitude and latitude) and a user-friendly representation of that coordinate. Taking a user-friendly location description (i.e., an address) and converting it to longitude and latitude is called *forward geocoding*. *Reverse geocoding* is converting a longitude and latitude into a user-friendly location description.

Geocoding is handled in Core Location by the CLGeocoder class. CLGeocoder works asynchronously in the background, querying the appropriate service. In the case of forward geocoding, CLGeocoder uses the built-in GPS functionality of your iPhone. For reverse geocoding, CLGeocoder queries a large database of coordinate data (in this case, it's Apple's database).

In almost all locations, reverse geocoding will be able to tell you the country and state or province that you're in. The more densely populated the area, the more information you're likely to get. If you're downtown in a large city, you might very well retrieve the street address of the building in which you are located. In most cities and towns, reverse geocoding will, at the very least, get you the name of the street you are on. The tricky thing is that you never know for sure what level of detail you're going to get back.

For this chapter's application, you're going to use the reverse geocoding functionality of CLGeocoder. To perform reverse geocoding, you start by creating an instance of CLGeocoder. You then call reverseGeocodeLocation:completionHandler: to perform the geocoding. The completionHandler: argument is a CLGeocodeCompletionHandler type, which is a *block*. A block is an anonymous inline function that encapsulates the lexical scope from where it is executed. For reverseGeocodeLocation:completionHandler:, the completionHandler: block is executed regardless of a successful or failed reverse geocoding attempt.

```
CLGeocoder *geocoder = [[CLGeocoder alloc] init];
[geocoder reverseGeocodeLocation:location completionHandler:^(NSArray *placemarks, NSError *error) {
    // process the location or errors
    ...
}
```

> **Note**    You can learn more about blocks from Apple. Their documentation on blocks starts here:
> https://developer.apple.com/library/ios/#featuredarticles/Short_Practical_
> Guide_Blocks/_index.html

If the reverse geocoding succeeds, the completion handler will be invoked with the placemarks array being populated. It should be an array with only one object, of type CLPlacemark. If there was an error during the reverse geocoding or the request was cancelled, then the placemarks array will be nil. In that case, the completion handler will receive an NSError object, detailing the failure.

Table 10-1 maps CLPlacemark's terminology to terms with which you might be more familiar.

Table 10-1. *CLPlacement Property Definitions*

| CLPlacemark Property | Meaning |
| --- | --- |
| Thoroughfare | Street address. First line if multiple lines. |
| subThoroughfare | Street address, second line (e.g., apartment or unit number, box number) |
| Locality | City |
| SubLocality | This might contain a neighborhood or landmark name, though it's often nil |
| administrativeArea | State, province, territory, or other similar unit |
| dministrativeArea | County |
| postalCode | ZIP code |
| Country | Country |
| countryCode | Two-digit ISO country code (see: http://en.wikipedia.org/wiki/ISO_3166-1_alpha-2) |

You know what? That's enough talking about Map Kit. Let's start actually using it.

# Building the MapMe Application

Let's build an application that shows some of the basic features of the Map Kit. Start by creating a new project in Xcode using the Single View Application template. Call the new project **MapMe**. You won't be using storyboards, so only the "Use Automatic Reference Counting" checkbox should be checked.

## Linking the Map Kit and Core Location Frameworks

Before you do any coding, you need to add the Core Location and Map Kit frameworks. Navigate to the Build Phases tab for the MapMe target in the Project Editor. Expand the Link Binary With Libraries (3 items). Click the + on the lower left. Select CoreLocation.framework and MapKit.framework (remember, you can ⌘-click to select multiple frameworks). Click the Add button. The two frameworks should appear in the Navigator pane. You can clean things up a little bit by dragging the CoreLocation.framework and MapKit.framework to the Frameworks group.

## Building the Interface

Select ViewController.xib to edit the user interface. Once Interface Builder opens, drag a round rect button from the library over to the view. Use the blue guidelines to align the button to the bottom right of the view. Double-click the newly placed button to edit its title, and type **Go**.

Drag a progress view from the library, and place it to the left of the button, with the top of the progress view and the top of the button aligned. Resize using the blue guidelines so it extends horizontally from the left margin to the right margin. It will overlap the button, and that's okay.

Next, drag a label from the library over to the view and place it below the progress bar. Resize it horizontally so that it takes up the entire width from the left margin guides to the right margin guides. Now, use the attribute inspector to center-align the label's text and change the font size to 13 so that the text will fit better. Lastly, delete the text "Label."

Find the map view (Figure 10-7) in the object library. Drag the map view over to the view. Align the top and left sides of the map view with view. Resize the map view to the width of the window view. Then resize the map view down toward the bottom, until the blue guideline appears, just above the progress bar and button you placed on the bottom earlier (Figure 10-8).

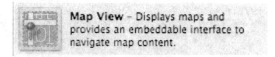

*Figure 10-7.  The map view as it appears in the Object library (List view)*

*Figure 10-8.  Laying out the map view, just above the progress bar and button*

Now, you make the Outlets and Action connections. Put the editor in Assistant mode (via the Toolbar). The Assistant should open ViewController.h to right of Interface Builder. Control-drag from the Go button to just below the @interface declaration. Be sure you have selected the button, not the (invisible) label. When the Connection pop-up appears, the Type field should be UIButton. Set the Connection to Outlet, and name it **button**. Next, control-drag from the Go button again, to just above the @end declaration. This time add an Action, and name it **findMe**.

Now control-drag from the progress bar to just below the `button` property you added. Create an Outlet named `progressBar`, making sure that the type is `UIProgressView`. Using the Attribute editor, click in the check box that's labeled Hidden so that the progress bar will not be visible until you want to report progress to the user.

Next, control-drag from the (invisible) label to below the `progressBar` property. You'll have to guess where the label is. Alternatively, you can drag from the label in the Object Dock, like you did in the last chapter. Either way, name the outlet **progressLabel**.

Finally, control-drag from the map view to below the `progressLabel` property declaration. Name this outlet `mapView`. Control-drag from the map view to the file's Owner icon in the Object Dock. When the Outlets pop-up appears, select delegate.

Save the XIB. Before moving on, put the editor back into Standard mode.

# Finishing the View Controller Interface

Select `ViewController.h` to edit it. For starters, import both the Map Kit and Core Location header files, because you're using both Core Location and Map Kit in this application.

```
#import <CoreLocation/CoreLocation.h>
#import <MapKit/MapKit.h>
```

You need conform your class to the following delegate protocols:

- `CLLocationManagerDelegate` so you can get notified by Core Location of the user's current location.

- `MKMapKitDelegate` because you're going to be your map view's delegate.

- `UIAlertViewDelegate` to handle the alert views that you'll use to inform the user if something went wrong.

```
@interface ViewController : UIViewController <CLLocationManagerDelegate, MKMapViewDelegate,
                                   UIAlertViewDelegate>
```

Right after the `@interface` declaration, you declare three instance variables to store the `CLLocationManager`, `CLGeocoder`, and `CLPlacemark` objects you'll use in the application. You declare them as instance variable and not properties since you don't need to expose these objects to your interface.

```
{
    CLLocationManager *manager;
    CLGeocoder *geocoder;
    CLPlacemark *placemark;
}
```

> **Note**    Although map views are capable of tracking the user's current location, you're going to track the user's location manually using Core Location in this application. By doing it manually, we can show you more Map Kit features. If you need to track the user's location in your own applications, just let the map view do it for you.

That's it. You declared the Outlets and Action you need via Interface Builder. Save `ViewController.h`. Before you work on the implementation file, you need to work on your annotation class.

# Writing the Annotation Object Class

You need to create a class to hold your annotation object. You're going to build a simple one that stores some address information, which you'll pull from the geocoder. Select the MapMe group in the Navigator pane. Create a new Objective-C class named **MapLocation** and make it a subclass of NSObject.

Once the new files have been created, single-click `MapLocation.h`. First, you need to include the Map Kit header.

```
#import <MapKit/MapKit.h>
```

You need to change `MapLocation` to adopt the `MKAnnotation` and `NSCoding` protocols.

```
@interface MapLocation : NSObject <MKAnnotation, NSCoding>
```

We did say that annotations were pretty standard data model classes, didn't we? We conformed this to `MKAnnotation` and also to `NSCoding`. You're not actually going to use the archiving functionality, but it's a good habit to conform data model classes to `NSCoding`.

Next, you need properties to store address data, along with a `CLLocationCoordinate2D`, which will be used to track this annotation's location on the map.

```
@property (strong, nonatomic) NSString *street;
@property (strong, nonatomic) NSString *city;
@property (strong, nonatomic) NSString *state;
@property (strong, nonatomic) NSString *zip;
@property (nonatomic, readwrite) CLLocationCoordinate2D coordinate;
```

Notice that you've specifically declared the `coordinate` property to be readwrite. The `MKAnnotation` protocol declares this property as readonly. You could have declared it that way as well, and then just set the `coordinate` property by using the underlying instance variable, but you are going to use the property to let other classes set your annotation's coordinates. It's okay to redefine properties to be more permissive than the same property as declared in a protocol to which you've conformed or as declared in your superclass. You can always redefine a readonly or writeonly property to be readwrite, but you must explicitly use the `readwrite` keyword. Most of the time, that keyword isn't used because it's the default value and unnecessary.

Save MapLocation.h and switch over to the implementation file, MapLocation.m. First, you implement the MKAnnotation protocol methods.

```
#pragma mark - MKAnnotation Protocol Methods

- (NSString *)title
{
    return NSLocalizedString(@"You are Here!", @"You are Here!");
}

- (NSString *)subtitle
{
    NSMutableString *result = [NSMutableString string];
    if (self.street)
        [result appendString:self.street];
    if (self.street && (self.city || self.state || self.zip))
        [result appendString:@", "];
    if (self.city)
        [result appendString:self.city];
    if (self.city && self.state)
        [result appendString:@", "];
    if (self.state)
        [result appendString:self.state];
    if (self.zip)
        [result appendFormat:@"  %@", self.zip];

    return result;
}
```

There really shouldn't be anything there that throws you for a loop. For the MKAnnotation protocol method of title, you just return "You are Here!" The subtitle method, however, is a little more complex. Because you don't know which data elements the reverse geocoder will give you, you have to build the subtitle string based on what you have. You do that by declaring a mutable string, and then appending the values from your non-nil, non-empty properties.

And you need to implement the NSCoder protocol methods.

```
#pragma mark - NSCoder Protocol Methods

- (void)encodeWithCoder:(NSCoder *)aCoder
{
    [aCoder encodeObject:self.street forKey:@"street"];
    [aCoder encodeObject:self.city forKey:@"city"];
    [aCoder encodeObject:self.state forKey:@"state"];
    [aCoder encodeObject:self.zip forKey:@"zip"];
}

- (id)initWithCoder:(NSCoder *)aDecoder
{
    self = [super init];
    if (self) {
        [self setStreet:[aDecoder decodeObjectForKey:@"street"]];
```

```
        [self setCity:[aDecoder decodeObjectForKey:@"city"]];
        [self setState:[aDecoder decodeObjectForKey:@"state"]];
        [self setZip:[aDecoder decodeObjectForKey:@"zip"]];
    }
    return self;
}
```

Everything else here is standard stuff to encode and decode the MapLocation class, so let's move on to implementing the ViewController class. Save MapLocation.m before proceeding.

## Implementing the MapMe ViewController

Single-click ViewController.m. Start by adding the import of the MapLocation header.

```
#import "MapLocation.h"
```

Next you define some private category methods for handling annotations and reverse geocoding. In the Category interface declaration, add these two method declarations:

```
@interface ViewController ()
- (void)openCallout:(id<MKAnnotation>)annotation;
- (void)reverseGeocode:(CLLocation *)location;
@end
```

Next, set the Map View map type in the viewDidLoad: method. Declare all three map types, with two of them commented out. This is just to make it easier for you to change the one you're using and experiment a little. Add these after the call to super.

```
self.mapView.mapType = MKMapTypeStandard;
//self.mapView.mapType = MKMapTypeSatellite;
//self.mapView.mapType = MKMapTypeHybrid;
```

Now implement the Action method findMe, which gets called when the user presses a button.

```
#pragma mark - Action Method

- (IBAction)findMe:(id)sender
{
    if (manager == nil)
        manager = [[CLLocationManager alloc] init];

    manager.delegate = self;
    manager.desiredAccuracy = kCLLocationAccuracyBest;
    [manager startUpdatingLocation];
```

```
    self.progressBar.hidden = NO;
    self.progressBar.progress = 0.0;
    self.progressLabel.text = NSLocalizedString(@"Determining Current Location",
                                        @"Determining Current Location");

    self.button.hidden = YES;
}
```

As discussed before, you could have used the map view's ability to track the user's location, but you're going the manual route to learn more functionality. Therefore, you allocate and initialize an instance of CLLocationManager to determine the user's location. You set self as the delegate, and tell the Location Manager you want the best accuracy available, before telling it to start updating the location. Then you unhide the progress bar and set the progress label to tell the user that you are trying to determine the current location. Lastly, you hide the button so the user can't press it again.

Now, you implement the private category methods you declared in the beginning of ViewController.m.

```
#pragma mark - (Private) Instance Methods

- (void)openCallout:(id<MKAnnotation>)annotation
{
    self.progressBar.progress = 1.0;
    self.progressLabel.text = NSLocalizedString(@"Showing Annotation", @"Showing Annotation");
    [self.mapView selectAnnotation:annotation animated:YES];
}
```

You'll use openCallout: a little later to select your annotation. You can't select the annotation when you add it to the map view. You have to wait until it's been added before you can select it. This method will allow you to select an annotation, which will open the annotation's callout by using performSelector:withObject:afterDelay:. All you do in this method is update the progress bar and progress label to show that you're at the last step, and then use the MKMapView's selectAnnotation:animated: method to select the annotation, which will cause its callout view to be shown.

You also declared another private method called reverseGeocode:. Again, you'll use it a little later. Given a CLLocation instance, it attempts to reverse geocode the location. If it succeeds, it will create a MapLocation annotation and send it to the Map View. If there's an error, it will pop up an alert dialog.

```
- (void)reverseGeocode:(CLLocation *)location
{
    if (!geocoder)
        geocoder = [[CLGeocoder alloc] init];

    [geocoder reverseGeocodeLocation:location completionHandler:^(NSArray* placemarks, NSError* error){
```

```
        if (nil != error) {
            UIAlertView *alert =
                [[UIAlertView alloc]
                    initWithTitle:NSLocalizedString(@"Error translating coordinates into location",
                                                    @"Error translating coordinates into location")
                    message:NSLocalizedString(@"Geocoder did not recognize coordinates",
                                              @"Geocoder did not recognize coordinates")
                    delegate:self
                    cancelButtonTitle:NSLocalizedString(@"OK", @"OK")
                    otherButtonTitles:nil];
            [alert show];

        }
        else if ([placemarks count] > 0) {
            placemark = [placemarks objectAtIndex:0];

            self.progressBar.progress = 0.5;
            self.progressLabel.text = NSLocalizedString(@"Location Determined",
                                                        @"Location Determined");

            MapLocation *annotation = [[MapLocation alloc] init];
            annotation.street = placemark.thoroughfare;
            annotation.city = placemark.locality;
            annotation.state = placemark.administrativeArea;
            annotation.zip = placemark.postalCode;
            annotation.coordinate = location.coordinate;

            [self.mapView addAnnotation:annotation];
        }
    }];
}
```

Next, add the CLLocationManagerDelegate methods.

```
#pragma mark - CLLocationManagerDelegate Methods

- (void)locationManager:(CLLocationManager *)aManager
    didUpdateToLocation:(CLLocation *)newLocation
            fromLocation:(CLLocation *)oldLocation
{
    if ([newLocation.timestamp timeIntervalSince1970] < [NSDate timeIntervalSinceReferenceDate] - 60)
        return;

    MKCoordinateRegion viewRegion =
        MKCoordinateRegionMakeWithDistance(newLocation.coordinate, 2000, 2000);
    MKCoordinateRegion adjustedRegion = [self.mapView regionThatFits:viewRegion];
    [self.mapView setRegion:adjustedRegion animated:YES];

    aManager.delegate = nil;
    [aManager stopUpdatingLocation];
```

```
    self.progressBar.progress = 0.25;
    self.progressLabel.text = NSLocalizedString(@"Reverse Geocoding Location",
                                                @"Reverse Geocoding Location");

    [self reverseGeocode:newLocation];
}
```

First, you check that you're operating with a fresh location, taken within the last minute, and not a cached one. You then use the MKCoordinateRegionMakeWithDistance() function to create a region that shows one kilometer on each side of the user's current location. You adjust that region to the aspect ratio of your map view and then tell the map view to show that new adjusted region. Now that you've gotten a non-cache location, you're going to stop having the location manager give you updates. Location updates are a drain on the battery, so when you don't want any more updates, you should shut the location manager down. Then you update the progress bar and label to let them know where you are in the whole process. This is the first of four steps after the Go button is pressed, so you set progress to .25, which will show a bar that is one-quarter blue. Finally, you call the reverseGeocoder: method to convert the new location to an annotation and update the map view.

If the location manager encounters an error, you just show an alert. Not the most robust error handling, but it'll do for this.

```
- (void)locationManager:(CLLocationManager *)manager didFailWithError:(NSError *)error
{
    NSString *errorType = (error.code == kCLErrorDenied)
                        ? NSLocalizedString(@"Access Denied", @"Access Denied")
                        : NSLocalizedString(@"Unknown Error", @"Unknown Error");

    UIAlertView *alert = [[UIAlertView alloc] initWithTitle:NSLocalizedString(@"Error getting Location",
                                                                              @"Error getting Location")
                                        message:errorType
                                        delegate:self
                              cancelButtonTitle:NSLocalizedString(@"OK", @"OK")
                              otherButtonTitles:nil];
    [alert show];
}
```

Now, you add the MapView delegate methods.

```
#pragma mark - MKMapViewDelegate Methods

- (MKAnnotationView *)mapView:(MKMapView *)aMapView viewForAnnotation:(id<MKAnnotation>)annotation
{
    static NSString *placemarkIdentifier = @"Map Location Identifier";
    if ([annotation isKindOfClass:[MapLocation class]]) {
        MKPinAnnotationView *annotationView =
          (MKPinAnnotationView *)[aMapView dequeueReusableAnnotationViewWithIdentifier:placemarkIdentifier];
        if (nil == annotationView) {
```

```
            annotationView = [[MKPinAnnotationView alloc] initWithAnnotation:annotation
                                           reuseIdentifier:placemarkIdentifier];
    }
    else
        annotationView.annotation = annotation;

    annotationView.enabled = YES;
    annotationView.animatesDrop = YES;
    annotationView.pinColor = MKPinAnnotationColorPurple;
    annotationView.canShowCallout = YES;
    [self performSelector:@selector(openCallout:) withObject:annotation afterDelay:0.5];

    self.progressBar.progress = 0.75;
    self.progressLabel.text = NSLocalizedString(@"Creating Annotation", @"Creating Annotation");

    return annotationView;
    }
    return nil;
}
```

When the map view for which you are the delegate needs an annotation view, it will call
`mapView:viewForAnnotation:`. The first thing you do is declare an identifier so you can dequeue
the right kind of annotation view, then you make sure the map view is asking you about a type
of annotation that you know about. If it is, you dequeue an instance of `MKPinAnnotationView`
with your identifier. If there are no dequeued views, you create one. You could also have used
`MKAnnotationView` here instead of `MKPinAnnotationView`. In fact, there's an alternate version of
this project in the project archive that shows how to use `MKAnnotationView` to display a custom
annotation view instead of a pin. If you didn't create a new view, it means you got a dequeued one
from the map view. In that case, you have to make sure the dequeued view is linked to the right
annotation. Then you do some configuration.

- You make sure the annotation view is enabled so it can be selected.

- You set `animatesDrop` to YES because this is a pin view, and you want it to drop
  onto the map the way pins are wont to do.

- You set the pin color to purple and make sure that it can show a callout.

- After that, you use `performSelector:withObject:afterDelay:` to call that private
  method you created earlier.

- You can't select an annotation until its view is actually being displayed on the
  map, so you wait half a second to make sure that's happened before selecting.
  This will also make sure that the pin has finished dropping before the callout is
  displayed.

- You need to update the progress bar and text label to let the user know that
  you're almost done.

- Then you return the annotation view. If the annotation wasn't one you recognize,
  you return nil and your map view will use the default annotation view for that
  kind of annotation.

■ You implement `mapViewDidFailLoadingMap:withError:` and inform the user if there was a problem loading the map. Again, your error checking in this application is very rudimentary; you just inform the user and stop everything.

```
- (void)mapViewDidFailLoadingMap:(MKMapView *)aMapView withError:(NSError *)error
{
    UIAlertView *alert = [[UIAlertView alloc] initWithTitle:NSLocalizedString(@"Error loading map",
                                                                              @"Error loading map")
                                        message:[error localizedDescription]
                                        delegate:nil
                                  cancelButtonTitle:NSLocalizedString(@"OK", @"OK")
                                  otherButtonTitles:nil];

    [alert show];
}
```

■ Finally, you implement the `UIAlertView` delegate method. It will hide the progress bar and set the progress label to an empty string. For simplicity's sake, we're just dead-ending the application if a problem occurs. In your apps, you'll probably want to do something a little more user-friendly.

```
#pragma mark - UIAlertViewDelegate Method

- (void)alertView:(UIAlertView *)alertView didDismissWithButtonIndex:(NSInteger)buttonIndex
{
    self.progressBar.hidden = YES;
    self.progressLabel.text = @"";
    self.button.hidden = NO;
}
```

You should now be able to build and run your application, so do that, and try it out.

> **Note**   When running in the Simulator, you may encounter problems. Try launching the application, but before pressing the Go button, use the Location Simulator in the Debug Jump Bar to set a location.

Experiment with the code. Change the map type, add more annotations, or try experimenting with custom annotation views.

## Go East, Young Programmer

That brings us to the end of the discussion of Map Kit. You saw the basics of how to use Map Kit, annotations, and the reverse geocoder. You saw how to create coordinate regions and coordinate spans to specify what area the map view should show to the user, and you've learned how to use Map Kit's reverse geocoder to turn a set of coordinates into a physical address.

Now, armed with your iPhone, Map Kit, and sheer determination, navigate your way one page to the East, err... right, so that we can talk about iOS Messaging.

# Chapter 11

# Messaging: Mail, SMS, and Social Media

Since the beginnings of the iOS SDK, Apple has provided the means for developers to send messages. It started with the MessageUI framework, which allowed developers to add support for sending e-mail message from within their applications. Then, Apple extended the MessageUI framework to include SMS messages. With iOS 5, Apple added support for Twitter with a new Twitter framework. Now, with iOS 6, Apple has migrated from the Twitter framework to the Social framework, adding support for Facebook, Sina Weibo, and Twitter. Let's go over how each messaging system works.

## This Chapter's Application

In this chapter, you're going to build an application that lets the user take a picture using their iPhone's camera or, if they don't have a camera because they're using the Simulator, then you'll allow them to select an image from the photo library. They can take the resulting image and send it to a friend via e-mail, SMS, Facebook, or Twitter without leaving the application.

> **Note**  While it is possible to send a photo via the Messages application, Apple has not exposed this functionality to developers. This functionality is called *Multimedia Messaging Service* or MMS for short. The iOS SDK only allows you to use *Short Message Service* (SMS) to send text messages. As a result, you'll just being sending a text message in your application.

Your application's interface will be quite simple (Figure 11-1). It will feature a single button to start the whole thing going. Tapping the button will bring up the camera picker controller, in a manner similar to the sample program in Chapter 20 of *Beginning iOS 6 Development* (Apress, 2012). Once the user has taken or selected an image, they'll be able to crop and/or scale the image (Figure 11-2).

Assuming they don't cancel, the image picker will return an image, and an activity view to ask the user how they want to send the message (Figure 11-3). Depending on their choice, you'll display the appropriate composition view (Figure 11-4). You'll populate the composition view with text and the selected image (unless it's an SMS message). Finally, once the message is sent, you'll provide some feedback confirming that the message was sent.

*Figure 11-1. The chapter's application has a very simple user interface consisting of a button*

*Figure 11-2.* *The user can take a picture with the camera or select an image from their photo library, and then crop and scale the image*

*Figure 11-3.* *After selecting and editing the image, you present the message selector view*

*Figure 11-4.  Mail, Twitter, and Facebook compose views*

**Caution**    The application in this chapter will run in the Simulator, but instead of using the camera, it will allow you to select an image from the Simulator's photo library. If you've ever used the *Reset Contents and Settings* menu item in the Simulator, then you have probably lost the photo album's default contents and will have no images available. You can rectify this by launching Mobile Safari in the simulator and navigating to an image on the Web. Make sure the image you are looking at is *not* a link, but a static image. This technique will not work with a linked image. Click and hold the mouse button with your cursor over an image, and an action sheet will pop up. One of the options will be Save Image. This will add the selected image to your iPhone's photo library.

In addition, note that you will not be able to send e-mail from within the simulator. You'll be able to create the e-mail, and the Simulator will say it sent it, but it's all lies. The e-mail just ends up in the circular file.

# The MessageUI Framework

To embed e-mail and SMS services in your application, use the MessageUI framework. It is one of the smallest frameworks in the iOS SDK. It's composed of two classes, `MFMailComposeViewController` and `MFMessageComposeViewController`, and their corresponding delegate protocols.

Each class comes with a static method to determine if the device supports the service. For MFMailComposeViewController, the method is canSendMail; for MFMessageComposeViewController, the method is canSendText. It's a good idea to check if your device can send an e-mail or SMS before attempting do so.

```
if ([MFMailComposeViewController canSendMail)] {
    // code to send email
    ...
}
if ([MFMessageComposeViewController canSendText]) {
    // code to send SMS
    ...
}
```

Let's start by reviewing the e-mail class, MFMailComposeViewController.

## Creating the Mail Compose View Controller

It's very simple to use the MFMailComposeViewController class. You create an instance, set its delegate, set any properties that you wish to prepopulate, and then present it modally. When the user is done with their e-mail and taps either the Send or Cancel button, the mail compose view controller notifies its delegate, which is responsible for dismissing the modal view. Here's how you create a mail compose view controller and set its delegate:

```
MFMailComposeViewController *mc = [[MFMailComposeViewController alloc] init];
mc.mailComposeDelegate = self;
```

## Populating the Subject Line

Before you present the mail compose view, you can preconfigure the various fields of the mail compose view controller, such as the subject and recipients (to:, cc:, and bcc:), as well as the body and attachments. You can populate the subject by calling the method setSubject: on the instance of MFMailComposeViewController, like this:

```
[mc setSubject:@"Hello, World!"];
```

## Populating Recipients

E-mails can go to three types of recipients. The main recipients of the e-mail are called the *to:* recipients and go on the line labeled *To:*. Recipients who are being cc:ed on the e-mail go on the *cc:* line. If you want to include somebody on the e-mail but not let the other recipients know that person is also receiving the e-mail, you can use the *bcc:* line, which stands for "blind carbon copy." You can populate all three of these fields when using MFMailComposeViewController.

To set the main recipients, use the method setToRecipients: and pass in an NSArray instance containing the e-mail addresses of all the recipients. Here's an example:

```
[mc setToRecipients:@[@"manny.sullivan@me.com"]];
```

Set the other two types of recipients in the same manner, though you'll use the methods setCcRecipients: for cc: recipients and setBccRecipients: for bcc: recipients.

```
[mc setCcRecipients:@[@"maru@boxes.co.jp"]];
[mc setBccRecipients:@[@"lassie@helpfuldogs.org"]];
```

## Setting the Message Body

You can also populate the message body with any text you'd like. You can either use a regular string to create a plain text e-mail or you can use HTML to create a formatted e-mail. To supply the mail compose view controller with a message body, use the method setMessageBody:isHTML:. If the string you pass in is plain text, you should pass NO as the second parameter, but if you're providing HTML markup in the first argument rather than a plain string, then you should pass YES in the second argument so your markup will be parsed before it is shown to the user.

```
[mc setMessageBody:@"Ohai!!!\n\nKThxBai" isHTML:NO];
[mc setMessageBody:@"<HTML><B>Ohai</B><BR/>I can has cheezburger?</HTML>" isHTML:YES];
```

## Adding Attachments

You can also add attachments to outgoing e-mails.  In order to do so, you must provide an instance of NSData containing the data to be attached, along with the mime type of the attachment and the file name to be used for the attachment. *Mime types*, which we discussed briefly back in Chapter 9 when we talked about interacting with web servers, are strings that define the type of data being transferred over the Internet. They're used when retrieving from or sending files to a web server, and they're also used when sending e-mail attachments. To add an attachment to an outgoing e-mail, use the method addAttachmentData:mimeType:fileName:. Here's an example of adding an image stored in your application's bundle as an attachment:

```
NSString *path = [[NSBundle mainBundle] pathForResource:@"surpriseCat" ofType:@"png"];
NSData *data = [NSData dataWithContentsOfFile:path];
[mc addAttachmentData:data mimeType:@"image/png" fileName:@"surpriseCat"];
```

## Presenting the Mail Compose View

Once you've configured the controller with all the data you want populated, you present the controller's view, as you've done before:

```
[self presentViewController:mc animated:YES completion:nil];
```

## The Mail Compose View Controller Delegate Method

The mail compose view controller delegate's method is contained in the formal protocol MFMailComposeViewControllerDelegate. Regardless of whether the user sends or cancels, and regardless of whether the system was able to send the message or not, the method mailComposeController:didFinishWithResult:error: gets called. As with most delegate methods, the first parameter is a pointer to the object that called the delegate method. The second parameter is a *result code* that tells you the fate of the outgoing e-mail, and the third is an NSError instance that will give you more detailed information if a problem was encountered. Regardless of what result code you received, it is your responsibility in this method to dismiss the mail compose view controller by calling dismissModalViewControllerAnimated:.

If the user tapped the Cancel button, your delegate will be sent the result code MFMailComposeResultCancelled. In that situation, the user changed their mind and decided not to send the e-mail. If the user tapped the Send button, the result code is going to depend on whether the MessageUI framework was able to successfully send the e-mail. If it was able to send the message, the result code will be MFMailComposeResultSent. If it tried, and failed, the result code will be MFMailComposeResultFailed, in which case, you probably want to check the provided NSError instance to see what went wrong. If the message couldn't be sent because there's currently no Internet connection, but the message was saved into the outbox to be sent later, you will get a result code of MFMailComposeResultSaved.

Here is a very simple implementation of the delegate method that just logs what happened:

```objc
- (void)mailComposeController:(MFMailComposeViewController*)controller
          didFinishWithResult:(MFMailComposeResult)result
                        error:(NSError*)error
{
    switch (result)
    {
        case MFMailComposeResultCancelled:
            NSLog(@"Mail send canceled...");
            break;
        case MFMailComposeResultSaved:
            NSLog(@"Mail saved...");
            break;
        case MFMailComposeResultSent:
            NSLog(@"Mail sent...");
            break;
        case MFMailComposeResultFailed:
            NSLog(@"Mail send error: %@...", [error localizedDescription]);
            break;
        default:
            break;
    }
    [controller dismissViewControllerAnimated:YES completion:nil];
}
```

## Message Compose View Controller

MFMessageComposeViewController is similar, but simpler than its e-mail counterpart. First, you create an instance and set its delegate.

```objc
MFMessageComposeViewController *mc = [[MFMessageComposeViewController alloc] init];
mc.messageComposeDelegate = self;
```

There are only two properties that you can populate: recipients and body. Unlike with e-mail, these can be accessed via direct properties on the class, as well as the method accessors. Recipients is an array of strings, where each string is a contact name from your Address Book or phone number. Body is the message you want to send.

```
mc.recipients = @[@"Manny Sullivan"];
mc.body = @"Hello, Manny!";
```

The message compose view controller delegate method behaves identically to its e-mail counterpart. There are only three possible results when sending an SMS: cancelled, sent, or failed.

```
- (void)messageComposeViewController:(MFMessageComposeViewController *)controller
                   didFinishWithResult:(MessageComposeResult)result
{
    switch (result)
    {
        case MessageComposeResultCancelled:
            NSLog(@"SMS sending canceled");
            break;
        case MessageComposeResultSent:
            NSLog(@"SMS sent");
            break;
        case MessageComposeResultFailed:
            NSLog(@"SMS sending failed");
            break;
        default:
            NSLog(@"SMS not sent");
            break;
    }
    [controller dismissViewControllerAnimated:YES completion:nil];
}
```

# The Social Framework

In iOS 5, Apple tightly integrated with Twitter (www.twitter.com). Basically, your Twitter account was available from the system. As a result, it was very easy to send messages ("tweets") to Twitter or perform Twitter API requests. In iOS 6, Apple abstracted and extended this feature into the Social framework. Along with Twitter, Apple integrated identical functionality for Facebook and Sina Weibo.

## SLComposeViewController

SLComposeViewController is very similar in design and principle to the e-mail and message view controller classes in the Message UI framework. However, there isn't a corresponding delegate class. Rather, SLComposeViewController has a completion handler property that can be assigned a block.

In order to confirm that your application can use a service, you call the static method isAvailableForServiceType:. For example, the check to see if you can send to Facebook is

```
if ([SLComposeViewController isAvailableForServiceType:SLServiceTypeFacebook]) {
    // code to send message to Facebook
    ...
}
```

isAvailableForServiceType: takes a String argument of possible service type constants. These service types are defined in the header file SLServiceTypes.h. Currently, Apple defines the following service type constant:

```
NSString *const SLServiceTypeFacebook;
NSString *const SLServiceTypeTwitter;
NSString *const SLServiceTypeSinaWeibo;
```

If you are able to send a send a message to the service, you start by creating an instance of the view controller.

```
SLComposeViewController *composeVC = [SLComposeViewController
                                composeViewControllerForServiceType:SLServiceTypeTwitter];
```

This example would create a view controller for sending a tweet. You're able to set the initial text, add images, and add URLs before presenting the view controller.

```
[composeVC setInitialText:@"Hello, Twitter!"];

UIImage *image = [UIImage imageWithContentsOfFile:@"surpriseCat.png"];
[composeVC addImage:image];

NSURL *url = [NSURL URLWithString:@"http://www.apporchard.com"];
[composeVC addURL:url];
```

These methods return YES if on success and NO on failure.

There are two convenience methods, removeAllImages and removeAllURLs, to remove any images or URLs you've added.

As mentioned earlier, you don't assign a delegate to handle message completion. Rather, you set the completionHandler property with a block.

```
[composeVC setCompletionHandler:^(SLComposeViewControllerResult result) {
    switch (result) {
        case SLComposeViewControllerResultCancelled:
            NSLog(@"Message cancelled.");
            break;
        case SLComposeViewControllerResultDone:
            NSLog(@"Message sent.");
            break;
        default:
            break;
    }
    [self dismissModalViewControllerAnimated:YES completion:nil];
}];
```

The block accepts one argument, which tells the result of the message. Again, you are expect to dismiss the view controller with a call to dismissModalViewControllerAnimated:completion:.

# SLRequest

SLComposeViewController is fine if you just want to post messages. What if you want to take advantage of the APIs these social media services offer? In that case you want to use SLRequest, which is basically a wrapper around an HTTP request that handles the authentication between your application and the social media service.

To create a request, you call the class method requestForServiceType:requestMethod:URL:parameters:.

```
SLRequest *request = [SLRequest requestForServiceType:SLServiceTypeFacebook
                                        requestMethod:SLRequestMethodPOST
                                                  URL:url
                                           parameters:params];
```

The first argument is the same service type String constant used in SLComposeViewController. requestMethod: is a subset of HTTP actions: GET, POST, and DELETE. Apple has defined an enumeration for this subset: SLRequestMethod:

```
SLRequestMethodGET
SLRequestMethodPOST
SLRequestMethodDELETE
```

URL: is a URL defined by the service provider. This is usually not the public "www" URL of the service. For example, Twitter's URL begins with http://api.twitter.com/. Finally, parameters: is a dictionary of HTTP parameters to send to the service. The contents of the dictionary depend on the service being called.

Once you've composed your request, you send it to the service provider:

```
[request performRequestWithHandler:^(NSData *responseData,
                                     NSHTTPURLResponse *urlResponse,
                                     NSError *error) {
    // Handle the response, process the data or error
    ...
}];
```

The handler is a block that returns the HTTP response object, along with any accompanying data. An error object is returned, which will be non-nil if an error occurred.

> **Note**    This is a pretty short overview of the SLRequest class. You can read more in the class documentation at https://developer.apple.com/library/ios/#documentation/Social/ Reference/SLRequest_Class/Reference/Reference.html.

# The Activity View Controller

In iOS 6, Apple introduced a new way to access the various services from within an application: the activity view controller (UIActivityViewController). In addition to giving applications access to standard iOS services, like copy and paste, the activity view controller provides a single unified interface for applications to send e-mail, SMS, or post content to social media services. You can even define your own custom service.

Using an activity view controller is simple. Initialize the activity view controller with the items you wish to send (i.e. text, images, etc.) and push it onto your current view controller.

```
NSString *text = @"some text";
UIImage *image = [[UIImage alloc] initWithContentsOfFile:@"some_image.png"];
NSArray *items = @[ text, image ];

UIActivityViewController *activityVC =
    [[UIActivityViewController alloc] initWithActivityItems:items applicationActivities:nil];

[self presentViewController:activityVC animated:YES completion:nil];
```

That's it. Pretty simple, right?

So all the magic happens here:

```
UIActivityViewController *activityVC =
                [[UIActivityViewController alloc] initWithActivityItems:items
applicationActivities:nil];
```

When you instantiate an activity view controller, you pass it an array of activity items. An activity item can be any object, and it depends on the application and activity service target. In the example code above, the activity items were a string and an image. If you want to use a custom object as an activity item, have it conform to the UIActivityItemSource protocol. Then you will have complete control over how your custom objects presents its data to the activity view controller.

applicationActivities: expects an array of UIActivity objects. If passed a value of nil, then the activity view controller will use a default set of Activity objects. Remember we said earlier you could define your own custom service? You accomplish that by subclassing UIActivity to define the communication to your service. Then you pass in your subclass as part of the array of application activities.

For the purposes of this chapter, you're going just going to use the default list of application activities. Ready? Let's go!

# Building the MessageImage Application

Create a new project in Xcode using the Single View Application template. Call the project MessageImage. Since this app only has one view controller, you won't need storyboards. But you're still using Automatic Reference Counting.

## Building the User Interface

Look back at Figure 11-1. The interface is pretty simple: a single button labeled Go. When you press the button, the application will activate your device's camera and allow you to take a picture.

Select `ViewController.xib`.

From the library, drag over a round rect button and place it anywhere on the window titled View. Double-click the button and give it a title of Go. Enter the assistant editor, which should split the Editor pane and open `ViewController.h`. Control-drag from the Go button to between the `@interface` and `@end` in `ViewController.h`. Add a new Action, and name it `selectAndMessageImage`.

Next, drag a label from the library to the view window. Place the label above the button, and resize it so that it stretches from the left margin all the way to the right margin. In the Attribute Inspector, change the text alignment to centered. Control-drag from the label to above the `selectAndMessageImage:` action you just created. Add a new outlet and name it `label`. Finally, double-click the label and erase the text "Label."

Put the editor back into Standard mode. Save the XIB file.

## Taking the Picture

Single-click `ViewController.h`. You need your view controller to conform to two delegate protocols:

```
@interface ViewController : UIViewController <UINavigationControllerDelegate,
                                              UIImagePickerControllerDelegate>
```

This is because the image picker controller you'll be using expects its delegate to conform to both `UINavigationControllerDelegate` and `UIImagePickerControllerDelegate`. You're using the image picker controller so you can use the camera and select an image to send. Now you need to add a property for the image you'll select.

```
@property (strong, nonatomic) UIImage *image;
```

That's all you need for now. Let's move on to the view controller implementation file.

## Calling the Camera

Select `ViewController.m` to open it in the editor.

You need to implement the action method when the button is pressed.

```
- (IBAction)selectAndMessageImage:(id)sender
{
    UIImagePickerControllerSourceType sourceType = UIImagePickerControllerSourceTypeCamera;
    if (![UIImagePickerController isSourceTypeAvailable:UIImagePickerControllerSourceTypeCamera]) {
        sourceType = UIImagePickerControllerSourceTypePhotoLibrary;
    }
```

```
    UIImagePickerController *picker = [[UIImagePickerController alloc] init];
    picker.delegate = self;
    picker.allowsEditing = YES;
    picker.sourceType = sourceType;
    [self presentViewController:picker animated:YES completion:nil];
}
```

Once the Go button is pressed, you set the image source to be the device's camera. If the camera is not available (if you're running on the Simulator), you fall back to using the photo library. You set the image picker delegate to be your view controller and allow the image to be edited. Finally, you display the image picker.

Since you set your view controller to be the image picker's delegate, you can add the delegate methods you need. Add the following below the selectAndMessageImage: method.

```
#pragma mark - UIImagePickerController Delegate Methods

- (void)imagePickerController:(UIImagePickerController *)picker
        didFinishPickingMediaWithInfo:(NSDictionary *)info
{
    [picker dismissViewControllerAnimated:YES completion:nil];
    self.image = [info objectForKey:UIImagePickerControllerEditedImage];
}

- (void)imagePickerControllerDidCancel:(UIImagePickerController *)picker
{
    [picker dismissViewControllerAnimated:YES completion:nil];
}
```

Both methods dismiss the image picker, but imagePickerController:didFinishPickingMediaWithInfo: also sets your image property to the picture you took (or chose).

Let's make sure everything is working. Run the application, take a picture, and click Use. Nothing should happen, but that's ok.

## Picking the Message Sender

Figure 11-3 shows the activity view controller that gets exposed after you select a picture. Let's set that up.

First, you'll define a method to show the activity view controller. Open ViewController.h and add the following method declaration:

```
- (void)showActivityViewController;
```

Now, select ViewController.m, and add the method implementation. We added ours after selectAndMessageImage:.

```
- (void)showActivityViewController
{
    NSString *message = NSLocalizedString(@"I took a picture on my iPhone",
                                          @"I took a picture on my iPhone");
    NSArray *activityItems = @[ message, self.image ];
    UIActivityViewController *activityVC =
        [[UIActivityViewController alloc] initWithActivityItems:activityItems
                                          applicationActivities:nil];
    [self presentViewController:activityVC animated:YES completion:nil];
}
```

Now, you need to call the showActivityViewController method after you've picked your picture. Add the following line to the end of imagePickerController:didFinishPickingMediaWithInfo:. You need to delay the presentation of the activity view controller slightly to allow the UIImagePickerController time to be removed from the root view controller.

```
[self performSelector:@selector(showActivityViewController) withObject:nil afterDelay:0.5];
```

Check your work so far. Run the application and confirm the alert sheet appears. That's it. Wow, that was simple.

> **Note** If you select a service and haven't configured your account information, iOS will pop an alert telling you to set up an account.

# Mailing It In...

In the course of this chapter, you saw how to send e-mail, SMS, or a post to social media services. You should be able to add this functionality to any of your applications. When you're ready to move on, turn the page to learn the art of iPod Fu.

# Chapter 12

# Media Library Access and Playback

Every iOS device, at its core, is a first class media player. Out of the box, people can listen to music, podcasts, and audio books, as well as watch movies and videos.

iOS SDK applications have always been able to play sounds and music, but Apple has been extending the functionality with each iOS release. iOS 3 gave us the MediaPlayer framework which, among other things, provided access to the user's audio library; iOS 5 extended this by giving us access to video stored in the user's library.

iOS 4 extended the AVFoundation framework, which offers finer control of playing, recording, and editing of media. This control comes at a cost, as most of the MediaPlayer framework's functionality is not directly implemented in AVFoundation. Rather, AVFoundation lets you implement custom controls for your specific needs.

In this chapter, you'll develop three applications: a simple audio player, a simple video player, and a combined audio/video player. The first two will use the MediaPlayer framework exclusively. The final application will use the MediaPlayer framework to access the user's media library, but then use AVFoundation for playback.

## The MediaPlayer Framework

The methods and objects used to access the media library are part of the MediaPlayer framework, which allows applications to play both audio and video. While the framework gives you access to all types of media from the user's library, there are some limitations that only allow you to work with audio files.

The collection of media on your iOS device was once referred as the *iPod library*, a term that we shall use interchangeably with *media library*. The latter is probably more accurate, as Apple has renamed the music player from iPod to Music and moved video media into an application called

Videos. More recently, Apple has gone even further, creating a Podcasts application to handle your podcast collections.

From the perspective of the MediaPlayer framework, the entire media library itself is represented by the class MPMediaLibrary. You won't use this object very often, however. It's primarily used only when you need to be notified of changes made to the library while your application is running. It was rare for changes to be made to the library while your application is running, since such changes usually happened as the result of synchronizing your device with your computer. Nowadays, you can synchronize your music collection directly with the iTunes Store, so you may need to monitor changes in the media library.

A media item is represented by the class MPMediaItem. If you wish to play songs from one of your user's playlists, you will use the class MPMediaPlaylist, which represents the playlists that were created in iTunes and synchronized to your user's device. To search for either media items or playlists in the iPod library, you use a media query, which is represented by the class MPMediaQuery. Media queries will return all media items or playlists that match whatever criteria you specify. To specify criteria for a media query, you use a special media-centric form of predicate called a media property predicate, represented by the class MPMediaPropertyPredicate.

Another way to let your user select media items is to use the media picker controller, which is an instance of MPMediaPickerController. The media picker controller allows your users to use the same basic interface they are accustomed to using from the iPod or Music application.

You can play media items using a player controller. There are two kinds of player controllers: MPMusicPlayerController and MPMoviePlayerController. The MPMusicPlayerController is not a view controller. It is responsible for playing audio and managing a list of audio items to be played. Generally speaking, you are expected to provide any necessary user interface elements, such as buttons to play, pause, skip forward, or backward. The MediaPlayer framework provides a view controller class, MPMoviePlayerViewController, to allow for the simple management of a full screen movie player within your applications.

If you want to specify a list of media items to be played by a player controller, you use a media item collection, represented by instances of the class MPMediaItemCollection. Media item collections are immutable collections of media items. A media item may appear in more than one spot in the collection, meaning you could conceivably create a collection that played "Happy Birthday to You" a thousand times, followed by a single playing of "Rock the Casbah." You could do that … if you really wanted to.

# Media Items

The class that represents media items, MPMediaItem, works a little differently than most Objective-C classes. You would probably expect MPMediaItem to include properties for things like title, artist, album name, and the like. But that is not the case. Other than those inherited from NSObject and the two NSCoding methods used to allow archiving, MPMediaItem includes only a single instance method called valueForProperty:.

valueForProperty: works much like an instance of NSDictionary, only with a limited set of defined keys. So, for example, if you wanted to retrieve a media item's title, you would call valueForProperty: and specify the key MPMediaItemPropertyTitle, and the method would return an NSString instance with the audio track's title. Media items are immutable on the iOS, so all MPMediaItem properties are read-only.

Some media item properties are said to be filterable. Filterable media item properties are those that can be searched on, a process you'll look at a little later in the chapter.

## Media Item Persistent ID

Every media item has a persistent identifier (or persistent ID), which is a number associated with the item that won't ever change. If you need to store a reference to a particular media item, you should store the persistent ID, because it is generated by iTunes and you can count on it staying the same over time.

You can retrieve the persistent ID of a media track using the property key MPMediaItemPropertyPersistentID, like so:

```
NSNumber *persistentId = [mediaItem valueForProperty:MPMediaItemPropertyPersistentID];
```

Persistent ID is a filterable property, which means that you can use a media query to find an item based on its persistent ID. Storing the media item's persistent ID is the surest way to guarantee you'll get the same object each time you search. We'll talk about media queries a bit later in the chapter.

## Media Type

All media items have a type associated with them. Currently, media items are classified using three categories: audio, video, and generic. You can determine a particular media item's type by asking for the MPMediaItemPropertyMediaType property, like so:

```
NSNumber *type = [mediaItem valueForProperty:MPMediaItemPropertyMediaType];
```

Media items may consist of more than a single type. A podcast, for example, could be a reading of an audio book. As a result, media type is implemented as a bit field (sometimes called bit flags).

> **Note**   Bit fields are commonly used in C, and Apple employs them in many places throughout its frameworks. If you're not completely sure how bit fields are used, you can check out Chapter 11 of *Learn C on the Mac for OS X and iOS* by David Mark and James Bucanek (Apress, 2012). You can find a good summary of the concept on Wikipedia as well at http://en.wikipedia.org/wiki/Bitwise_operation.

With bit fields, a single integer datatype is used to represent multiple, nonexclusive Boolean values, rather than a single number. To convert type (an object) into an NSInteger, which is the documented integer type used to hold media types, use the integerValue method, like so:

```
NSInteger mediaType = [type integerValue];
```

At this point, each bit of mediaType represents a single type. To determine if a media item is a particular type, you need to use the bitwise AND operator (&) to compare mediaType with system-defined constants that represent the available media types. Here is a list of the current constants:

- MPMediaTypeMusic: Used to check if the media is music.

- MPMediaTypePodcast: Used to check if the media is an audio podcast.

- MPMediaTypeAudioBook: Used to check if the media is an audio book.

- MPMediaTypeAudioAny: Used to check if the media is any audio type.

- MPMediaTypeMovie: Used to check if the media is a movie.

- MPMediaTypeTVShow: Used to check if the media is a television show.

- MPMediaTypeVideoPodcast: Used to check if the media is a video podcast.

- MPMediaTypeMusicVideo: Used to check if the media is a music video.

- MPMediaTypeITunesU: Used to check if the media is an iTunes University video.

- MPMediaTypeAnyVideo: Used to check if the media is any video type.

- MPMediaTypeAny: Used to check if the media is any known type.

To check if a given item contains music, for example, you take the mediaType you retrieved and do this:

```
if (mediaType & MPMediaTypeMusic) {
    // It is music...
}
```

MPMediaTypeMusic's bits are all set to 0, except for the one bit that's used to represent that a track contains music, which is set to 1. When you do a bitwise AND (&) between that constant and the retrieved mediaType value, the resulting value will have 0 in all bits except the one that's being checked. That bit will have a 1 if mediaType has the music bit set or 0 if it doesn't. In Objective-C, an if statement that evaluates a logical AND or OR operation will fire on any nonzero result; the code that follows will run if mediaType's music bit is set; otherwise, it will be skipped.

Media type is a filterable property, so you can specify in your media queries (which we'll talk about shortly) that they should return media of only specific types.

---

Bitwise Macros

Not every programmer is comfortable reading code with bitwise operators. If that describes you, don't despair. It's easy to create macros to turn these bitwise checks into C function macros, like so:

```
#define isMusic(x)      (x & MPMediaTypeMusic)
#define isPodcast(x)    (x & MPMediaTypePodcast)
#define isAudioBook(x)  (x & MPMediaTypeAudioBook)
```

Once these are defined, you can check the returned type using more accessible code, like this:

```
if (isMusic([type integerValue])) {
    // Do something
}
```

# Filterable Properties

There are several properties that you might want to retrieve from a media item, including the track's title, its genre, the artist, and the album name. In addition to MPMediaItemPropertyPersistentID and MPMediaItemPropertyMediaType, here are the filterable property constants you can use:

- MPMediaItemPropertyAlbumPersistentID: Returns the item's album's persistent ID.

- MPMediaItemPropertyArtistPersistentID: Returns the item's artist's persistent ID.

- MPMediaItemPropertyAlbumArtistPersistentID: Return item's album's principle artist's persistent ID.

- MPMediaItemPropertyGenrePersistentID: Return item's genre's persistent ID.

- MPMediaItemPropertyComposerPersistentID: Return item's composer's persistent ID.

- MPMediaItemPropertyPodcastPersistentID: Return item's podcast's persistent ID.

- MPMediaItemPropertyTitle: Returns the item's title, which usually means the name of the song.

- MPMediaItemPropertyAlbumTitle: Returns the name of the item's album.

- MPMediaItemPropertyArtist: Returns the name of the artist who recorded the item.

- MPMediaItemPropertyAlbumArtist: Returns the name of the principal artist behind the item's album.

- MPMediaItemPropertyGenre: Returns the item's genre (e.g., classical, rock, or alternative).

- MPMediaItemPropertyComposer: Returns the name of the item's composer.

- MPMediaItemPropertyIsCompilation: If the item is part of a compilation, returns true.

- MPMediaItemPropertyPodcastTitle: If the track is a podcast, returns the podcast's name.

Although the title and artist will almost always be known, none of these properties are guaranteed to return a value, so it's important to code defensively any time your program logic includes one of these values. Although unlikely, a media track can exist without a specified name or artist.

Here's an example that retrieves a string property from a media item:

```
NSString *title = [mediaItem valueForProperty:MPMediaItemPropertyTitle];
```

# Nonfilterable Numerical Attributes

Nearly anything that you can determine about an audio or video item in iTunes can be retrieved from a media item. The values in the following list are not filterable—in other words, you can't use them in your media property predicates. You can't, for example, retrieve all the tracks that are longer than four minutes in length. But once you have a media item, there's a wealth of information available about that item.

- MPMediaItemPropertyPlaybackDuration: Returns the length of the track in seconds.

- MPMediaItemPropertyAlbumTrackNumber: Returns the number of this track on its album.

- MPMediaItemPropertyAlbumTrackCount: Returns the number of tracks on this track's album.

- MPMediaItemPropertyDiscNumber: If the track is from a multiple-album collection, returns the track's disc number.

- MPMediaItemPropertyDiscCount: If the track is from a multiple-album collection, returns the total number of discs in that collection.

- MPMediaItemPropertyBeatsPerMinute: Returns the beats per minute of the item.

- MPMediaItemPropertyReleaseDate: Returns the release date of the item.

- MPMediaItemPropertyComments: Returns the item's comments entered in the Get Info tab.

Numeric attributes are always returned as instances of NSNumber. The track duration is an NSTimeInterval, which can be retrieved from NSNumber by using the doubleValue method. The rest are unsigned integers that can be retrieved using the unsignedIntegerValue method.

Here are a few examples of retrieving numeric properties from a media item:

```
NSNumber *durationNum = [mediaItem valueForProperty:MPMediaItemPropertyPlaybackDuration];
NSTimeInterval duration = [durationNum doubleValue];

NSNumber *trackNum = [mediaItem valueForProperty:MPMediaItemPropertyAlbumTrackNumber];
NSUInteger trackNumber = [trackNum unsignedIntegerValue];
```

## Retrieving Lyrics

If a media track has lyrics associated with it, you can retrieve those using the property key MPMediaItemPropertyLyrics. The lyrics will be returned in an instance of NSString, like so:

```
NSString *lyrics = [mediaItem valueForProperty:MPMediaItemPropertyLyrics];
```

## Retrieving Album Artwork

Some media tracks have a piece of artwork associated with them. In most instances, this will be the track's album's cover picture, though it could be something else. You retrieve the album artwork using the property key MPMediaItemPropertyArtwork, which returns an instance of the class MPMediaItemArtwork. The MPMediaItemArtwork class has a method that returns an instance of

UIImage to match a specified size. Here's some code to get the album artwork for a media item that would fit into a 100-by-100 pixel view:

```
MPMediaItemArtwork *art = [mediaItem valueForProperty:MPMediaItemPropertyArtwork];
CGSize imageSize = {100.0, 100.0};
UIImage *image = [art imageWithSize:imageSize];
```

## User-Defined Properties

Another set of data that you can retrieve from a media item are termed *User-Defined*. These are properties set on the media item based on the user's interaction. These include properties like play counts and ratings.

- MPMediaItemPropertyPlayCount: Returns the total number of times that this track has been played.

- MPMediaItemPropertySkipCount: Returns the total number of times this track has been skipped.

- MPMediaItemPropertyRating: Returns the track's rating, or 0 if the track has not been rated.

- MPMediaItemPropertyLastPlayedDate: Returns the date the track was last played.

- MPMediaItemPropertyUserGrouping: Returns the info from the Grouping tab from the iTunes Get Info panel.

## AssetURL Property

There is one last property to discuss was added in iOS 4, for use in AVFoundation. We'll mention it here, but discuss it later:

MPMediaItemPropertyAssetURL: An NSURL pointing to a media item in the user's media library.

# Media Item Collections

Media items can be grouped into collections, creatively called *media item collections*. In fact, this is how you specify a list of media items to be played by the player controllers. Media item collections, which are represented by the class MPMediaItemCollection, are immutable collections of media items. You can create new media item collections, but you can't change the contents of the collection once it has been created.

## Creating a New Collection

The easiest way to create a media item collection is to put all the media items you want to be in the collection into an instance of NSArray, in the order you want them. You can then pass the instance of NSArray to the factory method collectionWithItems:, like so:

```
NSArray *items = @[mediaItem1, mediaItem2];
MPMediaItemCollection *collection = [MPMediaItemCollection collectionWithItems:items];
```

## Retrieving Media Items

To retrieve a specific media item from a media item collection, you use the instance method items, which returns an NSArray instance containing all of the media items in the order they exist in the collection. If you want to retrieve the specific media item at a particular index, for example, you would do this:

```
MPMediaItem *item = [[mediaCollection items] objectAtIndex:5];
```

## Creating Derived Collections

Because media item collections are immutable, you can't add items to a collection, nor can you append the contents of another media item collection onto another one. Since you can get to an array of media items contained in a collection using the instance method items, however, you can make a mutable copy of the items array, manipulate the mutable array's contents, and then create a new collection based on the modified array.

Here's some code that appends a single media item onto the end of an existing collection:

```
NSMutableArray *items = [[originalCollection items] mutableCopy];
[items addObject:mediaItem];
MPMediaItemCollection *newCollection = [MPMediaItemCollection collectionWithItems:items];
```

Similarly, to combine two different collections, you combine their items and create a new collection from the combined array:

```
NSMutableArray *items = [[firstCollection items] mutableCopy];
[items addObjectsFromArray:[secondCollection items]];
MPMediaItemCollection *newCollection = [MPMediaItemCollection collectionWithItems:items];
```

To delete an item or items from an existing collection, you can use the same basic technique. You can retrieve a mutable copy of the items contained in the collection, delete the ones you want to remove, then create a new collection based on the modified copy of the items, like so:

```
NSMutableArray *items = [[originalCollection items] mutableCopy];
[items removeObject:mediaItemToDelete];
MPMediaItemCollection *newCollection = [MPMediaItemCollection collectionWithItems:items];
```

## Media Queries and Media Property Predicates

To search for media items in the media library, you use media queries, which are instances of the class MPMediaQuery. A number of factory methods can be used to retrieve media items from the library sorted by a particular property. For example, if you want a list of all media items sorted by artist, you can use the artistsQuery class method to create an instance of MPMediaQuery configured, like this:

```
MPMediaQuery *artistsQuery = [MPMediaQuery artistsQuery];
```

Table 12-1 lists the factory methods on MPMediaQuery.

*Table 12-1. MPMediaQuery Factory Methods*

| Factory Method | Included Media Types | Grouped/Sorted By |
|---|---|---|
| albumsQuery | Music | Album |
| artistsQuery | Music | Artist |
| audiobooksQuery | Audio Books | Title |
| compilationsQuery | Any | Album* |
| composersQuery | Any | Composer |
| genresQuery | Any | Genre |
| playlistsQuery | Any | Playlist |
| podcastsQuery | Podcasts | Podcast Title |
| songsQuery | Music | Title |

*\*Includes only albums with MPMediaItemPropertyIsCompilation set to YES.*

These factory methods are useful for displaying the entire contents of the user's library that meet preset conditions. That said, you will often want to restrict the query to an even smaller subset of items. You can do that using a media predicate. Media predicates can be created on any of the filterable properties of a media item, including the persistent ID, media type, or any of the string properties (like title, artist, or genre).

To create a media predicate on a filterable property, use the class MPMediaPropertyPredicate. Create new instances using the factory method predicateWithValue:forProperty:comparisonType:. Here, for example, is how to create a media predicate that searches for all songs with the title "Happy Birthday":

```
MPMediaPropertyPredicate *titlePredicate =
    [MPMediaPropertyPredicate predicateWithValue:@"Happy Birthday"
                              forProperty:MPMediaItemPropertyTitle
                         comparisonType:MPMediaPredicateComparisonContains];
```

The first value you pass—in this case, @"Happy Birthday"—is the comparison value. The second value is the filterable property you want that comparison value compared to. By specifying MPMediaItemPropertyTitle, you're saying you want the song titles compared to the string "Happy Birthday". The last item specifies the type of comparison to do. You can pass MPMediaPredicateComparisonEqualTo to look for an exact match to the specified string, or MPMediaPredicateComparisonContains to look for any item that contains the passed value as a substring.

> **Note** Media queries are always case-insensitive, regardless of the comparison type used. Therefore, the preceding example would also return songs called "HAPPY BIRTHDAY" and "Happy BirthDAY."

Because you've passed MPMediaPredicateComparisonContains, this predicate would match "Happy Birthday, the Opera" and "Slash Sings Happy Birthday," in addition to plain old "Happy Birthday."

Had you passed MPMediaPredicateComparisonEqualTo, then only the last one—the exact match—would be found.

You can create and pass multiple media property predicates to a single query. If you do, the query will use the AND logical operator and return only the media items that meet all of your predicates.

To create a media query based on media property predicates, you use the init method initWithFilterPredicates: and pass in an instance of NSSet containing all the predicates you want it to use, like so:

```
MPMediaQuery *query =
    [[MPMediaQuery alloc] initWithFilterPredicates:[NSSet setWithObject:titlePredicate]];
```

Once you have a query—whether it was created manually or retrieved using one of the factory methods—there are two ways you can execute the query and retrieve the items to be displayed:

■ You can use the items property of the query, which returns an instance of NSArray containing all the media items that meet the criteria specified in your media property predicates, like so:

```
NSArray *items = query.items;
```

■ You can use the property collections to retrieve the objects grouped by one of the filterable properties. You can tell the query which property to group the items by by setting the groupingType property to the property key for the filterable attribute you want it grouped by. If you don't set groupingType, it will default to grouping by title.

When you access the collections property, the query will instead return an array of MPMediaItemCollections, with one collection for each distinct value in your grouping type. So, if you specified a groupingType of MPMediaGroupingArtist, for example, the query would return an array with one MPMediaItemCollection for each artist who has at least one song that matches your criteria. Each collection would contain all the songs by that artist that meet the specified criteria. Here's what that might look like in code:

```
query.groupingType = MPMediaGroupingArtist;
NSArray *collections = query.collections;
for (MPMediaItemCollection *oneCollection in collections) {
    // oneCollection has all songs by one artist that meet criteria
}
```

You need to be very careful with media queries. They are synchronous and happen in the main thread, so if you specify a query that returns 100,000 media items, your user interface is going to hiccup while those items are found, retrieved, and stored in collections or an array. If you are using a media query that might return more than a dozen or so media items, you might want to consider moving that action off the main thread. You'll learn how to move operations off of the main thread in Chapter 14.

# The Media Picker Controller

If you want to let your users select specific media items from their library, you'll want to use the media picker controller. The media picker controller lets your users choose audio from their iPod library using an interface that's nearly identical to the one in the Music application they're already used to using. Your users will not be able to use Cover Flow, but they will be able to select from lists sorted by song title, artist, playlist, album, and genre, just as they can when selecting music in the Music application (Figure 12-1).

*Figure 12-1. The media picker controller by artist, song, and album*

The media picker controller is extremely easy to use. It works just like many of the other provided controller classes covered in the previous chapters, such as the image picker controller and the mail compose view controller that you used in Chapter 11. Create an instance of MPMediaPickerController, assign it a delegate, and then present it modally, like so:

```
MPMediaPickerController *picker = [[MPMediaPickerController alloc] initWithMediaTypes:MPMediaTypeMusic];
picker.delegate = self;
[picker setAllowsPickingMultipleItems:YES];
picker.prompt = NSLocalizedString(@"Select items to play", @"Select items to play");
[self presentModalViewController:picker animated:YES];
```

When you create the media picker controller instance, you need to specify a media type. This can be one of the three audio types mentioned earlier—MPMediaTypeMusic, MPMediaTypePodcast, or

MPMediaTypeAudioBook. You can also pass MPMediaTypeAnyAudio, which will currently return any audio item.

> **Note** Passing non-audio media types will not cause any errors in your code, but when the media picker appears, it will only display audio items.

You can also use the bitwise OR (|) operator to let your user select any combination of media types. For example, if you want to let your user select from podcasts and audio books, but not music, you could create your picker like this:

```
MPMediaPickerController *picker =
    [[MPMediaPickerController alloc] initWithMediaTypes:MPMediaTypePodcast | MPMediaTypeAudioBook ];
```

By using the bitwise OR operator with these constants, you end up passing an integer that has the bits representing both of these media types set to 1 and all the other bits set to 0.

Also notice that you need to tell the media picker controller to allow the user to select multiple items. The default behavior of the media picker is to let the user choose one, and only one, item. If that's the behavior you want, then you don't have to do anything, but if you want to let the user select multiple items, you must explicitly tell it so.

The media picker also has a property called prompt, which is a string that will be displayed above the navigation bar in the picker (see the top of Figure 12-1). This is optional, but generally a good idea.

The media picker controller's delegate needs to conform to the protocol MPMediaPickerControllerDelegate. This defines two methods: one that is called if the user taps the Cancel button and another that is called if the user chooses one or more songs.

## Handling Media Picker Cancels

If, after you present the media picker controller, the user hits the Cancel button, the delegate method mediaPickerDidCancel: will be called. You must implement this method on the media picker controller's delegate, even if you don't have any processing that needs to be done when the user cancels, since you must dismiss the modal view controller. Here is a minimal, but fairly standard, implementation of that method:

```
- (void)mediaPickerDidCancel:(MPMediaPickerController *)mediaPicker
{
    [self dismissModalViewControllerAnimated: YES];
}
```

## Handling Media Picker Selections

If the user selected one or more media items using the media picker controller, then the delegate method mediaPicker:didPickMediaItems: will be called. This method must be implemented, not only because it's the delegate's responsibility to dismiss the media picker controller, but also because this method is the only way to know which tracks your user selected. The selected items are grouped in a media item collection.

Here's a very simple example implementation of mediaPicker:didPickMediaItems: that assigns the returned collection to one of the delegate's properties:

```
- (void)mediaPicker:(MPMediaPickerController *)mediaPicker
       didPickMediaItems:(MPMediaItemCollection *)theCollection
{
    [self dismissModalViewControllerAnimated: YES];
    self.collection = theCollection;
}
```

# The Music Player Controller

As we discussed before, there are two player controllers in the MediaPlayer framework: the music player controller and movie player controller. We'll get to the movie player controller later. The music player controller allows you to play a queue of media items by specifying either a media item collection or a media query. As we stated earlier, the music player controller has no visual elements. It's an object that plays the audio. It allows you to manipulate the playback of that audio by skipping forward or backward, telling it which specific media item to play, adjusting the volume, or skipping to a specific playback time in the current item.

The MediaPlayer framework offers two completely different kinds of music player controllers: the iPod music player and the application music player. The way you use them is identical, but there's a key difference in how they work. The iPod music player is the one that's used by the Music app; as is the case with those apps, when you quit your app while music is playing, the music continues playing. In addition, when the user is listening to music and starts up an app that uses the iPod music player, the iPod music player will keep playing that music. In contrast, the application music player will kill the music when your app terminates.

There's a bit of a gotcha here in that both the iPod and the application music player controllers can be used at the same time. If you use the application music player controller to play audio, and the user is currently listening to music, both will play simultaneously. This may or may not be what you want to happen, so you will usually want to check the iPod music player to see if there is music currently playing, even if you actually plan to use the application music player controller for playback.

## Creating the Music Player Controller

To get either of the music player controllers, use one of the factory methods on MPMusicPlayerController. To retrieve the iPod music player, use the method iPodMusicPlayer, like so:

```
MPMusicPlayerController *thePlayer = [MPMusicPlayerController iPodMusicPlayer];
```

Retrieving the application music player controller is done similarly, using the applicationMusicPlayer method instead, like this:

```
MPMusicPlayerController *thePlayer = [MPMusicPlayerController applicationMusicPlayer];
```

## Determining If the Music Player Controller Is Playing

Once you create an application music player, you'll need to give it something to play. But if you grab the iPod music player controller, it could very well already be playing something. You can determine if it is by looking at the playbackState property of the player. If it's currently playing, it will be set to MPMusicPlaybackStatePlaying.

```
if (player.playbackState == MPMusicPlaybackStatePlaying) {
    // playing
}
```

## Specifying the Music Player Controller's Queue

There are two ways to specify the music player controller's queue of audio tracks: provide a media query or provide a media item collection. If you provide a media query, the music player controller's queue will be set to the media items returned by the items property. If you provide a media item collection, it will use the collection you pass as its queue. In either case, you will replace the existing queue with the items in the query or collection you pass in. Setting the queue will also reset the current track to the first item in the queue.

To set the music player's queue using a query, use the method setQueueWithQuery:. For example, here's how you would set the queue to all songs, sorted by artist:

```
MPMusicPlayerController *player = [MPMusicPlayerController iPodMusicPlayer];
MPMediaQuery *artistsQuery = [MPMediaQuery artistsQuery];
[player setQueueWithQuery:artistsQuery];
```

Setting the queue with a media item collection is accomplished with the method setQueueWithItemCollection:, like so:

```
MPMusicPlayerController *player = [MPMusicPlayerController iPodMusicPlayer];
NSArray *items = [NSArray arrayWithObjects:mediaItem1, mediaItem2, nil];
MPMediaItemCollection *collection = [MPMediaItemCollection collectionWithItems:items];
[items setQueueWithItemCollection:collection];
```

Unfortunately, there's currently no way to retrieve the music player controller's queue using public APIs. That means you will generally need to keep track of the queue independently of the music player controller if you want to be able to manipulate the queue.

## Getting or Setting the Currently Playing Media Item

You can get or set the current song using the nowPlayingItem property. This lets you determine which track is already playing if you're using the iPod music player controller and lets you specify a new song to play. Note that the media item you specify must already be in the music player controller's queue. Here's how you retrieve the currently playing item:

```
MPMediaItem *currentTrack = player.nowPlayingItem;
To switch to a different track, do this:
player.nowPlayingItem = newTrackToPlay; // must be in queue already
```

# Skipping Tracks

The music player controller allows you to skip forward one song using the method `skipToNextItem` or to skip back to the previous song using `skipToPreviousItem`. If there is no next or previous song to skip to, the music player controller stops playing. The music player controller also allows you to move back to the beginning of the current song using `skipToBeginning`.

Here is an example of all three methods:

```
[player skipToNextItem];
[player skipToPreviousItem];
[player skipToBeginning];
```

# Seeking

When you're using your iPhone, iPod touch, or iTunes to listen to music, if you press and hold the forward or back button, the music will start seeking forward or backward, playing the music at an ever-accelerating pace. This lets you, for example, stay in the same track, but skip over a part you don't want to listen to, or skip back to something you missed. This same functionality is available through the music player controller using the methods `beginSeekingForward` and `beginSeekingBackward`. With both methods, you stop the process with a call to `endSeeking`.

Here is a set of calls that demonstrate seeking forward and stopping, then seeking backwards and stopping:

```
[player beginSeekingForward];
[player endSeeking];

[player beginSeekingBackward];
[player endSeeking];
```

# Playback Time

Not to be confused with payback time (something we've dreamt of for years, ever since they replaced the excellent Dick York with the far blander Dick Sargent), playback time specifies how far into the current song you currently are. If the current song has been playing for five seconds, then the playback time will be 5.0.

You can retrieve and set the current playback time using the property `currentPlaybackTime`. You might use this, for example, when using an application music player controller, to resume a song at exactly the point where it was stopped when the application was last quit. Here's an example of using this property to skip forward ten seconds in the current song:

```
NSTimeInterval currentTime = player.currentPlaybackTime;
MPMediaItem *currentSong = player.nowPlayingItem;
NSNumber *duration = [currentSong valueForProperty:
MPMediaItemPropertyPlaybackDuration];
currentTime += 10.0;
if (currentTime > [duration doubleValue])
    currentTime = [duration doubleValue];
player.currentPlaybackTime = currentTime;
```

Notice that you check the duration of the currently playing song to make sure you don't pass in an invalid playback time.

## Repeat and Shuffle Modes

Music player controllers have ordered queues of songs and, most of the time, they play those songs in the order they exist in the queue, playing from the beginning of the queue to the end and then stopping. Your user can change this behavior by setting the repeat and shuffle properties in the iPod or Music application. You can also change the behavior by setting the music player controller's repeat and shuffle modes, represented by the properties repeatMode and shuffleMode. There are four repeat modes:

- MPMusicRepeatModeDefault: Uses the repeat mode last used in the iPod or Music application.

- MPMusicRepeatModeNone: Don't repeat at all. When the queue is done, stop playing.

- MPMusicRepeatModeOne: Keep repeating the currently playing track until your user goes insane. Ideal for playing "It's a Small World."

- MPMusicRepeatModeAll: When the queue is done, start over with the first track.

There are also four shuffle modes:

- MPMusicShuffleModeDefault: Use the shuffle mode last used in the iPod or Music application.

- MPMusicShuffleModeOff: Don't shuffle at all—just play the songs in the queue order.

- MPMusicShuffleModeSongs: Play all the songs in the queue in random order.

- MPMusicShuffleModeAlbums: Play all the songs from the currently playing song's album in random order.

Here is an example of turning off both repeat and shuffle:

```
player.repeatMode = MPMusicRepeatNone;
player.shuffleMode = MPMusicShuffleModeOff;
```

## Adjusting the Music Player Controller's Volume

The music player controller lets you manipulate the volume at which it plays the items in its queue. The volume can be adjusted using the property volume, which is a clamped floating-point value. Clamped values store numbers between 0.0 and 1.0. In the case of volume, setting the property to 1.0 means play the tracks at the maximum volume, and a value of 0.0 means turn off the volume. Any value between those two extremes represents a different percentage of the maximum volume, so setting volume to 0.5 is like turning a volume knob halfway up.

> **Caution**    Setting volume to 1.1 will not make the volume any louder than setting it to 1.0. Despite what Nigel might have told you, you can't set the volume to 11.

Here's how you set a player to maximum volume:

```
player.volume = 1.0;
```

And here's how you set the volume to its midpoint:

```
player.volume = 0.5;
```

## Music Player Controller Notifications

Music player controllers are capable of sending out notifications when any of three things happen:

- When the playback state (playing, stopped, paused, seeking, etc.) changes, the music player controller can send out the MPMusicPlayerControllerPlaybackStateDidChangeNotification notification.

- When the volume changes, it can send out the MPMusicPlayerControllerVolumeDidChangeNotification notification.

- When a new track starts playing, it can send out the MPMusicPlayerControllerNowPlayingItemDidChangeNotification notification.

Note that music player controllers don't send any notifications by default. You must tell an instance of MPMusicPlayerController to start generating notifications by calling the method beginGeneratingPlaybackNotifications. To have the controller stop generating notifications, call the method endGeneratingPlaybackNotifications.

If you need to receive any of these notifications, you first implement a handler method that takes one argument, an NSNotification *, and then register with the notification center for the notification of interest. For example, if you want a method to fire whenever the currently playing item changed, you could implement a method called nowPlayingItemChanged:, like so:

```
- (void)nowPlayingItemChanged:(NSNotification *)notification {
    NSLog(@"A new track started");
}
```

To start listening for those notifications, you could register with the notification for the type of notification you're interested in, and then have that music player controller start generating the notifications:

```
NSNotificationCenter *notificationCenter = [NSNotificationCenter defaultCenter];
[notificationCenter addObserver:self
                       selector:@selector(nowPlayingItemChanged:)
                           name:MPMusicPlayerControllerNowPlayingItemDidChangeNotification
                         object:player];
[player beginGeneratingPlaybackNotifications];
```

Once you do this, any time the track changes, your nowPlayingItemChanged: method will be called by the notification center.

When you're finished and no longer need the notifications, you unregister and tell the music player controller to stop generating notifications:

```
NSNotificationCenter *center = [NSNotificationCenter defaultCenter];
[center removeObserver:self
                name:MPMusicPlayerControllerNowPlayingItemDidChangeNotification
              object:player];
[player endGeneratingPlaybackNotifications];
```

Now that you have all that theory out of the way, let's build something!

# Simple Music Player

The first application you're going to build is going to take what you've covered so far to build a simple music player. The application will allow users to create a queue of songs via the MPMediaPickerController and play them back via the MPMusicPlayerController.

> **Note**    We'll use the term *queue* to describe the application's list of songs, rather than the term *playlist*. When working with the media library, the term *playlist* refers to actual playlists synchronized from iTunes. Those playlists can be read, but they can't be created using the SDK. To avoid confusion, we'll stick with the term *queue*.

When the application launches, it will check to see if music is currently playing. If so, it will allow that music to keep playing and will append any requested music to the end of the list of songs to be played.

> **Tip**    If your application needs to play a certain sound or music, you may feel that it's appropriate to turn off the user's currently playing music, but you should do that with caution. If you're just providing a soundtrack, you really should consider letting the music that's playing continue playing, or at least giving the users the choice about whether to turn off their chosen music in favor of your application's music. It is, of course, your call, but tread lightly when it comes to stomping on your user's music.

The application you'll build isn't very practical because everything you're offering to your users (and more) is already available in the Music application on your iOS device. But writing it will allow you to explore almost all of the tasks your own application might ever need to perform with regard to the media library.

> **Caution**    This chapter's application must be run on an actual iOS. The iOS Simulator does not have
> access to the iTunes library on your computer, and any of the calls related to the iTunes library access
> APIs will result in an error on the Simulator.

## Building the SimplePlayer Application

Your app will retrieve the iPod music player controller and allow you to add songs to the queue by
using the media picker. You'll provide some rudimentary playback controls to play/pause the music,
as well as to skip forward and backward in the queue.

> **Note**    As a reminder, the Simulator does not yet support the media library functionality. To get the most
> out of the SimplePlayer application, you need to run it on your iOS device, which means signing up for
> one of Apple's paid iOS Developer Programs. If you have not already done that, you might want to take
> a short break and head over to `http://developer.apple.com/programs/register/` and
> check it out.

Let's start by creating a new project in Xcode. Since this is a very simple application, you'll use
the Single View Application project template and name the new project SimplePlayer. Since you only
have one view, you don't need your project to use storyboards, though you can use them if
you wish.

Once your new project is created, you need to add the MediaPlayer framework to the project.
Select the SimplePlayer project at the top of the Navigator Pane. In the Project Editor, select the
SimplePlayer target and open the Build Phases pane. Find the Link Binary With Libraries (3 Items)
section and expand it. Click the + button at the bottom of the section and add the MediaPlayer
framework. If you've done this correctly, the `MediaPlayer.framework` should appear in the project
in the Navigator pane. Let's keep things clean, and move the `MediaPlayer.framework` to the
Frameworks group in your project.

## Building the User Interface

Single-click `ViewController.xib` to open Interface Builder. Let's take a look at Figure 12-2. There
are three labels along the top, an image view in the middle, and button bar on the bottom with four
buttons. Let's start from the bottom and work our way up.

*Figure 12-2. The SimplePlayer application playing a song*

Drag a UIToolbar from the object library to the bottom of the UIView. By default, the UIToolbar gives you a UIBarButtonItem aligned to the left side of the toolbar. Since you need four buttons in your toolbar, you'll keep this button. Drag a flexible space bar button item (Figure 12-3) to the left of the UIBarButtonItem. Make sure you use the flexible space, not the fixed space. If you placed it in the correct spot, the UIBarButtonItem should now be aligned to the right side of the UIToolbar (Figure 12-4).

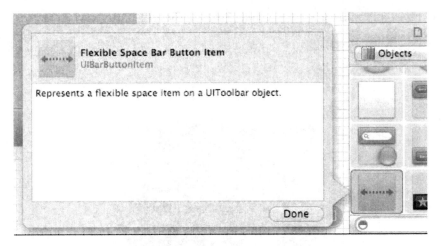

*Figure 12-3.* *The flexible space bar button item in the Object Library*

*Figure 12-4.* *The SimplePlayer toolbar with the flexible space*

Add three UIBarButtonItems to the left of the flexible space. These will be your playback control buttons. In order to center these buttons, you need to add one more flexible space bar button Item to left side of your UIToolbar (Figure 12-5). Select the left most button and open the Attribute

Inspector. Change the Identifier from Custom to Rewind (Figure 12-6). Select the button to the right of your new Rewind button and change the Identifier to Play. Change the Identifier to right of your Play button to Fast Forward. Select the rightmost button and change the Identifier to Add. When you're done, it should look like Figure 12-7.

*Figure 12-5.* *Toolbar with all your buttons*

*Figure 12-6.* *Changing the bar button item identifier to Rewind*

*Figure 12-7. The completed Toolbar*

Moving up the view, you need to add a UIImageView. Drag one onto your view, above the toolbar. Interface Builder will expand the UIImageView to fill the available area. Since you don't want that, open the Size Inspector in the Utility pane. The UIImageView should be selected, but if it isn't, select it to make sure you're adjusting the right component. The Size Inspector should show that your UIImageView width is 320. Change the height to match the width. Your image view should now be square. Center the image view in your view, using the guidelines to help.

Now you need to add the three labels across the top. Drag a label to the top of your application's view. Extend the area of the label to the width of your view. Open the Attribute Inspector, and change the label text from "Label" to "Now Playing." Change the label's color from black to white, and set the font to System Bold 17.0. Set the alignment to center. Finally, change the label's background color to black (Figure 12-8). Add another label below this label. Give it the same attributes as the first label, but set the text from "Label" to "Artist." Add one more label, below the Artist label, with the same attribute settings, and set the text to "Song."

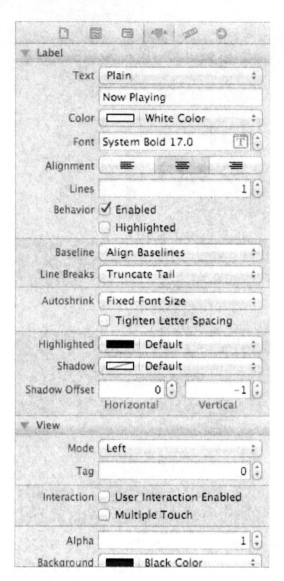

*Figure 12-8. Your SimplePlayer label attributes*

Finally, set the background of your view to black. Because black is cool.

## Declaring Outlets and Actions

In Interface Builder, switch from the standard editor to the assistant editor. The Editor pane should split to show Interface Builder on the left and `ViewController.h` on the right. Control-drag from the label with the text "Now Playing" to just below the `@interface` declaration. Create a `UILabel` outlet and name it "status." Repeat for the Artist and Song labels, naming the outlets "artist" and "song," respectively.

Control-drag from the image view to below the label outlets and create a `UIImageView` outlet named "imageView." Do the same for the Toolbar and the Play button. Now that you have your outlets set up, you need to add your actions.

Control-drag from the rewindButton, and create an action named "rewindPressed." Repeat for each button. Name the play action "playPausePressed," the fast forward action "fastForwardPressed," and the add action "addPressed."

Switch back to the standard editor and select `ViewController.h` to open it in the editor.

First, you need to have your `ViewController` conform to the `MPMediaPickerDelegate` protocol, so you can use the `MPMediaPicker` controller. In order to do that, you need to import the MediaPlayer header file, right after the UIKit header import:

```
#import <MediaPlayer/MediaPlayer.h>
```

Then you'll add the protocol declaration to `ViewController`:

```
@interface ViewController : UIViewController <MPMediaPickerControllerDelegate>
```

You need to add another `UIBarButtonItem` property to hold the pause button you'll display while music is playing. You also need to change the Play button property from weak to strong so you can toggle between the two.

```
@property (strong, nonatomic) IBOutlet UIBarButtonItem *play;
@property (strong, nonatomic)         UIBarButtonItem *pause;
```

You need two more properties: one to hold your `MPMediaPlayerController` instance, and the other to hold the `MPMediaItemCollection` that the player is playing.

```
@property (strong, nonatomic) MPMusicPlayerController *player;
@property (strong, nonatomic) MPMediaItemCollection   *collection;
```

When the `MPMusicPlayerController` starts playing a new media item, it sends a notification of type `MPMusicPlayerControllerNowPlayingItemDidChangeNotification`. You'll set up an observer for that notification to update the labels in your view.

```
- (void)nowPlayingItemChanged:(NSNotification *)notification;
```

Select `ViewController.m` to open it in the Editor pane. First you need to set up things for when the view loads. Find the `viewDidLoad` method. After the call to super, you need to instantiate the Pause button.

```
self.pause = [[UIBarButtonItem alloc] initWithBarButtonSystemItem:UIBarButtonSystemItemPause
                                              target:self
                                              action:@selector(playPausePressed:)];
[self.pause setStyle:UIBarButtonItemStyleBordered];
```

Next, create your `MPMusicPlayerController` instance.

```
self.player = [MPMusicPlayerController iPodMusicPlayer];
```

Then register for the notification when the Now Playing item changes in the player.

```
NSNotificationCenter *notificationCenter = [NSNotificationCenter defaultCenter];
[notificationCenter addObserver:self
                   selector:@selector(nowPlayingItemChanged:)
                       name:MPMusicPlayerControllerNowPlayingItemDidChangeNotification
                     object:self.player];
[self.player beginGeneratingPlaybackNotifications];
```

Note that you must tell the player to begin generating playback notifications. Since you registered for notifications, you have to remove your observer when view is released.

```
- (void)didReceiveMemoryWarning
{
    [super didReceiveMemoryWarning];
    // Dispose of any resources that can be recreated.
    [[NSNotificationCenter defaultCenter]
        removeObserver:self
                  name:MPMusicPlayerControllerNowPlayingItemDidChangeNotification
                object:self.player];
}
```

Let's work on the button actions next. When the user presses the Rewind button, you want the player to skip to the previous song in the queue. However, if it's at the first song in the queue, it'll just skip to the beginning of that song.

```
- (IBAction)rewindPressed:(id)sender
{
    if ([self.player indexOfNowPlayingItem] == 0) {
        [self.player skipToBeginning];
    }
    else {
        [self.player endSeeking];
        [self.player skipToPreviousItem];
    }
}
```

When the Play button is pressed, you want to start playing the music. You also want to the button to change to the Pause button. Then, if the player is already playing music, you want to player to pause (stop), and have the button change back to the Play button.

```
- (IBAction)playPausePressed:(id)sender
{
    MPMusicPlaybackState playbackState = [self.player playbackState];
    NSMutableArray *items = [NSMutableArray arrayWithArray:[self.toolbar items]];
    if (playbackState == MPMusicPlaybackStateStopped || playbackState == MPMusicPlaybackStatePaused) {
        [self.player play];
        [items replaceObjectAtIndex:2 withObject:self.pause];
    }
```

```
    else if (playbackState == MPMusicPlaybackStatePlaying) {
        [self.player pause];
        [items replaceObjectAtIndex:2 withObject:self.play];
    }
    [self.toolbar setItems:items animated:NO];
}
```

You query the player for its playback state, then use it to determine whether you should start or stop the player. In order to toggle between the Play and Pause buttons, you need to get the array of items in the toolbar and replace the third item (index of 2) with the appropriate button. Then you replace the entire array of bar button items for the toolbar.

The Fast Forward button works similarly to the Rewind button. When pressed, the player moves forward in the queue and plays the next song. If it's at the last song in the queue, it stops the player and resets the Play button.

```
- (IBAction)fastForwardPressed:(id)sender
{
    NSUInteger nowPlayingIndex = [self.player indexOfNowPlayingItem];
    [self.player endSeeking];
    [self.player skipToNextItem];
    if ([self.player nowPlayingItem] == nil) {
        if ([self.collection count] > nowPlayingIndex+1) {
            // added more songs while playing
            [self.player setQueueWithItemCollection:self.collection];
            MPMediaItem *item = [[self.collection items] objectAtIndex:nowPlayingIndex+1];
            [self.player setNowPlayingItem:item];
            [self.player play];
        }
        else {
            // no more songs
            [self.player stop];
            NSMutableArray *items = [NSMutableArray arrayWithArray:[self.toolbar items]];
            [items replaceObjectAtIndex:2 withObject:self.play];
            [self.toolbar setItems:items];
        }
    }
}
```

When the Add button is pressed, you need to modally display the MPMediaPickerController. You set it to display only music media types, and set its delegate to ViewController.

```
- (IBAction)addPressed:(id)sender
{
    MPMediaType mediaType = MPMediaTypeMusic;
    MPMediaPickerController *picker =
        [[MPMediaPickerController alloc] initWithMediaTypes:mediaType];
    picker.delegate = self;
    [picker setAllowsPickingMultipleItems:YES];
    picker.prompt = NSLocalizedString(@"Select items to play", @"Select items to play");
    [self presentViewController:picker animated:YES completion:nil];
}
```

This seems like a good point to add the MPMediaPickerControllerDelegate methods. There are only two methods that are defined in the protocol: mediaPicker:didPickMediaItems:, called when the user is done selecting; and mediaPickerDidCancel:, called when the user has cancelled the media selection.

```
#pragma mark - Media Picker Delegate Methods

- (void)mediaPicker:(MPMediaPickerController *)mediaPicker
      didPickMediaItems:(MPMediaItemCollection *)theCollection
{
    [mediaPicker dismissViewControllerAnimated:YES completion:nil];

    if (self.collection == nil) {
        self.collection = theCollection;
        [self.player setQueueWithItemCollection:self.collection];
        MPMediaItem *item = [[self.collection items] objectAtIndex:0];
        [self.player setNowPlayingItem:item];
        [self playPausePressed:self];
    }
    else {
        NSArray *oldItems = [self.collection items];
        NSArray *newItems = [oldItems arrayByAddingObjectsFromArray:[theCollection items]];
        self.collection = [[MPMediaItemCollection alloc] initWithItems:newItems];
    }
}

- (void)mediaPickerDidCancel:(MPMediaPickerController *) mediaPicker
{
    [mediaPicker dismissViewControllerAnimated:YES completion:nil];
}
```

When the user is done selecting, you dismiss the media picker controller. Then you look at the media collection property. If your ViewController collection property is nil, then you simply assign it to the media collection sent in the delegate call. If a collection exists, then you need to append the new media items to the existing collection. The mediaPickerDidCancel: method simply dismissed the media picker controller.

Lastly, you need to implement the notification method for when the now playing item changes.

```
#pragma mark - Notification Methods

- (void)nowPlayingItemChanged:(NSNotification *)notification
{
        MPMediaItem *currentItem = [self.player nowPlayingItem];
    if (currentItem == nil) {
        [self.imageView setImage:nil];
        [self.imageView setHidden:YES];
        [self.status setText:NSLocalizedString (@"Tap + to Add More Music", @"Add More Music")];
        [self.artist setText:nil];
        [self.song setText:nil];
    }
```

```
    else {
        MPMediaItemArtwork *artwork = [currentItem valueForProperty: MPMediaItemPropertyArtwork];
        if (artwork) {
            UIImage *artworkImage = [artwork imageWithSize:CGSizeMake(320, 320)];
            [imageView setImage:artworkImage];
            [imageView setHidden:NO];
        }

        // Display the artist and song name for the now-playing media item
        [self.status setText:NSLocalizedString(@"Now Playing", @"Now Playing")];
        [self.artist setText:[currentItem valueForProperty:MPMediaItemPropertyArtist]];
        [self.song setText:[currentItem valueForProperty:MPMediaItemPropertyTitle]];
    }
}
```

The nowPlayingItemChanged: method first queries the player for the media item that it is playing. If it is not playing anything, it resets the view and sets the status label to tell the user to add more music. If something is playing, then it retrieves the artwork for the media item using the MPMediaItemPropertyArtwork property. It checks to make sure the media item has artwork, and if it does, it puts it in your image view. Then you update the labels to tell you the artist and song name.

Build and run the SimplePlayer application. You should be able to select music from your media library and play it. This is a pretty simple player (duh) and doesn't give you much in terms of functionality, but you can see how to use the MediaPlayer framework to play music. Next, you'll use the MediaPlayer framework to playback video as well.

# MPMoviePlayerController

Playing back video with the MediaPlayer framework is very simple. First, you need the URL of the media item you wish to play back. The URL could point to either a video file in your media library or to a video resource on the Internet. If you want to play a video in your media library, you can retrieve the URL from an MPMediaItem via its MPMediaItemPropertyAssetURL.

```
// videoMediaItem is an instance of MPMediaItem that point to a video in our media library
NSURL *url = [videoMediaItem valueForProperty:MPMediaItemPropertyAssetURL];
```

Once you have your video URL, you use it to create an instance of MPMoviePlayerController. This view controller handles the playback of your video and the built-in playback controls. The MPMoviePlayerController has a UIView property where the playback is presented. This UIView can be integrated into your application's view (controller) hierarchy. It is much easier to use the MPMoviePlayerViewController class, which encapsulates the MPMoviePlayerController. Then you can push the MPMoviePlayerViewController into you view (controller) hierarchy modally, making it much easier to manage. The MPMoviePlayerViewController class gives you access to its underlying MPMoviePlayerController as a property.

In order to determine the state of your video media in the MPMoviePlayerController, a series of notifications are sent (Table 12-2).

*Table 12-2. MPMoviePlayerController Notifications*

| Notification | Description |
| --- | --- |
| MPMovieDurationAvailableNotification | The movie (video) duration (length) has been determined. |
| MPMovieMediaTypesAvailableNotification | The movie (video) media types (formats) have been determined. |
| MPMovieNaturalSizeAvailableNotification | The movie (video) natural (preferred) frame size has been determined or changed. |
| MPMoviePlayerDidEnterFullscreenNotification | The player has entered full screen mode. |
| MPMoviePlayerDidExitFullscreenNotification | The player has exited full screen mode. |
| MPMoviePlayerIsAirPlayVideoActiveDid ChangeNotification | The player has started or finished playing the movie (video) via AirPlay. |
| MPMoviePlayerLoadStateDidChangeNotification | The player (network) buffering state has changed. |
| MPMoviePlayerNowPlayingMovieDidChangeNotification | The current playing movie (video) has changed. |
| MPMoviePlayerPlaybackDidFinishNotification | The player is finished playing. The reason can be found via the MPMoviePlayerDidFinishReasonUserInfoKey. |
| MPMoviePlayerPlaybackStateDidChangeNotification | The player playback state has changed. |
| MPMoviePlayerScalingModeDidChangeNotification | The player scaling mode has changed. |
| MPMoviePlayerThumbnailImageRequest DidFinishNotification | A request to capture a thumbnail image has completed. It may have succeeded or failed. |
| MPMoviePlayerWillEnterFullscreenNotification | The player is about to enter full screen mode. |
| MPMoviePlayerWillExitFullscreenNotification | The player is about to exit full screen mode. |
| MPMovieSourceTypeAvailableNotification | The movie (video) source type was unknown and is now known. |

Generally, you only need to worry about these notifications if you use MPMoviePlayerController.

Enough talk. Let's build an app that plays both audio and video media from your Media Library.

# MPMediaPlayer

You're going to build a new app using the MediaPlayer framework that will allow you to play both audio and video content from your media library. You'll start with a tab bar controller with a tab for your audio content and another tab for your video content (Figure 12-9). You won't be using a queue to order your media choices. You'll keep this simple: the user picks a media item, the application will play it.

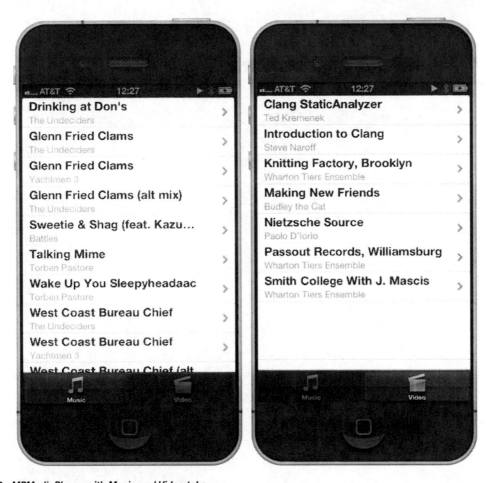

*Figure 12-9. MPMediaPlayer with Music and Video tabs*

Create a new project using the Tabbed Application template. Name the application MPMediaPlayer, and have the project use storyboards and Automatic Reference Counting. Add the MediaPlayer framework to the MPMediaPlayer target. If you're not sure how to do that, review how you did it in the SimplePlayer application.

Xcode will create two view controllers, FirstViewController and SecondViewController, and provide the tab bar icons in standard size (first.png, second.png) and double size (first@2x.png, second@2x.png). You're going to replace these controllers and images, so delete them. Select the controller files, FirstViewController.[hm] and SecondViewController.[hm], and the .png files in the Navigator pane. Delete files. When Xcode asks, move the files to the Trash. Select MainStoryboard.storyboard to open it in the storyboard editor. Select the first view controller scene and delete it. Repeat for the second view controller. The storyboard editor should consist of the tab bar controller only (Figure 12-10).

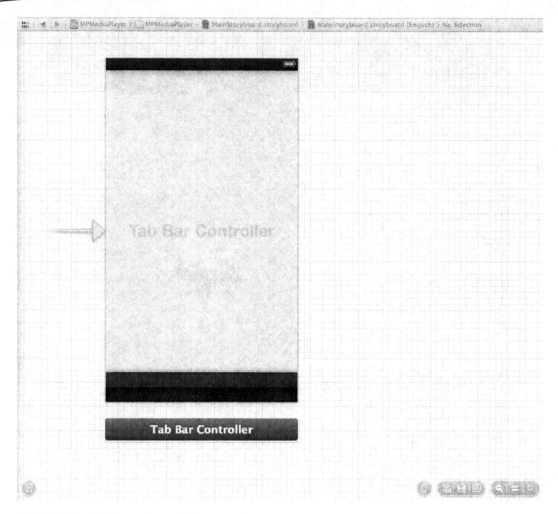

*Figure 12-10. Deleting the first and second view controllers*

Looking at Figure 12-9, you see that each tab controller is a table view controller. Drag a UITableViewController from the Object Library to the right of the tab bar controller in the storyboard editor. Control-drag from the tab bar view controller to the new table view controller. When the Segue pop-up menu appears, select the view controllers option under the Relationship Segue heading. Add a second UITableViewController and control-drag from the tab bar controller to it, selecting the view controllers option again. Align the two table view controllers and try to make your storyboard look like Figure 12-11.

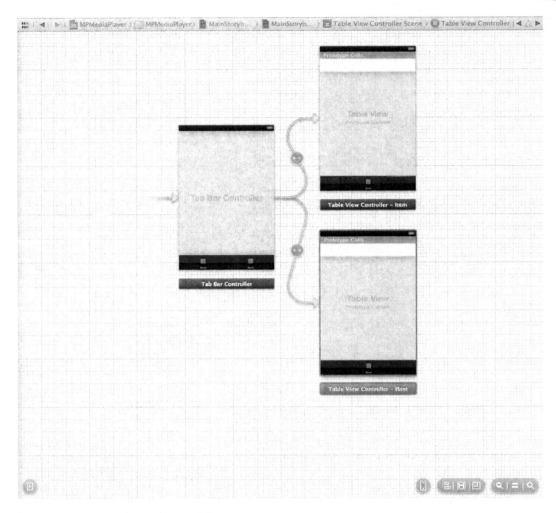

*Figure 12-11. Adding the new table view controllers*

Select the table view cell from the top table view controller. Open the Attribute Inspector and set the Style attribute to Subtitle. Give it an Identifier attribute a value of MediaCell. Set the Selection attribute to None, and the Accessory attribute to Disclosure Indicator. Repeat the attribute settings for the table view cell for the bottom table view controller.

You'll use the top table view controller for your audio media and the bottom table view controller for your video media. So you'll want an audio and video view controller. However, each view controller is really just a media view controller. So, you'll begin by creating a MediaViewController class, then subclass it. Create a new file using the Objective-C class template. Name the class MediaViewController, and make it subclass of UITableViewController.

You want the MediaViewController to be generic enough to handle both audio and video media. That means you need to store an array of media items and provide a method to load those items. Open MediaViewController.h. You'll need to import the MediaPlayer header to start. Add it after the UIKit header import.

```
#import <MediaPlayer/MediaPlayer.h>
```

We said you needed to store an array of media items. You'll declare that as a property of the `MediaViewController` class.

```
@property (strong, nonatomic) NSArray *mediaItems;
```

And you'll declare a method to populate the `mediaItems` depending on media type.

```
- (void)loadMediaItemsForMediaType:(MPMediaType)mediaType;
```

Select `MediaViewController.m` and adjust the implementation. First, you need to fix your table view data source methods to define the number of sections and rows per section in the table view.

```
- (NSInteger)numberOfSectionsInTableView:(UITableView *)tableView
{
    // Return the number of sections.
    return 1;
}


- (NSInteger)tableView:(UITableView *)tableView numberOfRowsInSection:(NSInteger)section
{
    // Return the number of rows in the section.
    return self.mediaItems.count;
}
```

Next, you want to adjust how the table view cell is populated.

```
- (UITableViewCell *)tableView:(UITableView *)tableView
        cellForRowAtIndexPath:(NSIndexPath *)indexPath
{
    static NSString *CellIdentifier = @"MediaCell";
    UITableViewCell *cell = [tableView dequeueReusableCellWithIdentifier:CellIdentifier
                                                        forIndexPath:indexPath];

    // Configure the cell...
    NSUInteger row = [indexPath row];
    MPMediaItem *item = [self.mediaItems objectAtIndex:row];
    cell.textLabel.text = [item valueForProperty:MPMediaItemPropertyTitle];
    cell.detailTextLabel.text = [item valueForProperty:MPMediaItemPropertyArtist];
    cell.tag = row;

    return cell;
}
```

Finally, you need to implement your `loadMediaItemsForMediaType:` method.

```
- (void)loadMediaItemsForMediaType:(MPMediaType)mediaType
{
    MPMediaQuery *query = [[MPMediaQuery alloc] init];
    NSNumber *mediaTypeNumber= [NSNumber numberWithInt:mediaType];
```

```
MPMediaPropertyPredicate *predicate =
    [MPMediaPropertyPredicate predicateWithValue:mediaTypeNumber
                                    forProperty:MPMediaItemPropertyMediaType];
[query addFilterPredicate:predicate];
self.mediaItems = [query items];
}
```

You've got your `MediaViewController` class defined. Let's create your audio and video subclasses. Create a new Objective-C class, named `AudioViewController`, which will be a subclass of `MediaViewController`. Repeat this process, this time naming the file `VideoViewController`. You only need to make two minor adjustments to each file. First, open `AudioViewController.m`, and add the following line to the `viewDidLoad` method, after the call to super:

```
[self loadMediaItemsForMediaType:MPMediaTypeMusic];
```

Do the same for `VideoViewController.m`, except this time you want to load videos.

```
[self loadMediaItemsForMediaType:MPMediaTypeAnyVideo];
```

Let's get your app to use your new view controllers. Select `MainStoryboard.storyboard` to open the storyboard editor. Select the top table view controller. In the Identity Inspector, change the Custom Class from a `UITableViewController` to `AudioViewController`. Change the bottom table view controller class to `VideoViewController`.

Before moving on, let's update the tabs for each view controller. Select the tab bar in the audio view controller. In the Attributes Inspector, set the Title to "Music" and set the Image to `music.png`. You can find the image files, `music.png` and `video.png`, in this chapter's download folder. Select the tab bar in the video view controller and set its title to "Video" and its image to `video.png`.

Build and run your app. You should see all your media library's music when selecting the Music tab, and all the media library's videos when selecting the Video tab. Great! Now you need to support playback. You'll be using the `MPMoviePlayerViewController` to playback video, but like the SimplePlayer, you need to make an audio playback view controller. You're going to make an even simpler version of your audio playback controller. Create a new Objective-C file named `PlayerViewController`, which will be a subclass of `UIViewController`.

Select the `MainStoryboard.storyboard` so you can work on the `PlayerViewController` scene. Drag a `UIViewController` to the right of the audio view controller. Select the new view controller, and open the Identity Inspector. Change its class from `UIViewController` to `PlayerViewController`. Control-drag from the table view cell in the audio view controller to the `UIViewController` and select the modal Manual Segue. Select the segue between `AudioViewController` and `PlayerViewController`, and name it "PlayerSegue" in the Attributes Inspector.

Your audio playback view controller will look like Figure 12-12 when you're done. Starting at the top, add two `UILabels`. Stretch them to width of the view. Like you did with the SimplePlayer, extend the labels to the width of the view and adjust their attributes (System Bold 17.0 font, center alignment, white foreground color, black background color). Set the top label text to "Artist" and the bottom label text to "Song."

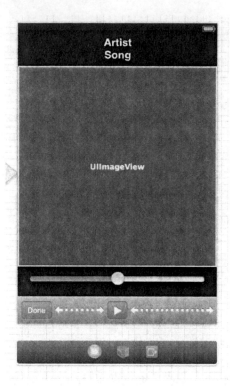

*Figure 12-12. MPMediaPlayer audio playback view controller*

Drag a `UIImageView` into the scene, just below the Song label. Use the blue guide lines to space it properly. Adjust the size of the image view to fit the width of the view, and make it square (320px by 320px). Just below the image view, drag a `UISlider`. Adjust the width of the slider, using the blue margin guidelines. Finally, drag a `UIToolbar` to the bottom of the `PlayerViewController` view. Select the `UIBarButtonItem` on the left side of the toolbar. Using the Attribute Inspector, change the Identifier from Custom to Done. Drag a flexible space bar button Item to the right of the Done button. Next, add a `UIBarButtonItem` to the right of the flexible space item. Select the new bar button item and change its Identifier to Play in the Attributes Inspector. Finally, to center your Play button, add another flexible space bar button item to the right of the Play button.

Just as you did with SimplePlayer, you need to create some outlets and actions for your `PlayerViewController`. Enter Assistant Editor mode. Control-drag from the Artist label to the `PlayerViewController` implementation, and create an outlet named "artist." Do the same for the Song label and name it song. Create outlets for the Image View, the slider, the toolbar and the Play button. The names of the outlets should be obvious (i.e. imageView for the Image View), except for the slider. You'll name the outlet "volume," since you're going to use the slider to control the volume level.

You need to define three actions. Control-drag from the volume slider, and create an action named volumeChanged: for the Value Changed event. Control-drag from the Done button to create a donePressed: action. Control-drag from the Play button to create a playPausePressed: event. Put the Editor back into Standard mode, and select `PlayerViewController.h`.

First, you need to import the MediaPlayer header file. You add the import declaration after the UIKIt header import.

```
#import <MediaPlayer/MediaPlayer.h>
```

As you did with the SimplePlayer, you need to redefine the play property outlet from weak to strong. You also declare your pause (button) property.

```
@property (strong, nonatomic) IBOutlet UIBarButtonItem *play;
@property (strong, nonatomic)         UIBarButtonItem *pause;
```

You need to add two more properties: one to hold the MPMusicPlayerController and one to hold the MPMediaItem that is being played.

```
@property (strong, nonatomic) MPMusicPlayerController *player;
@property (strong, nonatomic) MPMediaItem *mediaItem;
```

You need to know when the player state has changed and when the player media item has changed. Remember, these are handled via notifications. You'll declare some methods to register with the Notification Center.

```
- (void)playingItemChanged:(NSNotification *)notification;
- (void)playbackStateChanged:(NSNotification *)notification;
```

Let's move over to PlayerViewController.m and work on the implementation. You need to create your Pause button since it's not part of your storyboard scene. Find the viewDidLoad method, and create it after the call to super.

```
self.pause = [[UIBarButtonItem alloc] initWithBarButtonSystemItem:UIBarButtonSystemItemPause
target:self action:@selector(playPausePressed:)];
[self.pause setStyle:UIBarButtonItemStyleBordered];
```

You need a MPMusicPlayerController instance to play your music.

```
self.player = [MPMusicPlayerController applicationMusicPlayer];
```

You want to observe the player notifications, so you register for those and ask the player to start generating them.

```
NSNotificationCenter *notificationCenter = [NSNotificationCenter defaultCenter];
[notificationCenter addObserver:self
                    selector:@selector(playingItemChanged:)
                        name:MPMusicPlayerControllerNowPlayingItemDidChangeNotification
                      object:self.player];
[notificationCenter addObserver:self
                    selector:@selector(playbackStateChanged:)
                        name:MPMusicPlayerControllerPlaybackStateDidChangeNotification
                      object:self.player];
[self.player beginGeneratingPlaybackNotifications];
```

You need to pass your media item to the player. But the player takes `MPMediaItemCollections`, not individual an `MPMediaItem`. You'll do this assignment in the `viewDidAppear:` method where you'll create a collection and pass it to your player.

```
- (void)viewDidAppear:(BOOL)animated
{
    [super viewDidAppear:animated];
    MPMediaItemCollection *collection =
        [[MPMediaItemCollection alloc] initWithItems:@[self.mediaItem]];
    [self.player setQueueWithItemCollection:collection];
    [self.player play];
}
```

You need to stop generating notifications and unregister your observers when the `PlayerViewController` is released. Find the `didGenerateMemoryWarning` method, and add the following calls:

```
[self.player endGeneratingPlaybackNotifications];
[[NSNotificationCenter defaultCenter]
    removeObserver:self
            name:MPMusicPlayerControllerPlaybackStateDidChangeNotification
          object:self.player];
[[NSNotificationCenter defaultCenter]
    removeObserver:self
            name:MPMusicPlayerControllerNowPlayingItemDidChangeNotification
          object:self.player];
```

The `volumeChanged:` method simply needs to change the player volume to reflect the value of the volume slider.

```
- (IBAction)volumeChanged:(id)sender
{
    self.player.volume = [self.volume value];
}
```

The `donePressed:` method stops the player and dismisses the `PlayerViewController`.

```
- (IBAction)donePressed:(id)sender
{
    [self.player stop];
    [self dismissViewControllerAnimated:YES completion:nil];
}
```

Your `playPausePressed:` method is similar to the one in SimplePlayer. You don't update the Play/Pause button in the toolbar; you'll handle that in the `playbackStateChanged:` method.

```
- (IBAction)playPausePressed:(id)sender
{
    MPMusicPlaybackState playbackState = [self.player playbackState];
    if (playbackState == MPMusicPlaybackStateStopped || playbackState == MPMusicPlaybackStatePaused) {
        [self.player play];
    }
```

```
    else if (playbackState == MPMusicPlaybackStatePlaying) {
        [self.player pause];
    }
}
```

Implementing your notification observer methods is pretty straightforward. You update the view when the player media item changes. Again, it's similar to the same method in SimplePlayer.

```
- (void)playingItemChanged:(NSNotification *)notification
{
    MPMediaItem *currentItem = [self.player nowPlayingItem];
    if (nil == currentItem) {
        [self.imageView setImage:nil];
        [self.imageView setHidden:YES];
        [self.artist setText:nil];
        [self.song setText:nil];
    }
    else {
        MPMediaItemArtwork *artwork = [currentItem valueForProperty: MPMediaItemPropertyArtwork];
        if (artwork) {
            UIImage *artworkImage = [artwork imageWithSize:CGSizeMake(320, 320)];
            [self.imageView setImage:artworkImage];
            [self.imageView setHidden:NO];
        }

        // Display the artist and song name for the now-playing media item
        [self.artist setText:[currentItem valueForProperty:MPMediaItemPropertyArtist]];
        [self.song setText:[currentItem valueForProperty:MPMediaItemPropertyTitle]];
    }
}
```

The playbackStateChanged: notification observer method is new to you. You added this notification so that when the player automatically starts playing music in viewDidAppear:, it'll update the Play/Pause button state.

```
- (void)playbackStateChanged:(NSNotification *)notification
{
    MPMusicPlaybackState playbackState = [self.player playbackState];
    NSMutableArray *items = [NSMutableArray arrayWithArray:[self.toolbar items]];
    if (playbackState == MPMusicPlaybackStateStopped || playbackState == MPMusicPlaybackStatePaused) {
        [items replaceObjectAtIndex:2 withObject:self.play];
    }
    else if (playbackState == MPMusicPlaybackStatePlaying) {
        [items replaceObjectAtIndex:2 withObject:self.pause];
    }
    [self.toolbar setItems:items animated:NO];
}
```

You need to send the music media item from the `AudioViewController` when the table view cell is selected to the `PlayerViewController`. To do that, you need to modify your `AudioViewController` implementation. Select `AudioViewController.m` and add the following method:

```
- (void)prepareForSegue:(UIStoryboardSegue *)segue sender:(id)sender
{
    if ([segue.identifier isEqualToString:@"PlayerSegue"]) {
        UITableViewCell *cell = sender;
        NSUInteger index = [cell tag];
        PlayerViewController *pvc = segue.destinationViewController;
        pvc.mediaItem = [self.mediaItems objectAtIndex:index];
    }
}
```

One last thing: you need to import the `PlayerViewController` into the `AudioViewController.m`. At the top of the file, just below the import of `AudioViewController.h`, add this import:

```
#import "PlayerViewController.h"
```

Build and run the app. Select a music file to play. The app should transition the `PlayerViewController` and start playing automatically. Slide the volume slider and see how you can adjust the playback volume now. Next, let's add video playback. It's trivially easy with the MediaPlayer framework. Open `VideoViewController` and implement the table view delegate method `tableView:didSelectRowAtIndexPath:`, like so:

```
- (void)tableView:(UITableView *)tableView didSelectRowAtIndexPath:(NSIndexPath *)indexPath
{
    MPMediaItem *mediaItem = [self.mediaItems objectAtIndex:[indexPath row]];
    NSURL *mediaURL = [mediaItem valueForProperty:MPMediaItemPropertyAssetURL];
    MPMoviePlayerViewController *player =
        [[MPMoviePlayerViewController alloc] initWithContentURL:mediaURL];
    [self presentMoviePlayerViewControllerAnimated:player];
}
```

That's it. Build and run your application. Select the Video tab and pick a video to play. Easy!

# AVFoundation

The AVFoundation framework was originally introduced in iOS 3 with limited audio playback and recording functionality. iOS 4 expanded the framework to include video playback and recording, as well as the audio/video asset management.

At the core, AVFoundation represents an audio or video file as an AVAsset. It's important to understand that an AVAsset may have multiple tracks. For example, an audio AVAsset may have two tracks: one for the left channel and one for the right. A video AVAsset could have many more tracks; some for video, some for audio. Additionally, an AVAsset may encapsulate additional metadata about the media it represents. It's important to note that simply instantiating an AVAsset does not mean it will be ready for playback. It may take some time for the to analyze the data the AVAsset represents.

In order to give you fine grained control on how to playback an AVAsset, AVFoundation separates the presentation state of a media item from the AVAsset. This presentation state is represented by an AVPlayerItem. Each track within an AVPlayerItem is represented by an AVPlayerItemTrack. By using an AVPlayerItem and its AVPlayerItemTracks, you are allowed to determine how to present the item (i.e., mix the audio tracks or crop the video) via an AVPlayer object. If you wish to playback multiple AVPlayerItems, you use the AVPlayerQueue to schedule the playback of each AVPlayerItem.

Beyond giving finer control over media playback, AVFoundation gives you the ability to create media. You can leverage the device hardware to create your new media assets. The hardware is represented by an AVCaptureDevice. Where possible, you can configure the AVCaptureDevice to enable specific device functionality or settings. For example, you can set the flashMode of the AVCaptureDevice that represents your iPhone's camera to be on, off, or use auto sensing.

In order to use the output from the AVCaptureDevice, you need to use an AVCaptureSession. AVCaptureSession coordinates the management data from an AVCaptureDevice to its output form. This output is represented by an AVCaptureOutput class.

It's a complicated process to create media data using AVFoundation. First, you need to create an AVCaptureSession to coordinate the capture and creation of your media. You define and configure your AVCaptureDevice, which represents the actual physical device (such as your iPhone camera or microphone). From the AVCaptureDevice, you create an AVCaptureInput. AVCaptureInput is a <?> object that represents the data coming from the AVCaptureDevice. Each AVCaptureInput instance has a number of ports, where each port represents a data stream from the device. You can think of a port as a capture analogue of an AVAsset track. Once you've created your AVCaptureInput(s), you assign then to the AVCaptureSession. Each session can have multiple inputs.

You've got your capture session, and you've assigned inputs to your session. Now you have to save the data. You use the AVCaptureOutput class and add it to your AVCaptureSession. You can use a concrete AVCaptureOutput subclass to write your data to a file, or you can save it to a buffer for further processing.

Your AVCaptureSession is now configured to receive data from a device and save it. All you need to do is tell your session to startRunning. Once you're done, you send the stopRunning message to your session. Interestingly, it is possible to change your session's input or output while it is running. In order to insure a smooth transition, you would wrap these changes with a set of beginConfiguration / commitConfiguration messages.

Asset metadata is represented by the AVMetadataItem class. To add your own metadata to an asset, you use the mutable version, AVMutableMetadataItem, and assign it to your asset.

There are times where you may need to transform your media asset from one format to another. Similar to capturing media, you use an AVAssetExportSession class. You add your input asset to the export session object, then configure the export session to your new output format, and export the data.

Next, let's delve into the specifics of playing media via AVFoundation.

# AVMediaPlayer

At start, your AVFoundation-based media player will look identical to the MPMediaPlayer (Figure 12-9). Unlike MPMediaPlayer, your AVFoundation player will use a unified player view controller to play back both audio and video media. There are a couple of reasons for this, but it's primarily because AVFoundation does not give you a video playback view controller similar to `MPMoviePlayerViewController`. Rather, you need to define a `UIView` subclass to use an `AVPlayerLayer` view layer. Regardless of the media type, you use an `AVPlayer` instance to load the `AVAsset` and manage the playback controls.

Using Xcode, create a new project and name it AVMediaPlayer. Since AVMediaPlayer uses a tab bar controller, and behaves like MPMediaPlayer, follow the same steps you used for MPMediaPlayer, right up to the point where you add the MediaPlayer framework. You still need the MediaPlayer framework to access your media library. Since this project will use AVFoundation to play back media, you also need to add the AVFoundation framework.

Like MPMediaPlayer, AVMediaPlayer will use a generic `MediaViewController` as an abstract base class. Create a new Objective-C class named `MediaViewController`, subclassed from `UITableViewController`. Again, this `MediaViewController` class needs to be generic enough support both audio and video media. Also, similar to MPMediaPlayer `MediaViewController`, you need a way to load your media items. AVFoundation does not give access to your media library; that functionality only exists in the MediaPlayer framework. Since you intend to use the `AVPlayer` class to play back your media, you need to convert the MPMediaItems to AVAssets. First, you need to modify `MediaViewController.h`.

```
#import <UIKit/UIKit.h>
#import <MediaPlayer/MediaPlayer.h>

@interface MediaViewController : UITableViewController

@property (strong, nonatomic) NSArray *assets;
- (void)loadAssetsForMediaType:(MPMediaType)mediaType;

@end
```

This time, you named your `NSArray` property assets, as it is an array of AVAssets, rather than MPMediaItems. Correspondingly, you named your loader method `loadAssetsForMediaType:` for the same reason.

In `MediaViewController.m`, you need to update your table view data source methods. Before you do that, you need to import the AVFoundation header, right after the import of `MediaViewController.h`.

```
#import <AVFoundation/AVFoundation.h>
```

Now, find and update the table view data source methods.

```
- (NSInteger)numberOfSectionsInTableView:(UITableView *)tableView
{
    // Return the number of sections.
    return 1;
}

- (NSInteger)tableView:(UITableView *)tableView numberOfRowsInSection:(NSInteger)section
{
    // Return the number of rows in the section.
    return self.assets.count;
}
```

```
- (UITableViewCell *)tableView:(UITableView *)tableView
        cellForRowAtIndexPath:(NSIndexPath *)indexPath
{
    static NSString *CellIdentifier = @"MediaCell";
    UITableViewCell *cell = [tableView dequeueReusableCellWithIdentifier:CellIdentifier
                                                          forIndexPath:indexPath];

    // Configure the cell...
    NSUInteger row = [indexPath row];
    AVAsset *asset = [self.assets objectAtIndex:row];
    cell.textLabel.text = [asset description];
    cell.tag = row;

    return cell;
}
```

Again, this is similar to what you did in MPMediaPlayer. Notice that tableView:cellForRowAtIndexPath: retrieves an AVAsset from your assets array. Remember, AVAsset doesn't have an easy way to access its metadata properties like artist name, song title, or artwork. You'll get to loading that information in a little bit. For now, you'll just display the asset's description in the table view cell.

Now, you need to implement loadAssetsForMediaType: method. You'll add it to the bottom of MediaViewController.m, just before the @end declaration.

```
#pragma mark - Instance Methods

- (void)loadAssetsForMediaType:(MPMediaType)mediaType
{
    MPMediaQuery *query = [[MPMediaQuery alloc] init];
    NSNumber *mediaTypeNumber= [NSNumber numberWithInt:mediaType];
    MPMediaPropertyPredicate *predicate = [MPMediaPropertyPredicate predicateWithValue:mediaTypeNumber
                                                        forProperty:MPMediaItemPropertyMediaType];
    [query addFilterPredicate:predicate];

    NSMutableArray *mediaAssets = [[NSMutableArray alloc] initWithCapacity:[[query items] count]];
    for (MPMediaItem *item in [query items]) {
        [mediaAssets addObject:
            [AVAsset assetWithURL:[item valueForProperty:MPMediaItemPropertyAssetURL]]];
    }
    self.assets = mediaAssets;
}
```

The difference between this method and loadMediaItemsForMediaType: in MPMediaPlayer is that you use the MPMediaItemPropertyAssetURL to create your AVAssets.

You need to create two Objective-C classes: `AudioViewController` and `VideoViewController`. They are both subclasses of `MediaViewController`. Add the following to `AudioViewController.m` to have it load audio to your audio media:

```
- (void)viewDidLoad
{
    [super viewDidLoad];
    // Do any additional setup after loading the view.
    [self loadAssetsForMediaType:MPMediaTypeMusic];
}
```

Do the same for `VideoViewController.m`, except the media type you want to load is `MPMediaTypeAnyVideo`.

Open `MainStoryboard.storyboard` and change the custom classes for the two table view controllers to `AudioViewController` and `VideoViewController`, like you did in the MPMediaPlayer.

Build and run AVMediaPlayer. It looks like you're reading your media library, but its not very useful, yet. Let's fix it so you can get your asset metadata.

Recall that an AVAsset's information may not be available or loaded on instantiation. Asking an asset for information may block the call thread. If you were to do that in AVMediaPlayer, you would slow down the UI components, specifically the table views and their scrolling. In order to avoid this, you're going to load an asset's metadata asynchronously, using the AVAsset method `loadValuesAsynchro nouslyForKeys:completionHandler:`. Furthermore, you're going to encapsulate your AVAsset into a custom class to handle the loading and caching of this data.

Create a new Objective-C class named `AssetItem`, subclassed from `NSObject`. Once the files are created and in your project, select `AssetItem.h`. Since `AssetItem` is intended to encapsulate an AVAsset, you'll predeclare the AVAsset class for convenience. You'll also modify the `AssetItem` declaration to conform to the `NSCopying` protocol.

```
@class AVAsset;

@interface AssetItem : NSObject <NSCopying>
```

You need a property to hold your AVAsset instance. Since you're loading your AVAssets from a URL, you'll add property to hold your asset URL as well. This will allow you to load the AVAsset lazily, which should also help with performance.

```
@property (strong, nonatomic) NSURL *assetURL;
@property (strong, nonatomic) AVAsset *asset;
```

You define three read-only properties that represent the asset metadata you care most about for your application.

```
@property (strong, nonatomic, readonly) NSString *title;
@property (strong, nonatomic, readonly) NSString *artist;
@property (strong, nonatomic, readonly) UIImage *image;
```

Next, define two read-only properties to tell you the state of your `AssetItem`. Both are BOOLs. One, `metadataLoaded`, is a flag to tell you if you've already loaded the AVAsset's metadata. The second, `isVideo`, tells you if your AVAsset has video tracks.

```
@property (assign, nonatomic, readonly) BOOL metadataLoaded;
@property (assign, nonatomic, readonly) BOOL isVideo;
```

You need to declare two initializer methods. One creates an instance from a URL. The other creates a copy from another `AssetItem` instance; this is needed for the `NSCopying` protocol.

```
- (id)initWithURL:(NSURL *)aURL;
- (id)initWithAsset:(AssetItem *)assetItem;
```

You need a method to call that will asynchronously load your AVAsset's metadata.

```
- (void)loadAssetMetadataWithCompletionHandler:(void (^)(AssetItem *assetItem))completion;
```

Now you're ready to work on the implementation of `AssetItem`. Open `AssetItem.m`. To start, you need to import the AVFoundation header, right below the AssetItem header import. You'll also define a string constant, `kAssetItemDispatchQueue`. We'll explain why you need it in just a second.

```
#import <AVFoundation/AVFoundation.h>

#define kAssetItemDispatchQueue "AssetQueue"
```

You need to define a private property to hold your dispatch queue. We'll discuss dispatch queues in more detail in Chapter 14. Dispatch queues are part of the Grand Central Dispatch framework. You're using a dispatch queue to order your asset loading operations. As you load an AVAsset and perform your asynchronous loading requests, you'll put them into the dispatch queue. The benefits of this are two-fold. First, assets will be loaded in the order they are request, which should be the order they were requested. Second, this will keep your application from creating too many background requests. If your media library has hundreds or thousands of items, you could potentially spawn a process (thread) for each item. Create too many, and your application will freeze. A dispatch queue ensures that you keep your process (thread) count down. Your private category declaration starts like this:

```
@interface AssetItem ()
@property (strong, nonatomic) dispatch_queue_t dispatchQueue;
```

Your private category will also include a number of methods to help with the asynchronous nature of loading.

```
- (AVAsset *)assetCopyIfLoaded;
- (AVAsset *)localAsset;
- (NSString *)loadTitleForAsset:(AVAsset *)a;
- (NSString *)loadArtistForAsset:(AVAsset *)a;
- (UIImage *)loadImageForAsset:(AVAsset *)a;
@end
```

We'll discuss the specifics of these methods when we get to their implementations.

Since you have a number of read-only properties, you need to synthesize them, right after the @implementation declaration.

```
@synthesize title = _title;
@synthesize artist = _artist;
@synthesize image = _image;
```

Let's start your method implementation with your initializers.

```
- (id)initWithURL:(NSURL *)aURL
{
    self = [super init];
    if (self) {
        self.assetURL = aURL;
        self.dispatchQueue = dispatch_queue_create(kAssetItemDispatchQueue, DISPATCH_QUEUE_SERIAL);
    }
    return self;
}

- (id)initWithAsset:(AssetItem *)assetItem
{
    self = [super init];
    if (self) {
        self.assetURL = assetItem.assetURL;
        self.asset = [assetItem assetCopyIfLoaded];
        _title = assetItem.title;
        _artist = assetItem.artist;
        _image = assetItem.image;
        _metadataLoaded = assetItem.metadataLoaded;
        _isVideo = assetItem.isVideo;

        self.dispatchQueue = dispatch_queue_create(kAssetItemDispatchQueue, DISPATCH_QUEUE_SERIAL);
    }
    return self;
}
```

Both initializers should be straightforward. In both methods, you create a dispatch queue, with your constant string identifier, kAssetItemDispatchQueue, and as a serial queue. The initWithAsset: method copies the relevant properties. Note the use of the private method assetCopyIfLoaded when copying the AVAsset property.

Next, you'll define the methods you need to conform to the NSCopying protocol.

```
#pragma mark - NSCopying Protocol Methods

- (id)copyWithZone:(NSZone *)zone
{
        AssetItem *copy = [[AssetItem allocWithZone:zone] initWithAsset:self];
        return copy;
}
```

```objc
- (BOOL)isEqual:(id)anObject
{
        if (self == anObject)
                return YES;

        if ([anObject isKindOfClass:[AssetItem class]]) {
                AssetItem *assetItem = anObject;
                if (self.assetURL && assetItem.assetURL)
                        return [self.assetURL isEqual:assetItem.assetURL];
                return NO;
        }
        return NO;
}

- (NSUInteger)hash
{
    return (self.assetURL) ? [self.assetURL hash] : [super hash];
}
```

For the isEqual: and hash methods, you rely on the uniqueness of the asset's URL.

You'll override the accessors for some properties. To access an AssetItem's underlying AVAsset, you make a copy of the asset. This is because an AVAsset instance can only be accessed from one thread at a time. If you returned a reference to the AssetItem's actual AVAsset, you can't guarantee that it won't be accessed from different threads. Note that you don't copy the underlying AVAsset ivar; rather you've invoked the method localAsset.

```objc
#pragma mark - Property Overrides

// Make a copy since AVAsset can only be safely accessed from one thread at a time
- (AVAsset*)asset
{
        __block AVAsset *theAsset = nil;
        dispatch_sync(self.dispatchQueue, ^(void) {
                theAsset = [[self localAsset] copy];
        });
        return theAsset;
}

- (NSString *)title
{
    if (_title == nil)
        return [self.assetURL lastPathComponent];
    return _title;
}

- (NSString *)artist
{
    if (_artist == nil)
        return @"Unknown";
    return _artist;
}
```

The title and artist accessors check their respective ivars. If they are nil, you can assume either you haven't loaded the asset's metadata (yet), or the metadata values don't exists. In those cases, you use a fall back value. For the asset title, you use the last component of the asset URL. For artist name, you simply use the value Unknown.

Loading an asset's metadata can be a little complicated, so let's step through the implementation.

```
- (void)loadAssetMetadataWithCompletionHandler:(void (^)(AssetItem *assetItem))completion
{
    dispatch_async(self.dispatchQueue, ^(void){
```

The first thing you do is wrap the entire method body with a dispatch_async call to your dispatch queue. You'll be invoking this method from the main thread. The dispatch_async call ensures that the method will be placed in your dispatch queue and executed off the main thread. You retrieve your AVAsset and have it load its metadata asynchronously.

```
        AVAsset *a = [self localAsset];
        [a loadValuesAsynchronouslyForKeys:@[@"commonMetadata"] completionHandler:^{
            NSError *error;
            AVKeyValueStatus cmStatus = [a statusOfValueForKey:@"commonMetadata" error:&error];
            switch (cmStatus) {
                case AVKeyValueStatusLoaded:
                    _title = [self loadTitleForAsset:a];
                    _artist = [self loadArtistForAsset:a];
                    _image = [self loadImageForAsset:a];
                    _metadataLoaded = YES;
                    break;

                case AVKeyValueStatusFailed:
                case AVKeyValueStatusCancelled:
                    dispatch_async(dispatch_get_main_queue(), ^{
                        NSLog(@"The asset's available metadata formats were not loaded:\n%@",
                            [error localizedDescription]);
                    });
                    break;
            }
```

On completion of loadValuesAsychronouslyForKeys:completetionHandler:, the completion handler block checks the status of the commonMetadata key. If the load failed or was cancelled for some reason, you log the error. If the load was successful, you load the metadata properties you care about and set the metadataLoaded flag to YES.

```
            /* IMPORTANT: Must dispatch to main queue in order to operate on the
               AVPlayer and AVPlayerItem. */
            dispatch_async(dispatch_get_main_queue(), ^{
                if (completion)
                    completion(self);
            });
        }];
    });
}
```

Finally, you invoke the completion handler passed into your method. You dispatch this call back to the main queue as it will interact with your AVPlayer and AVPlayerItem instances.

Now let's implement your private category methods. One thing about these methods: they are implicitly or explicitly expected to be performed in the dispatch queue (thread). assetCopyIfLoaded is only used in the initWithAssetItem:initializer method to copy your AVAsset property. You dispatch the AVAsset copying to the dispatch queue to keep the copying from potentially blocking the main thread, which would cause the UI to freeze.

```
- (AVAsset*)assetCopyIfLoaded
{
        __block AVAsset *theAsset = nil;
        dispatch_sync(self.dispatchQueue, ^(void){
                theAsset = [_asset copy];
        });
        return theAsset;
}
```

The localAsset method is your private accessor to the AVAsset property/ivar. It follows a lazy loading logic to instantiate the _asset ivar if necessary. Remember, if you're invoking the localAsset method, you're operating from the dispatch queue thread, and it's only being invoke from another AssetItem method.

```
- (AVAsset*)localAsset
{
    if (_asset == nil) {
        _asset = [[AVURLAsset alloc] initWithURL:self.assetURL options:nil];
    }
    return _asset;
}
```

Take a look back at the loadAssetMetadataWithCompletionHandler: method. On successful loading of the metadata, you call loadTitleForAsset:, loadArtistForAsset:, and loadImageForAsset:. Let's step over each one, starting with loadTitleForAsset:. First, you extract the asset titles that are stored in the asset's commonMetadata property.

```
- (NSString *)loadTitleForAsset:(AVAsset *)a
{
    NSString *assetTitle = nil;
    NSArray *titles = [AVMetadataItem metadataItemsFromArray:[a commonMetadata]
                                             withKey:AVMetadataCommonKeyTitle
                                             keySpace:AVMetadataKeySpaceCommon];
```

If the titles array is not empty, then you need to find the title that matches the device user's preferred language and/or locale. Language and locale preference is a system setting. If there are multiple titles returned for a language/locale preference, you just return the first one.

```
    if ([titles count] > 0) {
        // Try to get a title that matches one of the user's preferred languages.
        NSArray *preferredLanguages = [NSLocale preferredLanguages];
```

```
        for (NSString *thisLanguage in preferredLanguages) {
            NSLocale *locale = [[NSLocale alloc] initWithLocaleIdentifier:thisLanguage];
            NSArray *titlesForLocale = [AVMetadataItem metadataItemsFromArray:titles
                                                            withLocale:locale];
            if ([titlesForLocale count] > 0) {
                assetTitle = [[titlesForLocale objectAtIndex:0] stringValue];
                break;
            }
        }
    }
```

If you haven't been able to match a title using the preferred language/locale, you just return the first one in your original titles array.

```
        // No matches in any of the preferred languages.
        // Just use the primary title metadata we find.
        if (assetTitle == nil) {
            assetTitle = [[titles objectAtIndex:0] stringValue];
        }
    }
    return assetTitle;
}
```

Finding the artist name from the asset metadata is pretty much identical, except you use the key AVMetadataCommonKeyArtist to extract the artist names array from the commonMetadata property.

```
- (NSString *)loadArtistForAsset:(AVAsset *)a
{
    NSString *assetArtist = nil;
    NSArray *titles = [AVMetadataItem metadataItemsFromArray:[a commonMetadata]
                                        withKey:AVMetadataCommonKeyArtist
                                        keySpace:AVMetadataKeySpaceCommon];
    if ([titles count] > 0) {
        // Try to get a artist that matches one of the user's preferred languages.
        NSArray *preferredLanguages = [NSLocale preferredLanguages];

        for (NSString *thisLanguage in preferredLanguages) {
            NSLocale *locale = [[NSLocale alloc] initWithLocaleIdentifier:thisLanguage];
            NSArray *titlesForLocale = [AVMetadataItem metadataItemsFromArray:titles
                                                            withLocale:locale];
            if ([titlesForLocale count] > 0) {
                assetArtist = [[titlesForLocale objectAtIndex:0] stringValue];
                break;
            }
        }

        // No matches in any of the preferred languages.
        // Just use the primary artist metadata we find.
        if (assetArtist == nil) {
```

```
            assetArtist = [[titles objectAtIndex:0] stringValue];
        }
    }
    return assetArtist;
}
```

Loading the asset artwork from the commonMetadata is much simpler. You load the potential array of images from the asset metadata. The first item in the images array can either be a dictionary or a block of data. If the item is a dictionary, the image data is stored under the key data. Either way, you can instantiate a UIImage from the data.

```
- (UIImage *)loadImageForAsset:(AVAsset *)a
{
    UIImage *assetImage = nil;
    NSArray *images = [AVMetadataItem metadataItemsFromArray:[a commonMetadata]
                                        withKey:AVMetadataCommonKeyArtwork
                                      keySpace:AVMetadataKeySpaceCommon];
    if ([images count] > 0) {
        AVMetadataItem *item = [images objectAtIndex:0];
        NSData *imageData = nil;
        if ([item.value isKindOfClass:[NSDictionary class]]) {
            NSDictionary *valueDict = (NSDictionary *)item.value;
            imageData = [valueDict objectForKey:@"data"];
        }
        else if ([item.value isKindOfClass:[NSData class]])
            imageData = (NSData *)item.value;
        assetImage = [UIImage imageWithData:imageData];
    }
    return assetImage;
}
```

Remember that you load an asset's metadata asynchronously. That means when you load the asset from your media library, you queue the request to load the asset metadata. Meanwhile, your application needs to populate the table view cells with something. By default, AssetItem will return the last path item of the asset URL for the title and "Unknown" for the artist. You need the table view cells to reload once the asset metadata has been loaded. You'll need to modify the MediaViewController class to do this.

MediaViewController will need to know about your new AssetItem class. Open MediaViewController.m and import the AssetItem header, right after the other header import declarations

```
#import "AssetItem.h"
```

Next, you'll add two private category methods. One will be use to configure the table view cell for a given index path. The other will be used at the completion handler when you invoke loadAssetMetadataWithCompletionHandler: on an AssetItem.

```
@interface MediaViewController ()
- (void)configureCell:(UITableViewCell *)cell forIndexPath:(NSIndexPath *)indexPath;
- (void)updateCellWithAssetItem:(AssetItem *)assetItem;
@end
```

Since configureCell:forIndexPath: will be used to configure your table view cells, you can modify table:cellForRowAtIndexPath: table view data source method.

```
- (UITableViewCell *)tableView:(UITableView *)tableView
         cellForRowAtIndexPath:(NSIndexPath *)indexPath
{
    static NSString *CellIdentifier = @"MediaCell";
    UITableViewCell *cell = [tableView dequeueReusableCellWithIdentifier:CellIdentifier
                                                           forIndexPath:indexPath];

    // Configure the cell...
    [self configureCell:cell forIndexPath:indexPath];

    return cell;
}
```

Now, you can implement configureCell:forIndexPath:.

```
- (void)configureCell:(UITableViewCell *)cell forIndexPath:(NSIndexPath *)indexPath
{
    NSInteger row = [indexPath row];

    AssetItem *assetItem = [self.assets objectAtIndex:row];
    if (!assetItem.metadataLoaded) {
        [assetItem loadAssetMetadataWithCompletionHandler:^(AssetItem *assetItem){
            [self updateCellWithAssetItem:assetItem];
        }];
    }

    cell.textLabel.text = [assetItem title];
    cell.detailTextLabel.text = [assetItem artist];
    cell.tag = row;
}
```

You find the AssetItem in the assets property array for the row of the given index path. You check if the AssetItem's metadata has been loaded. If not, you tell the AssetItem to load its metadata. Your completion handler block is a single call to updateCellWithAssetItem:. Finally, you populate the cell with the AssetItem title and artist.

Your completion handler, updateCellWithAssetItem:, will cause the table view cell that contains the passed in AssetItem to reload and redisplay itself. As a minor performance check, you only update the table view cell to update if it's currently visible.

```
- (void)updateCellWithAssetItem:(AssetItem *)assetItem
{
        NSArray *visibleIndexPaths = [self.tableView indexPathsForVisibleRows];
        for (NSIndexPath *indexPath in visibleIndexPaths) {
        AssetItem *visibleItem = [self.assets objectAtIndex:[indexPath row]];
            if ([assetItem isEqual:visibleItem]) {
                    UITableViewCell *cell = [self.tableView cellForRowAtIndexPath:indexPath];
                    [self configureCell:cell forIndexPath:indexPath];
```

```
                    [cell setNeedsLayout];
                    break;
            }
        }
    }
}
```

Finally, you need to populate your assets property with `AssetItems`. Locate the method `loadAssetsForMediaType:` and find the line

```
[mediaAssets addObject:[AVAsset assetWithURL:[item valueForProperty:MPMediaItemPropertyAssetURL]]];
```

and replace it with

```
[mediaAssets addObject:
    [[AssetItem alloc] initWithURL:[item valueForProperty:MPMediaItemPropertyAssetURL]]];
```

Build and run the app. You should see the audio view controller populate the table view cells, then refresh them with the correct metadata. If you have a large enough media library, you can scroll down and see the table view cells refresh themselves.

Your AVMediaPlayer can load your audio and video media from your media library, load them as AVAssets (encapsulated in your custom `AssetItem` class, and load and display the asset's metadata. What's left? You need to play your media!

Create a new Objective-C class. Name it `PlayerViewController` and make it subclass of `UIViewController`. That's all you need to do with this class for now. You'll return to this class when you lay out the scene in the storyboard.

Now, create another Objective-C class named `AVPlayerView`, which is a subclass of `UIView`. This is the view that you'll be using the play video media. It's a simple extension on `UIView`. Open `AVPlayerView.h`, and modify it to match this implementation:

```
#import <UIKit/UIKit.h>

@class AVPlayer;

@interface AVPlayerView : UIView

@property (strong, nonatomic) AVPlayer* player;
- (void)setVideoFillMode:(NSString *)fillMode;

@end
```

The implementation of `AVPlayerView` is a little trickier. Open `AVPlayerView.m`. First, you need to import the AVFoundation header file.

```
#import "AVPlayerView.h"
#import <AVFoundation/AVFoundation.h>

@implementation AVPlayerView
```

Next, you need to override the UIView method layerClass to return AVPlayerLayer.

```
+ (Class)layerClass
{
        return [AVPlayerLayer class];
}
```

Next, you override the player property to redirect to your view's layer.

```
- (AVPlayer *)player
{
        return [(AVPlayerLayer *)[self layer] player];
}

- (void)setPlayer:(AVPlayer *)player
{
        [(AVPlayerLayer*)[self layer] setPlayer:player];
}
```

Finally, you add the ability to adjust the video fill mode.

```
/* Specifies how the video is displayed within a player layer's bounds.
   (AVLayerVideoGravityResizeAspect is default) */
- (void)setVideoFillMode:(NSString *)fillMode
{
        AVPlayerLayer *playerLayer = (AVPlayerLayer*)[self layer];
        playerLayer.videoGravity = fillMode;
}
```

@end

Now you can work on building your player interface. Open MainStoryboard.storyboard. Drag a UIViewController to right of the AudioViewController and VideoViewController. Align it so it matches Figure 12-13. Control-drag from the prototype table view cell in the AudioViewController to the new UIViewController. In the pop-up menu, select Modal under the Selection Segue header. Repeat this process for the VideoViewController. Select the new UIViewController and change its class from UIViewController to PlayerViewController in the Identity Inspector. For AVMediaPlayer, the PlayerViewController will play both audio and video files.

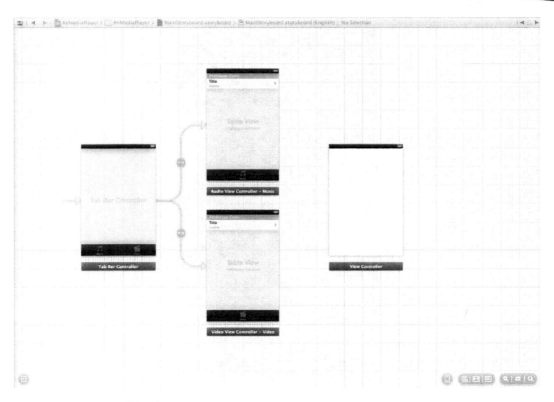

*Figure 12-13. Laying out your UIViewController*

Drag a UIView onto the PlayerViewController. It should expand to fill the entire scene. If not, adjust the size of the new UIView so it does. Open the Identity Inspector and change the view's class from UIView to AVPlayerView. Switch to the Attributes Inspector to change the background color from white to black. Switch to the assistant editor, and create a new outlet for the AVPlayerView. Name the outlet "playerView." Switch back to the standard editor.

Drag another UIView onto the PlayerViewController. Again, it should expand to fill the entire scene; adjust it if it doesn't. Unlike the playerView, you can keep the view's class as UIView. Open the Attributes Inspector and change the background color to Default (clear). Using the assistant editor, create a new outlet for this UIView and name it controlView. You're going to add the same control components to the controlView that you did for MPMediaPlayer, with some minor additions. Look at Figure 12-14 and compare it to Figure 12-12. You've added a UISlider with two UILabels on each side between the Song label and image view. Start by dragging a UILabel to the far left edge of the scene, right below the Song label. Change the text from "label" to "00:00," the color from black to white, the font to System 12.0, and right align the text. Add a UILabel to the far right edge, with the same attribute changes, except left align the text. Place a UISlider between the two labels, extending it to fill the space between the labels. Use the Attribute Inspector to change its current value from 0.5 to 0.0.

*Figure 12-14. AVMediaPlayer PlayerViewController layout*

You'll also add an additional `UIBarButtonItem` to the far right of the toolbar. Keep the button Identifier attribute as Custom, but change the Title to read 1.0x. You'll be using this button to toggle playback speed between different rates.

You need to add outlets for the UI components you added. Select the assistant editor. Create an outlet named "artist" for the label titled Artist. For the Song label, name the outlet "song." Create an outlet for the top slider, and name it "scrubber." Create an outlet for the label left of the scrubber slider, and name it "elapsedTime." For the label to the right of the scrubber slider, name the outlet "remainingTime." The `UIImageView` outlet should be named "imageView." And the bottom slider will be named "volume." You need outlets for the `UIToolbar` (toolbar), the Play button (play), and the 1.0x button (rate). Like with MPMediaPlayer, you don't need an outlet for the Done button.

Now you need to add the appropriate actions. Control-drag from the scrubber slider and add a new action named beginScrubbing for the `touchDown:` event. Control-drag from the scrubber slider again, and add a new action named scrub for the `valueChanged:` event. Finally, add a new ction named endScrubbing for the `touch up inside` event. Add a new action from the volume slider, named volumeChanged for the `valueChanged` event. For each of the toolbar buttons, add an action: the Done button (`donePressed`), the Play button (`playPressed`), and the Rate button (`ratePressed`).

Return to the standard editor, and select `PlayerViewController.h`. You need to import the following header files:

```
#import <AVFoundation/AVFoundation.h>
#import "AVPlayerView.h"
#import "AssetItem.h"
```

As you did before, you need to redefine the play property outlet from weak to strong. You also declare out pause (button) property.

```
@property (strong, nonatomic) IBOutlet UIBarButtonItem *play;
@property (strong, nonatomic)         UIBarButtonItem *pause;
```

You need to declare properties for an `AssetItem`, an `AVPlayerItem`, and `AVPlayer`.

```
@property (strong, nonatomic) AssetItem *assetItem;
@property (strong, nonatomic) AVPlayerItem *playerItem;
@property (strong, nonatomic) AVPlayer *player;
```

You going to have the Play and Pause buttons each have their own action, so declare the pause button action.

```
- (IBAction)pausePressed:(id)sender;
```

Before you can work on the `PlayerViewController` implementation, you need to add a method to your `AssetItem` to prepare the AVAsset for playback. Open `AssetItem.h` and add the following method declaration:

```
- (void)loadAssetForPlayingWithCompletionHandler:(void (^)(AssetItem *assetItem, NSArray *keys))
    completion;
```

Inside `AssetItem.m`, the implementation is pretty simple.

```
- (void)loadAssetForPlayingWithCompletionHandler:(void (^)(AssetItem *assetItem, NSArray *keys))
    completion;
{
    dispatch_async(self.dispatchQueue, ^(void){
        NSArray *keys = @[ @"tracks", @"playable" ];
        AVAsset *a = [self localAsset];
        [a loadValuesAsynchronouslyForKeys:keys completionHandler:^{
            /* IMPORTANT: Must dispatch to main queue in order to operate on the
               AVPlayer and AVPlayerItem. */
            dispatch_async(dispatch_get_main_queue(), ^{
                if (completion)
                    completion(self, keys);
            });
        }];
    });
}
```

You dispatch the asynchronous loading of the AVAsset tracks. Since you're loading two keys, you'll defer the check for each key to your completion handler. So all you do is invoke your completion handler on the main thread.

You need to implement the method `assetHasVideo:`. First, you declare it in your private category at the top of `AssetItem.m`.

```
- (BOOL)assetHasVideo:(AVAsset *)a;
```

Your implementation can be added at the bottom of the `AssetItem` implementation, after the other private category method implementations.

```
- (BOOL)assetHasVideo:(AVAsset *)a
{
    NSArray *videoTracks = [a tracksWithMediaType:AVMediaTypeVideo];
    return ([videoTracks count] > 0);
}
```

You simply query the asset for its video tracks.

Now you can work on the `PlayerViewController` implementation. First, you need to create the Pause button. Inside the `viewDidLoad` method, add the following lines:

```
    self.pause = [[UIBarButtonItem alloc] initWithBarButtonSystemItem:UIBarButtonSystemItemPause
                                                               target:self
                                                               action:@selector(pausePressed:)];
    [self.pause setStyle:UIBarButtonItemStyleBordered];
```

Next, you need to load prepare your asset for playback. You'll do this in the `viewDidAppear:` method.

```
- (void)viewDidAppear:(BOOL)animated
{
    if (self.assetItem) {
        [self.assetItem loadAssetForPlayingWithCompletionHandler:^(AssetItem *assetItem,
                                                                    NSArray *keys){
```

If you have an `assetItem`, you tell it to prepare it for playback by invoking `loadAssetForPlayingWithCompletionHandler:`. The first step of the completion handler is to check if the load status of each key.

```
            NSError *error = nil;
            AVAsset *asset = assetItem.asset;
            for (NSString *key in keys) {
                AVKeyValueStatus status = [asset statusOfValueForKey:key error:&error];
                if (status == AVKeyValueStatusFailed) {
                    NSLog(@"Asset Load Failed: %@ | %@",
                            [error localizedDescription], [error localizedFailureReason]);
                    return;
                }
                // handle AVKeyValueStatusCancelled
            }
```

As a sanity check, we see if the our underlying AVAsset is playable.

```
if (!asset.playable) {
    NSLog(@"Asset Can't be Played");
    return;
}
```

If you've already allocated your playerItem property, you need to remove an observer.

```
if (self.playerItem) {
    [self.playerItem removeObserver:self forKeyPath:@"status"];
    [[NSNotificationCenter defaultCenter]
        removeObserver:self
              name:AVPlayerItemDidPlayToEndTimeNotification
            object:self.playerItem];
}
```

You assign a new AVPlayerItem to your playerItem property. Since you're using ARC, any previous instance will be automatically released. This is why you removed the observer in the previous step.

```
self.playerItem = [AVPlayerItem playerItemWithAsset:asset];
```

You add an observer to your playerItem for the status key path.

```
[self.playerItem addObserver:self
                  forKeyPath:@"status"
                     options:NSKeyValueObservingOptionInitial | NSKeyValueObservingOptionNew
                     context:PlayerViewControllerStatusObservationContext];
```

Note the use of PlayerViewControllerStatusObservationContext. This is a special constant you'll declare in a little bit. You use this constant to ease the registration and identification of your AVPlayerItem notifications.

You add another observer, this time to the default notification center. You'll invoke the method playerItemDidReachEnd: for the AVPlayerItemDidPlayToEndTimeNotification.

```
[[NSNotificationCenter defaultCenter] addObserver:self
                                         selector:@selector(playerItemDidReachEnd:)
                                             name:AVPlayerItemDidPlayToEndTimeNotification
                                           object:self.playerItem];
```

If your player property is not assigned, you create one with your playerItem property. Then you add two observers to your player for the currentItem and rate key paths. Notice again that you've used two special constants, PlayerViewControllerCurrentItemObservationContext and AVPlayerViewControllerRateObservationContext.

```
if (self.player == nil) {
    self.player = [AVPlayer playerWithPlayerItem:self.playerItem];
    [self.player addObserver:self
                  forKeyPath:@"currentItem"
                     options:NSKeyValueObservingOptionInitial | NSKeyValueObservingOptionNew
                     context:PlayerViewControllerCurrentItemObservationContext];
```

```
        [self.player addObserver:self
                        forKeyPath:@"rate"
                            options:NSKeyValueObservingOptionInitial | NSKeyValueObservingOptionNew
                            context:AVPlayerViewControllerRateObservationContext];
    }
```

Next you make sure the player's `playerItem` is correct.

```
        if (self.player.currentItem != self.playerItem)
            [[self player] replaceCurrentItemWithPlayerItem:self.playerItem];
```

Finally, you do some initialization of UI components. If the asset is a video, you hide the image view, as you don't need it.

```
        self.artist.text = self.assetItem.artist;
        self.song.text = self.assetItem.title;
        self.imageView.image = self.assetItem.image;
        self.imageView.hidden = self.assetItem.isVideo;
        self.scrubber.value = 0.0f;
    }];
    }
}
```

Let's declare the three observation context constants you used. At the top of `PlayerViewController.m`, just after the import declaration, add the following:

```
static void *PlayerViewControllerStatusObservationContext =
    &PlayerViewControllerStatusObservationContext;
static void *PlayerViewControllerCurrentItemObservationContext =
    &PlayerViewControllerCurrentItemObservationContext;
static void *AVPlayerViewControllerRateObservationContext =
    &AVPlayerViewControllerRateObservationContext;
```

This is just a fancy way of defining some constant context values. You could have used string values if you wanted, but this is a bit cleaner.

So you added your `PlayerViewController` as an observer for your `AVPlayer` and `AVPlayerItem`. Unlike default notification center observers, you didn't specify what method to invoke. Rather the `AVPlayer` and `AVPlayerItem` observer will depend on a key-value observer. All you need to do is implement the method `observeValueForKeyPath:ofObject:change:context:`. This method will need to check the context value to decide what to do.

```
- (void)observeValueForKeyPath:(NSString *)path
                      ofObject:(id)object
                        change:(NSDictionary* )change
                       context:(void *)context
{
    /* AVPlayer "playerItem" property value observer. */
    if (context == PlayerViewControllerStatusObservationContext) {
    }
    /* AVPlayer "rate" property value observer. */
    else if (context == AVPlayerViewControllerRateObservationContext) {
```

```
        }
        /* AVPlayer "currentItem" property value observer. */
        else if (context == PlayerViewControllerCurrentItemObservationContext) {
        }
        else {
        NSLog(@"Other Context");
            [super observeValueForKeyPath:path ofObject:object change:change context:context];
        }
    }
}
```

You added hooks for each of the context constants you defined in your PlayerViewController. If the context is unknown, you pass it up the view controller hierarchy with a call to super. We've left each context section empty because handling each context is a discussion of itself, and we want to go over each one in detail.

We're doing to have you do some work that won't necessarily be clear right now, but will become clear once you implement your context handlers and action methods. First, you need to add the CoreMedia framework to your project. Select the project in the Navigator pane, and add the CoreMedia framework to the AVMediaPlayer target via the Build Phases pane. Return to editing PlayerViewController.m and import the CoreMedia header.

```
#import <CoreMedia/CoreMedia.h>
```

You're going to declare and implement some private category properties methods that you'll need for your context handlers and action methods.

```
@interface PlayerViewController ()
@property (assign, nonatomic) float prescrubRate;
@property (strong, nonatomic) id playerTimerObserver;

- (void)showPlay;
- (void)showPause;
- (void)updatePlayPause;
- (void)updateRate;

- (void)addPlayerTimerObserver;
- (void)removePlayerTimerObserver;
- (void)updateScrubber:(CMTime)currentTime;

- (void)playerItemDidReachEnd:(NSNotification *)notification;

- (void)handleStatusContext:(NSDictionary *)change;
- (void)handleRateContext:(NSDictionary *)change;
- (void)handleCurrentItemContext:(NSDictionary *)change;
@end
```

You'll discuss each of these as you implement them.

The showPlay and showPause methods are just convenience methods to toggle the Play and Pause buttons on the toolbar.

```
- (void)showPlay
{
    NSMutableArray *toolbarItems = [NSMutableArray arrayWithArray:self.toolbar.items];
    [toolbarItems replaceObjectAtIndex:2 withObject:self.play];
    self.toolbar.items = toolbarItems;
}

- (void)showPause
{
    NSMutableArray *toolbarItems = [NSMutableArray arrayWithArray:self.toolbar.items];
    [toolbarItems replaceObjectAtIndex:2 withObject:self.pause];
    self.toolbar.items = toolbarItems;
}
```

You need a method to check whether to show the Play or Pause button. You know if the media is playing based on the player's rate property. A rate of 0.0f means the media is not playing.

```
- (void)updatePlayPause
{
    if (self.player.rate == 0.0f)
        [self showPlay];
        else
        [self showPause];
}
```

The updateRate method is just used to set the text of the Rate button. You add a hook so the button shows "1.0x" if the actual player rate is 0.0f.

```
- (void)updateRate
{
    float rate = self.player.rate;
    if (rate == 0.0f)
        rate = 1.0f;
    self.rate.title = [NSString stringWithFormat:@"%.1fx", rate];
}
```

While the player is playing, you need to add an periodic observer to update the scrubber and time labels. You also need a method to remove the periodic observer.

```
- (void)addPlayerTimerObserver
{
    __block id blockSelf = self;
    self.playerTimerObserver =
        [self.player addPeriodicTimeObserverForInterval:CMTimeMakeWithSeconds(0.1f, NSEC_PER_SEC)
                    queue:nil
                    usingBlock:^(CMTime time){ [blockSelf updateScrubber:time]; }];
}
```

```
- (void)removePlayerTimerObserver
{
        if (self.playerTimerObserver) {
                [self.player removeTimeObserver:self.playerTimerObserver];
                self.playerTimerObserver = nil;
        }
}
```

Note that the AVPlayer periodic observer uses the CMTime structure. CMTime is defined in the CoreMedia framework, which is why you needed to include it in this project. You have the periodic observer fire every 0.1s and invoke the updateScrubber: method.

```
- (void)updateScrubber:(CMTime)currentTime
{
        if (CMTIME_IS_INVALID(self.playerItem.duration)) {
                self.scrubber.minimumValue = 0.0;
                return;
        }

        double duration = CMTimeGetSeconds(self.playerItem.duration);
        if (isfinite(duration)) {
            float minValue = [self.scrubber minimumValue];
            float maxValue = [self.scrubber maximumValue];
            double time = CMTimeGetSeconds([self.player currentTime]);
            [self.scrubber setValue:(maxValue - minValue) * time / duration + minValue];

            Float64 elapsedSeconds = CMTimeGetSeconds(currentTime);
            Float64 remainingSeconds = CMTimeGetSeconds(self.playerItem.duration) - elapsedSeconds;
            self.elapsedTime.text = [NSString stringWithFormat:@"%d:%02d",
                                                        (int)elapsedSeconds / 60,
                                                        (int)elapsedSeconds % 60];
            self.remainingTime.text = [NSString stringWithFormat:@"%d:%02d",
                                                        (int)remainingSeconds / 60,
                                                        (int)remainingSeconds % 60];

        }
}
```

updateScrubber: first performs a check on the CMTime value. If the time is invalid, you set the scrubber to 0.0 and return. If the time is valid, you query the playerItem for its duration. If the duration is finite, then you use it to determine where to set the scrubber value. Both the current time and duration are used to update the elapsedTime and remainingTime labels.

The notification handler method playerItemDidReachEnd: has the same effect as if you had tapped the Done button, so you simply call the donePressed: method.

Before you work on your context handlers, let's implement your action methods.

When you begin moving the scrubber, you need to remove the player's periodic observer to keep it from updating while the scrubber slider is being adjusted. You cache the current playback rate, and stop the player.

```
- (IBAction)beginScrubbing:(id)sender
{
    self.prescrubRate = self.player.rate;
    self.player.rate = 0.0f;
    [self removePlayerTimerObserver];
}
```

The scrub: action updates the player to the playback point that can be calculated from the scrubber value and playerItem duration. You then use those values to update the elapsedTime and remainingTime labels to reflect the new scrubber value.

```
- (IBAction)scrub:(id)sender
{
        if ([sender isKindOfClass:[UISlider class]]) {
                UISlider* slider = sender;
                if (CMTIME_IS_INVALID(self.playerItem.duration)) {
                        return;
                }

                double duration = CMTimeGetSeconds(self.playerItem.duration);
                if (isfinite(duration)) {
                    float minValue = [slider minimumValue];
                    float maxValue = [slider maximumValue];
                    float value = [slider value];
                    double time = duration * (value - minValue) / (maxValue - minValue);
                    [self.player seekToTime:CMTimeMakeWithSeconds(time, NSEC_PER_SEC)];

                    Float64 remainingSeconds = duration - time;
                    self.elapsedTime.text = [NSString stringWithFormat:@"%d:%02d",
                                                            (int)time / 60, (int)time % 60];
                    self.remainingTime.text = [NSString stringWithFormat:@"%d:%02d",
                                                            (int)remainingSeconds / 60,
                                                            (int)remainingSeconds % 60];
                }
        }
}
```

When you've completed scrubbing, you restore the player playback rate and periodic observer.

```
- (IBAction)endScrubbing:(id)sender
{
        if (self.playerTimerObserver == nil) {
            [self addPlayerTimerObserver];
    }

        if (self.prescrubRate != 0.0f) {
            self.player.rate = self.prescrubRate;
            self.prescrubRate = 0.0f;
        }
}
```

Changing the volume with an AVPlayer is much more complicated process. Your media asset could have multiple tracks, not just because of video; a stereo audio asset could have two tracks. As a result, you need to find all the audio tracks in an asset and adjust the audio mix to the new volume.

```objc
- (IBAction)volumeChanged:(id)sender
{
    float volume = [self.volume value];
    NSArray *audioTracks = [self.assetItem.asset tracksWithMediaType:AVMediaTypeAudio];

    NSMutableArray *allAudioParams = [NSMutableArray array];
    for (AVAssetTrack *track in audioTracks) {
        AVMutableAudioMixInputParameters *audioInputParams =
            [AVMutableAudioMixInputParameters audioMixInputParameters];
        [audioInputParams setVolume:volume atTime:kCMTimeZero];
        [audioInputParams setTrackID:[track trackID]];
        [allAudioParams addObject:audioInputParams];
    }

    AVMutableAudioMix *audioMix = [AVMutableAudioMix audioMix];
    [audioMix setInputParameters:allAudioParams];

    [self.playerItem setAudioMix:audioMix];
}
```

donePressed: will stop the player and return you to the MediaViewController.

```objc
- (IBAction)donePressed:(id)sender
{
    [self.player pause];
    [self dismissViewControllerAnimated:YES completion:nil];
}
```

playPressed: and pausePressed: update the player and toolbar as appropriate.

```objc
- (IBAction)playPressed:(id)sender
{
    [self.player play];
    [self updatePlayPause];
}

- (void)pausePressed:(id)sender
{
    [self.player pause];
    [self updatePlayPause];
}
```

The ratePressed: Action toggles the playback rate between three rates: 0.5, 1.0, and 2.0.

```objc
- (IBAction)ratePressed:(id)sender
{
    float rate = self.player.rate;
    rate *= 2.0f;
```

```
    if (rate > 2.0f)
        rate = 0.5;
    self.player.rate = rate;
}
```

Now you can implement your context handlers. For a change in `playerItem` status, you handle three possible statuses: unknown, ready to play, and failure.

```
- (void)handleStatusContext:(NSDictionary *)change
{
    [self updatePlayPause];

    AVPlayerStatus status = [[change objectForKey:NSKeyValueChangeNewKey] integerValue];
    switch (status) {
        case AVPlayerStatusUnknown:
            [self removePlayerTimerObserver];
            [self updateScrubber:CMTimeMake(0, NSEC_PER_SEC)];
            break;

        case AVPlayerStatusReadyToPlay:
            [self addPlayerTimerObserver];
            break;

        case AVPlayerStatusFailed:
            NSLog(@"Player Status Failed");
            break;
    }
}
```

When the player rate changes, you just perform a sanity check to make sure you're displaying the correct label on the Rate button.

```
- (void)handleRateContext:(NSDictionary *)change
{
    [self updatePlayPause];
    [self updateRate];
}
```

Finally, you only care about the player's `currentItem` when you've either created a new `AVPlayer` or `AVPlayerItem` instance. If you have a new `playerItem`, you need to make sure the `playerView` player is updated accordingly.

```
- (void)handleCurrentItemContext:(NSDictionary *)change
{
    // We've added/replaced the AVPlayer's AVPlayerItem
    AVPlayerItem *newPlayerItem = [change objectForKey:NSKeyValueChangeNewKey];
    if (newPlayerItem != (id)[NSNull null]) {
        // We really have a new AVPlayerItem
        self.playerView.player = self.player;
        [self.playerView setVideoFillMode:AVLayerVideoGravityResizeAspect];
    }
```

```
    else {
        // No AVPlayerItem
        NSLog(@"No AVPlayerItem");
    }
}
```

Your PlayerViewController is complete. Now you just need to ensure that your media AssetItem is set when selecting from the AudioViewController or VideoViewController. Open MediaViewController.m. Add an import directive for PlayerViewController.h.

```
#import "PlayerViewController.h"
```

Then add the implementation for prepareForSegue:sender:.

```
- (void)prepareForSegue:(UIStoryboardSegue *)segue sender:(id)sender
{
    PlayerViewController *pvc = segue.destinationViewController;
    UITableViewCell *cell = sender;
    pvc.assetItem = [self.assets objectAtIndex:cell.tag];
}
```

You don't need to check which segue is begin invoked, as there should only be one.

Build and run the AVMediaPlayer. Select a song or video to play. Slider the scrubber to change the playback point. Toggle the rate to see how you can change the playback rate. Pretty slick, right?

# Avast! Rough Waters Ahead!

In this chapter, you took a long but pleasant walk through the hills and valleys of using the iPod music library. You saw how to find media items using media queries, and how to let your users select songs using the media picker controller. You learned how to use and manipulate collections of media items. We showed you how to use music player controllers to play media items and how to manipulate the currently playing item by seeking or skipping. You also learned how to find out about the currently playing track, regardless of whether it's one your code played or one that the user chose using the iPod or Music application.

But now, shore leave is over, matey. It's time to set sail into the open waters of iOS security. Batten down the hatches and secure the ship!

# Locking It Down: iOS Security

Application security is an important aspect of development. Protecting your users' information is an essential feature that you need to think about while developing. It's important to remember that security is not a product, nor is it a check-mark that you can think about at the end of the development. Security is a process that has to be taken in to consideration during all stages of development, from design to implementation, through testing and release.

We'll go over some basic security issues you should keep in mind and how to handle them in iOS. Then we'll cover Security SDK, which provides three services: Certificate, Key, and Trust Services, which are used to manage certificates, keys, and trust policies; Keychain Services, which are used to manage keychain items; and Randomization Services, which are used to create cryptographically secure random numbers.

---

**Note**  An important security issue is sending and receiving data securely over the network. We won't be covering that in this chapter. Check Apple's Networking documentation. Start with Networking Overview (https://developer.apple.com/library/ios/#documentation/NetworkingInternetWeb/ Conceptual/NetworkingOverview/), then read Secure Transport Reference (https://developer.apple.com/library/ios/#documentation/Security/Reference/ secureTransportRef/). You may need to read the CFNetwork Programming Guide (https://developer.apple.com/library/ios/#documentation/Networking/Conceptual/ CFNetwork/) as well.

---

You're going to create an application that will list the keychain items. By default, your application will have no keychain items, so you'll embed two certificates (your self-signed root certificate and user certificate) into the application and add them to the keychain. Your keychain item detail view will allow you to encrypt and decrypt some text as a demonstration of functionality.

# Security Considerations

When you ask your user to provide some personal data, you are implicitly asking the user to trust that you, the application developer, will keep that information safe and secure. You are also implying that you are only asking for the information you need—and no more. If you send that data over the Internet, you have to make sure that the data is transmitted in a secure manner. When your application receives signed data, it's your job to verify those signatures and ensure that they can be trusted.

When asking your users for information, you need to take into consideration what could happen if that data were compromised. If your application is a game that only stores the user's high score, you probably don't need to worry too much if the database is accessed outside your application. However, if you are asking your users for passwords or other sensitive information, it is crucial that you do your best to protect your users' information. One possible solution is to encrypt the data, making it more difficult to read.

Many mobile applications routinely transmit information to a cloud-based service to centrally store and update data. If you are transmitting sensitive user information between your iOS application and a cloud server, you need to ensure the security of the data on both the client and server, and you must ensure that the data is transmitted securely. Furthermore, you need to make sure the communication won't be intercepted by a malicious third-party who will try to access your user's information or send back malicious data to aid in accessing your user's data on the device.

# Security Techniques

The following sections cover some common security techniques.

# Encryption

We're sure you all know what encrypting data is and means, but let's go over it anyway. At its simplest, it's a way of protecting data by transforming it into a non-readable form. In order to read it, you need to decrypt it. Decryption is accomplished by knowing the cipher—the technique used to encrypt the data. Ciphers work by applying a key, an additional piece of information, to the data in order to encrypt it. You encrypt data prior to transmitting it in order to protect it from being intercepted and read. You also encrypt data before storing it locally to prevent it from being read if the device is lost or stolen.

There are two major encryption techniques:

- *Symmetric*: A single key is shared between parties to encrypt and decrypt the data. Since the key is shared, if it is discovered, the data can be compromised.

- *Asymmetric*: Two mathematically related keys are used transform the data. Data encrypted with one key can be decrypted with the other. Generally, one key is shared between parties and the other key is kept private. Another term for asymmetric encryption is public key cryptography.

Asymmetric encryption can be computationally expensive. A common technique is to use asymmetric encryption to encrypt a shared key, then use symmetric encryption to share the actual data.

# Hashing

In cryptography, a *hash* is a smaller piece of data that is derived from a larger set of data. This smaller piece can then be used as a proxy for the larger data set. You can think of hashing as one-way encryption: you encrypt the data in to a unique value, but you can't decrypt it back. You may use hashing whenever you use a dictionary. The dictionary key is hashed to ensure it always points to the same value.

Hashing is typically used for checksumming. A large set of data is hashed using a well-known algorithm. After you download the data, you hash the data set and compare the hashed value with the expected one. If the values differ, you can assume the data has been compromised in some way.

# Certificates and Signatures

Using encryption and hashing, you're able to create certificates that will tie a public key to specific trusted source. Given a set of data (say an e-mail message or web page), the sender will compute the hash of the data and encrypt it with a private key. This encrypted hash is sent with the data and the sender's certificate. The receiver decrypts the sender's hash using the certificate's public key and compares the value to a locally computed hash. If the hashes match, then the data wasn't compromised and was sent by the certificate's owner. This process of hashing and encrypting using a certificate is called a *signature*. Users sign their data to prove that it came from them.

How can you trust the certificate used to sign the data? The certificate itself is signed by another source. That source may be trusted by both the sender and receiver, or that source's certificate may need to be signed by someone else. This series of certificate signing may continue until there is a certificate that the receiver trusts. This series of certificate signing is called the *chain of trust*. The last certificate in the chain is called the *anchor* or *root certificate*.

Signatures and certificates rely on someone being a certificate authority that everyone trusts on some level. The chain of trust is only as strong as the security of the certificate authority.

# Identity

Combining a certificate with a private key creates a digital identity. An identity is usually transferred using a password-protected format, PKCS #12, which typically has a .p12 extension.

# Security in iOS

Since iOS 4, developers have the option to leverage the built-in encryption hardware on iOS devices to further protect their application data. This feature leverages the passcode lock setting in iOS. When the device is locked, the data is inaccessible, even to the application. The device must be unlocked before you application can access the data. Remember, you might code for this functionality into your application, but unless the device user activates the passcode lock setting, it won't be used. Generally, it's better to add this feature. If your users then use the passcode lock setting, they'll have the extra level of protection.

To protect your application's file data, you need to specify the correct extended attribute to level of protection you want. You can set this attribute using either the NSData or NSFileManager class. For existing files, you use the setAttributes:ofItemAtPath:error: method on NSFileManager. The attributes parameter is an NSDictionary, where the key is NSFileProtectionKey. For new files, you use the NSData method writeToFile:options:error: method, using the correct options bitmask to specify the level of protection. The possible level of protections are shown in Table 13-1.

*Table 13-1. Levels of Protection*

| Level | Description | NSData Option Bitmask | NSFileManager Attribute Key |
|---|---|---|---|
| None | No file encryption. | NSDataWritingFileProtectionNone | NSFileProtectionNone |
| Complete | File is encrypted and inaccessible when device is locked. | NSDataWritingFileProtectionComplete | NSFileProtectionComplete |
| Complete, unless open | File is encrypted. Closed file is inaccessible until first unlock. | NSDataWritingFileProtectionComplete UnlessOpen | NSFileProtectionCompleteUntil FirstUserAuthentication |
| Complete, until first login | File is encrypted until device is (re)booted and first unlocked. | NSDataWritingFileProtectionComplete UntilFirstUserAuthentication | NSFileProtectionCompleteUntil FirstUserAuthentication |

> **Note**    NSData has three other writing options: NSDataWritingAtomic,
> NSDataWritingWithoutOverwriting, NSDataWritingFileProtectionMask. The first two
> have to do with how an NSData instance writes its files, while the last sets the permissions of the file itself.
> None of these options set the file protection with respect to password locking.

If you set a level of protection, then you must prepare for the file to potentially be inaccessible. In order to do that, you application needs to check file accessibility. There are a few ways to do this:

- Implement the applicationProtectedDataWillBecomeUnavailable: and applicationProtectedDataDidBecomeAvailable: methods in your AppDelegate.

- Register for the UIApplicationProtectedDataWillBecomeUnavailable and UIApplicationProtectedDataDidBecomeAvailable notifications.

- Check the protectedDataAvailable property in UIApplication.

# Randomization Keychains

The keychain is an encrypted container used to hold passwords, certificates, or other information. The keychain is encrypted and locked using the iOS passcode lock mechanism. When your iOS device is locked, no one can access the contents. Once you enter your passcode, iOS unlocks and decrypts the keychain for access. From the user's perspective, the keychain provides transparent authentication. Suppose your application communicates with services on the Internet. Each of those services require your users to provide login information. Rather than requiring your users to enter that information every time they access those Internet services, you can store that information in the keychain. Since the keychain is secure, you can count on that information being safe.

In iOS, each application has its own keychain. Each keychain contains a set of information called keychain items (or just items). A keychain Item consists of data and a set of attributes. Programmatically, a keychain item is a dictionary (specifically a CFDictionary). The item data may or may not be encrypted; this is determined by the type of data being store in the item (i.e., passwords or certificates).

When defining your keychain item dictionary, you must specify the item class using the key constant kSecClass. The possible values for kSecClass are a defined set of constants (Table 13-2).

*Table 13-2.  Possible Values for kSecClass*

| kSecClassGenericPassword | Generic password item |
| --- | --- |
| kSecClassInternetPassword | Internet password item |
| kSecClassCertificate | Certificate item |
| kSecClassKey | Cryptographic key item |
| kSecClassIdentity | Identity (certificate and private key) item |

Depending on the keychain item class value, there are a set of allowable attribute keys that can be used (see Table 13-3).

Table 13-3. Keychain Item Attribute Keys

| Attribute | Description | Allowable Values / Attribute Type | Item Class |
|---|---|---|---|
| kSecAttrAccessible | Does the application need to access data in this item? | kSecAttrAccessibleWhenUnlocked kSecAttrAccessibleAfterFirstUnlock kSecAttrAccessibleAlways kSecAttrAccessibleWhenUnlockedThisDeviceOnly kSecAttrAccessibleAfterFirstUnlockThisDeviceOnly kSecAttrAccessibleAlwaysThisDeviceOnly | ALL |
| kSecAttrCreationDate | Item creation date | CFDateRef | ALL |
| kSecAttrModificationDate | Item last modify date | CFDateRef | ALL |
| kSecAttrDescription | Item description | CFStringRef | ALL |
| kSecAttrComment | Item comment | CFStringRef | ALL |
| kSecAttrCreator | Number representation of creator | CFNumberRef | ALL |
| kSecAttrType | Number representation of item's type | CFNumberRef | ALL |
| kSecAttrLabel | Editable label for item | CFStringRef | ALL |
| kSecAttrIsInvisible | Boolean if item is visible or not | CFBooleanRef | ALL |
| kSecAttrIsNegative | Boolean is valid password in item | CFBooleanRef | ALL |
| kSecAttrAccount | Account name | CFStringRef | kSecClassGenericPassword kSecClassInternetPassword |
| kSecAttrService | Service name/type/description | CFStringRef | kSecClassGenericPassword |
| kSecAttrGeneric | User-defined attribute | CFDataRef | kSecClassGenericPassword |
| kSecAttrSecurityDomain | Internet security domain | CFStringRef | kSecClassInternetPassword |
| kSecAttrServer | Server's DNS name or IP address | CFStringRef | kSecClassInternetPassword |

| kSecAttrProtocol | Protocol for item | kSecClassInternetPassword |
|---|---|---|
| | kSecAttrProtocolFTP | |
| | kSecAttrProtocolFTPAccount | |
| | kSecAttrProtocolHTTP | |
| | kSecAttrProtocolIRC | |
| | kSecAttrProtocolNNTP | |
| | kSecAttrProtocolPOP3 | |
| | kSecAttrProtocolSMTP | |
| | kSecAttrProtocolSOCKS | |
| | kSecAttrProtocolIMAP | |
| | kSecAttrProtocolLDAP | |
| | kSecAttrProtocolAppleTalk | |
| | kSecAttrProtocolAFP | |
| | kSecAttrProtocolTelnet | |
| | kSecAttrProtocolSSH | |
| | kSecAttrProtocolFTPS | |
| | kSecAttrProtocolHTTPS | |
| | kSecAttrProtocolHTTPProxy | |
| | kSecAttrProtocolHTTPSProxy | |
| | kSecAttrProtocolFTPProxy | |
| | kSecAttrProtocolSMB | |
| | kSecAttrProtocolRTSP | |
| | kSecAttrProtocolRTSPProxy | |

(continued)

*Table 13-3. (continued)*

| Attribute | Description | Allowable Values / Attribute Type | Item Class |
|---|---|---|---|
| | | kSecAttrProtocolDAAP | |
| | | kSecAttrProtocolEPPC | |
| | | kSecAttrProtocolIPP | |
| | | kSecAttrProtocolNNTPS | |
| | | kSecAttrProtocolLDAPS | |
| | | kSecAttrProtocolTelnetS | |
| | | kSecAttrProtocolIMAPS | |
| | | kSecAttrProtocolRCS | |
| | | kSecAttrProtocolPOP3S | |
| kSecAttrAuthenticationType | Authentication scheme | kSecAttrAuthenticationTypeNTLM | ALL |
| | | kSecAttrAuthenticationTypeMSN | |
| | | kSecAttrAuthenticationTypeDPA | |
| | | kSecAttrAuthenticationTypeRPA | |
| | | kSecAttrAuthenticationTypeHTTPBasic | |
| | | kSecAttrAuthenticationTypeHTTPDigest | |
| | | kSecAttrAuthenticationTypeHTMLForm | |
| | | kSecAttrAuthenticationTypeDefault | |
| kSecAttrPort | Internet port number | CFNumberRef | kSecClassInternetPassword |
| kSecAttrPath | Path component of URL | CFStringRef | kSecClassInternetPassword |
| kSecAttrSubject | X.500 subject name of certificate | CFDataRef | kSecClassCertificate |
| kSecAttrIssuer | X.500 issuer name of certificate | CFDataRef | kSecClassCertificate |
| kSecAttrSerialNumber | Serial number data of certificate | CFDataRef | kSecClassCertificate |
| kSecAttrSubjectKeyID | Subject key ID of certificate | CFDataRef | kSecClassCertificate |

| kSecAttrPublicKeyHash | Public key hash of certificate | CFDataRef | kSecClassCertificate |
| kSecAttrCertificateType | Certificate type | CFNumberRef | kSecClassCertificate |
| kSecAttrCertificateEncoding | Certificate encoding method | CFNumberRef | kSecClassCertificate |
| kSecAttrKeyClass | Cryptographic key type | kSecAttrKeyClassPublic<br>kSecAttrKeyClassPrivate<br>kSecAttrKeyClassSymmetric | ALL |
| kSecAttrApplicationLabel | Application label key, intented for programmatic lookup | CFStringRef | ALL |
| kSecAttrIsPermanent | Store crytographic key permanently? | CFBooleanRef | ALL |
| kSecAttrApplicationTag | Private tag data | CFDataRef | ALL |
| kSecAttrKeyType | Algorithm attribute key | kSecAttrKeyTypeRSA | ALL |
| kSecAttrKeySizeInBits | Number of bits in cryptographic key | CFNumberRef | ALL |
| kSecAttrEffectiveKeySize | Number of bits in cryptographic key | CFNumberRef | ALL |
| kSecAttrCanEncrypt | Can key be used to encrypt data? | CFBooleanRef | ALL |
| kSecAttrCanDecrypt | Can key be used to decrypt data? | CFBooleanRef | ALL |
| kSecAttrCanDerive | Can key be used to derive another key? | CFBooleanRef | ALL |
| kSecAttrCanSign | Can key be used to create a digital signature? | CFBooleanRef | ALL |
| kSecAttrCanVerify | Can key be used to verify a digital signature? | CFBooleanRef | ALL |
| kSecAttrCanWrap | Can key be used to wrap ancther key? | CFBooleanRef | ALL |
| kSecAttrCanUnwrap | Can key be used to unwrap another key? | CFBooleanRef | ALL |
| kSecAttrAccessGroup | Access group key, used to share keychain items across applications | CFStringRef | ALL |

The Keychain SDK is a Core Foundation C API, not Objective-C. That's why everything is a Core Foundation data type. The API is a simple set of functions:

  ▪ SecItemAdd: Add an item to the keychain

  ▪ SecItemDelete: Remove an item from the keychain

  ▪ SecItemUpdate: Update an item in the keychain

  ▪ SecItemCopyMatching: Return an item matching the search criteria.

That's it.

# Certificates, Keys, and Trust Services

In order to make managing and using certificates easier, Apple added a number of functions in iOS to ease the management of certificates, generating keys, and evaluating your chain of trust. Specifically, you use the Certificate, Key, and Trust SDK to determine identity by matching a certificate to a private key; create and request certificates; import certificates, keys, and identities into your keychain; create public-private key pairs; and manage trust policies.

These services leverage the keychain to store certificates and keys. Like the Keychain SDK, the Certificate, Key and Trust SDK is a C API, not Objective-C. At the core, a set of security objects are defined:

  ▪ SecCertificate (SecCertificateRef): The certificate object

  ▪ SecIdentity (SecIdentityRef): The identity (certificate and private key) object

  ▪ SecKey (SecKeyRef): The (asymmetric) key object, both public and private

  ▪ SecPolicy (SecPolicyRef): The policy object

  ▪ SecTrust (SecTrustRef): The trust management object

Correspondingly, the Security framework provides a series of functions to manage certificates; manage identities; generate and use keys; plus manage policies and trust. We won't go over each function in detail, but we will cover some of them in this chapter's application. To learn more, read Apple's Certificate, Key, and Trust Services Programming Guide (https://developer.apple.com/library/ios/#documentation/Security/Conceptual/CertKeyTrustProgGuide/01introduction/) and Reference (https://developer.apple.com/library/ios/#documentation/Security/Reference/certifkeytrustservices/).

# Keychain Viewer Application

You're going to create a simple application that will show you how to use your application's keychain items. At the beginning, the keychain should be empty. You'll add functionality to import a self-signed root certificate and a digital identity created from that root certificate. You'll show the details of each certificate. Finally, you'll add a simple encryption/decryption example from the digital identity's public-private key pair.

Before you start building your application, you need to create your root certificate and digital identity. We'll be using the Certificate Assistant in the Keychain Access application on our Mac.

> **Note**    If you don't feel like learning how to create certificates and digital identities, you can skip this section. We've provided two files, `root.der` and `cert.p12`, in the book's download archive for this chapter. Feel free to use them instead.

## Create a Certificate Authority

Open `Keychain Access.app`. You can find in `/Application/Utilities`. Go to Keychain Access ➤ Certificate Assistant ➤ Create Certificate Authority (Figure 13-1). The Certificate Assistant should open with a form to create a new Certificate Authority (CA) (Figure 13-2). Give the CA a unique name, and fill in an e-mail address. Uncheck the "Make this CA the default" checkbox. The rest of defaults should be fine. Click Create. If the Certificate Assistant is successful, you should see a window like Figure 13-3. If you click the "Show Certificate Authority" button, it will open a Finder window to your `~/Library/Application Support/Certificate Authority/<CA Name>` directory. This is where the Certificate Assistant has placed the relevant CA files, including your root certificate.

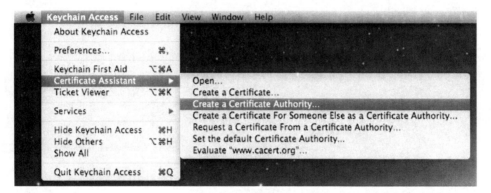

*Figure 13-1.  Creating a Certificate Authority*

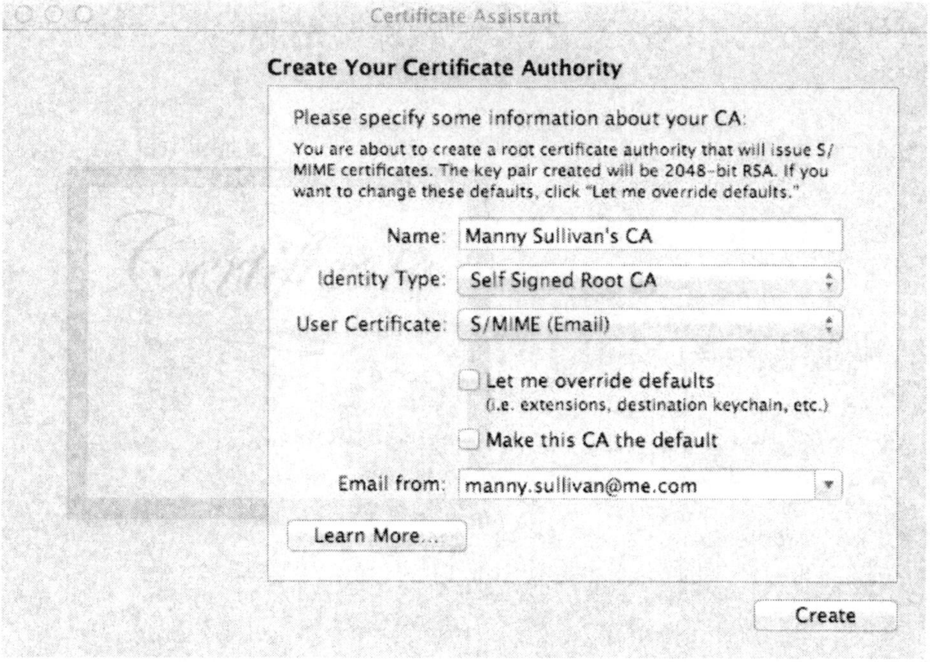

*Figure 13-2. Certificate Assistant*

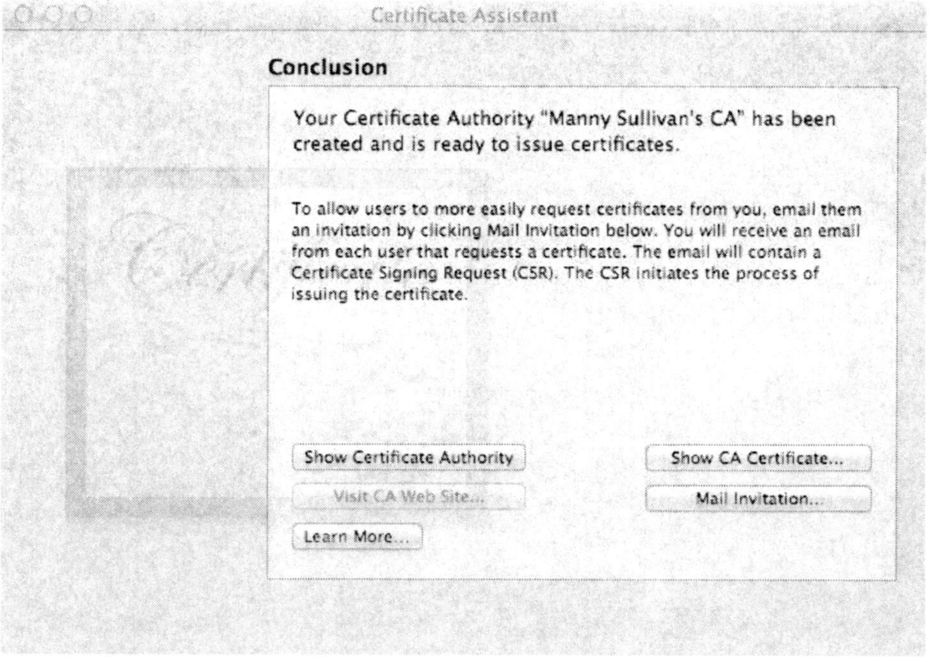

*Figure 13-3. Successful Certificate Authority creation*

Now you need to use your CA to create a new user certificate. Go back to `Keychain Access.app` and select Keychain Access ➤ Certificate Assistant ➤ Request a Certificate from a Certificate Authority. The Certificate Assistant should present a new form (Figure 13-4). Enter the e-mail address for the user and a common name (it doesn't have to be the name of a person). For the CA Email Address, enter the e-mail address you used when creating the CA (Figure 13-2). Since the CA is self-signed, select the "Save to disk" option. Click Continue. You will be presented with a Save dialog. Pick a location to save the file (the default name is fine), and click Save. When the Certificate Assistant is finished creating the certificate signing request, you can click Done to close the assistant.

*Figure 13-4. Creating a certificate signing request*

You're going to use this certificate signing request to create a new certificate. In `Keychain Access.app`, select Keychain Access ➤ Certificate Assistant ➤ Create a Certificate for Someone Else as a Certificate Authority. Drag the certificate signing request you just created into the specified area in the Certificate Assistant (Figure 13-5). The Certificate Assistant should change to ask you to specify the issuing CA. Select the CA name you created earlier. Leave the two checkboxes unchecked and click Continue. The Certificate Assistant will ask you for the same information again (to be honest, we're not sure why). Again, select the CA name you created earlier, leave the checkboxes unchecked, and click Continue (Figure 13-5). Once the Certificate Assistant is done, it will open `Mail.app` and create a draft e-mail with the certificate attached. You don't need this, so you can discard the message and close `Mail.app`. You should see the certificate information displayed in the Certificate Assistant (Figure 13-7). Click Done to close the assistant.

*Figure 13-5.* *Creating a certificate from your CSR*

Now you need to extract the digital identity from the user certificate. In Keychain Access.app, select the login keychain on the left, and select the Certificates category below that. Find the certificate you just created. It should have the common name you entered when creating the certificate signing request (Figure 13-6). Open the disclosure triangle next to the name. The private key should be exposed below the certificate, with the same name as the certificate. Select the private key, then File ➤ Export Items . Name the file cert in the Save dialog, making sure the file format is Personal Information Exchange (.p12). Click Save. You will be asked to provide a password for the .p12 file. It's a good idea to pick something the Password dialog thinks is secure. In our case, we used "@ Super2048Cat". After you click OK, you may be asked to enter your keychain password. This is your login password. Enter it and click Allow. On successful certificate creation, the Certificate Assistant will show you the details for your certificate (Figure 13-7). Notice that since it was self-signed, it's marked as being signed by an untrusted issuer.

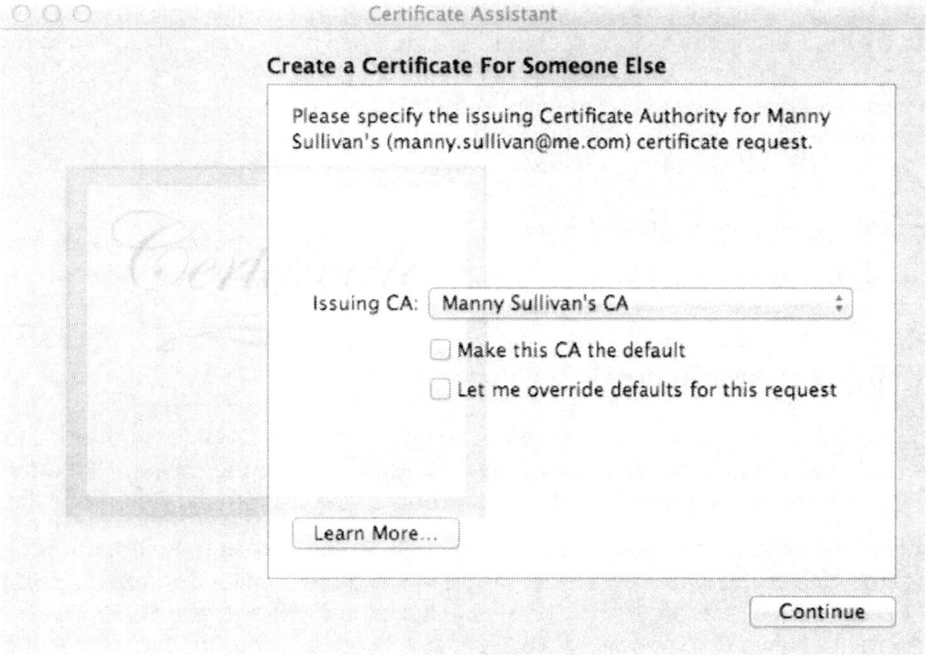

*Figure 13-6.  Select the Issuing Certificate Authority for your certificate*

*Figure 13-7.  Successful certificate creation*

One last thing. The Security framework expects your root certificate of DER format, not the PEM that's created by the Certificate Assistant. Open `Terminal.app` and change directories to the `~/Library/Application Support/Certificate Authority/<CA Name>` directory. You should see a file named `<CA Name>` certificates.pem. Enter this command

```
> openssl x509 -in <PEM file> -inform PEM -out root.der -outform DER
```

replacing <PEM file> with the name of the file.

Now you're ready to build your application.

# Creating the Keychain App

You're going to use the Tabbed Application template as the starting point for your application. Open Xcode and create a new project. Select the Tabbed Application template. Name the project KeychainViewer, and have the project use both storyboards and Automatic Reference Counting.

Once the project is created, you need to add the Security framework to it. Select the project in the Project Navigator. Select the Keychain Viewer target in the project editor and navigate to the Build Phases tab. Expand the Link Binary with Libraries (3 Items) section and add `Security.framework`. Clean up the Project Navigator by moving the `Security.framework` into the Frameworks group.

You're going to replace the `FirstViewController` and `SecondViewController` with different implementations. So select the files `FirstViewController.h`, `FirstViewController.m`, `SecondViewController.h`, and `SecondViewController.m` and delete them. You don't need to keep the files, so select Move to Trash when Xcode asks.

You'll delete the First View Controller and Second View Controller scenes in the main storyboard in a little bit. First, you'll define some keychain item classes. The Keychain API is a C language API, not Objective-C, so you're going to wrap it in an Objective-C class to make access easier. Create a new Objective-C class, in the Keychain Viewer group, named `KeychainItem`. Make it a subclass of `NSObject`.

Select `KeychainItem.h`, and add an import directive for the Security framework header file.

```
#import <Security/Security.h>
```

For each `KeychainItem` object, you need to know what type it might be (i.e. `kSecClassGenericPassword`), and the actual keychain item. Both of these can be captured using the `CFTypeRef` CoreFoundation type. `CFTypeRef` maps to the generic Objective-C object id. So you'll add two properties of type `id` to your `KeychainItem` class. You'll also define an `NSDictionary` property to hold the dictionary of attributes you get back for each keychain item. Finally, you'll have a property to hold the persistent reference of the keychain item.

```
@property (strong, nonatomic) id type;
@property (strong, nonatomic) id item;
@property (strong, nonatomic) NSDictionary *attributes;
@property (strong, nonatomic) id persistentRef;
```

You need an initializer that will take these two properties.

```
- (id)initWithItem:(CFTypeRef)item;
- (id)initWithData:(NSData *)data options:(NSDictionary *)options;
```

You'll use initWithItem: for when you create a keychain item via the Keychain API. initWithData:options: is intended for when you are loading a keychain item from a file or URL; the options dictionary is for when you need to pass additional information to load a keychain item.

You want to be able to save keychain items (i.e. write them to your keychain), so you'll implement a save method. The save method will return a BOOL to indicate success or failure. You'll pass in a pointer to an NSError pointer to allow you to send an error message on failure. You'll also add a convenience method, valueForAttribute:, to wrap the Keychain API call to retrieve value for the keychain item.

```
- (BOOL)save:(NSError **)error;
- (id)valueForAttribute:(CFTypeRef)attr;
```

Let's implement these methods.

Open KeychainItem.m and add your initializer.

```
- (id)initWithItem:(CFTypeRef)item
{
    self = [self init];
    if (self) {
        self.item = CFBridgingRelease(item);
    }
    return self;
}
```

This should be pretty standard fare by now. Note the use of the function CFBridgingRelease. This is part of the toll-free bridge between CoreFoundation and Objective-C. It converts a non-Objective-C pointer to an Objective-C object. It also transfers the memory management to ARC. The inverse of CFBridgingRelease is CFBridgingRetain, which you'll use a little later on. Notice that you haven't set the type property in the initializer. That's because you intend KeychainItem to be an *abstract base class*. Hopefully, you won't ever instantiate an instance of KeychainItem, but rather a subclass. It's in those subclasses where you'll set the type property.

Since KeychainItem is abstract, initWithData:options: should do nothing.

```
- (id)initWithData:(NSData *)data options:(NSDictionary *)options
{
    return nil;
}
```

The save: method turns out to be more complicated than you think.

```
- (BOOL)save:(NSError **)error
{
    NSDictionary *attributes = @{
        (__bridge id)kSecValueRef : self.item,
        (__bridge id)kSecReturnPersistentRef : (id)kCFBooleanTrue
    };
    CFTypeRef cfPersistentRef;
    OSStatus status = SecItemAdd((__bridge CFDictionaryRef)attributes, &cfPersistentRef);

    if (status != errSecSuccess) {
        NSDictionary *userInfo = nil;
        switch (status) {
            case errSecParam:
                userInfo = @{ NSLocalizedDescriptionKey : NSLocalizedString(@"errorSecParam",
                                @"One or more parameters passed to the function were not valid.") };
                break;
            case errSecAllocate:
                userInfo = @{ NSLocalizedDescriptionKey : NSLocalizedString(@"errSecAllocate",
                                @"Failed to allocate memory.") };
                break;
            case errSecDuplicateItem:
                userInfo = @{ NSLocalizedDescriptionKey : NSLocalizedString(@"errSecDuplicateItem",
                                @"The item already exists.") };
                break;
        }
        if (*error)
            *error = [NSError errorWithDomain:NSOSStatusErrorDomain code:status userInfo:userInfo];
        return NO;
    }

    self.persistentRef = CFBridgingRelease(cfPersistentRef);
    return YES;
}
```

The bulk of the method is taken up handling the different error conditions of the call to `SecItemAdd`, which adds the keychain item to the keychain, fails. You've got a bunch of casts that begin with __bridge. This is another part of the toll-free bridge. In this case, you don't want to transfer memory management to ARC (or in the case of (__bridge CFDictionaryRef) cast, away from ARC). You could have done this as pure CoreFoundation code, but you'd have to explicitly release your CoreFoundation objects with a call to CFRelease, and we thought this was easier.

`valueForAttribute:` is a simple wrapper to the `NSDictionary` method `valueForKey:` to make life easier for you, so you don't have to put (__bridge id) casts all over your code.

```
- (id)valueForAttribute:(CFTypeRef)attr
{
    return [self.attributes valueForKey:(__bridge id)attr];
}
```

Now you need to implement your concrete subclasses of `KeychainItem`. Recall that there are four keychain item types defined in the Security framework: `kSecClassGenericPassword`, `kSecClassInternetPassword`, `kSecClassCertificate`, and `kSecClassIdentity`. You're only going to work with two of them, Certificates and Identities. As a result, you only need to define two concrete subclasses for your application: KeychainCertificate and KeychainIdentity.

Create a new file using the Objective-C class template. Name the class KeychainCertificate, and make it a subclass of KeychainItem. Once the file is created, select KeychainCertificate.m, and implement the initializer methods.

```
- (id)init
{
    self = [super init];
    if (self) {
        self.type = [(__bridge id)kSecClassCertificate copy];
    }
    return self;
}

- (id)initWithData:(NSData *)data options:(NSDictionary *)options
{
    SecCertificateRef cert = SecCertificateCreateWithData(NULL, (__bridge CFDataRef)data);
    if (cert) {
        self = [self initWithItem:cert];
    }
    return self;
}
```

Use the generic init method to set the type property. The init method will override the default init in KeychainItem. When KeychainItem initWithItem: is invoked, it calls init. When you call initWithItem with a KeychainCertificate, you'll call this init method.

Now, let's create the KeychainIdentity class. Create a new Objective-C class, name it KeychainIdentity, and make it subclass of KeychainItem. Since this encapsulates a digital identity, you need a password when loading from a file.

```
- (id)init
{
    self = [super init];
    if (self) {
        self.type = [(__bridge id)kSecClassIdentity copy];
    }
    return self;
}

- (id)initWithData:(NSData *)data options:(NSDictionary *)options
{
    CFDataRef inPKCS12Data = (__bridge CFDataRef)data;
    CFArrayRef items = CFArrayCreate(NULL, 0, 0, NULL);
    // Options dictionary needs key kSecImportExportPassphrase with password used to protect file
    OSStatus status = SecPKCS12Import(inPKCS12Data, (__bridge CFDictionaryRef)options, &items);
    if (status != errSecSuccess) {
        NSLog(@"Error Reading P12 file");
        abort();
    }
```

```
    CFDictionaryRef myIdentityAndTrust = CFArrayGetValueAtIndex(items, 0);
    SecIdentityRef identity =
        (SecIdentityRef)CFDictionaryGetValue(myIdentityAndTrust, kSecImportItemIdentity);
    if (identity)
        self = [self initWithItem:identity];

    return self;
}
```

Again, you override the init method to set the type property; this time to kSecClassIdentity. initWithData:options: is used to load data in PKCS #12 format. Since this data is password protected, you need the options dictionary to have the key kSecImportExportPassphrase and the value of the password used when the file was created.

You need to define the view controller classes that will use these KeychainItem classes you just created. Create a new file using the Objective-C class template. Name the file KeychainItemsViewController and make it a subclass of UITableViewController. This will be your abstract base view controller class. Open KeychainItemsViewController.h and add the following property:

```
@property (strong, nonatomic) NSArray *items;
```

The items property will hold the array of keychain items you want to display. Open KeychainItemsViewController.m so you can work on all the changes you need to make. First, you need to import the KeychainItem header file.

```
#import "KeychainItem.h"
```

Next, you need to update the table view data source methods to return the correct number of sections and rows per section.

```
- (NSInteger)numberOfSectionsInTableView:(UITableView *)tableView
{
    // Return the number of sections.
    return 1;
}

- (NSInteger)tableView:(UITableView *)tableView numberOfRowsInSection:(NSInteger)section
{
    // Return the number of rows in the section.
    return self.items.count;
}
```

Finally, you need to use the keychain item to configure your table view cell.

```
- (UITableViewCell *)tableView:(UITableView *)tableView cellForRowAtIndexPath:(NSIndexPath *)
indexPath
{
    static NSString *CellIdentifier = @"KeychainItemCell";
    UITableViewCell *cell = [tableView dequeueReusableCellWithIdentifier:CellIdentifier
                                                          forIndexPath:indexPath];
```

```
    // Configure the cell...
    KeychainItem *item = self.items[indexPath.row];
    cell.textLabel.text = [item valueForAttribute:kSecAttrLabel];

    return cell;
}
```

That's all you need for your KeychainItemViewController. Let's define the concrete subclasses you'll actually use. Create a new Objective-C class file. Name it CertificatesViewController, subclass of KeychainItemsViewController. You don't need to modify the default code at this point. Create another KeychainItemsViewController subclass. This time name the class IdentitiesViewController.

Now, let's update the storyboard to use the KeychainCertificate and KeychainItem classes. Open the MainStoryboard.storyboard in the storyboard editor. Find the First View Controller and delete it. Repeat for the second view controller. Now drag a UITableViewController into the Editor pane. Control-drag from the tab bar controller to the table view controller. When the Segue Selector pop-up appears, select View Controllers under the Relationship Segue label. The table view controller should have a tab bar appear along the bottom with the label Item (Figure 13-8). Click the label and open the Attribute Inspector. Rename the title to Identities, and use the image called first.png.

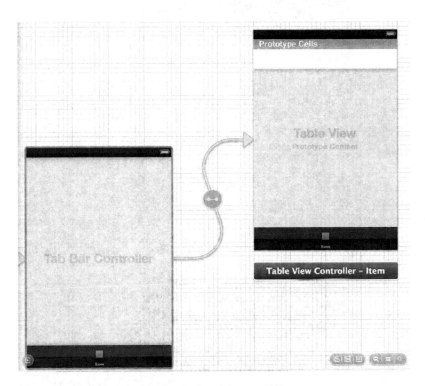

*Figure 13-8. Connecting the table view controller to the tab bar controller*

Select the table view controller, and in the Identity Inspector, change the class from `UITableViewController` to `IdentitiesViewController`. Select the table view cell under the Prototype Cells label. In the Attributes Inspector, change the style from Custom to Basic. Give the table view cell the identifier of `KeychainItemCell`. Change the accessory to Disclosure Indicator.

Drag another `UITableViewController` to the Editor pane. Control-drag from the tab bar controller to this table view controller, select the view controllers in the pop-up again. Relabel the tab bar to Certificates and use the `second.png` image. Change the table view controller class to `CertificatesViewController`. Adjust the table view cell to the Basic Style, give it the identifier of `KeychainItemCell`, and change the accessory to Disclosure Indicator.

Build and run the app (Figure 13-9). The table views are empty, since you haven't loaded the keychain identities or certificates to display.

*Figure 13-9. The Keychain Viewer application without any keychain items*

Edit CertificatesViewController.m. First, you need to import the KeychainCertificate.h
header file.

```
#import "KeychainCertificate.h"
```

And you need to update viewDidLoad to load your KeychainCertificates.

```
- (void)viewDidLoad
{
    [super viewDidLoad];
        // Do any additional setup after loading the view.
    self.items = [KeychainCertificate allKeychainCertificates];
}
```

You're invoking a KeychainCertificate class method, allKeychainCertificates, to populate your
items property. But you haven't defined that method yet. Open KeychainCertificate.h and add the
class method declaration.

```
+ (NSArray *)allKeychainCertificates;
```

Open KeychainCertificate.m so you can implement allKeychainCertificates.

```
+ (NSArray *)allKeychainCertificates
{
    NSMutableArray *certs = [NSMutableArray array];
    NSDictionary *query = @{
        (__bridge id)kSecClass               : (__bridge id)kSecClassCertificate,
        (__bridge id)kSecReturnRef           : (id)kCFBooleanTrue,
        (__bridge id)kSecReturnAttributes    : (id)kCFBooleanTrue,
        (__bridge id)kSecReturnPersistentRef : (id)kCFBooleanTrue,
        (__bridge id)kSecMatchLimit          : (__bridge id)kSecMatchLimitAll
    };
    CFTypeRef results = NULL;
    OSStatus status = SecItemCopyMatching((__bridge CFDictionaryRef)query, &results);
    if (status == errSecSuccess && results != NULL) {
        for (NSDictionary *result in (__bridge NSArray *)results) {
            id itemRef = [result valueForKey:(__bridge id)kSecValueRef];
            id persistentRef = [result valueForKey:(__bridge id)kSecValuePersistentRef];
            NSMutableDictionary *attrs = [NSMutableDictionary dictionaryWithDictionary:result];
            [attrs removeObjectForKey:(__bridge id)kSecValueRef];
            [attrs removeObjectForKey:(__bridge id)kSecValuePersistentRef];

            KeychainCertificate *cert =
                [[KeychainCertificate alloc] initWithItem:(__bridge CFTypeRef)itemRef];
            cert.persistentRef = persistentRef;
            cert.attributes = attrs;
            [certs addObject:cert];
        }
    }
    return certs;
}
```

You query the keychain for all certificates, asking for the certificates, their attributes, and their persistent references. The results come back as an array of dictionaries. You need to parse the dictionary to extract the certificate and persistent reference. The remaining dictionary are the attributes. You create a KeychainCertificate from each dictionary and return an array of KeychainCertificates back.

You need to repeat the process for the IdentitiesViewController. Edit IdentitiesViewController.m and import the KeychainIdentity.h header file.

```objc
#import "KeychainIdentity.h"
```

Modify viewDidLoad to load all the keychain identities.

```objc
- (void)viewDidLoad
{
    [super viewDidLoad];
        // Do any additional setup after loading the view.
    self.items = [KeychainIdentity allKeychainIdentities];
}
```

Now you need to define and implement the allKeychainIdentities class method on KeychainIdentity. Open KeychainIdentity.h to add the definition.

```objc
+ (NSArray *)allKeychainIdentities;
```

Add the implementation to KeychainIdentity.m.

```objc
+ (NSArray *)allKeychainIdentities
{
    NSMutableArray *idents = [NSMutableArray array];
    NSDictionary *query = @{
        (__bridge id)kSecClass               : (__bridge id)kSecClassIdentity,
        (__bridge id)kSecReturnRef           : (id)kCFBooleanTrue,
        (__bridge id)kSecReturnAttributes    : (id)kCFBooleanTrue,
        (__bridge id)kSecReturnPersistentRef : (id)kCFBooleanTrue,
        (__bridge id)kSecMatchLimit          : (__bridge id)kSecMatchLimitAll
    };
    CFTypeRef results = NULL;
    OSStatus status = SecItemCopyMatching((__bridge CFDictionaryRef)query, &results);
    if (status == errSecSuccess && results != NULL) {
        for (NSDictionary *result in (__bridge NSArray *)results) {
            id itemRef = [result valueForKey:(__bridge id)kSecValueRef];
            id persistentRef = [result valueForKey:(__bridge id)kSecValuePersistentRef];
            NSMutableDictionary *attrs = [NSMutableDictionary dictionaryWithDictionary:result];
            [attrs removeObjectForKey:(__bridge id)kSecValueRef];
            [attrs removeObjectForKey:(__bridge id)kSecValuePersistentRef];

            KeychainIdentity *ident =
                [[KeychainIdentity alloc] initWithItem:(__bridge CFTypeRef)itemRef];
            ident.persistentRef = persistentRef;
            ident.attributes = attrs;
```

```
            [idents addObject:ident];
        }
    }
    return idents;
}
```

This implementation is essentially identical to allKeychainCertificates, except you query for digital identities and create KeychainIdentities instead of KeychainCertificates. You could probably refactor the common code into a class method in KeychainItem, but this works for now.

Building and running the app still doesn't show any identities or certificates. Remember in iOS, keychains are only in the scope of the application. Your application doesn't have any keychain items. You're going to load the certificate and identity you created earlier.

First, let's add the two certificates you created earlier to your project. Select the Supporting Files group in the Project Navigator pane, and add the files root.cer and cert.p12 to the project. Make sure you check the "Copy items to destination group's folder (if needed)" checkbox.

You're going to load these items when you run your application, but you don't want to load them every time you launch your app. Open AppDelegate.m, and import your KeychainCertificate and KeychainIdentity header files.

```
#import "KeychainCertificate.h"
#import "KeychainIdentity.h"
```

Next, define a private category.

```
@interface AppDelegate ()
- (BOOL)isAnchorCertLoaded;
- (void)addAnchorCertificate;
- (void)addIdentity;
@end
```

You defined a method to check if your anchor certificate has been loaded, plus two methods to add the anchor certificate and digital identity. Before you implement those methods, you need to modify application:didFinishLoadingWithOptions:.

```
- (BOOL)application:(UIApplication *)application
        didFinishLaunchingWithOptions:(NSDictionary *)launchOptions
{
    // Override point for customization after application launch.
    if ([self isAnchorCertLoaded]) {
        [self addIdentity];
        [self addAnchorCertificate];
    }

    return YES;
}
```

Check if the anchor certificate is loaded. If not, load the digital identity and anchor certificate. The loading should happen only once, essentially at first launch of the application. The implementation of isAnchorCertLoaded is very simple.

```
- (BOOL)isAnchorCertLoaded
{
    return ([[NSUserDefaults standardUserDefaults] valueForKey:@"anchor_certificate"] == nil);
}
```

You just check if the key anchor_certificate exists in the application's User Defaults. If it doesn't, you assume the certificate and digital identity haven't been loaded. To load the certificate, you simply load the file, instantiate a KeychainCertificate, then save it. Remember your KeychainItem save: method writes the keychain item to the keychain.

```
- (void)addAnchorCertificate
{
    NSString *rootCertificatePath = [[NSBundle mainBundle] pathForResource:@"root" ofType:@"der"];
    NSData *data = [[NSData alloc] initWithContentsOfFile:rootCertificatePath];
    KeychainCertificate *cert = [[KeychainCertificate alloc] initWithData:data options:nil];
    if (cert) {
        NSError *error;
        BOOL saved = [cert save:&error];
        if (!saved) {
            NSLog(@"Error Saving Certificate: %@", [error localizedDescription]);
            abort();;
        }
        NSUserDefaults *userDefaults = [NSUserDefaults standardUserDefaults];
        [userDefaults setObject:cert.persistentRef forKey:@"anchor_certificate"];
        [userDefaults synchronize];
    }
}
```

As a final step, you write the certificate's persistent reference to your User Defaults, using the key anchor_certificates.

Adding a digital identity is similar to adding a certificate. You need send the password used to protect the identity file. You'll hard-code that value. In a production application, you'd probably use an Alert dialog asking the user to enter the password.

```
- (void)addIdentity
{
    NSString *identityPath = [[NSBundle mainBundle] pathForResource:@"cert" ofType:@"p12"];
    NSData *data = [[NSData alloc] initWithContentsOfFile:identityPath];
    NSString *password = @"@Super2048Cat";

    KeychainIdentity *ident =
        [[KeychainIdentity alloc] initWithData:data
                                       options:@{ (__bridge id)kSecImportExportPassphrase : password }];
    if (ident) {
        NSError *error;
        BOOL saved = [ident save:&error];
        if (!saved) {
            NSLog(@"Error Saving Identity: %@", [error localizedDescription]);
            abort();
        }
    }
}
```

You're assuming that if the certificate is loaded, that you've loaded the digital identity as well. Again, in a production application, you'd probably want a check for each keychain item you need.

Build and run your app. Now you should see your digital identity and certificates (Figure 13-10).

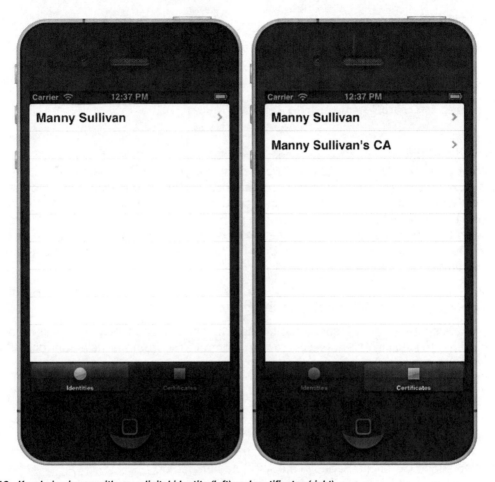

*Figure 13-10.* *Keychain viewer with your digital identity (left) and certificates (right)*

Let's add a detail view for your digital identity and certificates. You'll just use a simple text view to print out the attributes. You'll be presenting this view controller modally, so you'll add a single button to dismiss it.

Start by creating a new Objective-C class, named KeychainItemViewController, which will be a subclass of UIViewController. Once the class files are created, open KeychainItemViewController.h. Before the @interface declaration, you'll predeclare the KeychainItem class.

```
@class KeychainItem;
```

You do this because you want to have a KeychainItem property. In addition, you'll declare a UITextView property where you'll put the keychain item attribute information.

```
@property (strong, nonatomic) KeychainItem *item;
@property (weak, nonatomic) IBOutlet UITextView *textView;
```

Finally, you'll define an action that will dismiss your view controller when the user taps a button.

```
- (IBAction)done:(id)sender;
```

Open KeychainItemViewController.m, and implement the done: action.

```
- (IBAction)done:(id)sender
{
    [self dismissViewControllerAnimated:YES completion:nil];
}
```

You're ready to add the view controller scenes. Open MainStoryboard.storyboard. Drag a UIViewController from the Object Library to the storyboard editor next to the IdentitiesViewController. Drag another UIViewController, this time placing it next to the CertificatesViewController. Change the background color for both views to black. Next add a UITextView to both UIViewControllers. When you place them over the UIViewControllers, they should expand to fill the view. If they don't, that's okay. You want to adjust each one to be the width of the view (320.0 px), but have a height less than the full height of the view (we used 400.0 px). Delete the default text in each text view.

Drag a UIButton to each area below the text views. Use the blue guidelines to align the buttons to the left, below the text view. Change the button label text from Button to Done.

For each scene, use the Identity Inspector to change the class of each view controller from UIViewController to KeychainItemViewController. Control-drag from the view controller icon to the text view and select the textView outlet. Control-drag from the Done button to the view controller and select the done: Action.

Finally, control-drag from the table view cell in the IdentitiesViewController to the KeychainItemViewController right next to it. Select the modal Selection Segue in the pop-up menu that appears. Select the new segue and name it IdentitySegue in the Attributes Inspector. Repeat the process for the CertificatesViewController and the KeychainItemViewController next to it. This time, name the segue CertificateSegue in the Attributes Inspector.

You want to populate the text view with the keychain item's attributes. You'll use the UIViewController method viewWillAppear to populate the text view.

```
- (void)viewWillAppear:(BOOL)animated
{
    if (self.item) {
        NSMutableString *itemInfo = [NSMutableString string];
        [itemInfo appendFormat:@"AccessGroup: %@\n",
                               [self.item valueForAttribute:kSecAttrAccessGroup]];
        [itemInfo appendFormat:@"CreationDate: %@\n",
                               [self.item valueForAttribute:kSecAttrCreationDate]];
        [itemInfo appendFormat:@"CertificateEncoding: %@\n",
                               [self.item valueForAttribute:kSecAttrCertificateEncoding]];
        [itemInfo appendFormat:@"CreationDate: %@\n", [self.item valueForAttribute:kSecClass]];
        [itemInfo appendFormat:@"Issuer: %@\n", [self.item valueForAttribute:kSecAttrIssuer]];
```

```
        [itemInfo appendFormat:@"Label: %@\n", [self.item valueForAttribute:kSecAttrLabel]];
        [itemInfo appendFormat:@"ModificationDate: %@\n",
                            [self.item valueForAttribute:kSecAttrModificationDate]];
        [itemInfo appendFormat:@"Accessible: %@\n", [self.item valueForAttribute:kSecAttrAccessible]];
        [itemInfo appendFormat:@"PublicKeyHash: %@\n",
                            [self.item valueForAttribute:kSecAttrPublicKeyHash]];
        [itemInfo appendFormat:@"SerialNumber: %@\n",
                            [self.item valueForAttribute:kSecAttrSerialNumber]];
        [itemInfo appendFormat:@"Subject: %@\n", [self.item valueForAttribute:kSecAttrSubject]];
        self.textView.text = itemInfo;
    }
}
```

Next, check to see if you have a keychain item. If you do, you create and fill an NS(Mutable)String with some attribute values. That string is used to set the text view text.

For each table view controller, you need to implement prepareForSegue:sender: to set the keychain item for the KeychainItemViewController. Open CertificatesViewController.m and add import the KeychainItemViewController header file.

```
#import "KeychainItemViewController.h"
```

The implementation of prepareForSegue:sender: check the segue being called and sets the KeychainItem property for the KeychainItemViewController.

```
- (void)prepareForSegue:(UIStoryboardSegue *)segue sender:(id)sender
{
    if ([segue.identifier isEqualToString:@"CertificateSegue"]) {
        NSIndexPath *indexPath = [self.tableView indexPathForSelectedRow];
        KeychainCertificate *cert = self.items[indexPath.row];
        KeychainItemViewController *kivc = [segue destinationViewController];
        kivc.item = cert;
    }
}
```

You want to repeat the process for the IdentitiesViewController, with some minor changes.

```
- (void)prepareForSegue:(UIStoryboardSegue *)segue sender:(id)sender
{
    if ([segue.identifier isEqualToString:@"IdentitySegue"]) {
        NSIndexPath *indexPath = [self.tableView indexPathForSelectedRow];
        KeychainIdentity *ident = self.items[indexPath.row];
        KeychainItemViewController *kivc = [segue destinationViewController];
        kivc.item = ident;
    }
}
```

You check for the segue identifier IdentitySegue, and you're sending KeychainIdentity object rather than a KeychainCertificate.

Build and run your app. Select the digital identity and look at the attribute details. Dismiss the detail view and look at a certificate. You could extend this app to show the attributes that are specific to each keychain item. You're going to do something else. You're going to enhance the digital identity to allow you to encrypt and decrypt data.

Open KeychainIdentity.h. You want to add two methods.

```
- (NSData *)encrypt:(NSData *)data;
- (NSData *)decrypt:(NSData *)data;
```

For each method, you pass in an NSData object, whose data needs to be encrypted or decrypted. Each method will return a new NSData object with the transformed data.

Before you can use the public and private keys to encrypt and decrypt data, you need to know if the digital identity can be trusted. You only need to check trust once, so you'll do it lazily, checking only when you need it. You'll declare private ivar, _trusted, to tell you if the KeychainIdentity can be trusted. Since you don't want to check trust every time trusted is false, you'll also declare another property, trust, which is of type SecTrustRef.

```
@interface KeychainIdentity ()
@property (assign, nonatomic, readonly, getter=isTrusted) BOOL trusted;
@property (assign, nonatomic, readonly) SecTrustRef trust;
@property (assign, nonatomic, readonly) SecCertificateRef anchorCertificate;
@property (assign, nonatomic, readonly) SecCertificateRef certificate;
- (BOOL)recoverTrust;
@end
```

You also declared two additional properties, anchorCertificate and certificate, and a private method, recoverTrust, which you're going to need. We'll explain why when we get to the implementation.

Inside the implementation, you'll synthesize trusted, trust, anchorCertificate, and certificate so you have access to the ivars, _trusted, _trust _anchorCertificate and _certificate.

```
@synthesize trusted = _trusted;
@synthesize trust = _trust;
@synthesize anchorCertificate = _anchorCertificate;
@synthesize certificate = _certificate;
```

Let's update the init method to initialize these ivars.

```
- (id)init
{
    self = [super init];
    if (self) {
        self.type = [(__bridge id)kSecClassIdentity copy];
        _trusted = NO;
        _trust = NULL;
    }
    return self;
}
```

You need to implement the dealloc method to release the trust and certificate references, if necessary.

```
- (void)dealloc
{
    if (_trust)
        CFRelease(_trust);

    if (_certificate)
        CFRelease(_certificate);

    if (_anchorCertificate)
        CFRelease(_anchorCertificate);
}
```

Before you can implement methods for trust and trusted, you need to implement methods for anchorCertificate and certificate.

```
- (SecCertificateRef)anchorCertificate
{
    if (_anchorCertificate == NULL) {
        id persistentRef =
            [[NSUserDefaults standardUserDefaults] objectForKey:@"anchor_certificate"];
        NSDictionary *query = @{
                (__bridge id)kSecClass                 : (__bridge id)kSecClassCertificate,
                (__bridge id)kSecValuePersistentRef    : persistentRef,
                (__bridge id)kSecReturnRef             : (id)kCFBooleanTrue,
                (__bridge id)kSecMatchLimit            : (__bridge id)kSecMatchLimitOne
        };
        OSStatus status =
            SecItemCopyMatching((__bridge CFDictionaryRef)query, (CFTypeRef *)&_anchorCertificate);
        if (status != errSecSuccess || _anchorCertificate == NULL) {
            NSLog(@"Error loading Anchor Certificate");
            abort();
        }
    }
    return _anchorCertificate;
}
```

You lazily load the anchor certificate. This is the root certificate you loaded into the keychain in your AppDelegate. You retrieve the persistent reference you loaded into the User Defaults and use it to query the keychain for the anchor certificate. If you succeed, you set the _anchorCertificate ivar. If you fail, you've got a bigger problem, so you log an error and abort the application.

Loading the digital identity certificate is much easier.

```
- (SecCertificateRef)certificate
{
    if (_certificate == NULL) {
        OSStatus status =
            SecIdentityCopyCertificate((__bridge SecIdentityRef)self.item, &_certificate);
        if (status != errSecSuccess) {
```

```
            NSLog(@"Error retrieving Identity Certificate");
            return NULL;
        }
    }
    return _certificate;
}
```

You need to create a policy reference, and use that with the certificates to create a trust reference.

```
- (SecTrustRef)trust
{
    if (_trust == NULL) {
        SecPolicyRef policy = SecPolicyCreateBasicX509();
        NSArray *certs = @[ (__bridge id)self.certificate, (__bridge id)self.anchorCertificate ];
        OSStatus status =
            SecTrustCreateWithCertificates((__bridge CFTypeRef)certs, policy, &_trust);
        if (status != errSecSuccess) {
            NSLog(@"Error Creating Trust from Certificate");
            return NULL;
        }
    }
    return _trust;
}
```

You'll use these methods to implement the getter for the trusted property, isTrusted.

```
- (BOOL)isTrusted
{
    if (_trust == NULL) {
        SecTrustResultType trustResult;
        OSStatus status = SecTrustEvaluate(self.trust, &trustResult);
        if (status == errSecSuccess) {
            switch (trustResult) {
                case kSecTrustResultInvalid:
                case kSecTrustResultDeny:
                case kSecTrustResultFatalTrustFailure:
                case kSecTrustResultOtherError:
                    _trusted = NO;
                    break;
                case kSecTrustResultProceed:
                case kSecTrustResultConfirm:
                case kSecTrustResultUnspecified:
                    _trusted = YES;
                    break;
                case kSecTrustResultRecoverableTrustFailure:
                    _trusted = [self recoverTrust];
                    break;
            }
        }
```

```
        else
            _trusted = NO;
    }
    return _trusted;
}
```

You check if the `_trust` ivar is NULL or not. If it is, then you need to check if the digital identity can be trusted or not. You access the `trust` property and evaluate it. If the trust result code is not successful, then the digital identity cannot be trusted. The next three result codes, kSecTrustResultProceed, kSecTrustResultConfirm, kSecTrustResultUnspecified, indicate that that the digital identity can be trusted. The last, kSecTrustResultUnspecified, simply means that you haven't set an explicit trust setting for the underlying certificate.

With the last result code, kSecTrustResultRecoverableTrustFailure, means that you technically have failed, but there are ways to recover so that the digital identity can be trusted. In this specific application, the recoverable trust failure is because you are using a self-signed certificate authority. In order to recover from this, you need to explicitly tell the Security framework to trust your certificate authority. That's where the method `recoverTrust` comes in.

```
- (BOOL)recoverTrust
{
    NSArray *anchorCerts = @[ (__bridge id)self.anchorCertificate ];
    SecTrustSetAnchorCertificates(self.trust, (__bridge CFArrayRef)anchorCerts);
    SecTrustSetAnchorCertificatesOnly(self.trust, NO);
    SecTrustResultType trustResult;
    OSStatus status = SecTrustEvaluate(self.trust, &trustResult);
    if (status == errSecSuccess) {
        switch (trustResult) {
            case kSecTrustResultInvalid:
            case kSecTrustResultDeny:
            case kSecTrustResultFatalTrustFailure:
            case kSecTrustResultOtherError:
            case kSecTrustResultRecoverableTrustFailure:
                return NO;
                break;
            case kSecTrustResultProceed:
            case kSecTrustResultConfirm:
            case kSecTrustResultUnspecified:
                return YES;
                break;
        }
    }
    return NO;
}
```

You explicitly set the anchor certificate to your self-signed root certificate you created earlier and reevaluate the trust. You handle the trust result the same way as before, except this time, you treat a recoverable trust failure as a failure.

Now you can implement your encrypt: method.

```
- (NSData *)encrypt:(NSData *)data
{
    if (!self.isTrusted)
        return nil;
```

First, you check if your digital identity can be trusted. If not, you return nil.

Next, you copy your public key from your trust reference. You use it to determine the block size and the size, in bytes, that you can encrypt.

```
SecKeyRef publicKey = SecTrustCopyPublicKey(self.trust);
size_t keyBlockSize = SecKeyGetBlockSize(publicKey);
size_t bufferSize = keyBlockSize*sizeof(uint8_t);
```

You use the bufferSize to allocate the data buffers you'll use for encryption. Your source buffer needs to be shorted by 11 bytes due to the padding you're going to use.

```
uint8_t *srcBuffer = malloc(bufferSize);
size_t srcBufferLen = keyBlockSize - 11;

uint8_t *buffer = malloc(bufferSize);
size_t bufferLen = keyBlockSize;
```

You allocate your output NSData object. You actually use an NSMutableData instance so you can append data to it.

```
NSMutableData *result = [[NSMutableData alloc] init];
```

If your input NSData object is larger than the allowable block/buffer size, you need to encrypt the data in chunks and append them to your output NSMutableData instance.

```
NSRange range = NSMakeRange(0, keyBlockSize);
while (range.location < data.length) {
    memset(srcBuffer, 0x0, bufferSize);
    memset(buffer, 0x0, bufferSize);

    if (NSMaxRange(range) > data.length)
        range.length = data.length - range.location;

    [data getBytes:srcBuffer range:range];
    OSStatus status =
        SecKeyEncrypt(publicKey, kSecPaddingPKCS1, srcBuffer, srcBufferLen, buffer, &bufferLen);
    if (status != errSecSuccess) {
        NSLog(@"Error Encrypting Data");
        free(buffer);
        free(srcBuffer);
        free(publicKey);
        return nil;
    }
```

```
        [result appendBytes:buffer length:bufferLen];
        range.location += srcBufferLen;
    }
```

On an encryption error, you log an error and simply return nil.

Finally, you release the buffers and public key reference an return the encrypted data object.

```
    free(buffer);
    free(srcBuffer);
    free(publicKey);

    return result;
}
```

Decryption works in a similar fashion with one minor difference.

```
- (NSData *)decrypt:(NSData *)data
{
    if (!self.isTrusted)
        return nil;

    SecKeyRef privateKey;
    OSStatus status = SecIdentityCopyPrivateKey((__bridge SecIdentityRef)self.item, &privateKey);
    if (status != errSecSuccess && privateKey != NULL) {
        CFRelease(privateKey);
        privateKey = NULL;
                return nil;
    }

    size_t keyBlockSize = SecKeyGetBlockSize(privateKey);
    size_t bufferSize = keyBlockSize*sizeof(uint8_t);

    uint8_t *srcBuffer = malloc(bufferSize);

    uint8_t *buffer = malloc(bufferSize);
    size_t bufferLen = keyBlockSize;

    NSMutableData *result = [[NSMutableData alloc] init];

    NSRange range = NSMakeRange(0, keyBlockSize);
    while (range.location < data.length) {
        memset(srcBuffer, 0x0, bufferSize);
        memset(buffer, 0x0, bufferSize);

        if (NSMaxRange(range) > data.length)
            range.length = data.length - range.location;

        [data getBytes:srcBuffer range:range];
        OSStatus status =
            SecKeyDecrypt(privateKey, kSecPaddingPKCS1, srcBuffer, keyBlockSize, buffer, &bufferLen);
```

```
        if (status != errSecSuccess) {
            NSLog(@"Error Decrypting Data");
            free(buffer);
            free(srcBuffer);
            free(privateKey);
            return nil;
        }
        [result appendBytes:buffer length:bufferLen];
        range.location += keyBlockSize;
    }

    free(buffer);
    free(srcBuffer);
    free(privateKey);

    return result;
}
```

You retrieve the private key from the digital identity and check the return code to make sure you've successfully retrieved it.

Let's use the digital identity encrytion/decryption in the identity detail view controller. You need create a subclass of KeychainItemViewController, named IdentityViewController, first. You want to add a button to allow you to encrypt and decrypt the text view contents. Open IdentityViewController.h and declare the outlet and action for this button.

```
@property (weak, nonatomic) IBOutlet UIButton *cryptButton;
- (IBAction)crypt:(id)sender;
```

Open IdentityViewController.m. First you'll add some ivars and methods in a private category.

```
@interface IdentityViewController () {
    NSData *_encryptedData;
}
- (void)encrypt;
- (void)decrypt;
@end
```

_encryptedData will contain the encrypted data (obviously). You'll also use it determine if the data should be encrypted or decrypted. The methods, encrypt and decrypt, should be self-explanatory.

The crypt: action method is a simple check to determine which method to call.

```
- (IBAction)crypt:(id)sender
{
    if (_encryptedData)
        [self decrypt];
    else
        [self encrypt];
}
```

The encrypt method takes the contents of the text view and sends them to the KeychainIdentity encrypt method. The results are stored in the _encryptedData ivar. It's important to note that you encode the text view contents using UTF-8 encoding. This is important, as the Security framework works on an 8-bit data boundary.

```
- (void)encrypt
{
    KeychainIdentity *ident = (KeychainIdentity *)self.item;
    NSData *data = [self.textView.text dataUsingEncoding:NSUTF8StringEncoding];
    _encryptedData = [ident encrypt:data];
    if (_encryptedData == nil) {
        NSLog(@"Encryption Failed");
        return;
    }

    self.textView.text = [_encryptedData description];
    [self.cryptButton setTitle:@"Decrypt" forState:UIControlStateNormal];
}
```

Once you have the encrypted data, you display it in the text view and change the label on the crypt button Outlet.

The decrypt method works in the opposite manner.

```
- (void)decrypt
{
    KeychainIdentity *ident = (KeychainIdentity *)self.item;
    NSData *data = [ident decrypt:_encryptedData];
    if (data == nil) {
        NSLog(@"Decryption Failed");
        return;
    }

    NSString *decryptedString = [[NSString alloc] initWithBytes:[data bytes]
                                                 length:[data length]
                                               encoding:NSUTF8StringEncoding];
    _encryptedData = nil;
    self.textView.text = decryptedString;
    [self.cryptButton setTitle:@"Encrypt" forState:UIControlStateNormal];
}
```

Now you need to adjust the storyboard to use the new IdentityViewController. Select MainStoryboard.storyboard to open the storyboard editor. Find the KeychainItemViewController next to the IdentitiesViewController. Select it and change the class from KeychainItemViewController to IdentityViewController. Drag a UIButton to the bottom right of the view and use the blue guidelines to align it with the Done button and right side of the view. Change the label to read Encrypt. Control-drag from the view controller icon to the Encrypt button and bind it to the cryptButton outlet. Control-drag from the Encrypt button to the view controller icon and bind it to the crypt: Action.

Build and run your application. Select the digital identity to open the IdentityViewController. Click the Encrypt button to encrypt the text, then click the Decrypt button to decrypt the text (Figure 13-11).

*Figure 13-11. Encrypting (left) and decrypting (right) your digital identity information*

# Security Never Sleeps

As we stated at the beginning of the chapter, security is a process. It's something you need to think about every step of the way when developing your application, and beyond. We've given you a taste of the functionality that's available in iOS via the Security framework. Hopefully it's enough information to give you a solid basis for your future application development.

If you're interested in learning more, read Apple's Secure Coding Guide (https://developer.apple.com/library/ios/#documentation/Security/Conceptual/SecureCodingGuide/). Another general security resource is *Foundations of Security* by Christoph Kern, Anita Kesavan, and Neil Daswani (Apress, 2007). While this book is a few years old now, the principles it covers remain perfectly valid.

Next up, you're going work on keeping your interface responsive in iOS. It's quite a shift from what you just covered. Take a deep breath and turn the page.

# 14

# Keeping Your Interface Responsive

As we've mentioned a few times in this book, if you try to do too much at one time in an action or delegate method, or in a method called from one of those methods, your application's interface can skip or even freeze while the long-running method does its job. As a general rule, you do not want your application's user interface to ever become unresponsive. Your user will expect to be able to interact with your application at all times, or at the very least will expect to be kept updated by your user interface when they aren't allowed to interact with it.

In computer programming, the ability to have multiple sets of operations happening at the same time is referred to, generally, as *concurrency*. In this chapter, we're going to look at some more general-purpose solutions for adding concurrency to your application. These solutions will allow your user interface to stay responsive even when your application is performing long-running tasks. Although there are many ways to add concurrency to an application, we're going to look at just two, but these two, combined with what you already know about run loop scheduling for networking, should allow you to accommodate just about any long-running task.

The first mechanism we're going to look at is the *timer*. Timers are objects that can be scheduled with the run loop, much like the networking classes you've worked with. Timers can call methods on specific objects at set intervals. You can set a timer to call a method on one of your controller classes, for example, ten times per second. Once you kick it off, approximately every tenth of a second, your method will fire until you tell the timer to stop.

Neither run loop scheduling nor timers are what some people would consider "true" forms of concurrency. Most people refer to run loops and timers as asynchronous computing, where tasks are run in the background, hidden from the application's user facing operations. In both cases, the application's main run loop will check for certain conditions, and if those conditions are met, it will call out to a specific method on a specific object. If the method that gets called runs for too long, however, your interface will become unresponsive. But, working with run loops and timers is considerably less complex than implementing what we might call "true" concurrency, which is to have multiple tasks (and multiple run loops) functioning at the same time.

The other mechanism we're going to look at is relatively new in the Objective-C world. It's called an *operation queue*, and it works together with special objects you create called *operations*. The operation queue can manage multiple operations at the same time, and it makes sure that those operations get processing time based on some simple rules that you set down. Each operation has a specific set of commands that take the form of a method you write, and the operation queue will make sure that each operation's method gets run in such a way as to make good use of the available system resources.

Operation queues are really nice because they are a high-level abstraction and hide the nitty-gritty implementation details involved with implementing true concurrency. In iOS, queues leverage an operating system feature called *threads* to give processing time to the various operations they manage. Apple is currently recommending the use of operation queues rather than threads, not only because operation queues are easier to use, but also because they give your application other advantages.

> **Note**   Even though it's not available when using the iPhone SDK, another form of concurrency is multiprocessing, using the UNIX system calls `fork()` and `exec()` or Cocoa's `NSTask` class. Using multiple processes is more heavy-weight than using threads.

Grand Central Dispatch (GCD) is a technology that allows applications to take greater advantage of the fact that modern computers have multiple processing cores and sometimes multiple processors. If you used an operation queue in your program back before GCD was released, when you recompiled your application for iOS, your code automatically received the benefit of GCD for free. If you had used another form of concurrency, such as threads, instead of operation queues, your application would not have automatically benefitted from GCD.

You can probably see why we're limiting our discussion of "true" concurrency to operation queues. They are clearly the way of the future for both Cocoa and Cocoa Touch. They make our lives as programmers considerably easier and they help us take advantage of technologies that haven't even been written yet. What could be better?

Let's start with a little detour to look at the problem that concurrency solves.

# Exploring the Concurrency Problem

Before we explore ways of solving the concurrency problem, let's make sure you understand the problem. You're going to build a small application that will demonstrate the problem that arises when you try to do too much at one time on the application's main thread. Every application has at least one thread of execution, and that's the one where the application's main run loop is running. All action methods fire on the main thread and all event processing and user interface updating is also done from the main thread. If any method that fires on the main thread takes too long to finish, the user interface will freeze up and become unresponsive.

Your small application is going to calculate square roots. Lots and lots of square roots. The user will be able to enter a number, and you'll calculate the square root for every number from 1 up to the number they specify (Figure 14-1). Your only goal in this exercise is to burn processor cycles.

*Figure 14-1. The Stalled application will demonstrate the problem of trying to do too much work on the application's main thread*

With a sufficiently large number entered, when the Go button is tapped, the user interface will become completely unresponsive for several seconds or even longer. The progress bar and progress label, whose properties will be set each time through the loop, won't actually show any changes to the user until all the values in the loop have been calculated. Only the last calculation will be reflected in the user interface.

# Creating the Stalled Application

In Xcode, create a new project using the Single View Application template and call this project Stalled. You'll start by designing your interface and declaring your outlets and actions. Then you'll write the implementation of your view controller and try it out.

## Designing the Interface

Select ViewController.xib to enter Interface Builder mode. Drag a round rect button from the library to the view, placing the button against the upper-right margins using the blue guides. Double-click the button and change its title to Go.

Drag a text field from the library and place it to the left of the button. Use the blue guides to line up the text field and place it the correct distance from the button. Resize the text field to about two-third of its original size, or use the size inspector and change its width to 70 pixels. Double-click the text field and set its default value to 100000. In the Attribute Inspector, change the Keyboard from Default to Number Pad to restrict entry to only numbers.

Drag a label from the library and place it to the left of the text field. Double-click it to change its text to read # of Operations and then adjust its size and placement to fit in the available space. You can use Figure 14-1 as a guide.

Bring over a progress view and place it below the three items already on the interface. We placed it a little more than the minimum distance below them as indicated by the blue guides, but exact placement really doesn't matter much with this application. Once you place the progress bar, use the resize handles to change its width so it takes up all the space from the left margin to the right margin. Next, use the Attribute Inspector to change the Progress field to 0.0.

Place one more label below the progress view. Resize the label so it is stretches from the left to the right margins. Use the Attributes Inspector to change the text alignment from Left Alignment to Center Alignment.

Press the Assistant Mode toggle on the toolbar so you can set up your outlets and actions. Control-drag from the text field to just below the @interface declaration in ViewController.h. Create an outlet named numberOfOperations. Control-drag from the progress view and create an outlet named progressBar. For the last outlet, control-drag from the label below the progress view and name it progressLabel. While you're here, double-click the label text and delete it.

Finally, control-drag from the Go Button to just above the @end declaration. Create an action named go.

Save your XIB. Put the editor back into Standard mode.

# Implementing the Stalled View Controller

You need to implement the go method in ViewController.m.

```
- (IBAction)go:(id)sender
{
```

The method starts by retrieving the number from the text field.

```
    NSInteger operationCount = [self.numberOfOperations.text integerValue];
```

You loop so you can calculate all of the square roots.

```
    for (NSInteger i = 0; i<= operationCount; i++) {
```

Let's log which calculation you're working on.

```
        NSLog(@"Calculating Square Root of %d", i);
```

In shipping applications, you generally wouldn't log like this, but logging serves two purposes in this chapter. First, you'll be able to see, using Xcode's debugger console, the application is working even when your application's user interface isn't responding. Second, logging takes a non-trivial amount of time. In real-world applications, that would generally be bad, but since your goal is just to do processing to show how concurrency works, this slow-down actually works to your advantage. If you choose to remove the NSLog() statements, you will need to increase the number of calculations by an order of magnitude because the iPhone is actually capable of doing tens of thousands of square root operations per second and it will hardly break a sweat doing ten thousand without the NSLog() statement in the loop to throttle the speed.

> **Caution**   Logging using NSLog() takes considerably longer when running on the device launched from Xcode because the results of every NSLog() statement have to be transferred through the USB connection to Xcode. Although this chapter's applications will work just fine on the device, you may wish to consider restricting yourself to the simulator for testing and debugging in this chapter, or else commenting out the NSLog() statements when running on the device.

Then you calculate the square root of i.

```
double squareRootOfI = sqrt((double)i);
```

And update the progress bar and label to reflect the last calculation made, and that's the end of your loop.

```
self.progressBar.progress = ((float)i / (float)operationCount);
self.progressLabel.text =
    [NSString stringWithFormat:@"Square Root of %d is %.6f", i, squareRootOfI];
    }
}
```

The problem with this method isn't so much what you're doing as where you're doing it. As we stated earlier, action methods fire on the main thread, which is also where user interface updates happen, and where system events, such as those that are generated by taps and touches, are processed. If any method firing on the main thread takes too much time, it will affect your application's user experience. In less severe cases, your application will seem to hiccup or stall at times. In severe cases, like here, your application's entire user interface will freeze up.

Save ViewController.m and build and run the application. Press the Go button and watch what happens. Not much, huh? If you keep an eye on the debug console in Xcode, you'll see that it is working away on those calculations (Figure 14-2) thanks to the NSLog() statement in your code, but the user interface doesn't update until all of the calculations are done, does it?

```
2012-10-02 14:03:11.968 Stalled[97901:c07] Calculating Square Root of 99945
2012-10-02 14:03:11.968 Stalled[97901:c07] Calculating Square Root of 99946
2012-10-02 14:03:11.982 Stalled[97901:c07] Calculating Square Root of 99947
2012-10-02 14:03:11.983 Stalled[97901:c07] Calculating Square Root of 99948
2012-10-02 14:03:11.984 Stalled[97901:c07] Calculating Square Root of 99949
2012-10-02 14:03:11.984 Stalled[97901:c07] Calculating Square Root of 99950
2012-10-02 14:03:11.985 Stalled[97901:c07] Calculating Square Root of 99951
2012-10-02 14:03:11.986 Stalled[97901:c07] Calculating Square Root of 99952
2012-10-02 14:03:11.988 Stalled[97901:c07] Calculating Square Root of 99953
2012-10-02 14:03:11.989 Stalled[97901:c07] Calculating Square Root of 99954
2012-10-02 14:03:11.990 Stalled[97901:c07] Calculating Square Root of 99955
2012-10-02 14:03:11.991 Stalled[97901:c07] Calculating Square Root of 99956
2012-10-02 14:03:12.030 Stalled[97901:c07] Calculating Square Root of 99957
2012-10-02 14:03:12.032 Stalled[97901:c07] Calculating Square Root of 99958
2012-10-02 14:03:12.038 Stalled[97901:c07] Calculating Square Root of 99959
2012-10-02 14:03:12.040 Stalled[97901:c07] Calculating Square Root of 99960
2012-10-02 14:03:12.041 Stalled[97901:c07] Calculating Square Root of 99961
2012-10-02 14:03:12.048 Stalled[97901:c07] Calculating Square Root of 99962
2012-10-02 14:03:12.049 Stalled[97901:c07] Calculating Square Root of 99963
2012-10-02 14:03:12.051 Stalled[97901:c07] Calculating Square Root of 99964
2012-10-02 14:03:12.051 Stalled[97901:c07] Calculating Square Root of 99965
2012-10-02 14:03:12.053 Stalled[97901:c07] Calculating Square Root of 99966
2012-10-02 14:03:12.054 Stalled[97901:c07] Calculating Square Root of 99967
2012-10-02 14:03:12.055 Stalled[97901:c07] Calculating Square Root of 99968
2012-10-02 14:03:12.056 Stalled[97901:c07] Calculating Square Root of 99969
2012-10-02 14:03:12.058 Stalled[97901:c07] Calculating Square Root of 99970
2012-10-02 14:03:12.059 Stalled[97901:c07] Calculating Square Root of 99971
2012-10-02 14:03:12.060 Stalled[97901:c07] Calculating Square Root of 99972
2012-10-02 14:03:12.060 Stalled[97901:c07] Calculating Square Root of 99973
2012-10-02 14:03:12.061 Stalled[97901:c07] Calculating Square Root of 99974
2012-10-02 14:03:12.061 Stalled[97901:c07] Calculating Square Root of 99975
2012-10-02 14:03:12.104 Stalled[97901:c07] Calculating Square Root of 99976
2012-10-02 14:03:12.105 Stalled[97901:c07] Calculating Square Root of 99977
2012-10-02 14:03:12.106 Stalled[97901:c07] Calculating Square Root of 99978
2012-10-02 14:03:12.109 Stalled[97901:c07] Calculating Square Root of 99979
2012-10-02 14:03:12.110 Stalled[97901:c07] Calculating Square Root of 99980
2012-10-02 14:03:12.111 Stalled[97901:c07] Calculating Square Root of 99981
2012-10-02 14:03:12.114 Stalled[97901:c07] Calculating Square Root of 99982
2012-10-02 14:03:12.115 Stalled[97901:c07] Calculating Square Root of 99983
2012-10-02 14:03:12.115 Stalled[97901:c07] Calculating Square Root of 99984
```

*Figure 14-2. The debug console in Xcode shows that the application is working, but the user interface is locked up*

Note that if you do click in the text field, the numeric keypad will not disappear when you tap the Go button. Since there's nothing being hidden by the keypad, this isn't a problem. In the final version of the application, you'll add a table that will be hidden by the keypad. You'll add some code to hide the keypad when you press Go.

**Tip**    Running the Stalled app for 100,000 iterations can take a really long time. You may want to make the default smaller (say 10,000).

If you have code that takes a long time to run, you've basically got two choices if you want to keep your interface responsive: you can break your code into smaller chunks that can be processed in pieces, or you can move the code to a separate thread of execution, which will allow your application's run loop to return to updating the user interface and responding to taps and other system events. We'll look at both options in this chapter.

First, you'll fix the application by using a *timer* to perform the requested calculations in batches, making sure not to take more than a fraction of a second each time so that the main thread can continue to process events and update the interface. After that, you'll look at using an operation queue to move the calculations off of the application's main thread, leaving the main thread free to process events.

# Timers

In the Foundation framework shared by Cocoa and Cocoa Touch, there's a class called NSTimer that you can use to call methods on a specific object at periodic intervals. Timers are created, and then scheduled with a run loop, much like some of the networking classes you've worked with. Once a timer is scheduled, it will fire after a specified interval. If the timer is set to repeat, it will continue to call its target method repeatedly each time the specified interval elapses.

Timers are not guaranteed to fire exactly at the specified interval. Because of the way the run loop functions, there's no way to guarantee the exact moment when a timer will fire. The timer will fire on the first pass through the run loop that happens after the specified amount of time has elapsed. That means a timer will never fire before the specified interval, but it may fire after. Usually, the actual interval is only milliseconds longer than the one specified, but you can't rely on that being the case. If a long-running method runs on the main loop, like the one in Stalled, then the run loop won't get to fire the scheduled timers until that long-running method has finished, potentially a long time after the requested interval.

Timers fire on the thread whose run loop they are scheduled into. In most situations, unless you specifically intend to do otherwise, your timers will get created on the main thread and the methods that they fire will also execute on the main thread. This means that you have to follow the same rules as with action methods. If you try to do too much in a method that is called by a timer, you will stall your user interface.

As a result, if you want to use timers as a mechanism for keeping your user interface responsive, you need to break your work down into smaller chunks, only doing a small amount of work each time it fires. We'll show you a technique for doing that in a minute.

# Creating a Timer

Creating an instance of NSTimer is quite straightforward. If you want to create it, but not schedule it with the run loop right away, use the factory method timerWithTimeInterval:target:selector: userInfo:repeats:, like so:

```
NSTimer *timer = [NSTimer timerWithTimeInterval:1.0/10.0
                              target:self
                            selector:@selector(myTimerMethod:)
                            userInfo:nil repeats:YES];
```

The first argument to this method specifies how frequently you would like the timer to fire and call its method. In this example, you're passing in a tenth of a second, so this timer will fire approximately ten times a second. The next two arguments work exactly like the target and action properties of a control. The second argument, target, is the object on which the timer should call a method, and selector points to the actual method the timer should call when it fires. The method specified by the selector must take a single argument, which will be the instance of NSTimer that called the method. The fourth argument, userInfo, is designed for application use. If you pass in an object here, that object will go along with the timer and be available in the method the timer calls when it fires. The last argument specifies whether the timer repeats or fires just once.

> **Note**    Non-repeating timers are no longer very commonly used because you can achieve exactly the same affect much more easily by calling the method performSelector:withObject:afterDelay: as you've done a few times in this book.

Once you've got a timer and are ready for it to start firing, you get a reference to the run loop you want to schedule it into, and then add the timer. Here's an example of scheduling the timer into the main run loop:

```
NSRunLoop *loop=[NSRunLoop mainRunLoop];
[loop addTimer:timer forMode:NSDefaultRunLoopMode];
```

When you schedule the timer, the run loop retains the timer until you stop the timer

If you want to create a timer that's already scheduled with the run loop, letting you skip the previous two lines of code, you can use the factory method scheduledTimerWithTimeInterval:target: selector:userInfo:repeats:, which takes exactly the same arguments as timerWithTimeInterval: target:selector:userInfo:repeats:.

```
NSTimer *timer = [NSTimer scheduledTimerWithTimeInterval:1.0/10.0
                                 target:self
                                 selector:@selector(myTimerMethod:)
                                 userInfo:nil
                                  repeats:YES];
```

## Stopping a Timer

When you no longer need a timer, you can unschedule it from the run loop by calling the invalidate method on the instance. Invalidating a timer will stop it from firing any further and remove it from the run loop, which will release the timer and cause it to be deallocated unless it's been retained elsewhere. Here's how you invalidate a timer:

```
[timer invalidate];
```

## Limitations of Timers

Timers are very handy for any number of purposes. As a tool for keeping your interface responsive, they do have some limitations, however. The first and foremost of these limitations is that you have to make some assumptions about how much time is available for the process that you're implementing.  If you have more than a couple of timers running, things can easily get complex and the logic to make sure that each timer's method gets an appropriate share of the available time without taking too much time away from the main thread can get very complex and abstruse.

Timers are great for when you have one, or at most, a small number, of long-running tasks that can be easily broken down into discrete chunks for processing. When you have more than that, or when the processes don't lend themselves to being performed in chunks, timers become far too much trouble and just aren't the right tool for the job.

Let's use a timer to get the Stalled application working the way your users will expect it to work, then you'll move on and look at how to handle scenarios where you have more than a couple of processes.

# Fixing Stalled with a Timer

You're going to keep working with the Stalled application, but before you proceed, make a copy of the Stalled project folder. You're going to fix the project using two different techniques, so you will need two copies of the project in order to play along at home. If you run into problems, you can always copy the 14 – Stalled project in the project archive that accompanies this book as your starting point for both this exercise and the next one.

## Creating the Batch Object

Before you start modifying your controller class, create a class to represent your batch of calculations. This object will keep track of how many calculations need to be performed as well as how many already have. You'll also move the actual calculations into the batch object as well. Having this object will make it much easier to do processing in chunks, since the batch will be self-contained in a single object.

Create a new file that is an Objective-C class in the Stalled Group in the Navigator pane. Name the class SquareRootBatch, and make sure it is a subclass of NSObject. When presented with the Save dialog, make sure it is assigned to the Stalled target. You'll modify the interface file first. Select SquareRootBatch.h to open it in the editor.

You need define two properties for the maximum number whose square root will be calculated and the current number whose square root is being calculated. This will allow you to keep track of where you are between timer method calls.

```
@property (assign, nonatomic) NSInteger max;
@property (assign, nonatomic) NSInteger current;
```

Next, you declare an initializer method that takes one argument, the maximum number for which you are to calculate the square root.

```
- (id)initWithMaxNumber:(NSInteger)maxNumber;
```

The next two methods will enable your batch to work similarly to an enumerator. You can find out if you still have numbers to calculate by calling hasNext, and actually perform the next calculation by calling next, which returns the calculated value.

```
- (BOOL)hasNext;
- (double)next;
```

After that, you have two more methods used to retrieve values for updating the progress bar and progress label.

```
- (float)percentCompleted;
- (NSString *)percentCompletedText;
```

And that's all she wrote for this header file. Save SquareRootBatch.h and then flip over to SquareRootBatch.m.

You start off by defining a string that will be used for throwing an exception. If you exceed the number of calculations you've specified, you will throw an exception with this name. Put this #define before the @implementation declaration.

```
#define kExceededMaxException @"Exceeded Max"
```

Now you can implement the methods you defined in the interface file. First, the initializer:

```
- (id)initWithMaxNumber:(NSInteger)maxNumber
{
    self = [super init];
    if (self) {
        self.current = 0;
        self.max = maxNumber;
    }
    return self;
}
```

The current Property is set to zero, indicating that you are starting from the beginning. You set the max Property to the maxNumber argument.

Next, your "enumerator" methods. hasNext simply checks that you haven't reached the maximum number you initialized with.

```
- (BOOL)hasNext
{
    return self.current <= self.max;
}

- (double)next
{
    if (self.current > self.max)
        [NSException raise:kExceededMaxException
                    format:@"Requested a calculation from completed batch"];

    return sqrt((double)++self.current);
}
```

The next method increments the current Property, then returns its square root. Before you do that, you check to make sure that haven't reached (and passed) the maximum number.

Finally, you implement the methods to calculate your progress and format your label text.

```
- (float)percentCompleted
{
    return (float)self.current / (float)self.max;
}

- (NSString *)percentCompletedText
{
    return [NSString stringWithFormat:@"Square Root of %d is %.6f",
                           self.current, sqrt((double)self.current)];
}
```

Basically, you've taken the logic from your go method and distributed it throughout this little class. By doing so, you make the batch completely self-contained, which will allow you to pass the batch along to the method fired by the timer by making use of the userInfo argument.

> **Note**    In this implementation, you might notice that you're actually calculating the square root twice, once in next, and again in percentCompletedText. For your purposes, this is actually good because it burns more processor cycles. In a real application, you would probably want to store off the result of the calculation in an instance variable so that you have access to the last calculation performed without having to perform the calculation again.

## Updating the Nib

Select ViewController.xib in the Navigator pane. Once in Interface Builder mode, switch the editor to Assistant mode. The interface file, ViewController.h, should open in the right pane of the editor. Control-drag from Go button to just below the last @property declaration. Create a new outlet for the Go Button, and name it goStopButton. That's the only change you need, so save the XIB.

## Updating the View Controller Header

Rewrite your controller class to use this new timer. Since your user interface will be useable while the batch is running, you want to make the Go button become a Stop button while the batch is running. It's generally a good idea to give users a way to stop long-running processes if feasible. Open ViewController.h in the editor and add the following method declaration:

```
- (void)processChunk:(NSTimer *)timer;
```

That's all you need to do. Save ViewController.h and open ViewController.m.

# Updating the View Controller Implementation

The first will import the header of the batch object you created. Add this as the second #import declaration.

```
#import "SquareRootBatch.h"
```

Next, you'll define two constants.

```
#define kTimerInterval (1.0/60.0)
#define kBatchSize     10
```

The first constant you defined—kTimerInterval—will be used to determine how often the timer fires. You're going to start by firing approximately 60 times a second. If you need to tweak the value to keep your user interface responsive, you can do that as you test. The second constant, kBatchSize, will be used in the method that the timer calls. In the method, you're going to check how much time has elapsed as you do calculations because you don't want to spend more than one timer interval in that method. In fact, you need to spend a little less than the timer interval because you need to make resources available for the run loop to do other things. However, it would be wasteful to check the elapsed time after every calculation, so you'll do a certain number of calculations before checking the elapsed time, and that's what kBatchSize is for. You can tweak the batch size for better performance as well.

Next, you add a private property in the Category.

```
@interface ViewController ()
@property (assign, nonatomic) BOOL processRunning;
@end
```

You need to rewrite the go method to

```
- (IBAction)go:(id)sender
{
    if (!self.processRunning) {
        NSInteger operationCount = [numberOfOperations.text integerValue];
        SquareRootBatch *batch = [[SquareRootBatch alloc] initWithMaxNumber:operationCount];

        [NSTimer scheduledTimerWithTimeInterval:kTimerInterval
                                         target:self
                                       selector:@selector(processChunk:)
                                       userInfo:batch repeats:YES];
        [goStopButton setTitle:@"Stop" forState:UIControlStateNormal];
        self.processRunning = YES;
    }
    else {
        self.processRunning = NO;
        [goStopButton setTitle:@"Go" forState:UIControlStateNormal];
    }
}
```

You start the method out by checking to see if a batch is already running. If it isn't, then you grab the number from the text field, just as the old version did. You create a new `SquareRootBatch` instance, initialized with the number pulled from the text field. After creating the batch object, you create a scheduled timer, telling it to call your `processChunk:` method every sixtieth of a second. You pass the batch object in the `userInfo` argument so it will be available to the timer method. Because the run loop retains the timer, you don't even declare a pointer to the timer you create. Next, you set the button's title to Stop and set `processRunning` to reflect that the process has started.

If the batch had already been started, then you just change the button's title back to Go and set `processRunning` to NO, which will tell the `processChunk:` method to stop processing.

Now that you've updated your go method, you need to implement the `processChunk:` method. You'll add it below the go method you just rewrote.

```
- (void)processChunk:(NSTimer *)timer
{
```

The first thing this method does is check if the user has tapped the Stop button since the last time the method was called. If it was, you invalidate the timer, which will prevent this method from being called any more by this timer, ending the processing of this batch. You also update the progress label to tell the user that you canceled.

```
if (!self.processRunning) {
    // Cancelled
    [timer invalidate];
    progressLabel.text = @"Calculations Cancelled";
    return;
}
```

Next, you retrieve the batch from the timer.

```
SquareRootBatch *batch = (SquareRootBatch *)[timer userInfo];
```

After that, you calculate when to stop processing this batch. For starters, you're going to spend half of the time available to you working on the batch. That should leave plenty of time for the run loop to receive system events and update the UI, but you can always tweak the value if necessary.

```
NSTimeInterval endTime = [NSDate timeIntervalSinceReferenceDate] + (kTimerInterval / 2.0);
```

You set a Boolean that you'll use to identify if you have reached the end of the batch. You'll set this to YES if hasNext returns NO.

```
BOOL isDone = NO;
```

Then, you go into a loop until you either reach the end time you calculated earlier or there's no calculations left to do.

```
while ((([NSDate timeIntervalSinceReferenceDate] < endTime) && !isDone) {
```

You're going to calculate the square root for several numbers at a time rather than checking the date after every one, so you go into another loop based on the batch size you defined earlier.

```
for (int i = 0; i < kBatchSize; i++) {
```

In that loop, you make sure there's more work to be done. If there isn't, you set isDone to YES and set i to the batch size to end this loop.

```
if (![batch hasNext]) {
    isDone = YES;
    i = kBatchSize;
}
```

If there is another number to calculate, you grab the current value and its square root and log the fact to the debug console.

```
        else {
            NSInteger current = batch.current;
            double nextSquareRoot = [batch next];
            NSLog(@"Calculated square root of %d as %.6f", current, nextSquareRoot);
        }
    }
}
```

After you're done with processing a chunk, you update the progress bar and label.

```
progressLabel.text = [batch percentCompletedText];
progressBar.progress = [batch percentCompleted];
```

And, if you're all out of rows to process, you invalidate the timer and update the progress label and button.

```
    if (isDone) {
        [timer invalidate];
        self.processRunning = NO;
        progressLabel.text = @"Calculations Finished";
        [goStopButton setTitle:@"Go" forState:UIControlStateNormal];
    }
}
```

Go ahead and take this new version for a spin. Build and run your project and try entering different numbers. As the calculations happen, your user interface should get updated (Figure 14-3) and the progress bar should make its way across the screen. While a batch is processing, you should be able to tap the Stop button to cancel the processing.

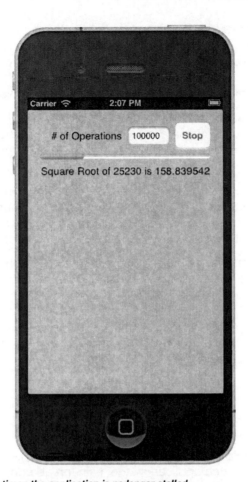

*Figure 14-3. Now that you're using a timer, the application is no longer stalled*

That's great, and your users are now able to start and stop the process and can continue to use the application while the calculations are being performed. But, if you had more tasks going on in the background, this option wouldn't be ideal. Trying to calculate how much time to let each batch use would be non-trivial. Fortunately, Apple has given you the operation queue and has put all sorts of non-trivial logic in it so that you don't have to reinvent the wheel. Let's take a look at operation queues now.

# Operation Queues and Concurrency

There are times when your application will need to run more than just a few concurrent tasks. When you get to more than a handful of tasks, the amount of complexity quickly escalates, making it very difficult to use any form of run loop scheduling to share time amongst all the tasks. When your application needs to manage many independent sets of instructions, you have to look at other mechanisms besides run loop scheduling to add concurrency.

As we've mentioned before, one of the traditional tools for adding concurrency at the application level is called threads. Threads are a mechanism provided by the operating system that allows multiple sets of instructions to operate at the same time within a single application. In iOS, threading functionality is provided by the POSIX Threads API (often referred to as pthreads). You should rarely, if ever, need to actually use that API in Cocoa Touch applications, however.

The Foundation framework has, for many years, contained a class called NSThread, which is far easier to work with than pthreads, which are implemented as a procedural C API. NSThread was the recommended way, until fairly recently, to add and manage threads in a Cocoa application.

Relatively recently, Apple introduced some new classes for implementing concurrency and is strongly recommending the use of these new classes instead of using NSThread directly. NSOperationQueue is a class that manages a queue of instances of a subclass of NSOperation. Each NSOperation (or subclass) contains a set of instructions to perform a specific task. The operation queue will spawn and manage threads as needed to run the queued operations.

The use of operation queues makes implementing concurrency quite a bit easier than the traditional NSThread-based approach, and worlds easier than using pthreads directly. The benefits of using operation queues are so clear and compelling that we're not even going to show you how to use the lower-level mechanisms directly. We are going to discuss threads a bit, but only enough to inform your use of NSOperationQueue. Although NSOperationQueue does make many aspects of concurrency easier, there are still a few gotchas associated with concurrency and threads that you need to be aware of when using operation queues.

# Threads

As we've mentioned before, every application has at least one thread, which is a sequence of instructions. The thread that begins executing when the program is launched is called the main thread. In the case of a Cocoa Touch application, the main thread contains the application's main run loop, which is responsible for handling inputs and updating the user interface. Although there are some instances where Cocoa Touch uses additional threads implicitly, pretty much all application code that you will write will fire on the main thread unless you specifically spawn a thread or use an operation in an operation queue.

To implement concurrency, additional threads are spawned, each tasked to perform a specific set of instructions. Each thread has equal access to all of your application's memory. This means that any object, except local variables, can potentially be modified, used, and changed in any thread. Generally speaking, there's no way to predict how long a thread will run, and if there are multiple threads, there's no way to predict, with any certainty, which thread will finish first.

These two thread traits—the fact that they all share access to the same memory and that there's no way to predict what share of the processing time each will get—are the root cause of a number of problems that come along for the ride when doing concurrent programming. Operation queues provide some relief from the timing problem, since you can set priorities and dependencies, which we'll look at a little later, but the memory sharing issue is still very much a concern.

# Race Conditions

The fact that every thread can access the same memory can cause any number of problems if you're not conscious of that fact while programming. When a program doesn't give the expected result because shared data is accessed concurrently by multiple threads, a *race condition* is said to exist. Race conditions can happen when any thread operates on the assumption that it is the sole user of a resource that is actually shared with other threads.

Take a look at the following code:

```
static int i;
for (i = 0; i < 25; i++) {
    NSLog(@"i = %d", i);
}
```

There's not really any reason why somebody would declare i to be static in this example, but it illustrates one classic form of race condition. When you declare a variable static, it becomes a single shared variable used whenever this method fires on any object. If this code runs in a program with only a single thread, it will work completely fine. The fact that there is only one variable i shared by multiple objects simply isn't a problem because as long as you're in the loop, no other code can fire and change the value of i.

The second you add concurrency into the mix, that's no longer true. If, for example, you had this code running in multiple threads, they would all be sharing the same copy of i. When one thread increments i, it increments it for all the other threads as well. Instead of each thread looping 25 times, which is likely the intent, all the threads combined would loop a total of 25 times. The output in such a case might look like this:

| Thread 1: | Thread 2: | Thread 3: |
|-----------|-----------|-----------|
| i = 0 | i = 2 | i = 5 |
| i = 1 | i = 3 | i = 10 |
| i = 4 | i = 6 | i = 13 |
| i = 7 | i = 8 | i = 18 |
| i = 9 | i = 11 | i = 19 |
| i = 12 | i = 14 | i = 24 |
| i = 15 | i – 17 | |
| i = 16 | i = 21 | |
| i = 20 | i = 22 | |
| i = 23 | | |

This behavior is almost certainly not what was intended. In this case, the solution is simple: remove the static operator from i. It won't always be quite as obvious as this, but you should understand the potential for problems now with shared memory.

Another example of a race condition can happen with accessors and mutators. Let's say, for example, that you have an object that represents a person with two properties, one to hold their first name and another to hold their last name.

```
@implementation Person : NSObject

@property (nonatomic, strong) NSString *firstName;
@property (nonatomic, strong) NSString *lastName;

@end
```

If an instance of Person is being accessed from multiple threads, you could have problems. Let's say, for example, that the instance is being updated in one thread and read in another thread. Now, let's say that the first thread, the one that is updating the object, is changing both firstName and lastName. For the sake of argument, let's say that you have an instance of Person called person, and it starts out with a firstName value of *George* and a lastName value of *Washington*. The code executing in the first thread is changing both firstName and lastName to new values, like so:

```
person.firstName = @"Manny";
person.lastName = @"Sullivan";
```

Now, concurrently with that, another thread is reading the values from person.

```
NSLog(@"Now processing %@ %@.", person.firstName, person.lastName);
```

If the NSLog() statement from the second thread fires between the two assignments you showed from the first thread, the result would be this:

```
Now processing Manny Washington.
```

There is no such person as Manny Washington. There's George Washington and there's Manny Sullivan. But, as far as that second thread's NSLog() statement is concerned, person represented Manny Washington.

Operation queues do not eliminate the problem of race conditions, so it's important to be aware of them. Sometimes you can give each thread its own copy of a shared resource, perhaps an object or block of data, instead of accessing that shared resource from multiple threads. This will ensure that one thread doesn't change the resource out from under a competing thread. That said, there's some overhead with making multiple copies of data. Often, duplicating resources is just not a viable option, however, because you need to know the current value, not the value as it was when your thread started. In those cases, you need to take additional steps to ensure data integrity and avoid race conditions. The main tool you use to avoid race conditions is the *mutex lock*.

## Mutex Locks and @synchronized

A mutex lock is a mechanism used to ensure that while a piece of code is firing, other threads can't fire that same piece of code or related code. The term "mutex" is a portmanteau of the words "mutual" and "exclusion" and, as you might suspect based on that, locks are essentially a way to specify that only one thread can execute particular sections of code at a given time.

Originally, locks were always implemented using the class NSLock. Although NSLock is still available, there's now a language-level feature for locking down segments of code: @synchronized blocks.

If you wrap a section of code in a @synchronized block, that code can only fire on one thread at a time. Here's an example of a @synchronized block:

```
@synchronized(self) {
    person.firstName = @"Samantha";
    person.lastName = @"Stephens";
}
```

Notice that after the @synchronize keyword, there's a value in parentheses: self. This argument is called a *mutual exclusion semaphore* or a *mutex*. To understand semaphores in the context of concurrency, the best real-world metaphor is the bathroom key you might find in some small gas stations. There's a single key to the bathroom, usually attached to a large keychain. Only the person who has the key can use the bathroom. If there's only one key, it's a mutual exclusion semaphore or mutex, because only one person can use the bathroom at a time.

@synchronize works pretty much the same way. When a thread gets to a synchronized block of code, it will check to see if anyone else is using the mutex, which is to say, if any other synchronized chunks of code that take the same semaphore are currently executing. If they are, then the thread will *block* until no other code is using that semaphore. A thread that is blocked is not executing any code. When the mutex becomes available, the thread will unblock and execute the synchronized code.

This is the main mechanism you'll use in Cocoa Touch to avoid race conditions and to make your objects *thread safe*.

## Atomicity and Thread Safety

Throughout *Beginning iOS 6 Development* (Apress), and up until now in this book, we've always had you use the nonatomic keyword when declaring properties. We've never fully explained what nonatomic does, we just said that atomic properties added overhead that we didn't need. A good chunk of the overhead we were referring to is mutex locking. When you don't specify nonatomic, the accessors and mutators get created as if the @synchronized keyword was used with self as the mutex. Now, the exact form of the mutator and accessor methods varies depending on the other keywords and the property's datatype, but here's a simple example of what a nonatomic accessor might look like:

```
- (NSMutableString *)foo {
    return foo;
}
```

As a contrast, here's what the atomic version might look like:

```
- (NSMutableString *)foo {
    NSString *ret;
    @synchronized(self) {
        ret = foo;
    }
    return ret;
}
```

Here's what the atomic version does that the nonatomic doesn't do: it uses self as a mutex around all the code except the return statement and variable declaration. This means that no other code that uses self as a mutex can run while the next line of code is executing. All atomic accessors and mutators block when any other atomic accessor or mutator on the same object is executing on another thread. This helps to ensure data integrity.

When we declare a property to be nonatomic, we're removing these protections because, for some reason, we don't think we need them. So far, this has always been fine because we've only been accessing and setting object properties from the main thread. For outlets, it's still the case that you can pretty much always declare them nonatomic, because you shouldn't use outlets on threads other than the main thread. Most of the UIKit is not thread-safe, which means it's generally not safe to set or retrieve values from threads other than the main thread.

But, if you're creating objects that are used in threads or in operation queues, then you almost certainly want to leave off the nonatomic keyword because the protection from atomic properties is valuable enough to offset the small amount of overhead.

It's important to note, however, that there's a difference between the concepts of atomicity and thread safety, and the fact that you've used atomic properties does not make your class thread-safe. In some simple cases, having atomic properties may be all that an object needs to be thread-safe, but thread-safety is an object-level trait. In the earlier example with the Person object, removing the nonatomic keyword from the two properties would not make the object thread-safe because the problem we illustrated earlier could still happen. You could still have one thread reading the object after firstName had been changed, but before lastName had been changed. To make the object truly "thread-safe," you'd need to not just synchronize the individual accessors and mutators, but also any transaction involving dependent data. In this case, you would need to synchronize code that sets the first and last name so that other code accessing either firstName or lastName would block until the transaction was finished.

The example that demonstrated @synchronized a few pages back shows an excellent way to ensure that the transaction is atomic. You need to lock down the transaction to make sure that no other code can read either value until both have been changed. In the Person class, you might consider adding a method called something like setFirstName:lastName: to synchronize the entire transaction, like this:

```
- (void)setFirstName:(NSString *)inFirst lastName:(NSString *)inLast {
    @synchronized (self) {
        self.firstName = inFirst;
        self.lastName = inLast;
    }
}
```

Notice that you've used mutator methods to set first and last name, even though those mutators are atomic, which means the code in that mutator will also by synchronized. This is okay, because @synchronized is what's called a *recursive mutex*, which means that a synchronized block can call another synchronized block safely as long as the two blocks share the same mutex.

However, you never want to call a synchronized block from within another synchronized block if they don't use the same mutex. Doing so puts you at risk of a situation known as a *deadlock*.

> **Tip**   Apple's API documentation will tell you if a class is thread-safe. If the API documentation doesn't say anything on the topic, then you should assume that the class is ***not*** thread-safe.

## Deadlocks

Sometimes solutions have their own problems, and mutex locks, which are the primary solution to race conditions in concurrency, indeed have a very big problem of their own, which is known as a *deadlock*. A deadlock occurs when a thread blocks and then waits for a condition that can never be met. This can happen, for example, if two threads each have synchronized code that calls synchronized code on the other thread. If both threads are using one mutex and waiting for the one the other thread has, neither thread will ever be able to continue. They will block forever.

There's no simple solution to deadlock scenarios, but one really good rule of thumb that will help you avoid deadlocks is never to have a synchronized block of code call another synchronized block of code that uses a different mutex.

If you find yourself needing to call a method or function with synchronized code in it, you may need to actually replicate the code from that method inside the synchronized block instead of calling the other method. This seems to violate the idea we've been pounding throughout this book that code shouldn't be unnecessarily duplicated. However, if you don't duplicate the code when necessary and attempt to call synchronized code from synchronized code, you could end up deadlocked.

## Sleepy Time

If too many threads are executing, the system can get bogged down. This is especially true on older iPhones that have only a single CPU with a single core. Even if you're using threads, your user interface can start to skip or respond slowly if you're trying to do too much in too many threads. One solution to this, of course, is to spawn fewer threads. This is something that NSOperationQueue can actually handle for you, as you'll see in a few moments.

There's another thing that threads (and by extension operations) can do to help keep your application responsive, which is to *sleep*. A thread can choose to sleep either for a set interval or until a set point in time. If a thread sleeps, it blocks until it's done sleeping, which yields processor cycles to the other threads. Putting sleep calls in a thread or operation essentially throttles it, slowing it down to make sure that there's plenty of processor time available for the main thread.

To cause the thread where your code is executing to sleep, you can use one of two class methods on the class NSThread. To sleep for a specified number of seconds, you use the method sleepForTimeInterval:. So, for example, to sleep for two and a half seconds, you do this:

```
[NSThread sleepForTimeInterval:2.5];
```

To sleep until a specific date and time represented by an instance of NSDate, you could alternatively use sleepUntilDate:. As a result, the previous example could be rewritten like this:

```
[NSThread sleepUntilDate:[NSDate dateWithTimeIntervalSinceNow:2.5]];
```

Note that you should never, ever (and we really mean never) use either of these sleep methods (or their pthreads API counterparts) on the main thread. Why? The main thread is the only thread that handles events and can update the user interface. If you put the main thread to sleep, your interface will just plain stop.

## Operations

We're going to look at operation queues in a moment, but before we do that, you need to know about operations, which are the objects that contain the sets of instructions that the operation queue manages. Operations usually take the form of custom subclasses of NSOperation. You write the subclass and, in it, you put the code that needs to be run concurrently.

> **Note** There are two subclasses of NSOperation, NSInvocationOperation and NSBlockOperation, that will allow you to run code concurrently without creating your own subclasses of NSOperation. NSInvocationOperation allows you to specify an object and selector to use as the basis for the operation. NSBlockOperation allows you specify one or more blocks to use as the basis for the operation. In all but the simplest cases, however, you will want to subclass NSOperation because doing so gives you a lot more control over the process.

When implementing an operation for use in an operation queue, there are a few steps you need to take. First, you create a subclass of NSOperation and define any properties that you'll need as inputs or outputs from the operation. In your square root example, you will create a subclass of NSOperation and define properties for current and max on it.

The only other thing you have to do is to override the method called main, which is where you put the code that makes up the operation. There are a couple of things you need to do in your main method. The first thing you need to do is wrap all of your logic in a @try block so you can catch any exceptions. It's very important that an operation's main method not throw any exceptions. They must be caught and handled without being rethrown. An uncaught exception in an operation will result in a fatal application crash.

The second thing you have to do in main is to create a new autorelease pool. Different threads cannot share the same autorelease pool. The operation will be running in a separate thread, so it can't use the main thread's autorelease pool, so it's important to allocate a new one.

Here's what a skeleton main method for an NSOperation subclass looks like:

```
- (void)main {
    @try {
        @autoreleasepool {
        // Do work here...
        }
    }
    @catch (NSException * e) {
        // Important that we don't re-throw exception here
        NSLog(@"Exception: %@", e);
    }
}
```

## Operation Dependencies

Any operation can optionally have one or more dependencies. A dependency is another instance of NSOperation that has to complete before this operation can be executed. An operation queue will know not to run an operation that has dependencies that have not yet finished. You can add dependencies to an operation using the addDependency: method, like so:

```
MyOperation *firstOperation = [[MyOperation alloc] init];
MyOperation *secondOperation = [[MyOperation alloc] init];
[secondOperation addDependency:firstOperation];
...
```

In this example, if both firstOperation and secondOperation are added to a queue at the same time, they will not be run concurrently even if the queue has free threads available for both operations. Because firstOperation is a dependency of secondOperation, secondOperation will not start executing until firstOperation has finished.

You can get an array of an operation's dependencies by using the dependencies method.

```
NSArray *dependencies = [secondOperation dependencies];
```

You can remove dependencies using the removeDependency: method. To remove the firstOperation as a dependency from secondOperation, you would do this:

```
[secondOperation removeDependency:firstOperation];
```

## Operation Priority

Every operation has a priority that the queue uses to decide which operation gets run when and that dictates how much of the available processing this operation will get to use. You can set a queue's priority using the setQueuePriority: method, passing in one of the following values:

- NSOperationQueuePriorityVeryLow
- NSOperationQueuePriorityLow
- NSOperationQueuePriorityNormal

- NSOperationQueuePriorityHigh

- NSOperationQueuePriorityVeryHigh

Instances of NSOperation default to NSOperationQueuePriorityNormal. Here's how you would change it to a higher priority:

```
[firstOperation setQueuePriority:NSOperationQueuePriorityVeryHigh];
```

Although higher priority operations will execute before lower priority ones, no operation executes if it's not ready. So, for example, an operation with a very high priority that has unmet dependencies will not be run, so a lower priority operation could go in front of it. But, among operations that are ready to execute (which can be determined using the isReady property), the operation with the highest priority will be selected.

You can determine the current priority of an operation by calling the queuePriority method on it, like so:

```
NSOperationQueuePriority *priority = [firstOperation queuePriority];
```

## Other Operation State

By subclassing NSOperation, your class will inherit several properties that can be used to determine aspects of its current state. To determine if an operation has been cancelled, you can check the isCancelled property. The code in an operation's main method should periodically check the isCancelled property to see if the operation has been cancelled. If it has been cancelled, your main method should immediately stop processing and return, which will end the operation.

If an operation's main method is currently being executed, the isExecuting property will return YES. If it returns NO, then it means that the operation hasn't been kicked off yet for some reason. This could be because the operation was just created, because it has a dependency that hasn't finished running yet, or because the queue's maximum number of threads have already been created and none are available yet for this operation to use.

When an operation's main method returns, that will trigger the method's isFinished property to be set to YES, which will cause it to be removed from its queue.

> **Note**    NSOperation has another property called isConcurrent. As of iOS 4, it does nothing. The operation queue will always create a new thread for your operation. Dave Dribin (now at Apple) had a posting about it at www.dribin.org/dave/blog/archives/2009/09/13/snowy_concurrent_operations/.

## Cancelling an Operation

You can cancel operations by calling the `cancel` method, like so:

```
[firstOperation cancel];
```

This will cause the operation's `isCancelled` property to be set to `YES`. It is, however, the operation's responsibility to check for this in its `main` method. Calling `cancel` will not cause the operation to be force cancelled. It just sets the property and it's the `main` method's responsibility to finish processing and return when it detects that the operation has been cancelled.

The fact that cancellations are tracked at the operation level and not by the operation queue does cause some behavior that may seem wrong at first. If an operation in a queue that is not yet executing gets cancelled, the operation will stay in the queue. Calling `cancel` on a pending operation doesn't remove the operation from the queue, and the operation queue doesn't provide a mechanism for removing operations. Cancelled operations don't get removed until they are done executing. The operation will have to wait until it starts executing to realize it's been cancelled and return, triggering its removal from the queue.

# Operation Queues

Now you know how to create operations, so let's look at the object that manages operations, `NSOperationQueue`. Operation queues are created like any other object. You allocate and initialize the queue, like so:

```
NSOperationQueue *queue = [[NSOperationQueue alloc] init];
```

## Adding Operations to the Queue

At this point, the queue is ready to use. You can start adding operations to it immediately without doing anything else. Adding operations is accomplished by using the `addOperation:` method, like so:

```
[queue addOperation:newOperation];
```

Once the operation is added to the queue, it will execute as soon as there is a thread available for it and it is ready to execute. It can even start executing operations while you're still adding other operations. Operation queues, by default, set the number of threads based on the hardware available. A queue running on a multi-processor or multi-core device will tend to create more threads than one running on a single-processor, single-core device.

## Setting the Maximum Concurrent Operation Count

It is generally advisable to let the operation queue decide the number of threads to use. This will, in most cases, ensure that your application makes the best use of available resources now and in the future. However, there may be situations where you want to take control over the number of threads. For example, if you have operations that yield a lot of time by blocking for some reason, you might want to have more threads running than the operation queue thinks it should have. You can do that using the method setMaxConcurrentOperationCount:. To create a serial queue, which is one that only has a single thread, you would to this:

```
[queue setMaxConcurrentOperationCount:1];
```

To tell the queue to reset the maximum number of operations based on the hardware available, you can use the constant NSOperationQueueDefaultMaxConcurrentOperationCount, like so:

```
[queue setMaxConcurrentOperationCount:NSOperationQueueDefaultMaxConcurrentOperationCount];
```

## Suspending the Queue

An operation queue can be paused (or *suspended*). This causes it to stop executing new operations. Operations that have already started executing will continue, unless cancelled, but new ones will not be started as long as the queue is suspended. Suspending the queue is accomplished using the method setSuspended:, passing YES to pause the queue, and NO to resume the queue.

# Fixing Stalled with an Operation Queue

Now that you've got a good grasp on operation queues and concurrency, let's use that knowledge to fix the Stalled application one last time. Open up that copy of the Stalled application we had you make earlier. If you didn't do that, you can just copy the 14 – Stalled application from the project archives and use it as your starting point for this section.

This time, you're going to fix the Stalled application by using an operation queue. Tapping the Go button will add another process to the queue, and you'll add a table that shows the number of operations in the queue along with some information about their status. As you can see from Figure 14-4, the individual rows have a red button. You're using the red button to cancel operations in the operation queue. To create that button, you'll need to grab the image remove.png from the project archive and add it to the Supporting Files group of this project. Do that now before proceeding.

*Figure 14-4.* *The final version of the Stalled application will use an operation queue to manage a variable number of square root operations*

# Creating SquareRootApplication

You're going to start by creating your NSOperation subclass. Create a new Objective-C class file inside the Stalled group in the Navigator pane. Name the class SquareRootOperation and enter NSOperation as the subclass. Save the file, making sure it is part of the Stalled target.

Select SquareRootOperation.h so you can edit it. You start off by defining two constants. Declare them right after the #import at the top of the file.

```
#define kBatchSize      100
#define kUpdateFrequency 0.5
```

The first, kBatchSize, will be used to set how many calculations you perform before checking to see if your operation has been cancelled. The second, kUIUpdateFrequency, specifies how often, in seconds, you update the user interface. You are going to be doing, literally, thousands of calculations a second. If you update the interface from every thread every time you do an update, that's an awful lot of updates. Remember, updates to the user interface have to be done on the main thread. We'll show you how to safely do that from an operation in a moment, but doing so incurs overhead. Different threads can't talk to each other directly.

You don't need to understand the process that threads use to communicate, but you do need to understand that there is overhead associated with sending messages between threads. Fortunately, as you'll see in a moment, the complexity of inter-thread communication is hidden from us. But there's still a cost involved with that communication that will slow things down if you do it too frequently. By reducing the updates to every half a second, you eliminate a lot of unnecessary inter-thread communications. As you test your application, you might want to tweak this value. You might find that more or less frequent updates give a better user experience, but these settings seem to be a good starting point and give decent results both on the device and on the simulator.

After that, you create a protocol for your thread's delegate. Your operation's delegate will be the controller class for your application's main view: StalledViewController. You'll call this protocol's only method to tell that controller that changes have been made that need to be reflected in the row that represents your operation in the table view.

```
@class SquareRootOperation;

@protocol SquareRootOperationDelegate
- (void)operationProgressChanged:(SquareRootOperation *)operation;
@end
```

Things are pretty similar to your SquareRootBatch class from the timer example, except instead of subclassing NSObject, you subclass NSOperation. In addition to the instance variables and properties for current and max calculation, you also have an instance variable and property for your delegate.

```
@property (assign, nonatomic) NSInteger max;
@property (assign, nonatomic) NSInteger current;
@property (strong, nonatomic) id<SquareRootOperationDelegate> delegate;
```

You have an init method that takes the max number of calculations and a delegate.

```
- (id)initWithMaxNumber:(NSInteger)maxNumber delegate:(id<SquareRootOperationDelegate>)aDelegate;
```

And you have two methods that can be called by your delegate to get the current values for the progress bar and label.

```
- (float)percentComplete;
- (NSString *)progressString;
```

Make sure you save SquareRootOperation.h and then switch over to SquareRootOperation.m. Your initializer method shouldn't have any surprises.

```
- (id)initWithMaxNumber:(NSInteger)maxNumber delegate:(id<SquareRootOperationDelegate>)aDelegate
{
    if (self = [super init]) {
        self.max = maxNumber;
        self.current = 0;
        self.delegate = aDelegate;
    }
    return self;
}
```

percentComplete method is just like the one you created earlier in the chapter for the timer-based version of the application.

```
- (float)percentComplete
{
    return (float)self.current / (float)self.max;
}
```

progressString, however, is different.

```
- (NSString *)progressString
{
    if ([self isCancelled])
        return @"Cancelled...";
    if (![self isExecuting])
        return @"Waiting...";

    return [NSString stringWithFormat:@"Completed %d of %d", self.current, self.max];
}
```

All this does is return a string that represents the current amount of progress in the operation and will be used in the cell that represents this row (see Figure 14-4). The one extra step you take here to set the label to Cancelled... if the operation has been cancelled. Remember, earlier, we said that cancelled operations that haven't started executing sit in the queue with their isCancelled property set to YES until they get kicked off, at which point they don't do any processing and fall out of the queue. Since you don't have any way to remove these operations from the queue, you do the next best thing and update the label that is displayed in the table to show that the user requested that this operation be cancelled. Otherwise, you return Waiting... if the operation hasn't started yet, or a string identifying how many square roots you've calculated so far if you are executing.

The next method is the soul of the operation, and it warrants some special attention. The main method is the one that gets called when this operation gets kicked off by the queue. Your operation is going to be running in a thread, so you start off by wrapping everything in a @try block and @autoreleasepool block.

```
- (void)main
{
    @try {
        @autoreleasepool {
```

Then you declare and initialize a variable that will be used to keep track of how much time has elapsed since the last time you updated the user interface.

```
NSTimeInterval lastUIUpdate = [NSDate timeIntervalSinceReferenceDate];
```

Next, you start your loop until your operation is cancelled or `current` is equal to `max`.

```
while (!self.isCancelled && self.current < self.max) {
```

If your operation hasn't been cancelled, you increment `current`, calculate its square root, and log the result.

```
        self.current++;
        double squareRoot = sqrt((double)self.current);
        NSLog(@"Operation %@ reports the square root of %d is %.6f",
            self, self.current, squareRoot);
```

You then use modulus math to determine if you should check the time. Remember, you specified a batch size constant that tells how often you should check if it's time to do a user interface update, so every time `current` modulo `kBatchSize` equals zero, then you've reached a multiple of `kBatchSize` and should check to see if it's time to update the user interface.

```
if (self.current % kBatchSize == 0) {
```

If you've processed an entire batch, you check the current time and compare it to the time of the last update added to the update frequency. If the current time is greater than those values added together, it's time to push another update out to your controller so it can get reflected in the user interface.

```
if ([NSDate timeIntervalSinceReferenceDate] > lastUIUpdate + kUpdateFrequency) {
```

Make sure you have a delegate and that it responds to the correct selector before using `perform Selector:onMainThread:withObject:waitUntilDone:` to let the controller know that the row that represents this operation should be updated. This is a great method that allows you to communicate back to the main thread without having to deal with the nitty-gritty aspects of inter-thread communications. It's an absolutely lovely method; just ask anybody who's had to do it the old-fashioned way using Mach ports.

```
if ((NSObject *)self.delegate respondsToSelector:@selector(operationProgressChanged:)]) {
    [(NSObject *)self.delegate performSelectorOnMainThread:@selector(operationProgressChanged:)
                                    withObject:self
                                    waitUntilDone:NO];
}
```

After you update the interface, you're going to sleep for a fraction of a second. This is optional, and the exact value to use here would probably get adjusted as you tested your application, but it's often a good idea to block periodically to yield some time.

```
[NSThread sleepForTimeInterval:0.05];
```

You update lastUIUpdate with the current time so the next time through the loop, you know how long has passed since you updated the user interface.

```
                    lastUIUpdate = [NSDate timeIntervalSinceReferenceDate];
                }
            }
        }
    }
}
```

Finally, you catch any exceptions. In this application, you just log them. If you need to do something else here, like show an alert, make sure that you call methods on the main thread to do it. Do not do any UI work directly in an operation because UIKit is not thread safe. Yes, we did say that already, but it's important.

```
@catch (NSException *e) {
    NSLog(@"Exception: %@", e);
}
```

Oh, and by the way? UIKit is not thread safe.

Also, whatever you do, do not throw an exception here. Because this operation is executing on a non-main thread, there is no higher-level exception handler available to catch that exception. This means that any exceptions thrown here will be uncaught exceptions, which is a fatal condition at runtime (as in a fatal crash).

Make sure you save SquareRootOperation.m before moving on.

# Custom ProgressCell

Looking at Figure 14-4, you can see that you no longer have a single progress view and progress label in your user interface. Rather, you have a table view that shows the operation queue's operations. Each table view cell has a progress view and progress label, along with a cancel button. Let's build that table view cell as a custom table view cell.

First, create a new Objective-C class file, making it a subclass of UITableViewCell; named ProgressCell. Once the files are created, select ProgressCell.h and add the following properties:

```
@property (weak, nonatomic) IBOutlet UIProgressView *progressBar;
@property (weak, nonatomic) IBOutlet UILabel *progressLabel;
```

Save ProgressCell.h.

You don't have a XIB file for ProgressCell, so why did you declare those properties as outlets? We'll explain that soon, but first you'll create the XIB. Create a new file. Choose the User Interface group in the New File Assistant, and select Empty. Click Next, and make sure the Device Family is iPhone. When asked to save the file, the name is ProgressCell.xib. If it doesn't open Interface Builder, select ProgressCell.xib.

Drag a table view cell on to the Interface Builder. Next, drag a round rect button to the far right edge of the table view cell. In the Attribute Inspector, change the button Type to Custom, and enter remove.png in the Image field. Drag a progress view from the Object Library to the table view cell, above the center guideline, aligning the left edge using the blue guidelines. Extend the right edge of the progress view to the left edge of the button. In the Attribute Inspector, change the Progress field from 0.5 to 0.0. Next, drag a label to just below the progress view. Adjust the width to be the same as the progress view. Use the Attribute Inspector to change the Alignment to Center Alignment.

Now, this is where things are a little different. In the Class Dock, on the left side of the Interface Builder, select the table view cell. Open the Identity Inspector in the Utility pane, and change the Class Field from `UITableViewCell` to `ProgressCell`. Switch to the Attribute Inspector and enter `OperationQueueCell` in the Identifier field. While you're here, change the Selection from Blue to None.

Control-drag from the table view cell in the Class Dock to the progress view. On the Outlet pop-up, select `progressBar`. Control-drag from the table view cell to the label. This time select `progressLabel`.

That's it for now. You'll be coming back to this file, but save `ProgressCell.xib` for now.

## Adjusting the User Interface

Select `ViewController.xib`. In Interface Builder, select the view window and open the Identity Inspector. Change the underlying class from `UIView` to `UIControl`. This will allow background taps to trigger action methods.

Single-click the progress view and hit the delete key. Then single-click the progress label (the empty label below the progress bar) and press delete again.

Look in the library for a table view and drag it over to the Control window. Place it in the window, then use the resize handles so that it takes up all of the window from the left side to the right (not the margins, the full window), and from the very bottom of the window until just below the existing text field, button, and label, using the blue guidelines for proper distance.

Switch to Assistant mode, and control-drag from the table view to just below the last @property declaration in `ViewController.h`. Create a new outlet named tableView. Control-drag back from the table view to File's Owner twice. The first time, select the delegate outlet, the second time select the dataSource outlet.

While still in Assistant mode, select the File's Owner in the Class Dock and switch the Utility pane to the Connections Inspector. Look for the circle to the right of Touch Down. Drag from that circle to below the go method in `ViewController.h` and create a new action named backgroundTap.

Put the editor back into Standard mode and save the XIB.

## Changes to ViewController.h

Open `ViewController.h` in the editor. First, import the `SquareRootOperation` and `ProgressCell` interface files.

```
#import "SquareRootOperation.h"
#import "ProgressCell.h"
```

Next, redeclare the ViewController to conform to the protocols you need.

```
@interface ViewController : UIViewController<UITableViewDataSource, UITableViewDelegate,
SquareRootOperationDelegate>
```

You don't need the progressBar nor progressLabel properties, so you delete them. You created the tableView property via Interface Builder. You need to declare a property for an operation queue. You also declare a progress cell property (don't worry, we'll explain it soon!).

```
@property (weak, nonatomic) IBOutlet UIProgressView *progressBar;
@property (weak, nonatomic) IBOutlet UILabel *progressLabel;
@property (weak, nonatomic) IBOutlet UITableView *tableView;
@property (strong, nonatomic) NSOperationQueue *queue;
@property (strong, nonatomic) IBOutlet ProgressCell *progressCell;
```

Lastly, you add a new method, cancelOperation:, that will be called when the user taps the cancel button of a row in the table.

```
- (IBAction)cancelOperation:(id)sender;
```

Save ViewController.h.

# Updating ViewController.m

Select ViewController.m so you can make your final changes. At the top of the file, you need to add a private Property in the Category declaration.

```
@interface ViewController ()
@property (assign, nonatomic) NSInteger cancelledIndex;
@end
```

You get rid of the @synthesize statements for the two deleted outlets.

```
@synthesize progressBar;
@synthesize progressLabel;
```

Next, look for the go method and replace the current implementation with this new one:

```
- (IBAction)go:(id)sender
{
    NSInteger operationCount = [numberOfOperations.text integerValue];
    SquareRootOperation *newOperation =
        [[SquareRootOperation alloc] initWithMaxNumber:operationCount delegate:self];
    [self.queue addOperation:newOperation];
}
```

First, you retrieve the number of operations, just as you did in the last two versions. Next, you create an instance of SquareRootOperation with that number, passing self as the delegate so that you get notified of changes that impact the user interface. Finally, you add the operation to the queue.

After the go method, replace the backgroundClick: method stub with this implementation:

```
- (IBAction)backgroundClick:(id)sender
{
    [self.numberOfOperations resignFirstResponder];
}
```

This method you just added just tells the text field to resign the first responder so that the keyboard will retract and you can see the whole table.

Now you need to implement the cancelOperation: method. You ask the sender for its tag value and use that as the table view row index. You use that index to retrieve an operation from the operation queue and cancel it. You check to see if the operation was executing, and if it wasn't, you trigger a reload of the table data so that the row's text gets changed from Waiting… to Cancelled….

```
- (IBAction)cancelOperation:(id)sender
{
    self.cancelledIndex = [sender tag];
    NSOperation *operation = [[self.queue operations] objectAtIndex:self.cancelledIndex];
    [operation cancel];
    if (![operation isExecuting])
        [self.tableView reloadData];
}
```

Back up a little bit and find the viewDidLoad method. Add the following after the call to super:

```
    self.queue = [[NSOperationQueue alloc] init];
    [self.queue addObserver:self
                forKeyPath:@"operations"
                    options:(NSKeyValueObservingOptionNew | NSKeyValueObservingOptionOld)
                    context:NULL];
    self.cancelledIndex = -1;
```

The first thing you do in viewDidLoad is create a new instance of NSOperationQueue and assign it to queue. Then you do something kind of neat. You use something called KVO. That's not a typo. We're not talking about KVC, but it's a related concept. KVO stands for key-value observation, and it's a mechanism that lets you get notified when a particular property on another object gets changed. You're registering self as an observer of queue for the key path called operations. That key path is the name of the property that returns an array with all of the operations in the queue. Whenever an operation is added or gets removed from the queue, your controller class will get notified of that fact thanks to KVO. The options parameter allows you to request additional information about the change, such as the previous value of the changed property. You don't need anything over and above what basic KVO provides, so you pass 0. You also pass NULL into the final argument because you don't have any objects that you want to get passed along to the notification method.

Now that you've registered for the KVO notification, you have to implement a method called observeValueForKeyPath:ofObject:change:context:. Let's add that method to your class and then talk about what it's doing. Insert the following new method at the bottom of the file, before @end:

```
#pragma mark - KVO method

- (void)observeValueForKeyPath:(NSString *)keyPath
                      ofObject:(id)object
                        change:(NSDictionary *)change
                       context:(void *)context
{
```

Any change to properties you observe using KVO will trigger a call to this method. The first argument to the method is the key path that you're watching, and the second is the object that you are observing. In your case, since you're only watching one key path on one object, you don't need to do anything with these values. If you were observing multiple values, you would probably need to check these arguments to know what to do. The third argument, change, is a dictionary that contains a whole bunch of information about the change that happened. You didn't pass in a value for context earlier when you observed queue, so you won't receive anything in context when this method gets called.

> **Note**  KVO is a neat feature of Cocoa Touch, but one that we're not covering in-depth. If you're interested in leveraging KVO in your own applications, a great place to start is Apple's *Key Value Observing Programming Guide* available at https://developer.apple.com/library/ios/#documentation/Cocoa/Conceptual/KeyValueObserving/KeyValueObserving.html.

The first thing you do in this method is retrieve the value stored under NSKeyValueChangeKindKey. This will return an NSNumber that, when converted to an integer, will tell you if change happened. If there was a change, then the integer representation will equal the constant NSKeyValueChangeSetting.

```
NSNumber *kind = [change objectForKey:NSKeyValueChangeKindKey];
```

Next, you get the NSArray stored under NSKeyValueChangeOldKey. This will return the array before you performed any work on it. Next, you get the NSArray stored under NSKeyValueChangeNewKey. This will give you the array after the action is completed.

```
NSArray *old = (NSArray *)[change objectForKey:NSKeyValueChangeOldKey];
NSArray *new = (NSArray *)[change objectForKey:NSKeyValueChangeNewKey];
```

Now, you check that change has occurred. If a change has occurred, you'll be updating the table view, so you prepare the table view.

```
if ([kind integerValue] == NSKeyValueChangeSetting) {
    [self.tableView beginUpdates];
```

If the number of elements in the old array is smaller than the new array, then you've inserted a new operation and you update the table view accordingly.

```
    if ([old count] < [new count]) {
        NSArray *indexPaths =
            [NSArray arrayWithObject:[NSIndexPath indexPathForRow:([new count]-1) inSection:0]];
        [self.tableView insertRowsAtIndexPaths:indexPaths
                            withRowAnimation:UITableViewRowAnimationFade];
    }
```

Otherwise, if the old array is larger than the new array, then you know you've deleted an operation.

```
    else if ([old count] > [new count]) {
        NSArray *indexPaths =
            [NSArray arrayWithObject:[NSIndexPath indexPathForRow:self.cancelledIndex inSection:0]];
        [self.tableView deleteRowsAtIndexPaths:indexPaths
                            withRowAnimation:UITableViewRowAnimationFade];
        self.cancelledIndex = -1;
    }
```
Then you tell the table view you're done making changes, so it can update itself.
```
        [self.tableView endUpdates];
    }
}
```

Almost there, friends. Almost there. At the bottom of the class you have a few more methods to add. First, you need to add your SquareRootOperationDelegate method, where you update the user interface.

```
#pragma mark  - SquareRootOperation Delegate Method

- (void)operationProgressChanged:(SquareRootOperation *)op {
    NSUInteger opIndex = [[self.queue operations] indexOfObject:op];
    NSUInteger reloadIndices[] = {0, opIndex};
    NSIndexPath *reloadIndexPath = [NSIndexPath indexPathWithIndexes:reloadIndices length:2];
    ProgressCell *cell = (ProgressCell *)[tableView cellForRowAtIndexPath:reloadIndexPath];
    if (cell) {
        UIProgressView *progressView = cell.progressBar;
        progressView.progress = [op percentComplete];
        UILabel *progressLabel = cell.progressLabel;
        progressLabel.text = [op progressString];

        [self.tableView beginUpdates];
        [self.tableView reloadRowsAtIndexPaths:[NSArray arrayWithObject:reloadIndexPath]
                            withRowAnimation:UITableViewRowAnimationNone];
        [self.tableView endUpdates];
    }
}
```

You take the SquareRootOperation instance that called the method and find its index in the operations array. You use that information to build an index path that points to the row that corresponds to the operation that triggered the method call. You use that index path to get a reference to the cell that displays the updated operation. If there is no corresponding cell, then the row isn't currently visible and you don't need to do anything. If the row is visible, you grab the `percentComplete` and `progressString` values from the operation and use them to set the label and progress view for the operation's cell.

All that's left are the table view methods, and you all are old hands at these by now, so just insert the following methods:

```
#pragma mark - Table View Data Source Methods

- (NSInteger)tableView:(UITableView *)theTableView numberOfRowsInSection:(NSInteger)section
{
    if (nil == [self.queue operations])
        NSLog(@"NIL QUEUE OPERATIONS");
    else
        NSLog(@"%d", [[self.queue operations] count]);

    return [[self.queue operations] count];
}

- (UITableViewCell *)tableView:(UITableView *)theTableView cellForRowAtIndexPath:
(NSIndexPath *)indexPath {
    static NSString *identifier = @"OperationQueueCell";
    ProgressCell *cell = [theTableView dequeueReusableCellWithIdentifier:identifier];
    if (cell == nil) {
        [[NSBundle mainBundle] loadNibNamed:@"ProgressCell" owner:self options:nil];
        cell = (ProgressCell *)self.progressCell;
        self.progressCell = nil;
    }
    SquareRootOperation *rowOp =
        (SquareRootOperation *)[[self.queue operations] objectAtIndex:[indexPath row]];
    UIProgressView *progressView = cell.progressBar;
    progressView.progress = [rowOp percentComplete];

    UILabel *progressLabel = cell.progressLabel;
    progressLabel.text = [rowOp progressString];
    cell.accessoryView.tag = [indexPath row];

    return cell;
}
```

The only thing that might be new for you are these lines:

```
    static NSString *identifier = @"OperationQueueCell";
    ProgressCell *cell = [theTableView dequeueReusableCellWithIdentifier:identifier];
    if (cell == nil) {
        [[NSBundle mainBundle] loadNibNamed:@"ProgressCell" owner:self options:nil];
        cell = (ProgressCell *)self.progressCell;
        self.progressCell = nil;
    }
```

You try to dequeue a ProgressCell with the identifier "OperationQueueCell". If you recall, that's the identifier you gave the table view cell in ProgressView.xib. If the dequeue method returns nil, you load the ProgressCell Nib (XIB). Loading the XIB will instantiate a ProgressCell and assign it to the ViewController progressCell property. You assign that property to your local cell variable. Finally, you set the progressCell property to nil.

> **Note**   You can read more in the "Loading Custom Table-View Cells From Nib Files" section of Apple's *Table View Programming Guide for iOS* at https://developer.apple.com/library/ios/#documentation/UserExperience/Conceptual/TableView_iPhone/TableViewCells/TableViewCells.html.

You need to do two more things in order for this XIB loading to work. Save ViewController.m, and select ProgressCell.xib to open Interface Builder. Select the File's Owner in the Class Dock and open the Identity Inspector in the Utility pane. Change the Class field from NSObject to ViewController. Control-drag from the File's Owner to the table view cell, and select progressCell in the Outlet pop-up. Next control-drag from the red remove button to the File's Owner and connect to the cancelOperation: action.

# Queue 'em Up

Build and run the application and take it for a spin. You probably want to run this one in the Simulator. Try spawning a whole bunch of operations and then watch them run, keeping an eye both on Xcode's debugger console and the application itself. Try deleting both executing and pending operations to see how they behave. If you want to run the application on your phone, you might want to consider commenting out the NSLog() statement in the main method of SquareRootOperation.m, but if you do, make sure you add a few zeros on to the number of calculations to perform or else increase the amount of time that each operation sleeps; otherwise the operations will finish so fast you won't even see the table update.

Make note of how many running operations there are when you run it on the device versus the simulator. Try experimenting by setting the maximum number of concurrent operations in the queue and see how performance is impacted.

This chapter was just an introduction to concurrency, but you should have enough of a grip on both operation queues and timers to be able to effectively use both techniques in your iOS applications. Once you've digested it all, turn the page and you'll get into the final frontier: unit testing, debugging, and instruments.

# 15

# Unit Testing, Debugging, and Instruments

One of the fundamental truths of computer programming (and life) is that not everything works perfectly. No matter how much you plan, and no matter how long you've been programming, it's rare for an application you write to work perfectly the first time and then forever under all circumstances and possible uses. Knowing how to properly architect your application and write well-formed code is important. Knowing how to find out why things aren't working the way they're supposed to, and fixing them, is equally important.

There are three techniques you can leverage to help identify and solve these problems: *unit testing*, *debugging*, and *profiling*.

- *Unit testing* is the idea of isolating the smallest piece of testable code and determining if that code behaves as expected. Each unit of code is tested in isolation before testing the application, which can be seen as the integration of all the units of code. That's it. Apple has provided a unit-testing framework and integrated it into Xcode.

- *Debugging*, as you're probably aware, is the task of eliminating errors, or *bugs*, from your application. While it may refer to any process you use to correct bugs, generally it means using a *debugger* to find and identify bugs in your code.

- *Profiling* is the measurement and analysis of your application while running. You usually perform profiling with the goal of optimizing application performance. Profiling can be used to monitor CPU or memory usage to help determine where your application is expending resources. With iOS, Apple has provided a GUI tool called Instruments to make application profiling easier.

We'll cover each of these techniques briefly. Our goal here is not to be a comprehensive guide for these techniques. Rather, we want to provide an introduction to these techniques. If you want a more detailed explanation, you may want to read *Pro iOS Tools: Xcode Instruments and Build Tools* (Apress, 2011).

In this chapter, you're not going to build and debug a complex application. Instead, you're going to create a project from a template, then we'll show you how to implement each technique, one at a time, by adding code to demonstrate specific problems.

# Unit Tests

Let's start by creating a simple project.  Open Xcode, and create a new project. Select the Master-Detail Application template. Call it DebugTest, and make sure you check the "Include Unit Tests" check box (Figure 15-1), along with "Use Core Data" and "Use Automatic Reference Counting."

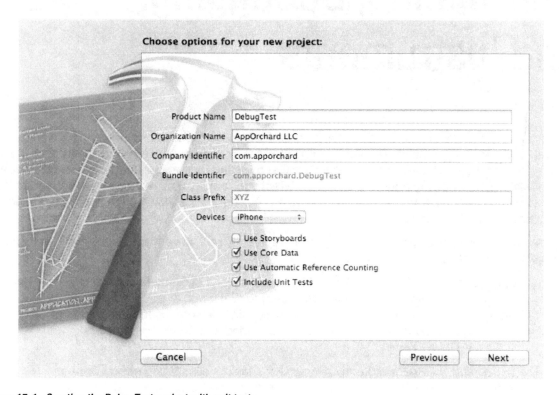

*Figure 15-1.  Creating the DebugTest project with unit tests*

Let's take a quick look at the project. Select the project in the Navigator pane and look at the resulting Project Editor (Figure 15-2). Notice there are two targets: the application, DebugTest, and a bundle, DebugTestTests. This bundle is where the unit tests you'll be writing will reside. The DebugTestTests target depends on the DebugTest target (application). This means that when you build the unit testing bundle, it will build the application first.

*Figure 15-2. Two project targets: the application and the unit testing bundle*

How do you run your tests? If you look at the Xcode scheme pop-up menu in the toolbar, there is no scheme for DebugTestTests, only one for DebugTest (Figure 15-3).

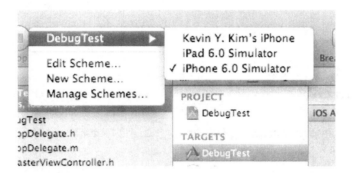

*Figure 15-3. Where is the DebugTestTests scheme?*

Xcode automagically manages this for you. When you select Product ➤ Test on the DebugTest scheme, Xcode knows to execute the DebugTestTests target.

Now run the unit test bundle and see what happens. Select Product ➤ Test.

Xcode should have notified you that the test(s) failed. The Issue Navigator should tell you where the error occurred. If you select the failure, the editor should go to the failed test in DebugTestTests.m (Figure 15-4).

*Figure 15-4. The failed test in Xcode*

This seems like a good time to discuss the format of the unit tests. In the Project Navigator, open the group named DebugTestTests, and select DebugTestTests.h.

```
#import <SenTestingKit/SenTestingKit.h>

@interface DebugTestTests : SenTestCase

@end
```

This is a very simple header file. It imports the header SenTestingKit.h and declares the class DebugTestTests to inherit from SenTestCase. What is SenTestingKit? The unit testing framework Xcode uses is called OCUnit. OCUnit was developed by a company called SenTe (www.sente.ch/software/ocunit/). They define OCUnit as three components: SenTestingKit, a framework to help write tests; otest, a testing tool to execute tests; and a set of files and utilities to integrate testing with Xcode. So while you may use OCUnit and SenTestingKit interchangeably, OCUnit refers to the entire testing suite, while SenTestingKit is the Objective-C framework to write tests.

Let's look at DebugMeTests.m.

```
#import "DebugTestTests.h"

@implementation DebugTestTests
```

```objc
- (void)setUp
{
    [super setUp];

    // Set-up code here.
}

- (void)tearDown
{
    // Tear-down code here.

    [super tearDown];
}

- (void)testExample
{
    STFail(@"Unit tests are not implemented yet in DebugTestTests");
}

@end
```

Each unit test follows a simple process: set up the test, execute the test, tear down the test. Using OCUnit, each test is defined as a method prepended by the word *test*. Since each test needs to run in isolation, each test method follows the set up/test/tear down cycle.

In the case of DebugMeTests.m, you can see the one test method, testExample. The body of that method consists of one line, which invokes the function STFail. STFail is an *assertion* that forces the test to fail. Let's fix this to pass. Replace STFail with this:

```objc
- (void)testExample
{
    STAssertTrue(YES, @"Make this test pass");
}
```

> **Note** For a complete list of test assertions, check the file SenTestCase.h in the SenTestingKit framework.

Run the tests again (to shortcut this, hit CMD-U). This time they should succeed.

What have you done here? You made a test pass without actually fixing or testing anything. This is a very important point: unit testing is not a silver bullet. The tests are only as good as you write them. It's important to make sure you write meaningful tests. A generally accepted practice is called *Test First*: write your test, write your application code such that your test fails, then adjust the code to make the test pass. An interesting side effect is that your code tends to be shorter, clearer, and more concise.

Let's define an object with some simple methods that you can test. Create a new file, choosing the Objective-C class. Name the class DebugMe and make it a subclass of NSObject. When you save the file, make sure it is assigned only to the DebugTest target (Figure 15-5).

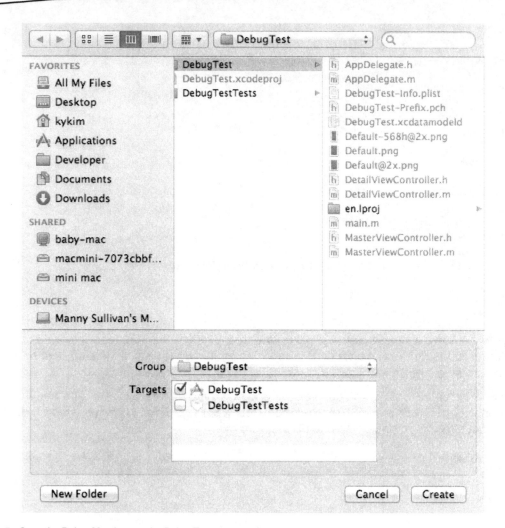

*Figure 15-5. Save the DebugMe class to the DebugTest target only*

Select DebugMe.h and edit it to appear as follows:

```
#import <Foundation/Foundation.h>

@interface DebugMe : NSObject

@property (nonatomic, strong) NSString *string;

- (BOOL)isTrue;
- (BOOL)isFalse;
- (NSString *)helloWorld;

@end
```

Pretty simple. I think you can guess what DebugMe.m will look like.

```
#import "DebugMe.h"

@implementation DebugMe

- (BOOL)isTrue
{
    return YES;
}

- (BOOL)isFalse
{
    return NO;
}

- (NSString *)helloWorld
{
    return @"Hello, World!";
}

@end
```

Again, very simple. Your classes will probably be far more complex than this, but we're just doing this as an example.

In order to test the DebugMe class, you need to create a DebugMeTests class. Create a new file, selecting the Objective-C test case class (Figure 15-6). Name the class DebugMeTests (Figure 15-7). When saving the file, make sure you are adding it to the DebugTestTests target only (Figure 15-8). Now, let's update your test class. Start with DebugMeTests.h.

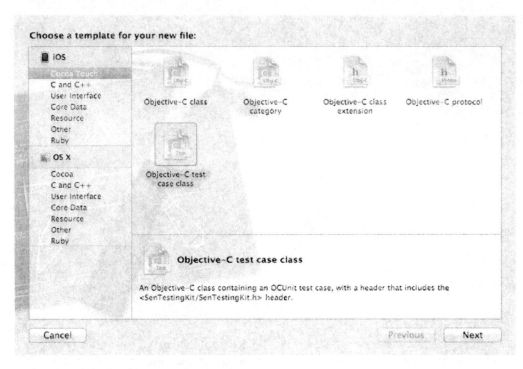

*Figure 15-6.  Select the Objective-C test case class template*

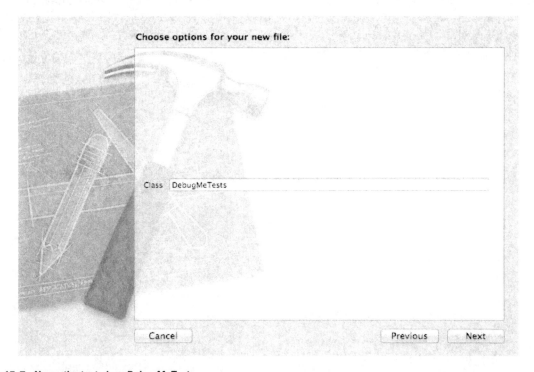

*Figure 15-7.  Name the test class DebugMeTests*

*Figure 15-8. Add DebugMeTests to the DebugTestTests target only*

```
#import <SenTestingKit/SenTestingKit.h>
#import "DebugMe.h"

@interface DebugMeTests : SenTestCase

@property (nonatomic, strong) DebugMe *debugMe;

@end
```

You import the DebugMe header file, and add the property debugMe. You'll be using this property in the implementation. Select DebugMeTests.m to open the implementation file in the editor. Before you write any tests, you need to implement your setUp and tearDown methods. You'll use setUp to instantiate your debugMe property and tearDown to release it.

```
- (void)setUp
{
    [super setUp];

    // Set-up code here.
    self.debugMe = [[DebugMe alloc] init];
}

- (void)tearDown
{
    // Tear-down code here.
    self.debugMe = nil;

    [super tearDown];
}
```

Let's start by thinking about what you want to test in the DebugMe class. DebugMe has a property named string. We could argue that you don't need to test that this property is present. Or we could argue that you should. In the end, it's going to depend on your preferences and project. We'll define a test as an exercise.

```
- (void)testDebugMeHasStringProperty
{
    STAssertTrue([self.debugMe respondsToSelector:@selector(string)],
                 @"expected DebugMe to have 'string' selector");
}
```

You're only checking to see if you have an accessor method for the string property. You could also check that you have a setter method (setString:) as well. Which raises another point: do you put that check in this test, or do you create another test? Again, there is no correct answer; what you do is going to depend on your personal preferences and project.

At this point, it's a good idea to test the project again. Generally, you only add a new test when all your existing tests pass. So before you proceed, run this test and make sure it passes.

Your test should have passed, so let's move on to testing the isTrue method.

```
- (void)testDebugMeIsTrue
{
    BOOL result = [self.debugMe isTrue];
    STAssertTrue(result, @"expected DebugMe isTrue to be true, got %@", result);
}
```

Next, you write a test for the isFalse method.

```
- (void)testDebugMeIsFalse
{
    BOOL result = [self.debugMe isFalse];
    STAssertFalse(result, @"expected DebugMe isFalse to be false, got %@", result);
}
```

Finally, you write a test for the `helloWorld` method.

```
- (void)testDebugMeHelloWorld
{
    NSString *result = [self.debugMe helloWorld];
    STAssertEquals(result, @"Hello, World!",
                   @"expected DebugMe helloWorld to be 'Hello, World!', got '%@'", result);
}
```

Running your tests at this point will return a failure. Why did your tests fail? Look at the Issues Navigator. The failure message reads:

```
error: testDebugMeHelloWorld (DebugMeTests) failed: '<7c7d0000>' should be equal to '<f8b23d07>':
expected DebugMe helloWorld to be 'Hello, World!', got 'Hello, World!'
```

You told the test to expect "Hello, World!", and the method returned "Hello, World!" What's going on? Well, it turns out that `STAssertEquals` expects the two string objects to be equal, not their values. You need to use `STAssertEqualObjects`. So make that change and try again.

Success! You've written your first unit test cases.

As a general practice, you'll want to write a test class for each class in your application. There is a methodology called *test-driven development* (TDD) that suggests you should write your test cases first, then write your application code. A side effect of TDD is that you know how your application is supposed to behave before you start coding (isn't that a good idea?).

> **Note**   You may want to read up on test-driven development (TDD). An excellent introduction can be found at the Agile Data web site (`www.agiledata.org/essays/tdd.html`). Kent Beck wrote an excellent book called *Test Driven Development* (Addison-Wesley, 2003) that we highly recommend.

> **Note**   There is an additional concept that is very useful when writing tests: *mocking*. When the code you are testing is dependent on another object, you can define a *mock object* to emulate the dependent object. This helps maintain the *isolation* of each unit test. A good mocking framework is OCMock, by Mulle Kyberkinetik (`http://ocmock.org/`).

# Debugging

As you probably have noticed, when you create a project in Xcode, the project defaults into what's called the *debug configuration*. If you've ever compiled an application for the App Store or for ad hoc distribution, then you're aware of the fact that applications usually start with two configurations, one called debug and another called release.

So, how is the debug configuration different than the release or distribution configuration? There are actually a number of differences between them, but the key difference between them is that the *Debug* configuration builds *debug symbols* into your application. These debug symbols are like little bookmarks in your compiled application that make it possible to match up any command that fires in your application with a specific piece of source code in your project. Xcode includes a piece of software known as a *debugger*, which uses the debug symbols to go from bytes of machine code to the specific functions and methods in the source code that generated that machine code.

> **Caution**   If you try to use the debugger with the release or distribution configuration, you will get very odd results since those configurations don't include debug symbols. The debugger will try its best, but ultimately will become morose and limp quietly away.

One of the big changes in Xcode 4 was the integration of the debugger into the main window (Figure 15-9). Prior versions of Xcode had their own separate debugger console. Now Xcode changes a number of panes when debugging. We'll discuss the contents of each pane later.

*Figure 15-9. Xcode in debugger mode*

# Breakpoints

Probably the most important debugging tool in your arsenal is the *breakpoint*. A breakpoint is an instruction to the debugger to pause execution of your application at a specific place in your code and wait for you. By pausing, but not stopping, the execution of your program, your application is still running and you can do things like look at the value of variables and step through lines of code one at a time. A breakpoint can also be set up so that instead of pausing the program's execution, a command or script gets executed and then the program resumes execution. You'll look at both types of breakpoints in this chapter, but you'll probably use the former a lot more than the latter.

The most common breakpoint type that you'll set in Xcode is the *line number breakpoint*. This type of breakpoint allows you to specify that the debugger should stop at a specific line of code in a specific file. To set a line number breakpoint in Xcode, you just click in the space to the left of the source code file in the editing pane. Let's do that now so you can see how it works.

Single-click `MasterViewController.m`. Look for the method called `viewDidLoad`. It should be one of the early methods in the file. On the left side of the Editing pane, you should see a column with numbers, as in Figure 15-10. This is called the *gutter*, and it's one way to set line number breakpoints.

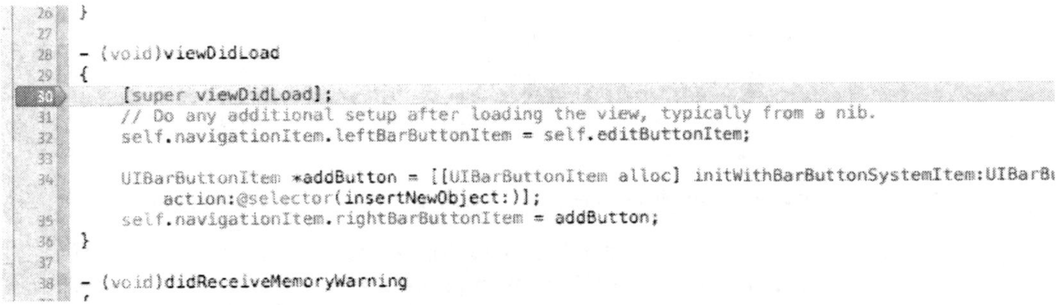

```
26   }
27
28   - (void)viewDidLoad
29   {
30       [super viewDidLoad];
31       // Do any additional setup after loading the view, typically from a nib.
32       self.navigationItem.leftBarButtonItem = self.editButtonItem;
33
34       UIBarButtonItem *addButton = [[UIBarButtonItem alloc] initWithBarButtonSystemItem:UIBarB
             action:@selector(insertNewObject:)];
35       self.navigationItem.rightBarButtonItem = addButton;
36   }
37
38   - (void)didReceiveMemoryWarning
```

*Figure 15-10. To the left of the editing pane is a column that usually shows line numbers. This is where you set breakpoints*

> **Tip**   If you don't see line numbers or the gutter, open Xcode's preferences and go to the Text Editing pane and select the Editing tab (Figure 15-11). The first check box in that section is "Show: Line numbers." It's much easier to set breakpoints if you can see the line numbers.

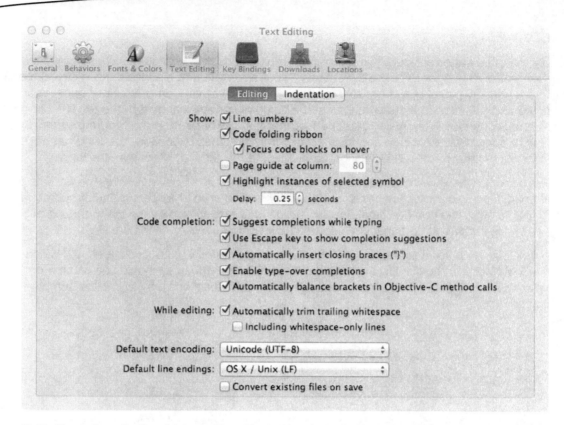

*Figure 15-11. Expose the gutter by making sure Show: Line numbers is checked in the Text Editing pane of Xcode Preferences*

Look for the first line of code in viewDidLoad, which should be a call to super. In Figure 15-10, this line of code is at line 30, though it may be a different line number for you. Single-click in the gutter to the left of that line, and a little arrow should appear in the gutter pointing at the line of code. You now have a breakpoint set in the MasterViewController.m file at a specific line number.

You can remove breakpoints by dragging them off of the gutter, and move them by dragging them to a new location on the gutter. You can temporarily disable existing breakpoints by single-clicking them, which will cause them to change from a darker color to a lighter color. To re-enable a disabled breakpoint, you just click it again to change it back to the darker color.

Before we talk about all the things you can do with breakpoints, let's try out the basic functionality. Select **Product ➤ Run**. The program will start to launch normally, then before the view gets fully shown, you'll be brought back to Xcode, and the project window will come forward, showing the line of code about to be executed and its associated breakpoint (Figure 15-10).

**Note**    In the toolbar at the top of the debug and project windows is an icon labeled Breakpoints. As its name implies, clicking that icon toggles between breakpoints on or breakpoints off. This allows you to enable or disable all your breakpoints without losing them.

Remember we said we'd talk about the Xcode debugger layout? Let's do that now.

# The Debug Navigator

When Xcode enters debugging mode, the Navigation pane (on the left) activates the Debug Navigator (Figure 15-12). This view shows you the Stack Trace of the application, the method and function calls that got you here. In this case, it highlights the call to viewDidLoad in the MasterViewController. The greyed out rows indicate the classes and methods you don't have access to in the source code. You can see the next method is the view from UIViewController. Since UIViewController is part of the UIKit framework, it's not surprising you don't have the source code.

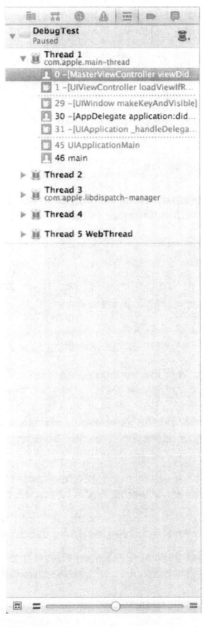

*Figure 15-12. Debug Navigator, displaying the stack trace*

If you go further up the call stack, you see that [AppDelegate application:didFinishLaun chingWithOptions:] was called. If you click on that line, the Editor pane will change to show the file AppDelegate.m, highlighting the line that was last called before reaching the breakpoint. This is a very useful feature. It allows you to track the flow of method and function calls that lead up to a problem.

## The Debug Area

The area underneath the Editor Area is called the Debug Area (Figure 15-13). It's composed of three components. Along the top is the Debug Bar. Below the Debug Bar, to the left, is the Variable List. To the right of the Variable List is the Console Pane. Let's discuss each one, starting with the Variable List.

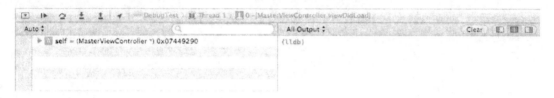

*Figure 15-13. Debug Area, located below the Editor Area*

The Variable List displays all the variables that are currently *in scope*. A variable is in scope if it is an argument or local variable from the current method, or if it is an instance variable from the object that contains the method.

> **Note**    The variable list will also let you change a variable's value. If you double-click any value, it will become editable, and when you press return to commit your change, the underlying variable will also change in the application.

By default, the Variable List will display local variables. You may change this by selecting the drop-down at the upper left of the Variable List pane. There are three options available: Auto; Local; and All Variables, Registers, Globals and Statics. Auto displays the variables Xcode thinks you'll be interested based on the given context. All Variables… will all variables and processor registers. Suffice to say, if you are handling processor registers, you're doing some pretty advanced work, far beyond the scope of this chapter.

The Console Pane gives you direct access to the debugger command line and output. While using the debugger console command is very powerful, we're not going to discuss it in detail here.

It's important to note that output (i.e. NSLog() statement) will direct you to the Console Pane. So it's useful to look there and see what output is generated while debugging.

Finally, the Debug Bar contains a set of controls (Figure 15-14) and a stack trace jump bar. The jump bar displays the current location of the current thread in the application. This is just a distillation of the Debug Navigator view.

*Figure 15-14. Debug Bar controls*

The Debug Bar controls provide a series of buttons to help control your debugging session. From the left, the first button is a disclosure button to minimize the Debug Area. When minimized, only the Debug Bar is visible. Next is the Continue button. The Continue button resumes execution of your program. It will pick up right where it left off and continue executing as normal unless another breakpoint or an error condition is encountered. The Step Over and Step Into buttons allow you to execute a single line of code at a time. The difference between the two is that Step Over will fire any method or function call as a single line of code, skipping to the next line of code in the current method or function, while Step Into will go to the first line of code in the method or function that's called and stop there. The Step Out button finishes execution of the current method and returns to the method that called it. This effectively pops the current method off the stack trace's stack (you didn't think that name was accidental did you?) and the method that called this method becomes the top of the stack trace.

The final button on the Debug Bar is the Location button. This allows you to simulate a location for an application that uses Core Location.

That might be a little clearer if you try it out. Stop your program. Note that even though your program might be paused at a breakpoint, it is still executing. To stop it, click on the stop sign in the Xcode or select **Stop** from the **Product** menu. You're going to add some code that might make the use of Step Over, Step Into, and Step Out a little clearer.

## NESTED CALLS

Nested method calls like this combine two commands in the same line of code:

```
[[NSArray alloc] initWithObject:@"Hello"];
```

If you nest several methods together, you will skip over several actual commands with a single click of the Step Over button, making it impossible to set a breakpoint between the different nested statements. This is the primary reason to avoid excessive nesting of message calls. Other than the standard nesting of `alloc` and `init` methods, we generally prefer not to nest messages.

Dot notation has changed this somewhat. Remember, dot notation is just shorthand for calling a method, so this line of code is also two commands:

```
[self.tableView reloadData];
```

Before the call to `reloadData`, there is a call to the accessor method `tableView`. If it makes sense to use an accessor, we will often use dot notation right in the message call rather than using two separate lines of code, but be careful. It's easy to forget that dot notation results in a method call, so you can inadvertently create code that is hard to debug by nesting several method calls on one line of code.

# Trying Out the Debug Controls

Select MasterViewController.m. Add the following two methods, right after the @implementation declaration:

```
@implementation MasterViewController

- (float)processBar:(float)inBar {
    float newBar = inBar * 2.0;
    return newBar;
}

- (NSInteger)processFoo:(NSInteger)inFoo {
    NSInteger newFoo = inFoo * 2;
    return newFoo;
}

- (id)initWithNibName:(NSString *)nibNameOrNil bundle:(NSBundle *)nibBundleOrNil
{
...
```

And insert the following (bold) lines of code into the existing viewDidLoad method:

```
- (void)viewDidLoad
{
    [super viewDidLoad];
        // Do any additional setup after loading the view, typically from a nib.
    NSInteger foo = 25;
    float bar = 374.3494;
    NSLog(@"foo: %d, bar: %f", foo, bar);

    foo = [self processFoo:foo];
    bar = [self processBar:bar];

    NSLog(@"foo: %d, bar: %f", foo, bar);

    self.navigationItem.leftBarButtonItem = self.editButtonItem;

    UIBarButtonItem *addButton =
        [[UIBarButtonItem alloc] initWithBarButtonSystemItem:UIBarButtonSystemItemAdd
                                        target:self
                                        action:@selector(insertNewObject:)];
    self.navigationItem.rightBarButtonItem = addButton;
}
```

Your breakpoint should still be set at the first line of the method. Xcode does a pretty good job of moving breakpoints around when you insert or delete text from above or below it. Even though you just added two methods above your breakpoint and the method now starts at a new line number, the breakpoint is still set to the correct line of code, which is nice. If the breakpoint somehow got moved, no worries; you're going to move it anyway.

Click and drag the breakpoint down until it's lined up with the line of code that reads

```
NSInteger foo = 25;
```

Now, choose Run from the Project menu to compile the changes and launch the program again. You should see the breakpoint at the first new line of code you added to viewDidLoad.

The first two lines of code are just declaring variables and assigning values to them. These lines don't call any methods or functions, so the Step Over and Step Into buttons will function identically here. To test that out, click the Step Over button to cause the next line of code to execute, then click Step Into to cause the second new line of code to execute.

Before using any more of the debugger controls, check out the variable list (Figure 15-15). The two variables you just declared are in the variable list under the Local heading with their current values. Also, notice that the value for bar is blue. That means it was just assigned or changed by the last command that executed.

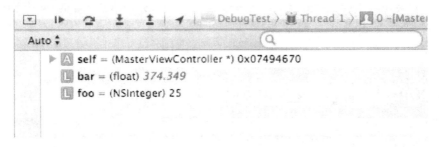

**Figure 15-15.** *When a variable was changed by the last command that fired, it will turn blue in the variable list*

> **Note**    As you are probably aware, numbers are represented in memory as sums of powers of 2 or powers of ½ for fractional parts. This means that some numbers will end up stored in memory with values slightly different than the value specified in the source code. Though you set bar to a value of 374.3494, the closest representation was 374.349396. Close enough, right?

There's another way you can see the value of a variable. If you move your cursor so it's above the word *foo* anywhere it exists in the editor pane, a little box will pop up similar to a tooltip that will tell you the variable's current value and type (Figure 15-16).

```
39    {
40        [super viewDidLoad];
41        // Do any additional setup after loading the view, typically from a nib.
42        NSInteger foo = 25;
43        float bar = 3    NSInteger    foo         25
44        NSLog(@"foo: %d, bar: %f", foo, bar);
45
46        foo = [self processFoo:foo];
47        bar = [self processBar:bar];
```

**Figure 15-16.** *Hovering your mouse over a variable in the editing pane will tell you both the variable's datatype and its current value*

The next line of code is just a log statement, so click the Step Over button again to let it fire.

The next two lines of code each call a method. You're going to step into one and step over the other. Click the Step Into button now.

The green arrow and highlighted line of code should just have moved to the first line of the processFoo method. If you look at the stack trace now, you'll see that viewDidLoad is no longer the first row in the stack. It has been superseded by processFoo. Instead of one black row in the stack trace, there are now two, because you wrote both processFoo and viewDidLoad. You can step through the lines of this method if you like. When you're ready to move back to viewDidLoad, click the Step Out button. That will return you to viewDidLoad. processFoo will get popped off of the stack trace's stack, and the green indicator and highlight will be at the line of code after the call to processFoo.

Next, for processBar, you're going to use Step Over. You'll never see processBar on the stack trace when you do that. The debugger is going to run the entire method and then stop execution after it returns. The green arrow and highlight will move forward one line (excluding empty lines and comments). You'll be able to see the results of processBar by looking at the value of bar, which should now be double what it was, but the method itself happened as if it was just a single line of code.

## The Breakpoint Navigator and Symbolic Breakpoints

You've now seen the basics of working with breakpoints, but there's far more to breakpoints. In the Xcode Navigator pane, select the Breakpoints tab on the Navigation bar (Figure 15-17). This pane shows you all the breakpoints that are currently set in your project. You can delete breakpoints here by selecting them and pressing the delete key. You can also add another kind of breakpoint here, which is called a *symbolic breakpoint*. Instead of breaking on a specific line in a specific source code file, you can tell the debugger to break whenever it reaches a certain one of those debug symbols built into the application when using the debug configuration. As a reminder, debug symbols are human-readable names derived from method and function names.

*Figure 15-17. The breakpoint navigator allows you to see all the breakpoints in your project*

Single-click the existing breakpoint (select the first line in the right-hand pane) and press the delete key on your keyboard to delete it. Now, click the + button on the lower left of the Breakpoint Navigator and select "Add Symbolic Breakpoint" (Figure 15-18). In the pop-up dialog, enter viewDidLoad for the Symbol. In the Module field, enter DebugMe and click the Done button. The Breakpoint Navigator will update with a line that reads viewDidLoad with a stylized sigma icon before it (Figure 15-19). The sigma icon is to remind you this is symbolic breakpoint.

**Figure 15-18.** *Adding a symbolic breakpoint*

**Figure 15-19.** *Breakpoint list updated with your symbolic breakpoint*

Restart the application by clicking the Run button on the toolbar. If Xcode tells you the application is already running, then stop it. This time, your application should stop again, at the first line of code in viewDidLoad.

## Conditional Breakpoints

Both the symbolic and line number breakpoints you've set so far have been *unconditional breakpoints*, meaning they always stop when the debugger gets to them. If the program reaches the breakpoint, it stops. But you can also create *conditional breakpoints*, which pause execution only in certain situations.

If your program is still running, stop it, and in the breakpoint window, delete the symbolic breakpoint you just created. In MasterViewController.m, add the following (bold) lines of code, right after the call to super, in viewDidLoad:

```
[super viewDidLoad];
    // Do any additional setup after loading the view, typically from a nib.
for (int i=0; i < 25; i++) {
    NSLog(@"i = %d", i);
}

NSInteger foo = 25;
float bar = 374.3494;
...
```

Save the file. Now, set a line number breakpoint by clicking to the left of the line that reads

```
for (int i=0; i < 25; i++) {
```

Control-click the breakpoint, and select "Edit Breakpoint" from the context menu (Figure 15-20). A dialog should appear, pointing to the breakpoint (Figure 15-21). Enter i > 15 in the Condition field and click Done.

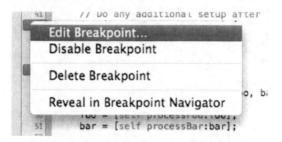

*Figure 15-20. The context menu of a breakpoint*

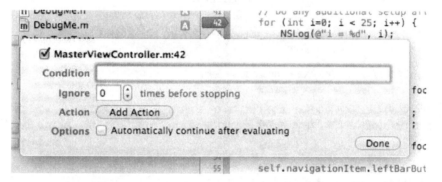

*Figure 15-21. Editing the condition of a breakpoint*

Build and debug your application again. This time it should stop at the breakpoint just like it has done in the past, but look in your debug console, and you should see this:

```
2012-09-25 14:19:53.927 DebugTest[53411:c07] i = 0
2012-09-25 14:19:53.940 DebugTest[53411:c07] i = 1
2012-09-25 14:19:53.952 DebugTest[53411:c07] i = 2
2012-09-25 14:19:53.959 DebugTest[53411:c07] i = 3
2012-09-25 14:19:53.965 DebugTest[53411:c07] i = 4
2012-09-25 14:19:53.971 DebugTest[53411:c07] i = 5
2012-09-25 14:19:53.978 DebugTest[53411:c07] i = 6
2012-09-25 14:19:53.984 DebugTest[53411:c07] i = 7
2012-09-25 14:19:54.008 DebugTest[53411:c07] i = 8
2012-09-25 14:19:54.014 DebugTest[53411:c07] i = 9
2012-09-25 14:19:54.022 DebugTest[53411:c07] i = 10
2012-09-25 14:19:54.072 DebugTest[53411:c07] i = 11
2012-09-25 14:19:54.079 DebugTest[53411:c07] i = 12
2012-09-25 14:19:54.085 DebugTest[53411:c07] i = 13
```

```
2012-09-25 14:19:54.093 DebugTest[53411:c07] i = 14
2012-09-25 14:19:54.099 DebugTest[53411:c07] i = 15
2012-09-25 14:19:54.106 DebugTest[53411:c07] i = 16
```

If you look in the Variable List, you should see *i* has a value of 16. So, the first 16 times through the loop, it didn't pause execution; instead, it just kept going because the condition you set wasn't met.

This can be an incredibly useful tool when you've got an error that occurs in a very long loop. Without conditional breakpoints, you'd be stuck stepping through the loop until the error happened, which is tedious. It's also useful in methods that are called a lot but are only exhibiting problems in certain situations. By setting a condition, you can tell the debugger to ignore situations that you know work properly.

> **Tip**   The Ignore field, just below the Condition field, is pretty cool too—it's a value decremented every time the breakpoint is hit. So you might place the value 16 into the column to have your code stop on the 16th time through the breakpoint. You can even combine these approaches, using Ignore with a condition. Cool beans, eh?

## Breakpoint Actions

If you look at the Breakpoint Editor again (Figure 15-21), you'll see an Action label. This allows you to set a *breakpoint action*, which is very useful.

Stop your application.

Edit the breakpoint, and delete the condition you just added. To do that, just clear the Condition field. Now you'll add the breakpoint action. Next to the Action label, click over the text that reads "Click to add an Action." The area should expand to reveal the breakpoint actions interface (Figure 15-22).

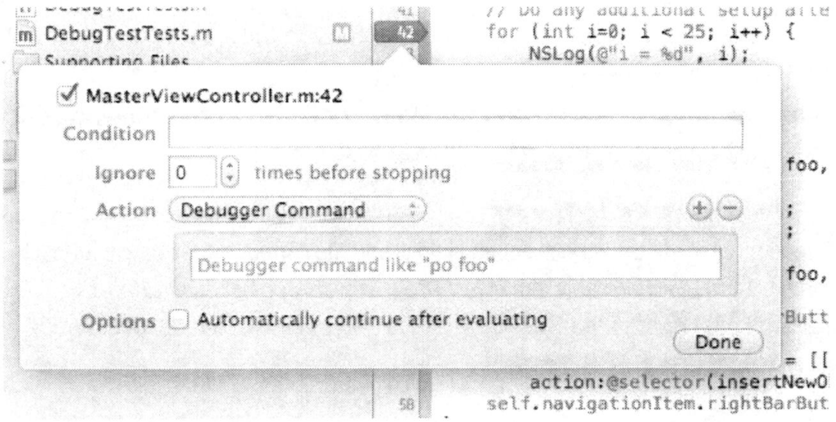

*Figure 15-22.  The breakpoint actions interface revealed*

There are a number of different options to choose from (Figure 15-23). You can run a debugger command or add a statement to the console log. You can also play a sound, or fire off a shell script or AppleScript. As you can see, there's a lot you can do while debugging your application without having to litter up your code with debug-specific functionality.

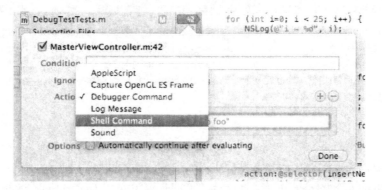

**Figure 15-23.** *Breakpoint actions allow you to fire debugger commands, add statements to the log, play a sound, or fire a shell script or AppleScript*

From the **Debugger Command** pop-up menu, select **Log Message**, which will allow you to add information to the debugger console without writing another NSLog() statement. When you compile this application for distribution, this breakpoint won't exist, so there's no chance of accidentally shipping this log command in your application. In the white text area below the pop-up menu, add the following log command:

```
Reached %B again. Hit this breakpoint %H times. Current value of i is @(int)i@
```

The %B is a special substitution variable that will be replaced at runtime with the name of the breakpoint. The %H is a substitution variable that will be replaced with the number of times this breakpoint has been reached. The text between the two @ characters is a debugger expression that tells it to print the value of i, which is an integer.

Any breakpoint can have one or more actions associated with it. Click the + button at the right side to add another action to this breakpoint.

Next, check the Options box that reads "Automatically continue after evaluating action," so that the breakpoint doesn't cause the program's execution to stop.

> **Tip**  You can read more about the various debug actions and the correct syntax to use for each one in the *Xcode 4 Users Guide* available at http://developer.apple.com/library/ mac/#documentation/ToolsLanguages/Conceptual/Xcode4UserGuide/000-About_ Xcode/about.html.

Build and debug your application again. This time, you should see additional information printed in the debug console log, between the values printed by your NSLog() statement (Figure 15-24). While statements logged using NSLog() are printed in bold, those done by breakpoint actions are printed in non-bold characters.

```
▼  I▶  ⟳  ⬇  ⬆  |  ◀  | ⌐ DebugTest ⟩ 🔳 Thread 1 ⟩ 🔟 0 -[MasterViewController viewDidLoad]

All Output ⟺

Reached -viewDidLoad again. Hit this breakpoint 1 times. Current value of i is 0
Reached -viewDidLoad again. Hit this breakpoint 2 times. Current value of i is 0
Reached -viewDidLoad again. Hit this breakpoint 3 times. Current value of i is 1
Reached -viewDidLoad again. Hit this breakpoint 4 times. Current value of i is 2
Reached -viewDidLoad again. Hit this breakpoint 5 times. Current value of i is 3
Reached -viewDidLoad again. Hit this breakpoint 6 times. Current value of i is 4
Reached -viewDidLoad again. Hit this breakpoint 7 times. Current value of i is 5
Reached -viewDidLoad again. Hit this breakpoint 8 times. Current value of i is 6
Reached -viewDidLoad again. Hit this breakpoint 9 times. Current value of i is 7
2012-09-25 14:25:53.371 DebugTest[53667:c07] i = 0
Reached -viewDidLoad again. Hit this breakpoint 10 times. Current value of i is 8
Reached -viewDidLoad again. Hit this breakpoint 11 times. Current value of i is 9
Reached -viewDidLoad again. Hit this breakpoint 12 times. Current value of i is 10
Reached -viewDidLoad again. Hit this breakpoint 13 times. Current value of i is 11
2012-09-25 14:25:53.383 DebugTest[53667:c07] i = 1
2012-09-25 14:25:53.391 DebugTest[53667:c07] i = 2
2012-09-25 14:25:53.401 DebugTest[53667:c07] i = 3
2012-09-25 14:25:53.407 DebugTest[53667:c07] i = 4
2012-09-25 14:25:53.414 DebugTest[53667:c07] i = 5
2012-09-25 14:25:53.420 DebugTest[53667:c07] i = 6
2012-09-25 14:25:53.446 DebugTest[53667:c07] i = 7
2012-09-25 14:25:53.454 DebugTest[53667:c07] i = 8
Reached -viewDidLoad again. Hit this breakpoint 14 times. Current value of i is 12
2012-09-25 14:25:53.461 DebugTest[53667:c07] i = 9
2012-09-25 14:25:53.470 DebugTest[53667:c07] i = 10
2012-09-25 14:25:53.475 DebugTest[53667:c07] i = 11
2012-09-25 14:25:53.482 DebugTest[53667:c07] i = 12
2012-09-25 14:25:53.525 DebugTest[53667:c07] i = 13
Reached -viewDidLoad again. Hit this breakpoint 15 times. Current value of i is 13
2012-09-25 14:25:53.580 DebugTest[53667:c07] i = 14
Reached -viewDidLoad again. Hit this breakpoint 16 times. Current value of i is 14
2012-09-25 14:25:53.588 DebugTest[53667:c07] i = 15
Reached -viewDidLoad again. Hit this breakpoint 17 times. Current value of i is 15
Reached -viewDidLoad again. Hit this breakpoint 18 times. Current value of i is 16
2012-09-25 14:25:53.594 DebugTest[53667:c07] i = 16
2012-09-25 14:25:53.600 DebugTest[53667:c07] i = 17
Reached -viewDidLoad again. Hit this breakpoint 19 times. Current value of i is 17
2012-09-25 14:25:53.607 DebugTest[53667:c07] i = 18
Reached -viewDidLoad again. Hit this breakpoint 20 times. Current value of i is 18
2012-09-25 14:25:53.615 DebugTest[53667:c07] i = 19
Reached -viewDidLoad again. Hit this breakpoint 21 times. Current value of i is 19
Reached -viewDidLoad again. Hit this breakpoint 22 times. Current value of i is 20
Reached -viewDidLoad again. Hit this breakpoint 23 times. Current value of i is 21
2012-09-25 14:25:53.621 DebugTest[53667:c07] i = 20
2012-09-25 14:25:53.640 DebugTest[53667:c07] i = 21
2012-09-25 14:25:53.658 DebugTest[53667:c07] i = 22
Reached -viewDidLoad again. Hit this breakpoint 24 times. Current value of i is 22
2012-09-25 14:25:53.666 DebugTest[53667:c07] i = 23
Reached -viewDidLoad again. Hit this breakpoint 25 times. Current value of i is 23
Reached -viewDidLoad again. Hit this breakpoint 26 times. Current value of i is 24
2012-09-25 14:25:53.674 DebugTest[53667:c07] i = 24
(lldb)
```

*Figure 15-24.  Breakpoint log actions get printed to the debugger console but, unlike the results of NSLog() commands, are not printed in bold*

That's not all there is to breakpoints, but it's the fundamentals and should give you a good foundation for finding and fixing problems in your applications.

# Static Analysis

Under the **Product** menu in Xcode, there is a menu item labeled **Analyze**. This option compiles your code and runs a *static analysis* on your code that is capable of detecting any number of common problems. Normally, when you build a project, you will see yellow icons in the build results window that represent build warnings and red icons that represent build errors. When you build and analyze, you may also see rows with blue icons that represent potential problems found by the static analyzer. Although static analysis is imperfect and can sometimes identify problems that aren't actually problems (referred to as *false positives*), it's very good at finding certain types of bugs, most notably code that leaks memory. Let's introduce a leak into your code and then analyze it.

If your application is running, stop it.

In `MasterViewController.m`, in the `viewDidLoad` method, add the following code just after the call to `super`:

```
NSArray *myArray = [[NSArray alloc] initWithObjects:@"Hello", @"Goodbye", "So Long", nil];
```

Before you analyze, it's a good idea to select **Clean** from the **Product** menu. Only files that get compiled will be analyzed. Code that hasn't been changed since the last time it was compiled won't get compiled again and won't get analyzed. In this case, that wouldn't be an issue, since you just changed the file where you introduced the bug, but it's good practice to analyze your entire project. Once the project is done cleaning, select **Analyze** from the **Product** menu.

You'll now get a warning about an unused variable, which is true. You declared and initialized `myArray`, but never used it. If you look in the Issue Navigator (Figure 15-25), you'll also see two additional rows in the build results from the static analyzer, one that tells you that `myArray` is never read after initialization. This is essentially telling you the same thing as the unused variable warning from the compiler. The next one, however, is one the compiler doesn't catch. It says: *Argument to 'NSArray' method 'initWithObjects:' should be an Objective-C pointer type, not 'char *'*. That's the static analyzer telling you that you passed the wrong kind of pointer to your array. To find out more, click the disclosure triangle to the left of the message, then click lower message. Pretty informative, eh?

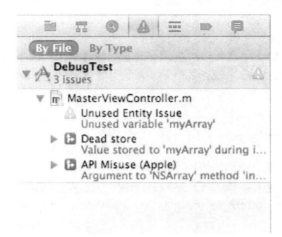

*Figure 15-25. Issues Navigator after running the Static Analyzer*

Before you begin testing any application, you should run Build and Analyze and look at every item it points out. It can save you a lot of aggravation and trouble.

## One More Thing About Debugging

You now know the basic tools of debugging. We haven't discussed all the features of either Xcode or LLDB, but we've covered the essentials. It would take far more than a single chapter to cover this topic exhaustively, but you've now seen the tools that you'll use in 95% or more of your debugging efforts. Unfortunately, the best way to get better at debugging is to do a lot of it, and that can be frustrating early on. The first time you see a particular type of problem, you often aren't sure how to tackle it. So, to give you a bit of a kick-start, we're going to show you a couple of the most common problems that occur in Cocoa Touch programs and show you how to find and fix those problems when they happen to you.

Debugging can be one of the most difficult and frustrating tasks on this green Earth. It's also extremely important, and tracking down a problem that's been plaguing your code can be extremely gratifying. The reason the debugging process is so hard is that modern applications are complex, the libraries we use to build them are complex, and modern operating systems themselves are very complex. At any given time, there's an awful lot of code loaded, running, and interacting.

## Profiling With Instruments

We're not going to dive deep into Instruments. That's a topic for another book (like *Pro iOS Tools*). Let's take a look at how to start Instruments and what it offers. Select Product ➤ Profile in Xcode. Xcode will build the application (if necessary) and launch Instruments.

> **Note**  You can read more about Instruments in Apple's documentation as well. It's located at
> `http://developer.apple.com/library/ios/documentation/DeveloperTools/`
> `Conceptual/InstrumentsUserGuide.`

Instruments operates by creating a trace document to determine what it monitors during your application's execution. Each trace document can be composed of many *instruments*. Each instrument collects different aspects of your application's running state.

On startup, Instruments offers a series of trace document templates to help begin your Instruments session. It also offers a blank template, allowing you to define your own set of instruments to use (Figure 15-26).

*Figure 15-26. Launching Instruments from Xcode*

Let's review what templates Instruments offers:

- *Blank*: An empty template for you to customize.

- *Allocations*: Template to track memory usage on an object basis.

- *Leaks*: Another memory usage template, focused on finding memory leaks.

- *Activity Monitor*: Monitor system resource usage of the application.

- *Zombies*: Another memory usage template, focused on finding overreleased memory.

- *Time Profiler*: Sample processes running the CPU.

- *System Trace*: Monitors application threads moving between system and user space.

- *Automation*: Scripting tool to allow simulation of user interaction.

- *File Activity*: Monitors file system usage by application.

- *Core Data*: Monitors Core Data activity within the application.

Let's just start with the Allocations template. Double click it, and Instruments should open (Figure 15-27). The application should launch in Simulator and you will note that you are now tracking memory usage.

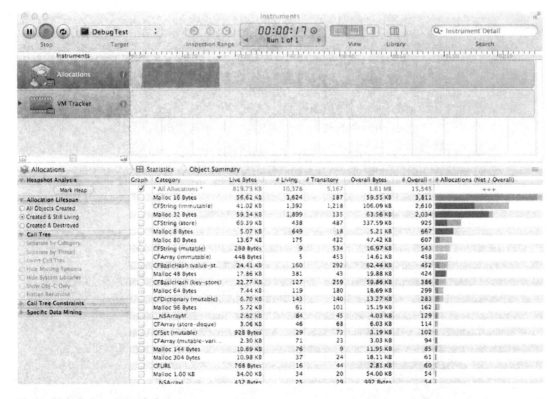

*Figure 15-27. Main Instruments window*

Add some items to your application, then delete them. You should see Instruments trace memory usage.

While running one trace instrument is useful, the real power behind Instruments is the ability to run many traces simultaneously and determine where your application may have performance issues.

Play around with Instruments and see if it helps you optimize your applications.

# End Of The Road

As we stated at the beginning of the chapter, there's no teacher like experience when it comes to unit testing, debugging, and profiling, so you just need to get out there and start making your own mistakes and then fixing them. Don't hesitate to use search engines or to ask more experienced developers for help if you truly do get stuck, but don't let those resources become a crutch, either. Put in an effort to find and fix each bug you encounter before you start looking for help. Yes, it will be frustrating at times, but it's good for you. It builds character.

And with that, we're close to the end of our journey together. We do have one more chapter, though, a farewell bit of guidance as you move forward in your iOS development travels. So, when you're ready for it, turn the page.

# The Road Goes Ever On…

You've survived another journey with us. Great! At this point, you know a lot more than when you first opened this book. We would love to tell you that you now know it all, but when it comes to technology, you never know it all. This is particularly true of iOS development technologies. The programming language and frameworks you've been working with in this book are the result of well over 25 years of evolution. Our engineering friends at Apple are always feverishly working on that Next Cool New Thing.™ Despite being much more mature than it was when it first launched, the iOS platform has still just begun to blossom. There is so much more to come.

Before we started working on this edition of the book, the co-founder and chairman of Apple, Steve Jobs, passed away. When people ask Alex what it was like to work with Steve at NeXT and then Apple, he would always tell them that it was the most exhilarating experience of his life. It was an environment where he was always sure that nothing less than excellence was expected from him at all times. It was an environment where he knew this expectation was shared by the folks he worked closely with. An environment infused with passion and great talent; who could ask for more? While we mourn the loss of Steve, we acknowledge that Apple is infused with his DNA and the pursuit of excellence continues as Apple advances our beloved iOS platform.

By making it through another book, you've built yourself an even sturdier foundation. You've acquired a solid knowledge of Objective-C, Cocoa Touch, and the tools that bring these technologies together to create incredible new iOS applications. You understand the iOS software architecture and the design patterns that make Cocoa Touch sing. In short, you are even more ready to chart your own course.

## Getting Unstuck

At its core, programming is about problem solvingfiguring things out. It is both fun and rewarding. But there will be times when you run up against a puzzle that seems insurmountable, a problem that does not appear to have a solution.

Sometimes, the answer just appears—a result of a bit of time away from the problem. A good night's sleep or a few hours of doing something different can often be all that you need to get through it.

Believe us, sometimes you can stare at the same problem for hours, overanalyzing and getting yourself so worked up that you miss an obvious solution.

And then there are times when even a change of scenery doesn't help. In those situations, it's good to have friends in high places. Here are some resources you can turn to when you're in a bind.

# Apple's Documentation

Become one with Xcode's documentation browser. The documentation browser is a front end to a wealth of incredibly valuable sample source code, concept guides, API references, video tutorials, and a whole lot more.

There are few areas of iOS that you won't be able to learn more about by making your way through Apple's documentation. And the more comfortable you get with Apple's documentation, the easier it will be for you to make your way through uncharted territories and new technologies as Apple rolls them out.

# Mailing Lists

The following are some useful mailing lists that are maintained by Apple:

- `http://lists.apple.com/mailman/listinfo/cocoa-dev`: A moderately high-volume list, primarily focused on Cocoa for Mac OS X. Because of the common heritage shared by Cocoa and Cocoa Touch, many of the people on this list may be able to help you. Make sure to search the list archives before asking your question, though.

- `http://lists.apple.com/mailman/listinfo/xcode-users`: A mailing list specific to questions and problems related to Xcode.

- `http://lists.apple.com/mailman/listinfo/quartz-dev`: A mailing list for discussion of Quartz 2D and Core Graphics technologies.

# Discussion Forums

These are some discussion forums you may like to join:

- `http://forum.learncocoa.org/`: Forums set up by Jack Nutting, author of *Beginning iOS Development*. We've set up a forum for this book as well. The most current version of the project archives that accompany this book are here, updated with all errata and running on the most current release of the iOS SDK.

- `http://devforums.apple.com/`: Apple's new developer community forums for Mac and iPhone software developers. These require logging in, but that means you can discuss new functionality that's still under NDA. Apple's engineers are known to check in periodically and answer questions.

- `www.iphonedevsdk.com/`: A web forum where iPhone programmers, both new and experienced, help each other out with problems and advice.

- `http://forums.macrumors.com/forumdisplay.php?f=135`: A forum for iPhone programmers hosted by the nice folks at MacRumors.

# Web Sites

Here are some web sites that you may want to visit:

- `http://www.cocoadevcentral.com/`: A portal that contains links to a great many Cocoa-related web sites and tutorials.

- `http://cocoaheads.org/`: The CocoaHeads site. CocoaHeads is a group dedicated to peer support and promotion of Cocoa. It focuses on local groups with regular meetings where Cocoa developers can get together and even socialize a bit. There's nothing better than knowing a real person who can help you out, so if there's a CocoaHeads group in your area, check it out. If there isn't one, why not start one up?

- `http://cocoablogs.com/`: A portal that contains links to a great many blogs related to Cocoa programming.

- `http://stackoverflow.com/questions/tagged/ios`: The iOS tagged question for the free programming Q&A web site. Overall, a great source for finding answers to questions. Many experienced and knowledgeable iPhone programmers, including some who work at Apple, contribute to this site by answering questions and posting sample code.

- `http://www.quora.com/iOS-Development`: Another excellent Q&A web site. Though not focused on programming, this tag is for iOS development questions.

# Blogs

Check out these blogs:

- `http://blog.kykim.com/`: Kevin's blog with a little bit of everything, including sprinkles of iOS development information.

- `http://iphonedevelopment.blogspot.com/`: Jeff's iPhone development blog. Jeff posts sample code, tutorials, and other information of interest to iPhone developers.

- `http://davemark.com/`: Dave's little spot in the sun. Not at all technical, just full of whimsical ephemera that catches Dave's interest and he hopes you'll enjoy, too.

- `http://nuthole.com/`: Jack Nutting's blog.

- `http://theocacao.com`: Scott Stevenson, an experienced Cocoa programmer.

- `http://blog.wilshipley.com/`: Wil Shipley's blog. Wil is one of the most experienced Objective-C programmers on the planet. His "Pimp My Code" series of blog postings should be required reading for any Objective-C programmer.

- `http://rentzsch.lumblr.com/`: Wolf Rentzsch's blog. Wolf is an experienced, independent Cocoa programmer and the founder of the C4 Independent Developers conference.

- `http://www.cimgf.com/`: The Cocoa Is My Girlfriend site, which covers software development on both the Mac and iPhone using Objective-C.

- `http://raywenderlich.com/`: Ray Wenderlich's blog and tutorial site. Ray runs an excellent site for supplemental tutorials and information.

## And If All Else Fails...

Drop Kevin an e-mail at `moreiphonedev@kykim.com`.

## Farewell

We sure are glad you came along on this journey with us. We wish you the best of luck, and we hope that you enjoy iOS programming as much as we do.

# Index

## G, H

## I, J, K, L

## M, N

# O

CPSIA information can be obtained at www.ICGtesting.com
Printed in the USA
LVOW111608261212

313293LV00002B/3/P